AF323787

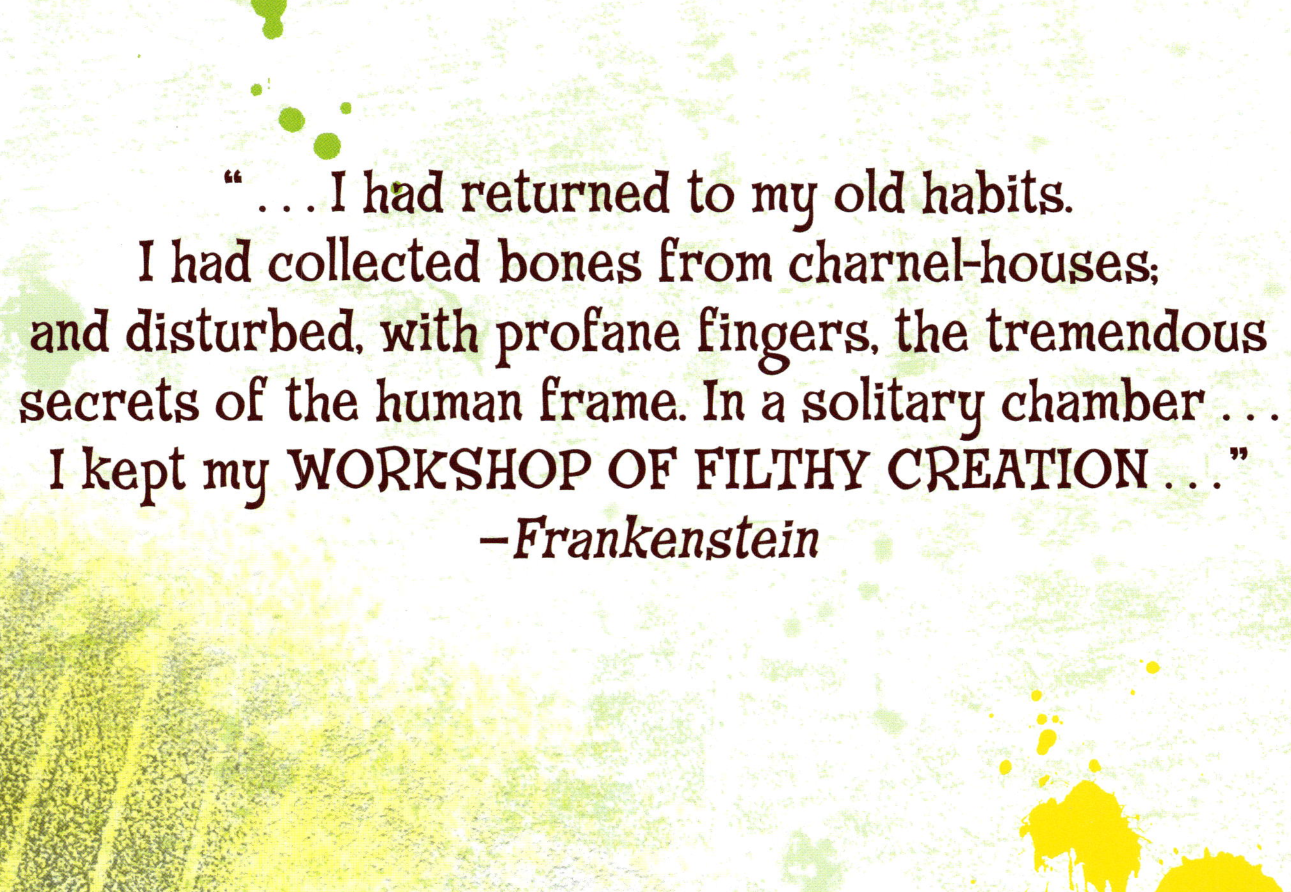

" . . . I had returned to my old habits.
I had collected bones from charnel-houses;
and disturbed, with profane fingers, the tremendous
secrets of the human frame. In a solitary chamber . . .
I kept my WORKSHOP OF FILTHY CREATION . . ."
–Frankenstein

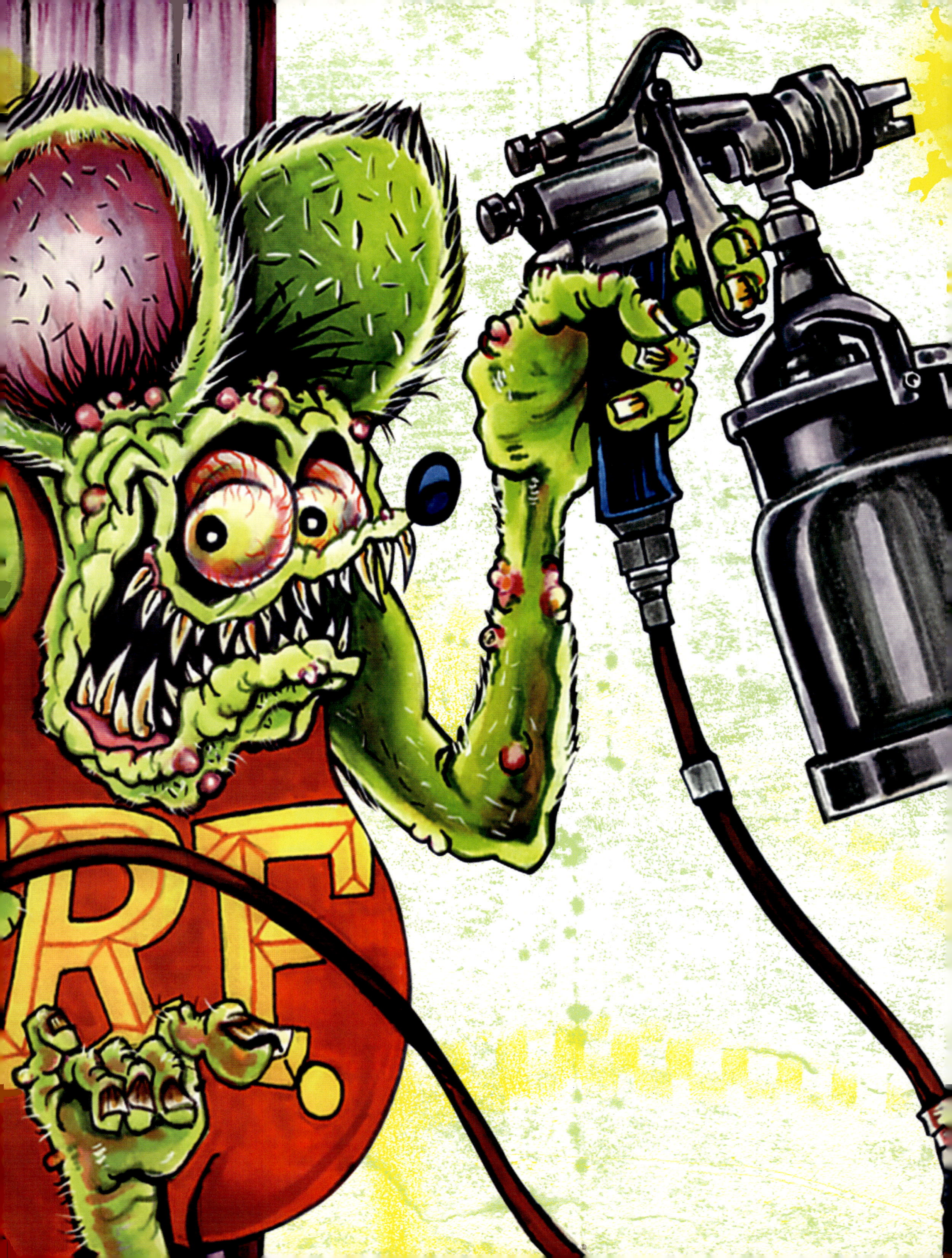
RF.

THE WORKSHOP OF FILTHY CREATION

THE ART OF JOHNNY ACE AND KALI VERRA

FOREWORD BY THE PIZZ

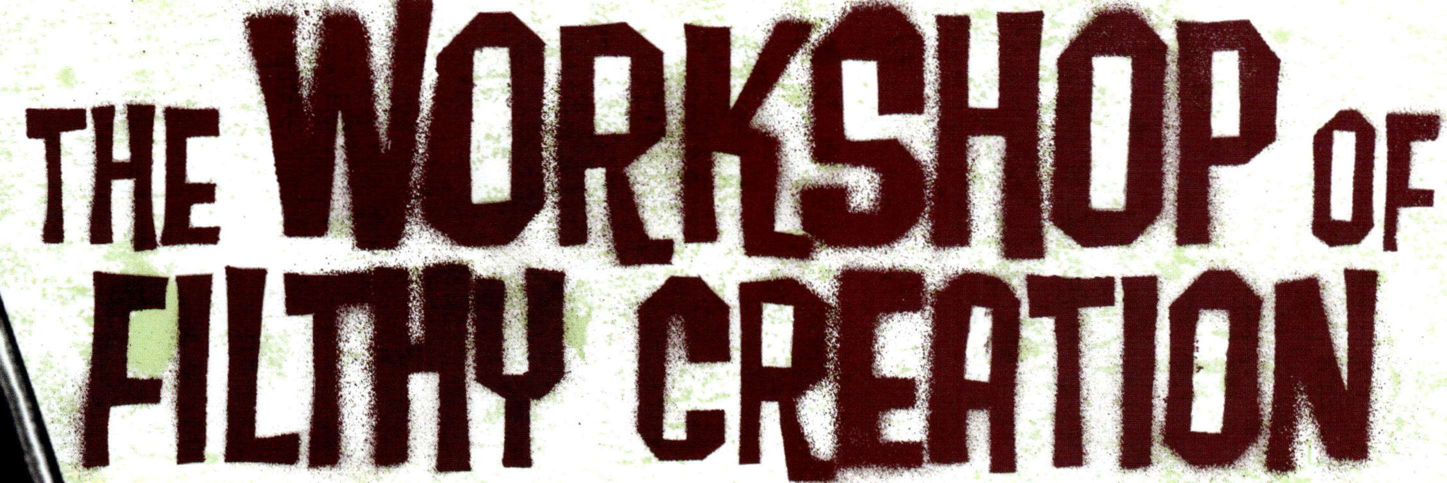

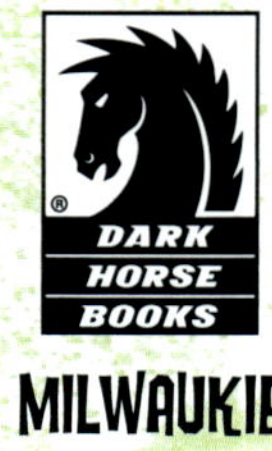

DARK HORSE BOOKS

MILWAUKIE

WE DEDICATE THIS WORK TO EACH OTHER:
"IN SICKNESS AND IN HEALTH . . . "

SPECIAL DEDICATIONS:
To our daughter, Abigail Raven, who thinks we're
"the coolest parents in the world!"

To Ed "Big Daddy" Roth for being there for us through thick and thin . . .
Good night, Big Daddy, wherever you are . . .

ACKNOWLEDGMENTS AND THANKS:
Ilene Roth, Ed "Big Daddy" Roth, Inc., Ed "Newt" Newton, Darryl Roth,
Roth Originals, Road Devils C.C., The Pizz, Hans' Rod & Cycle, Smokin'
Shutdown, Bill Campbell, Stanley "Mouse!" Miller, Anna Marco, Car Kulture
Deluxe, Sal Canzonieri, Electric Frankenstein, Lisa Petrucci, Chris Warner
and everyone at Dark Horse, Chris Kong and everybody at Garageworks
Industries, Mel "Dirtyest Devil" Stultz, *Garage* Magazine, Lev @ Toy Tokyo,
Showroom NYC, Colleen Zwickler, Murph & Susan Graham (Hey group,
cool it with the boom-booms!), and to the memories of Tom Sutton,
Kenneth "Von Dutch" Howard, Basil Wolverton, Pete "Mad Daddy" Meyers,
Bill Ward, Wally Wood, R.K. Sloane, Johnny Craig, Pete Millar, Don Knotts,
and Biscuit (the last of the Red-Hot Round Boys).

ALL ARTWORK, PHOTOGRAPHY, AND SCULPTURE BY
JOHNNY ACE AND KALI VERRA, EXCEPT WHERE NOTED.

ADDITIONAL PHOTOGRAPHY:
Dave Molloy/Pro Photography (page 66), Brandon Gouthier (page 101),
Gloria Uberdelli (page 72), Mark Moriarity (page 29), Todd Huber (pages
11 & 52), Hank Cash (page 103), Blake Burwell (page 104), Larry Garland
(page 52), Carson Vester (page 41).

THE WORKSHOP OF FILTHY CREATION:
THE ART OF JOHNNY ACE AND KALI VERRA

Dark Horse Books
A division of Dark Horse Comics, Inc.
10956 S.E. Main Street
Milwaukie OR 97222

darkhorse.com

acekustoms.com

10 9 8 7 6 5 4 3 2 1

First edition: July 2008
ISBN 978-1-59307-924-6

Printed in Hong Kong

FOREWORD

Johnny Ace . . .

. . . Waaaaaaaaaaaaaaaaaaaaay back before they rolled the Big-Tent Holy-Roller Kustom Kulture Revival into town, before they had to prop up the dead corpse of Von Dutch to sell pink panties to pubescent girls and he was actually alive and spitting, before Robert Williams had a cologne named after him and when Big Daddy Roth was still in command of the entire three-ring circus, we had a little pow-wow get-together called the Rat Fink Reunion. This was back in the early '80s. The glory days of the Klassic Rat Fink Era were twenty years past, and we were the few determined holdouts and disciples who hung onto the vision, like moths to the flame . . .

Two, three times Roth had passed me the baton to be the auctioneer, which was a burden as much as it was a great honor; being the auctioneer couldn't bid on shit. And what really fucking cool shit it was! See, although everything was signed "Big Daddy Roth Studios," we knew that there was a stable of stars who had worked or did work for Roth or were influenced by him . . . Such notables in attendance were Robert Williams, leading scion of Lowbrow; Ed Newton, the inventor of The Chrome School; the ever-nasty Von Dutch . . . as well as a buncha bums like Von Franko, XNO, Eric Pigors, and that no-goodnik, The Pizz . . .

Von Franko would jibe: "Hey! I never see our stuff here! Do you suppose they sell our shit at the Rat Fink Party in Tex-Ass??" Well, that gets us to the point of this scrawl: Just whose shit were we looking at, and did it come from Texas? Uh-huh! One of Roth's toiling minions was a husband-wife team from Texas, and the ugly half of the team was Johnny Ace.

Johnny Ace was working for Big Daddy at just about the same time I was. While Roth kept me toiling in the new Rat Fink adventures in the wonderful world of comix, a Mr. Ace was cranking out Rat Fink art in the classic vein. Roth had a knack for recognizing and nurturing talent and gathered up artists like a giant junkyard magnet. Out of an entire auditorium of people, Roth could find the two or three freaks hanging out who GOT IT. See, Rat Fink was more than just a character, a set of guidelines, and PMS colors to be used to hawk candy

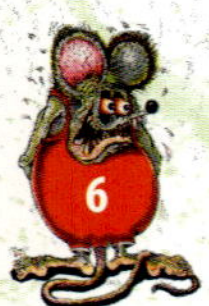

bars and hamburgers; Rat Fink was a vibe, a buzzing undercurrent of adolescent angst and raw power, the seedier side of the Amerikan Dream, the one that kept the 7/11s open all night and worked on weird little projects in the wee hours . . .

Johnny Ace is a Classic Rat Fink Artist. He ascribes to the look of the classic '60s vintage Fink, he actually DID work for Roth, and he has the cranky demeanor that most Roth veterans have. A superb draftsman skilled in the automotive arts, chops honed by years of tutelage in The School Of Roth, Master of the More Bang For The Buck theory of compositional development, with an easily recognizable palette and style . . . Far from being a dilettante artist who tries on a Rat Fink style like some poofter with the latest fashions, only to discard them when the party's over, Johnny Ace is a straight shot of the real stuff, off the cuff and garage-tuff . . .

Roth told Ace that he wouldn't introduce him to me, as he didn't want the tender Ace to be influenced by me . . . end quote. Whether this was a lifestyle issue or a matter of stylistic flourish, we'll never know, but as usual it seems like the Big Daddy knew better after all . . .

I finally got to meet Mr. Ace and his spazzmatic cool-chick wife, Kali, at a showing of vintage Roth originals in Hollywood, and it was like meeting a long-lost brother. Here's his book of work—it's a labor of love from a real guy who Gets It, and I think Big Daddy Roth would be proud . . .

—The Pizz, "The Beatnik's Beatnik®"
Long Beach CA
January 2008

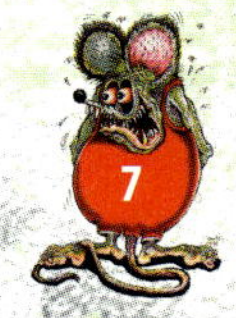

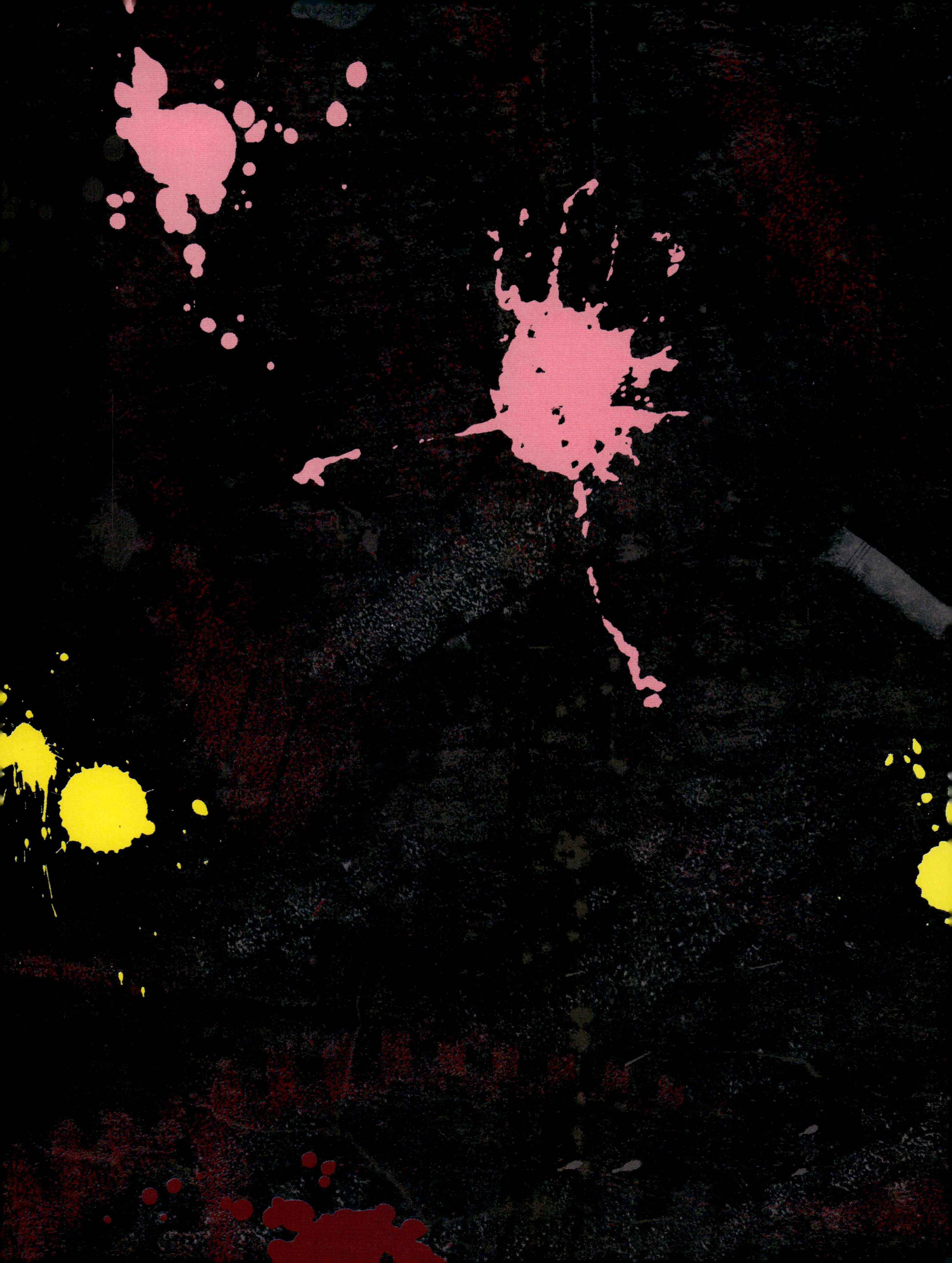

PUTRID POSTERS & AWFUL ALBUM COVERS

"The form of the monster on whom I had bestowed existence was for ever before my eyes, and I raved incessantly concerning him"

PUTRID POSTERS & AWFUL ALBUM COVERS

"The form of the monster on whom I had bestowed existence
was for ever before my eyes, and I raved incessantly concerning him."

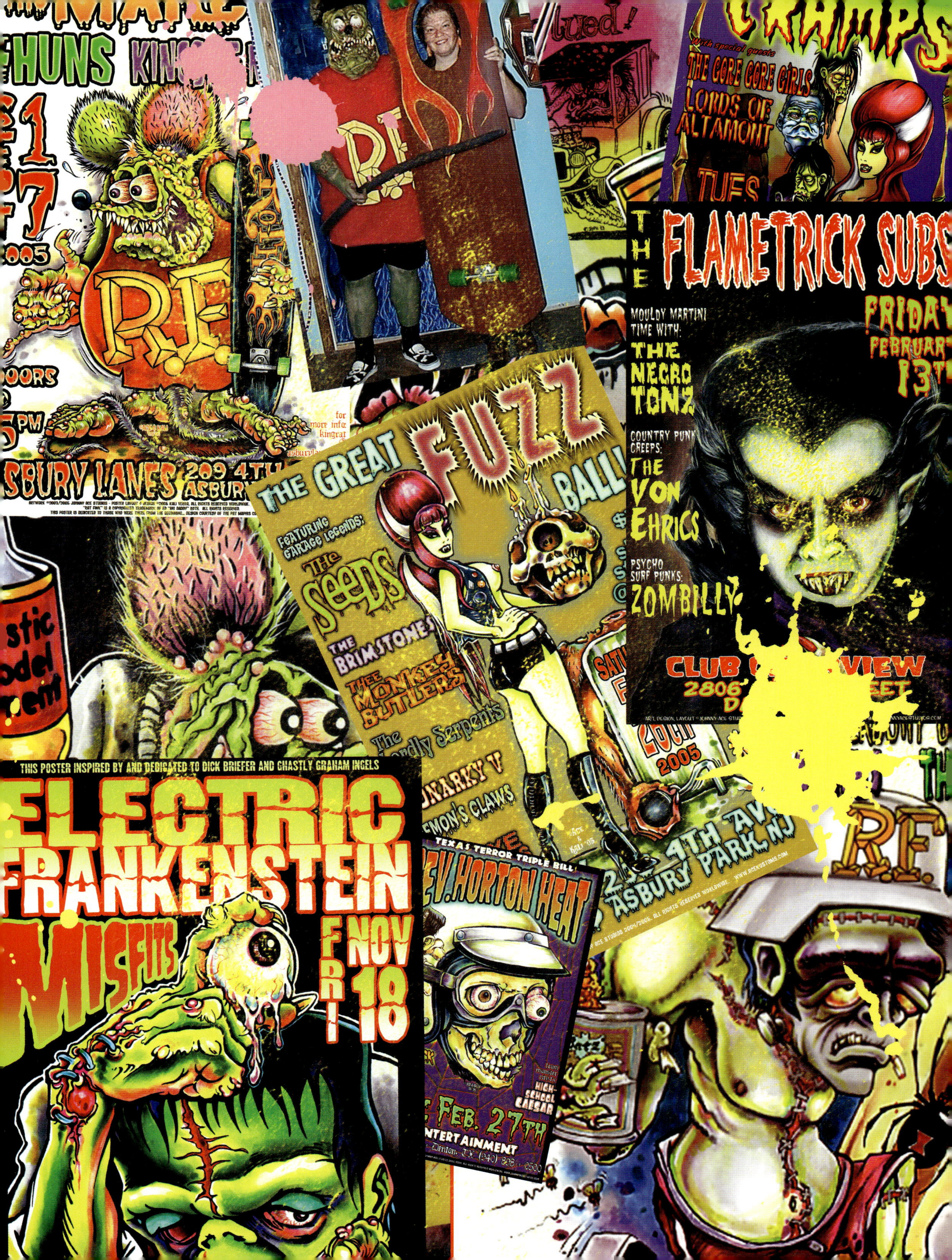
HUNS
KING
1
7
005
R.F.
DOORS
5 PM
SBURY LANES 209 4TH
ASBUR
THIS POSTER IS DEDICATED TO THOSE WHO WILL PASS FROM THE BEGINNING.
CRAMPS
THE GORE GORE GIRLS
LORDS OF ALTAMONT
TUES
THE FLAMETRICK SUBS
MOULDY MARTINI TIME WITH:
THE NECRO TONZ
COUNTRY PUNK CREEPS:
THE VON EHRICS
PSYCHO SURF PUNKS:
ZOMBILLY
CLUB RIVERVIEW
2806
2005
stic
odel
ent
THE GREAT FUZZ
FEATURING GARAGE LEGENDS:
THE SEEDS
THE BRIMSTONES
THEE MONKEY BUTLERS
The Deadly Serpents
BALL
SNARKY V
emon's Claws
TEXAS TERROR TRIPLE BILL
REV. HORTON HEAT
4TH AVE
ASBURY PARK, NJ
WWW. NEKUSTONZ.COM
THIS POSTER INSPIRED BY AND DEDICATED TO DICK BRIEFER AND GHASTLY GRAHAM INGELS
ELECTRIC FRANKENSTEIN
MISFITS
FRI
NOV
18
NICK
RIGGL
CAESAR
E FEB. 27TH
NTERTAINMENT
Denton TX (940) 308
R.F.

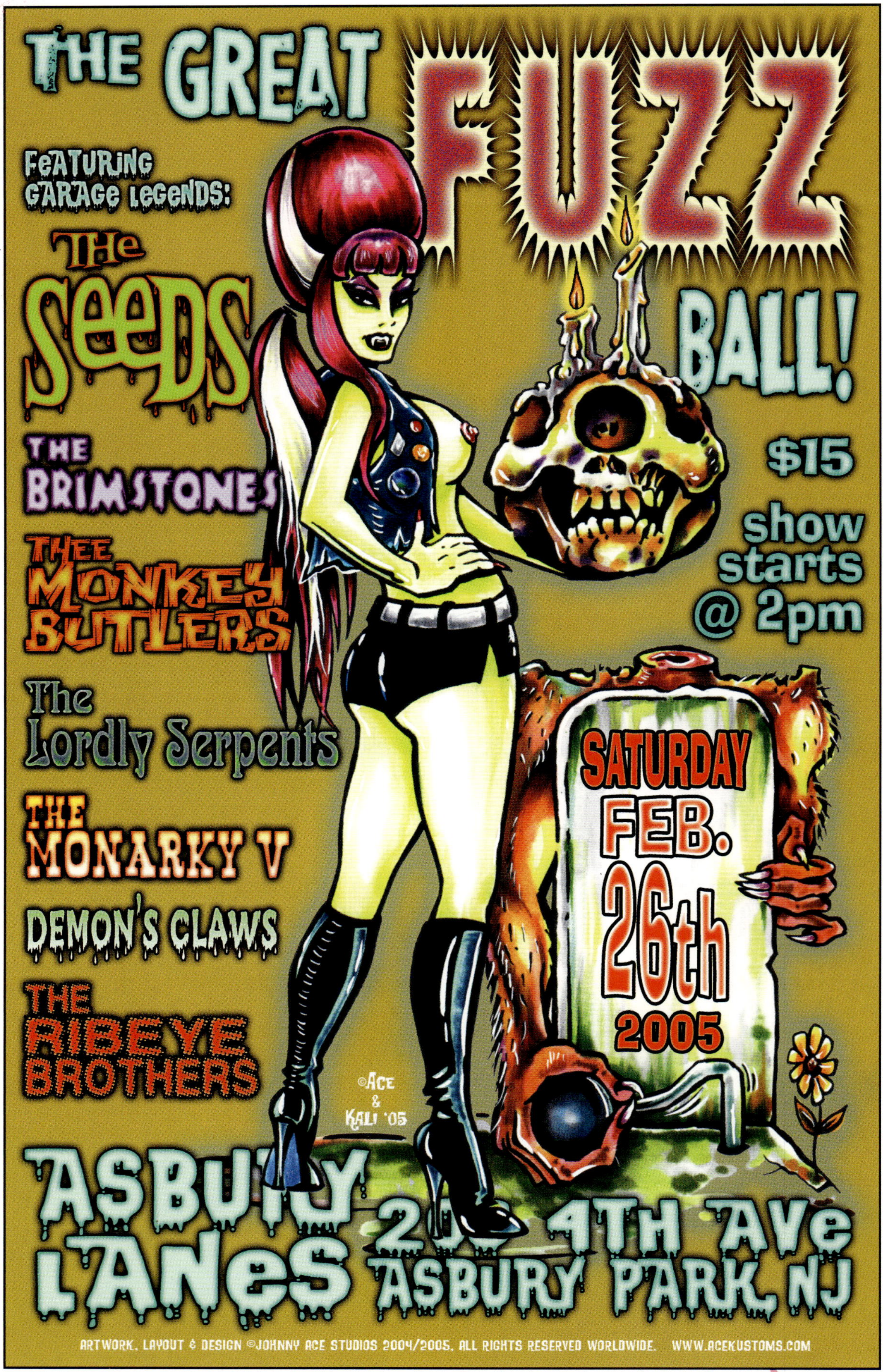

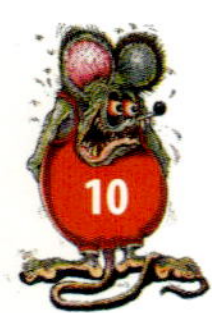

When in California, Visit Roth Studios! 2005.
Dedicated to Ed "Newt" Newton, Robt. Williams, and Ed Fuller.

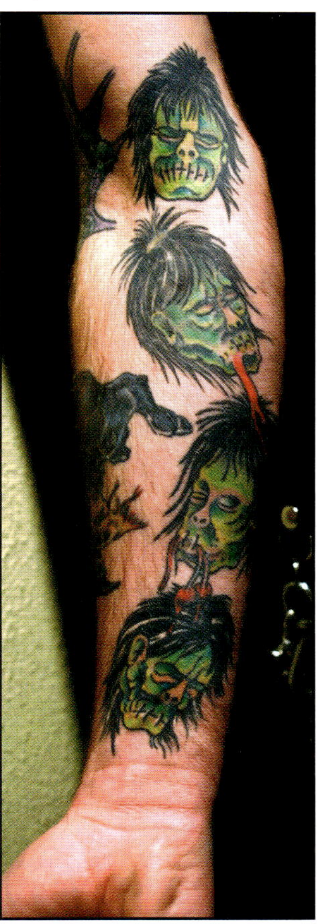

1. *Stay Sick and Turn Blue!* 2003. Dedicated to Ernie "Ghoulardi" Anderson and all the Purple Knifs!

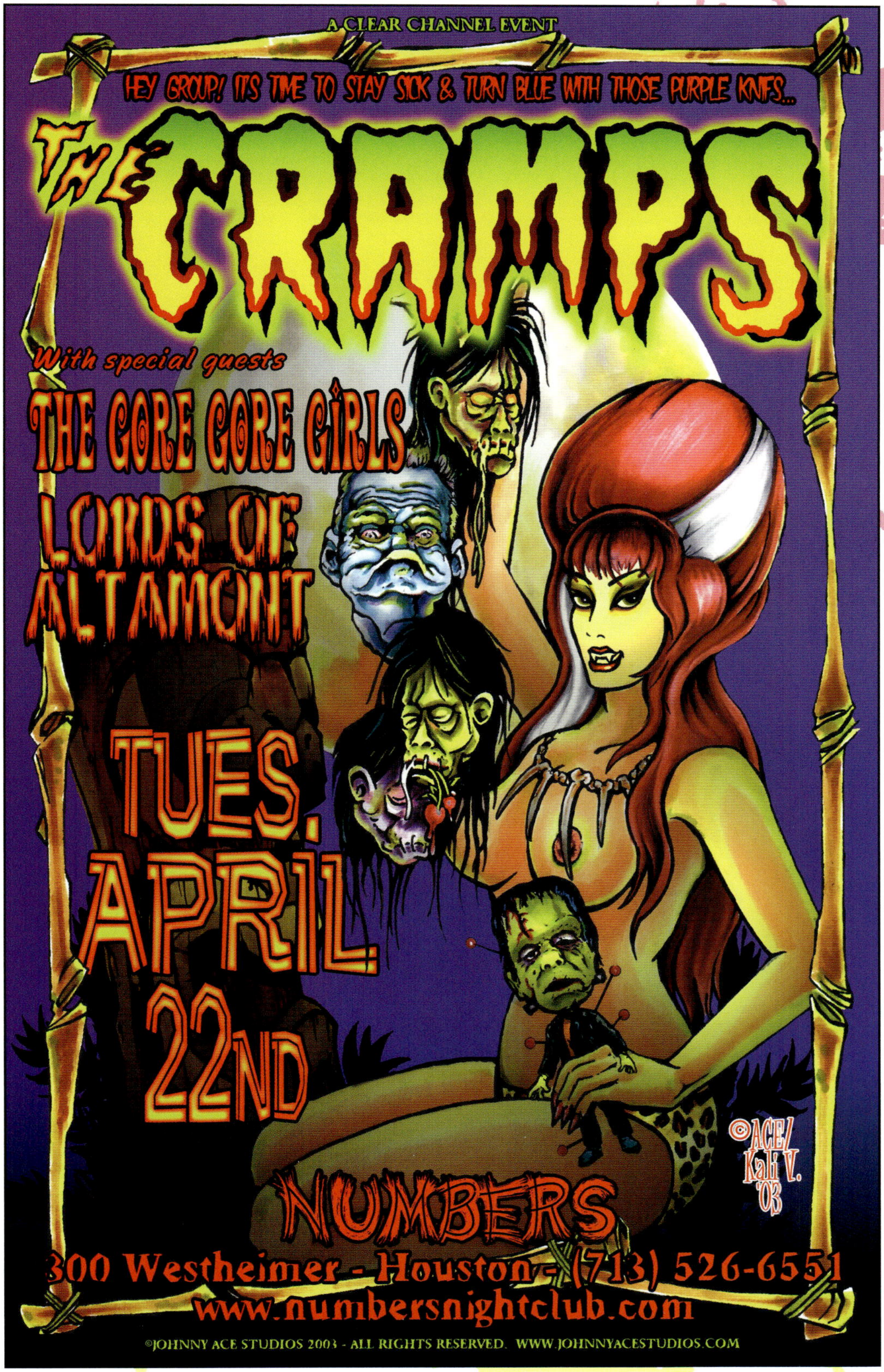

2. The Cramps bassist, Chopper Von, with tattoo featuring Johnny Ace Studios' detailing from Cramps show poster art. Photo © 2005 by Todd Huber.

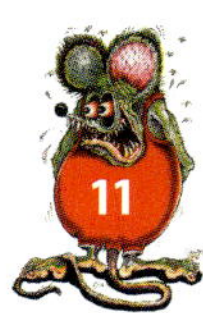

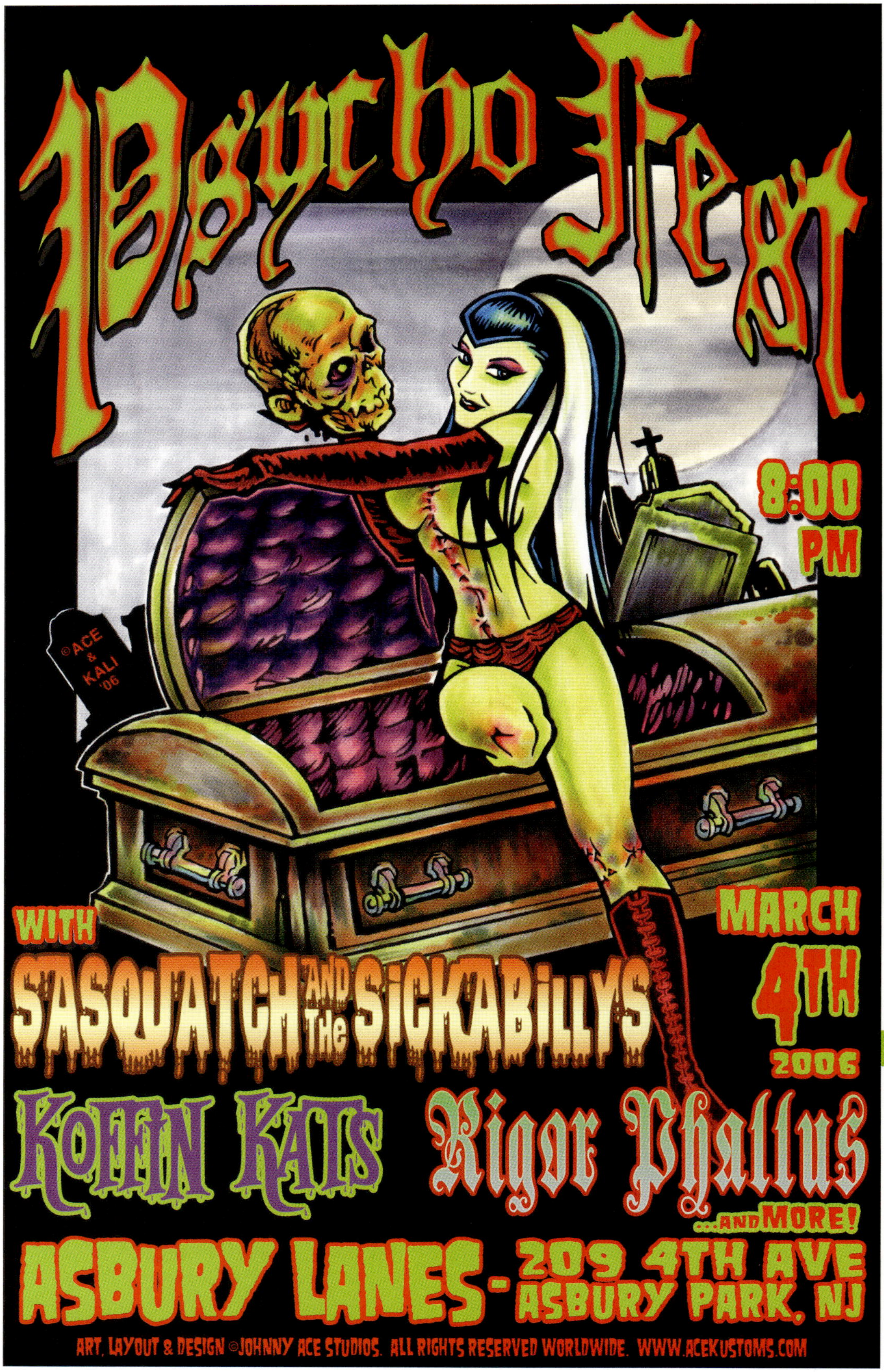

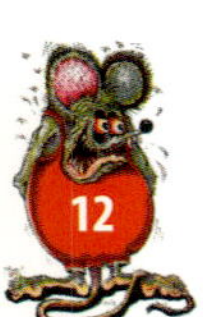

Kasket Kutie/Gruesome Goodies. 2005.
Our "Kadaverella" character makes another appearance, with Kali serving as the perfect model!

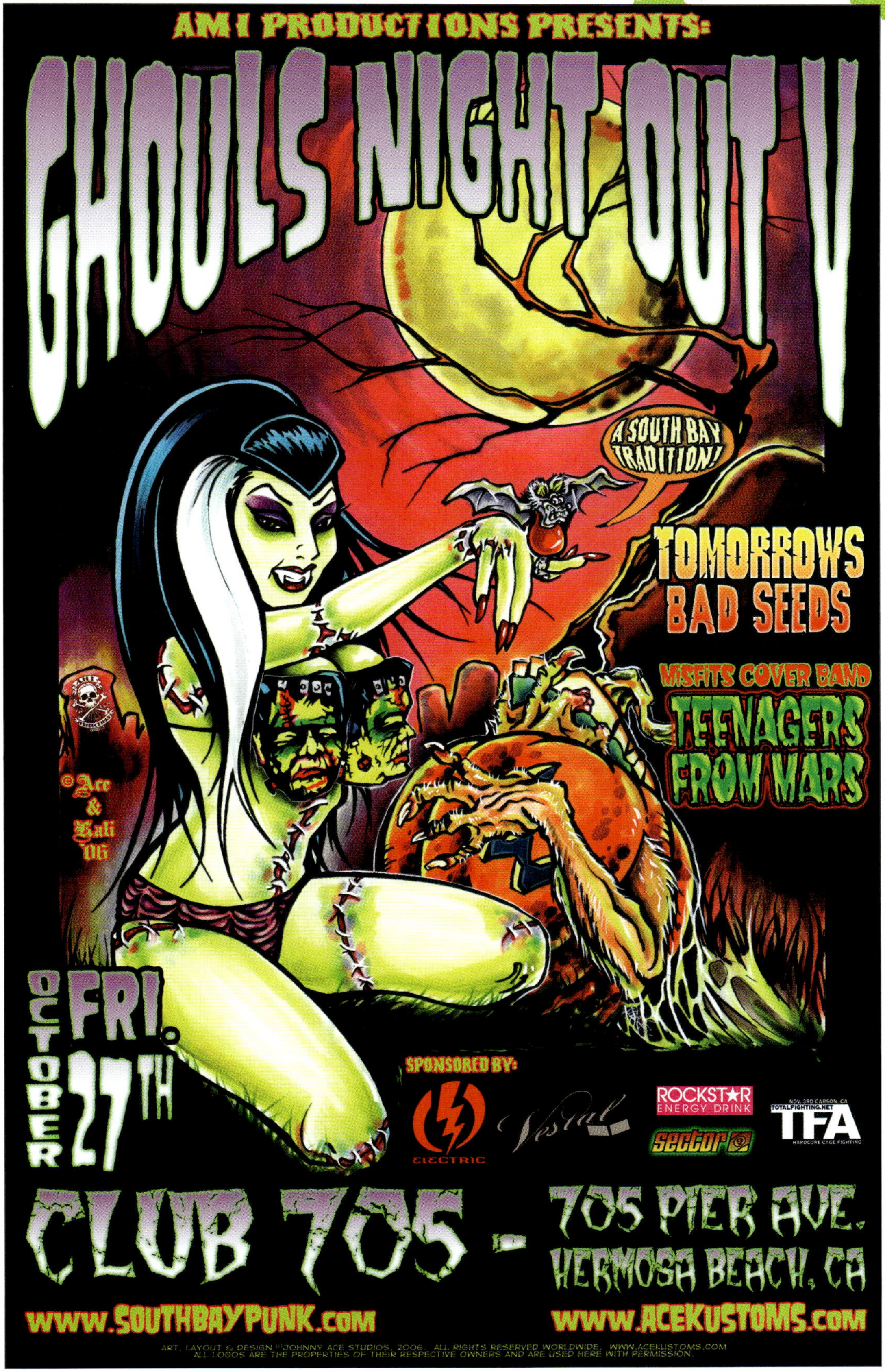

Kadaverella with Frankenbra (a.k.a. Ben Cooper's Secret!). 2006.

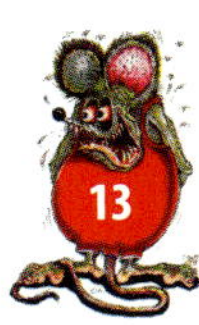

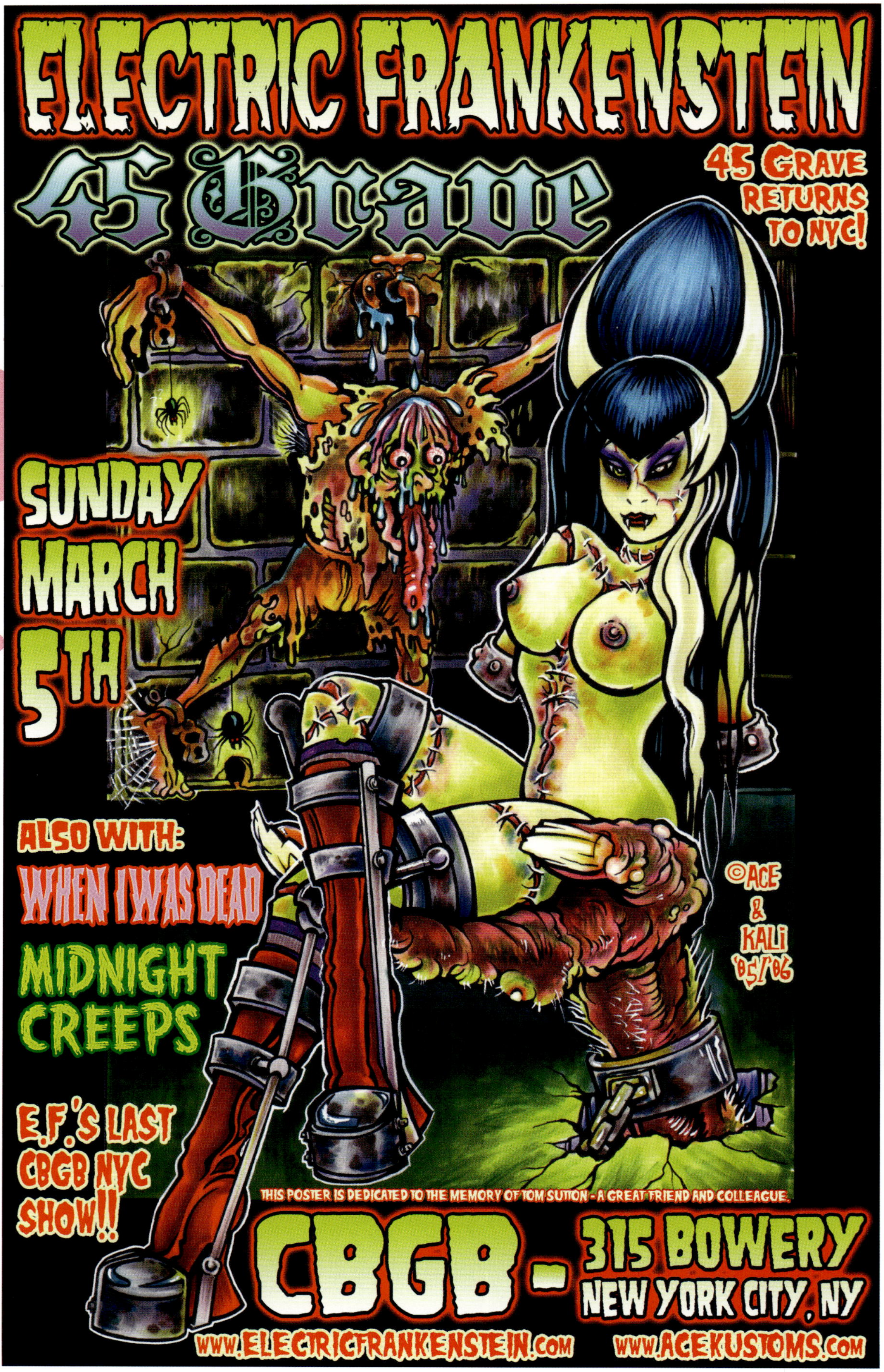

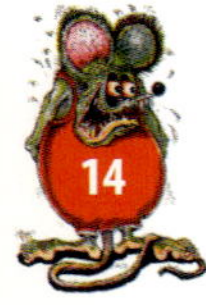

Frankenbabe (a.k.a. FrankenTease). 2005.
Dedicated to the memory of Tom Sutton, a great friend and colleague.

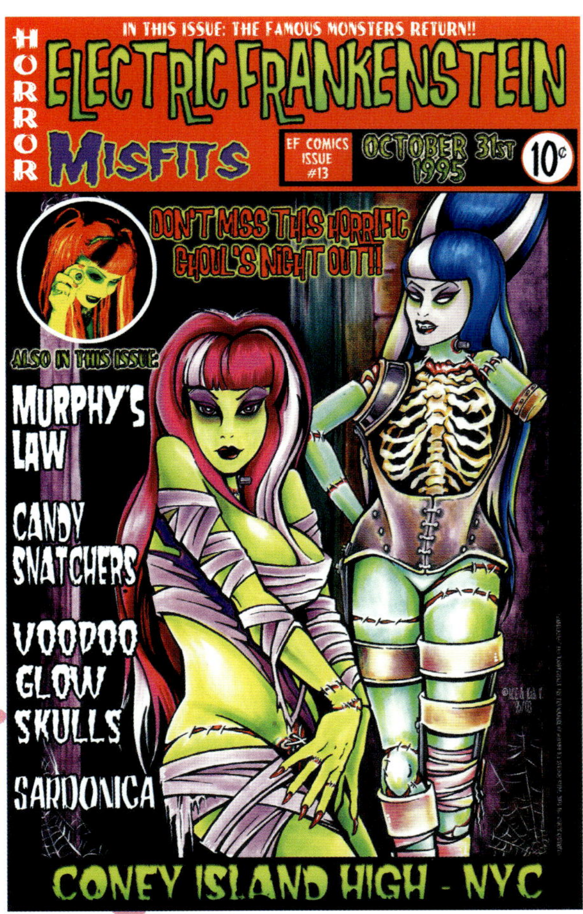

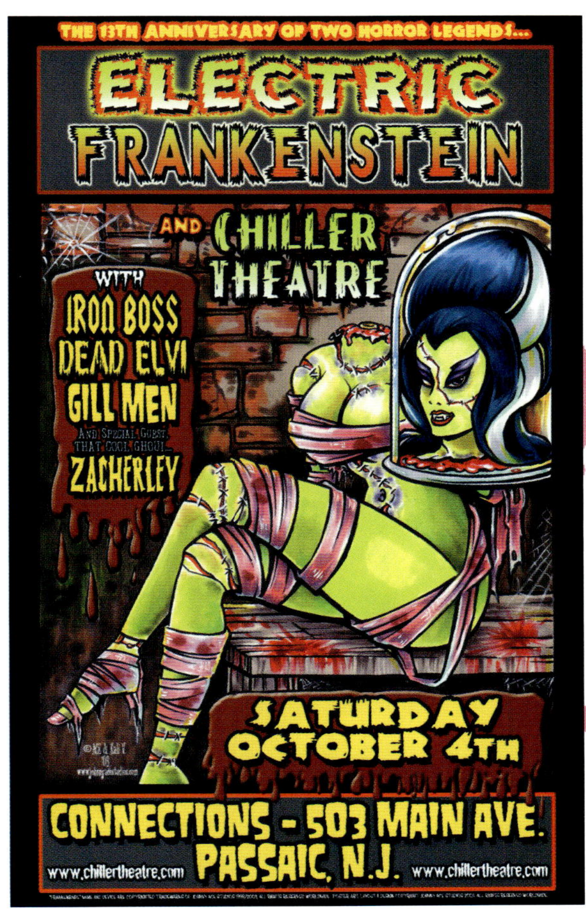

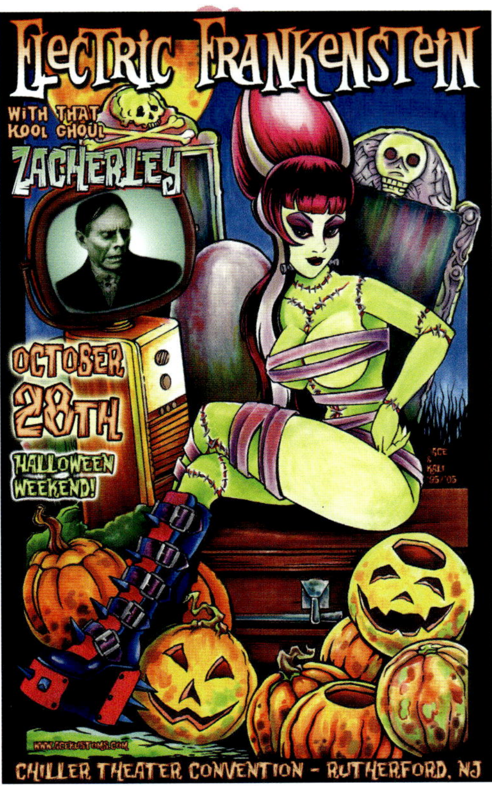

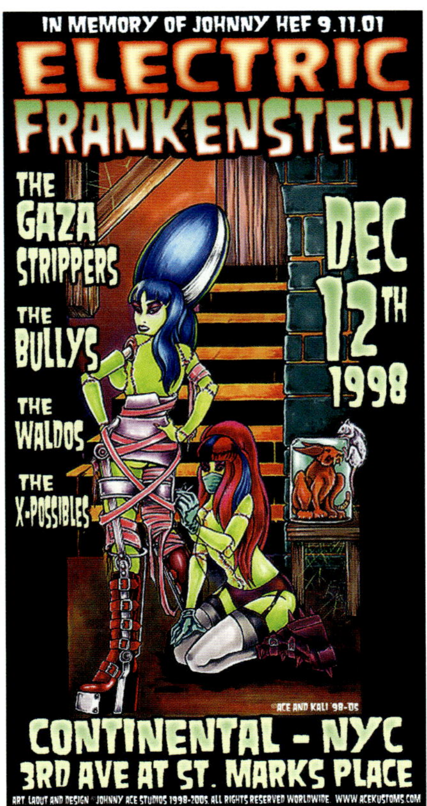

Frankenbabe and Kadaverella making more appearances on Electric Frankenstein gig posters . . . Many of our monster girl characters are done in the spirit of the infamous cover art from the Myron and Irving Fass publications of the mid-'60s to early '70s. With titles such as *Weird, Horror Tales, Terror Tales*, etc., these repackaged '50s pre-code horror comics often featured examples of scantily-clad, stitched, heavy mascara-laden vampire women, gory lab scenes, and brutal monster battles . . . Although the Warren publications (*Creepy, Eerie, Vampirella, Famous Monsters*) were the first choice when spending hard-earned cash, these lurid but extremely high-energy magazines made great trading fodder . . . Personally being unable to illustrate traditional pin-up girls, our studio standard became these types almost by default. No matter how hard we tried, they always came out like the examples pictured within these pages!

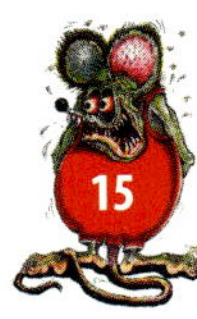

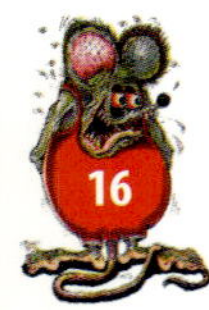

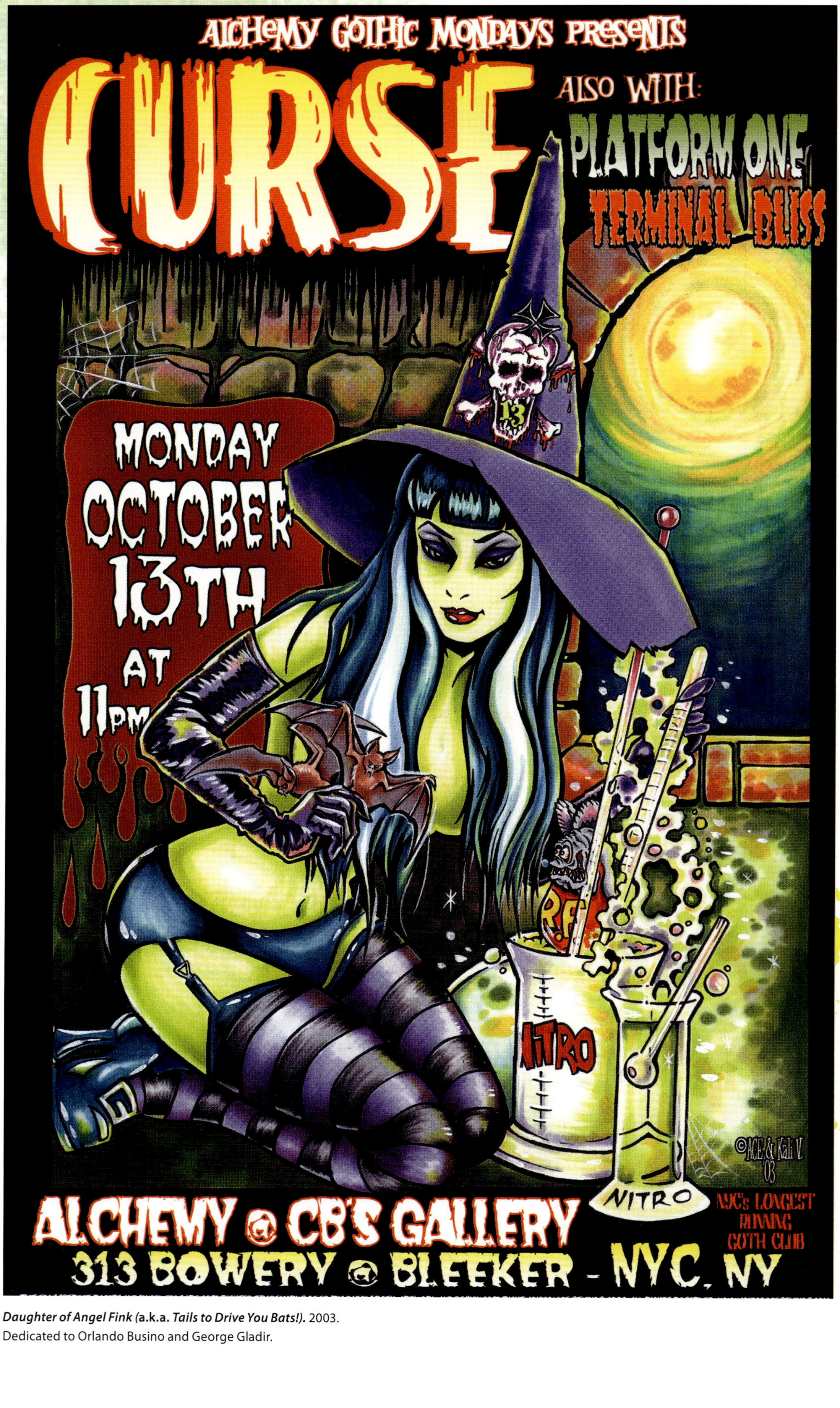

Daughter of Angel Fink (a.k.a. Tails to Drive You Bats!). 2003.
Dedicated to Orlando Busino and George Gladir.

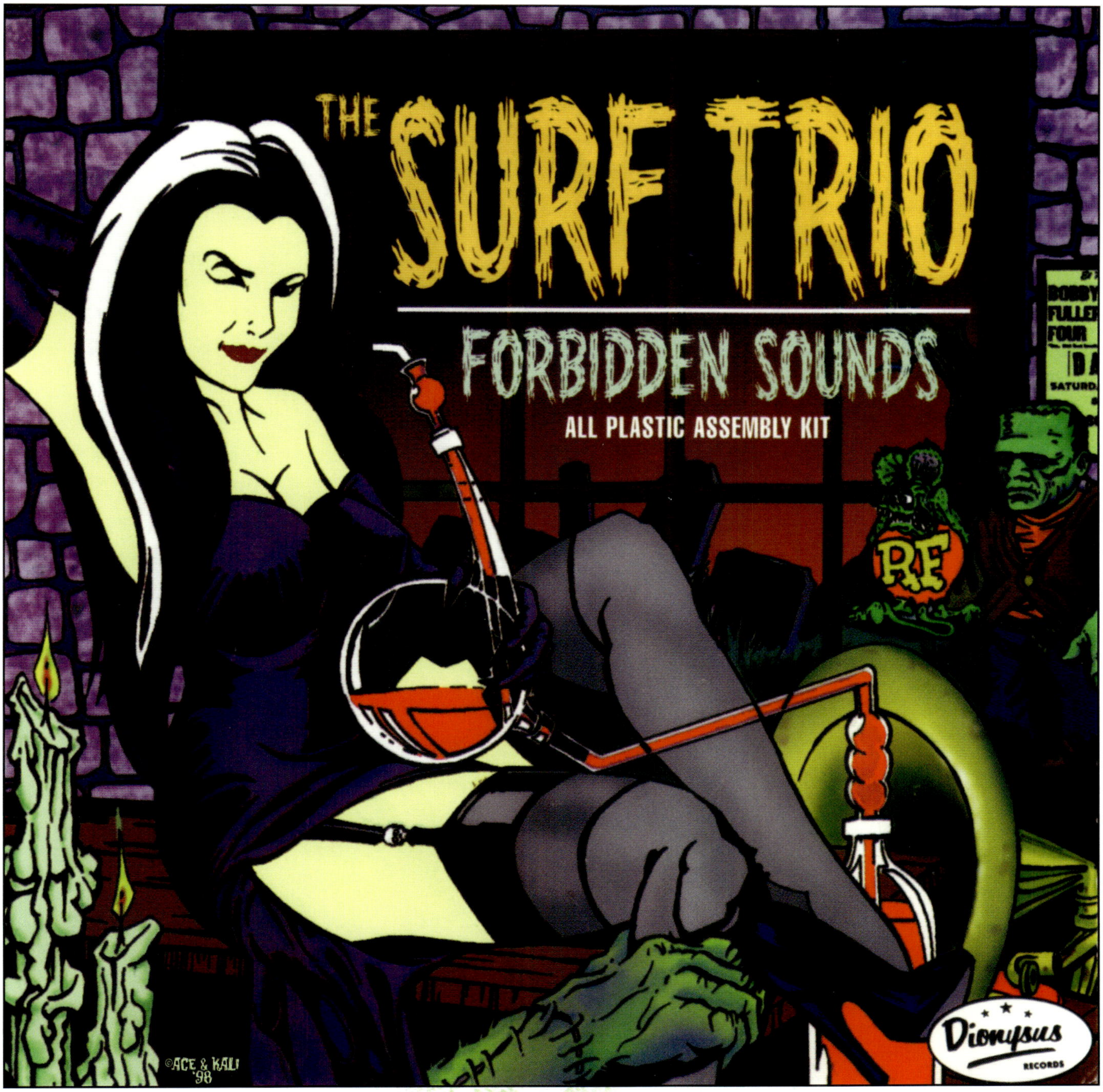

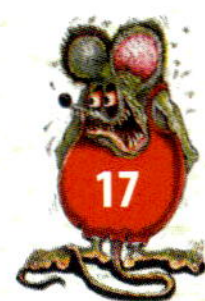

The Surf Trio: Forbidden Sounds LP. Dionysus Records, 1999.

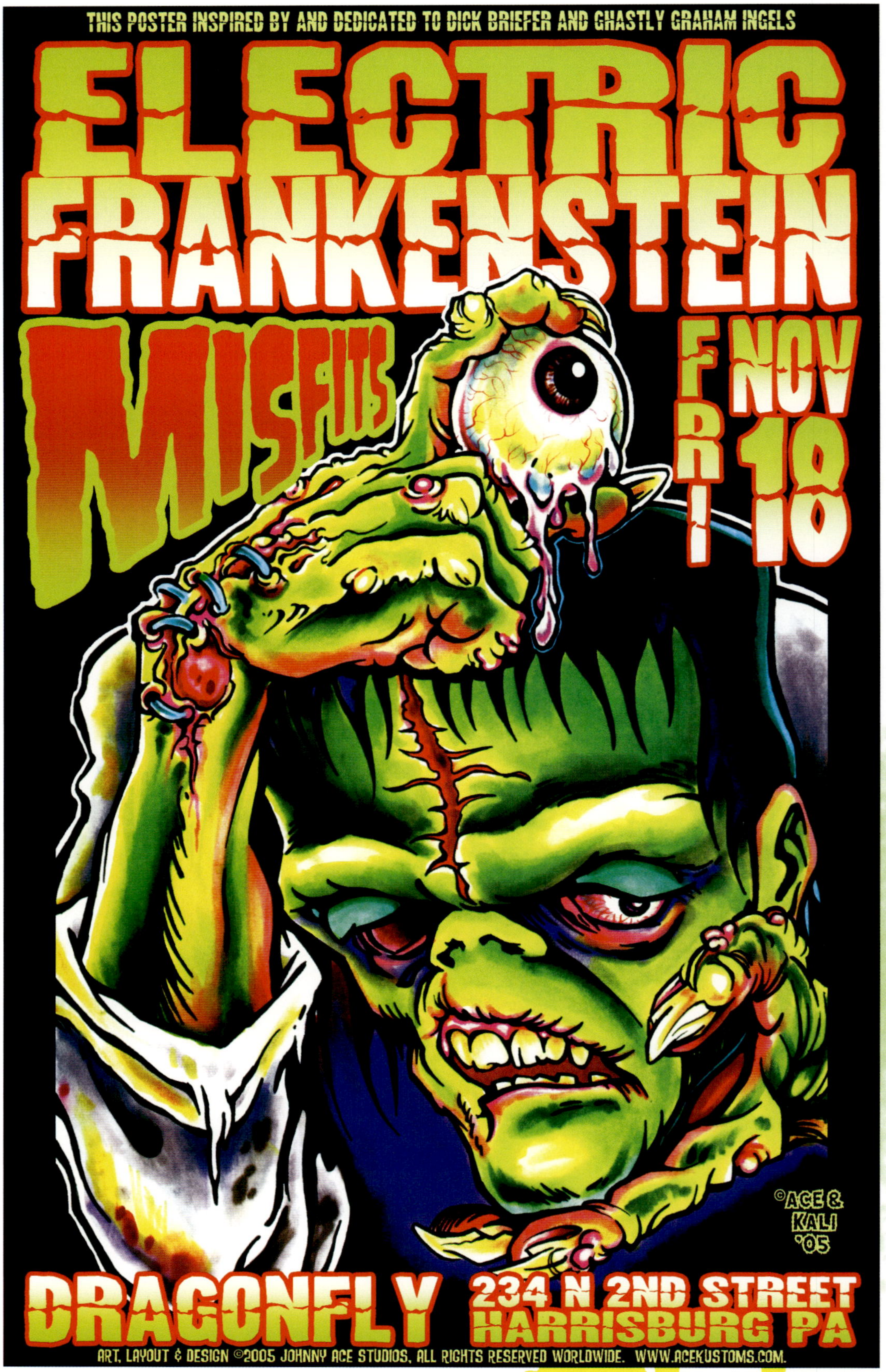

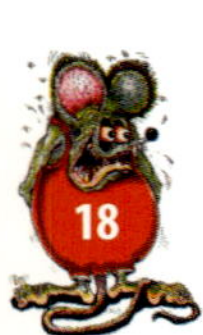

Electric Frankenstein/Misfits. 2005.
Inspired by and dedicated to Dick Briefer and Ghastly Graham Ingels.

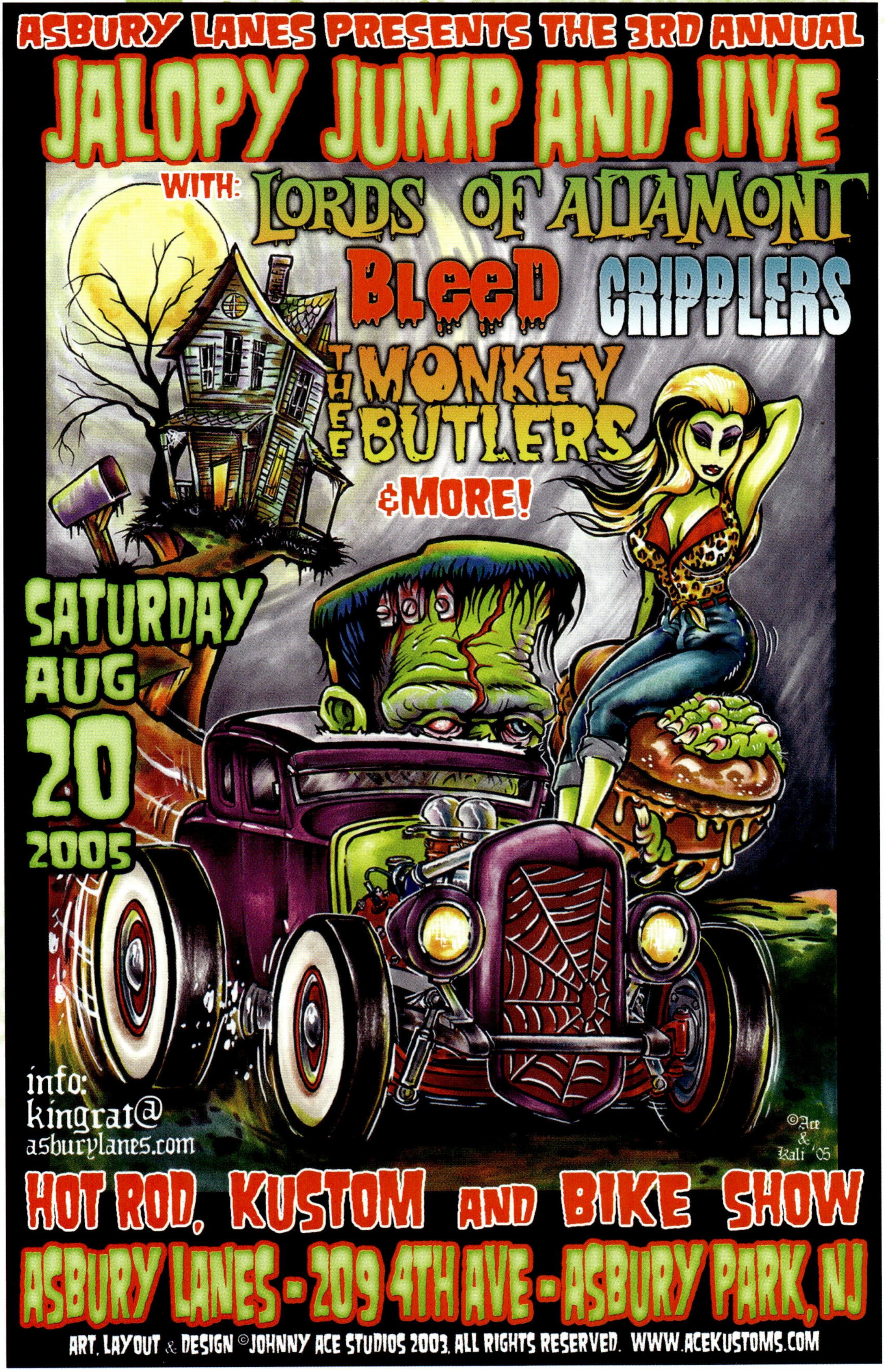

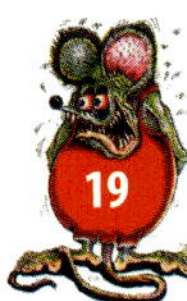

Flatheads Forever (Return of The Untouchables). 2003.
In addition to this event poster, this artwork also became a DVD cover and menu for a really cool drive-in feature collection that included *Atom Age Vampire*, *Terror In the Haunted House*, *Burger Town*, and *Hot Rod Girl*.

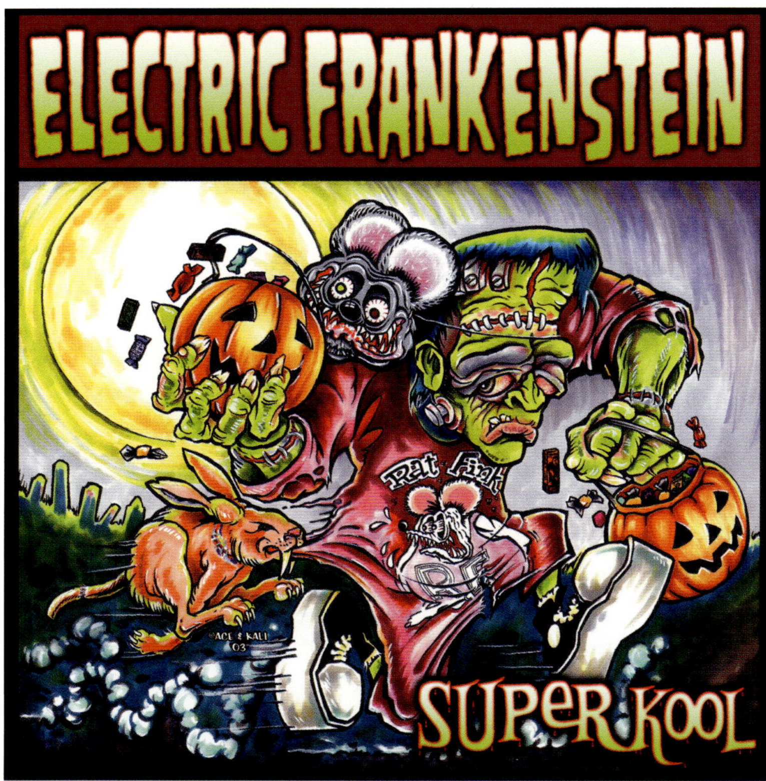

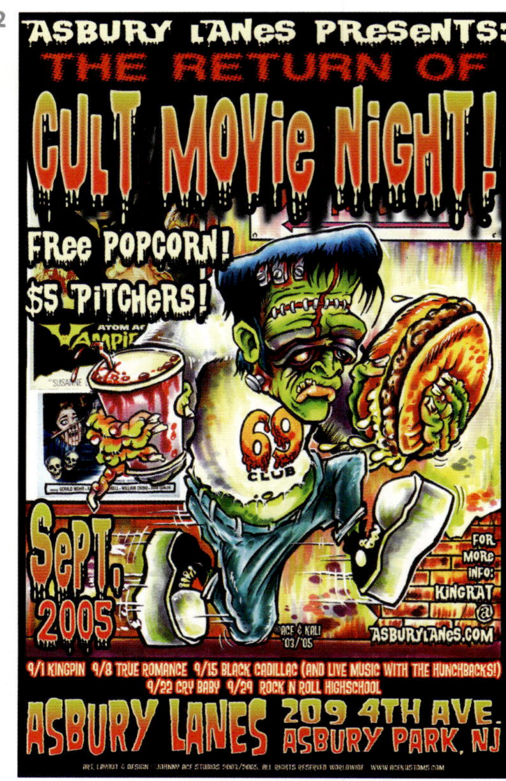

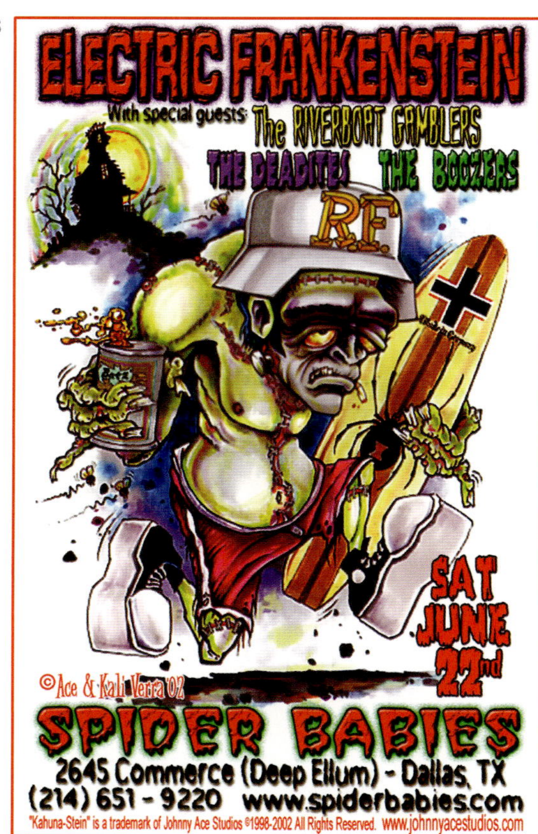

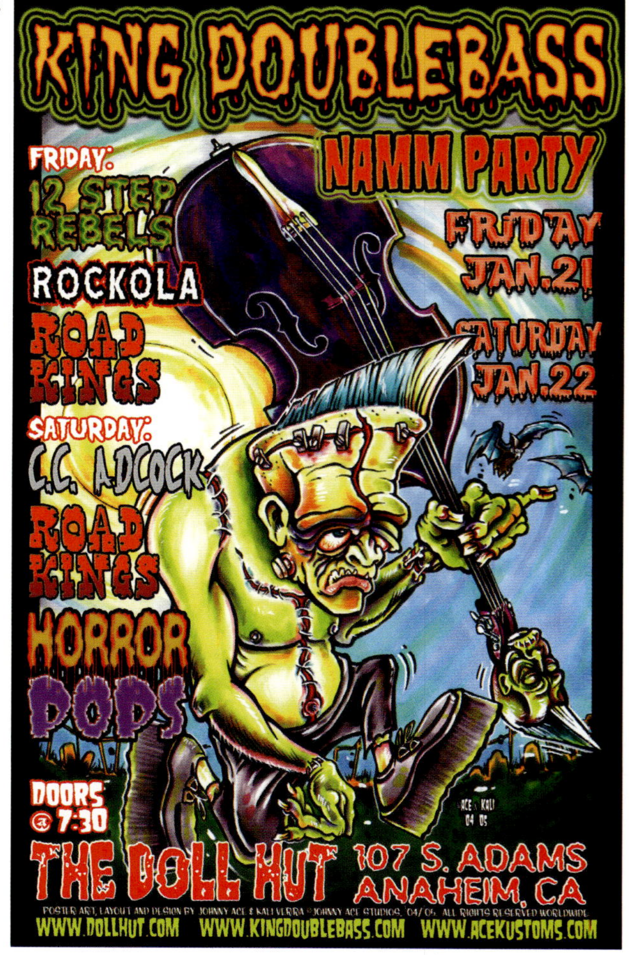

1. *Halloween Hodad (Electric Frankenstein: Super Kool* LP). 2003.

2. *Lord Beastnik, The Hip Prometheus (a.k.a. Scarf-Fink).* 2003.

3. *KahunaStein (a.k.a. Genuine German Parts).* 1998.

4. *Frigid Jr./Son of Formalde-Head.* 2004.

If *one* running Frankenstein monster is good for you, then several must be GREAT, apparently . . .

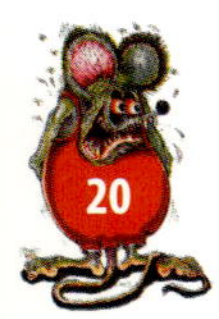

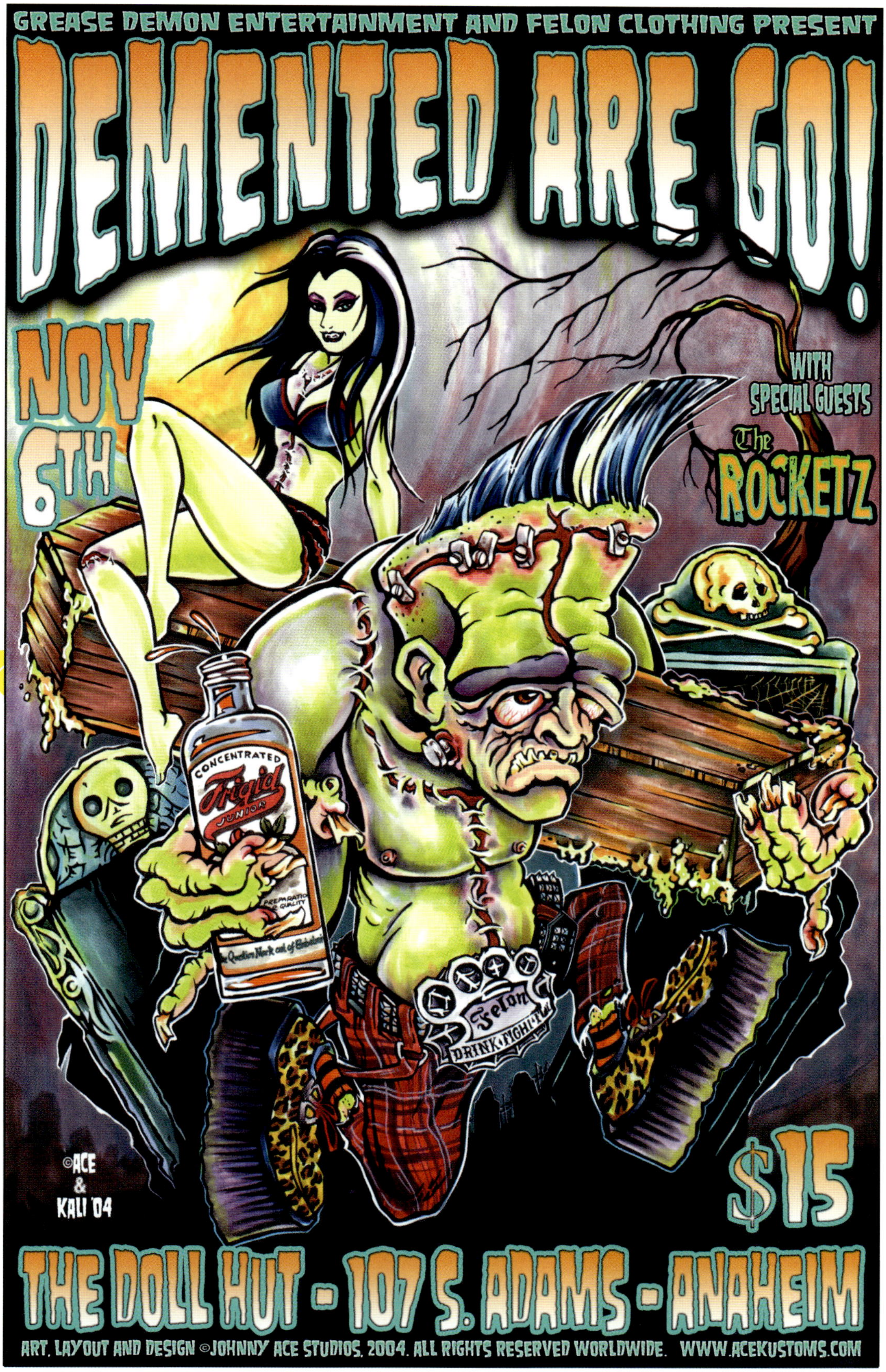

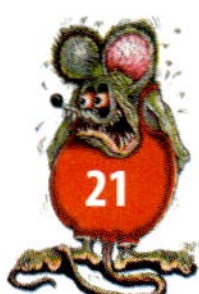

Frigid Jr. & Kasket Kutie. 2004.
Poster and full color artwork © 2004 by Johnny Ace Studios. All Rights Reserved.
"Steal Your Women/Drink Your Beer" design © 2005 by Felon Clothing.

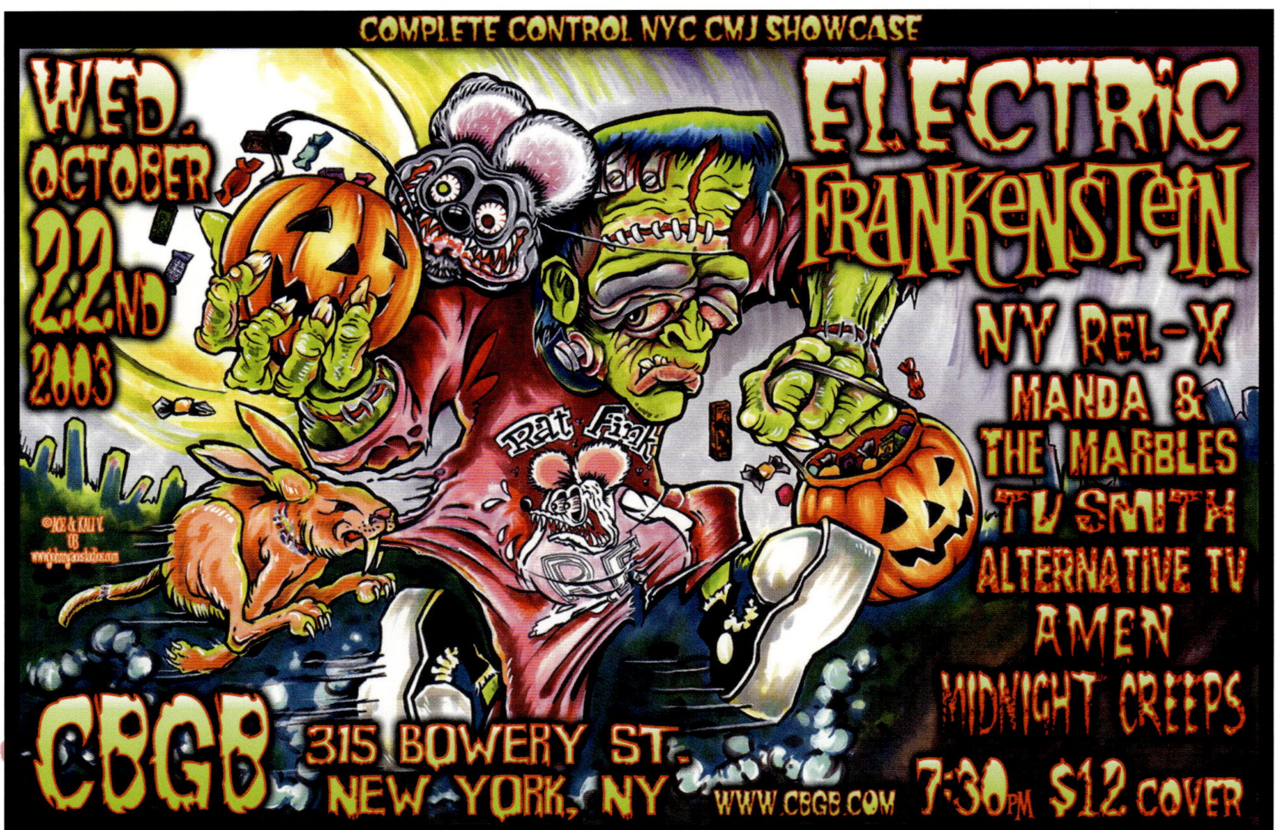

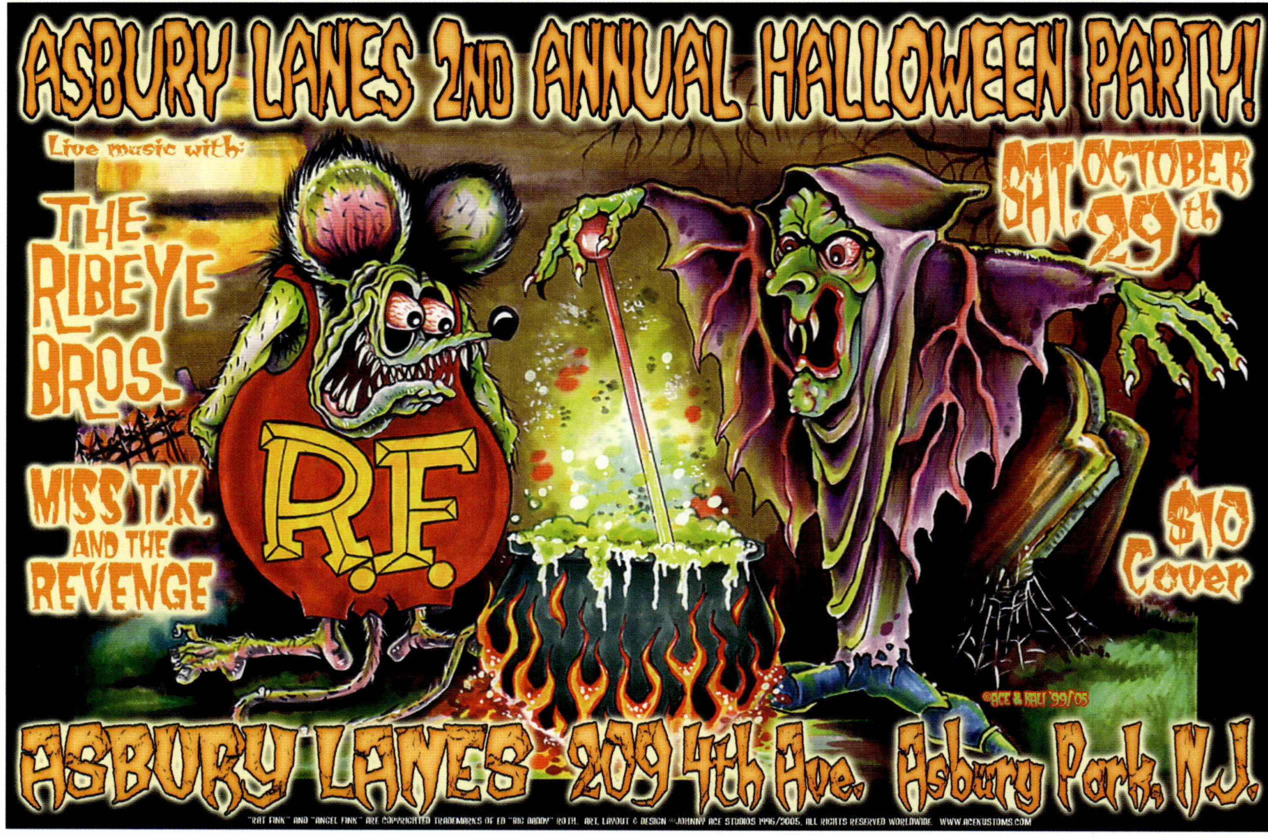

1. *Halloween Hodad (Genuine Ben Cooper Parts).* 2003.

2. *Halloween Hootenanny (Rat Fink Meets Angel Fink).* 1999.

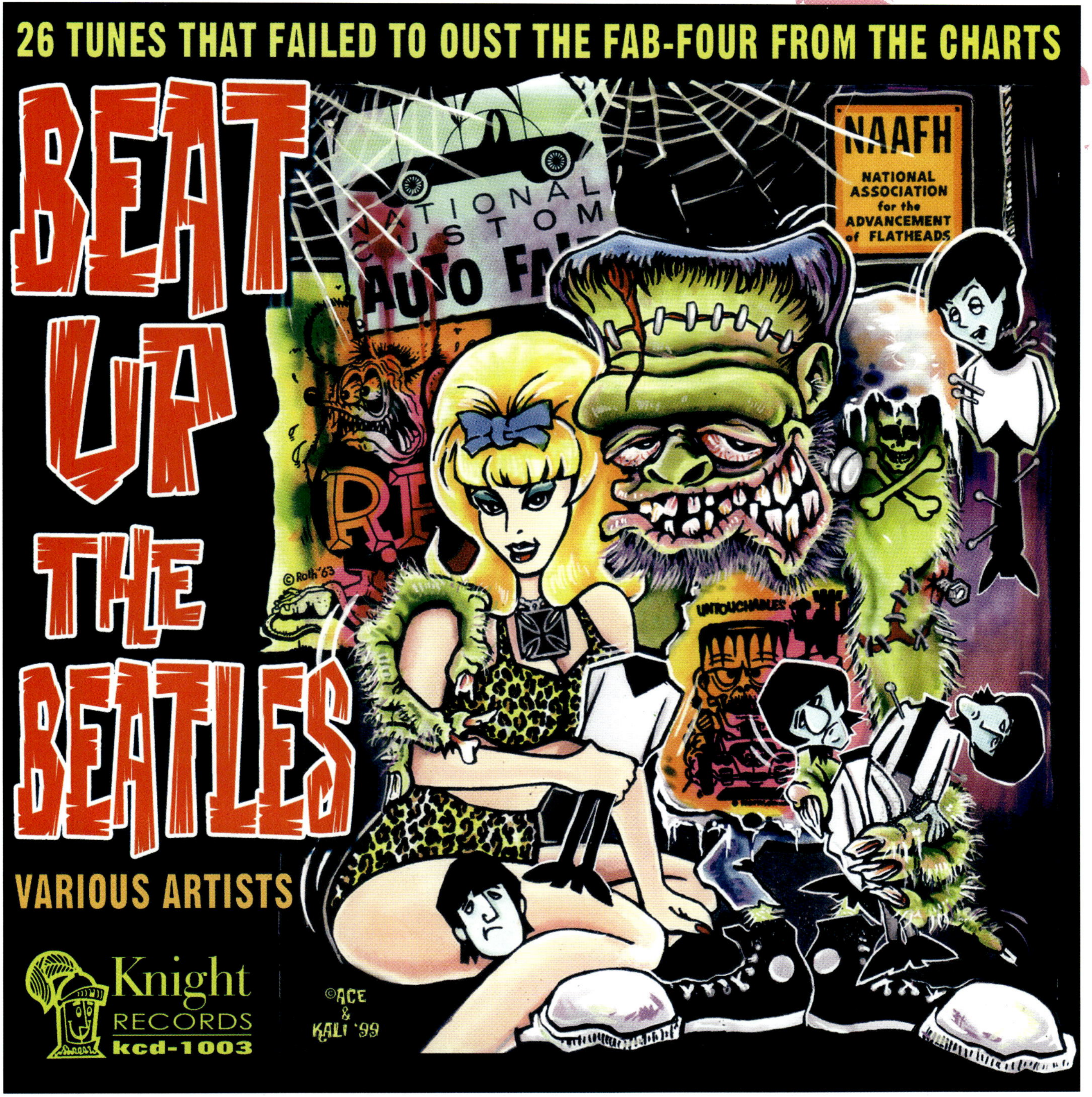

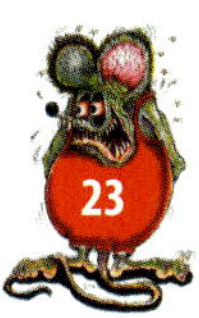

Beat Up The Beatles (Knight Records). 1999. Released as *Better Than The Beatles*.
The cover artwork for this collection of anti-Beatles novelty tunes was our tribute to Ed
"Big Daddy" Roth's legendary dislike of the Fab Four and their impact on teen culture.
He blamed the British Invasion as being one of the main distractions that kept American
youth from pursuing more constructive and creative endeavors—hot rodding, car
building, and surfing—in the early to mid '60s.

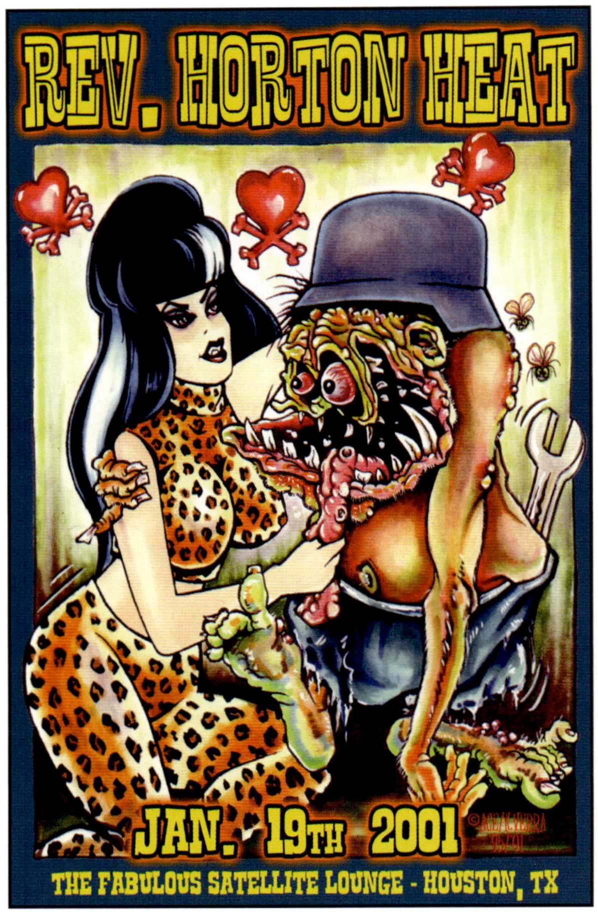

REV. HORTON HEAT
JAN. 19TH 2001
THE FABULOUS SATELLITE LOUNGE - HOUSTON, TX

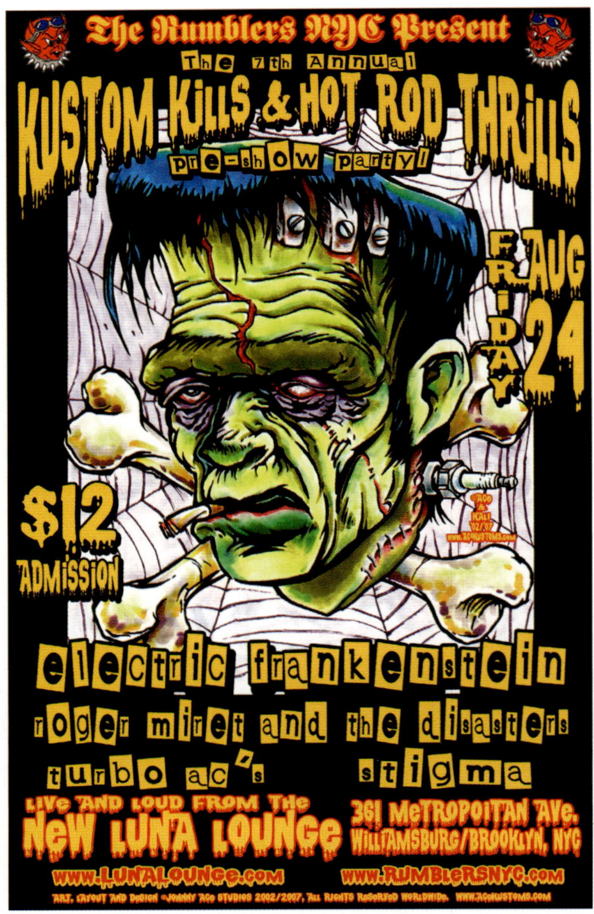

The Rumblers NYC Present
The 7th Annual
KUSTOM KILLS & HOT ROD THRILLS
pre-show party!
FRIDAY AUG 24
$12 ADMISSION
electric frankenstein
roger miret and the disasters
turbo ac's
stigma
LIVE AND LOUD FROM THE
NEW LUNA LOUNGE
361 METROPOITAN AVE.
WILLIAMSBURG/BROOKLYN, NYC
www.LUNALOUNGE.com
www.RUMBLERSNYC.com
ART, LAYOUT AND DESIGN ~JOHNNY ACE STUDIOS 2002/2007, ALL RIGHTS RESERVED WORLDWIDE. WWW.ACEKUSTOMS.COM

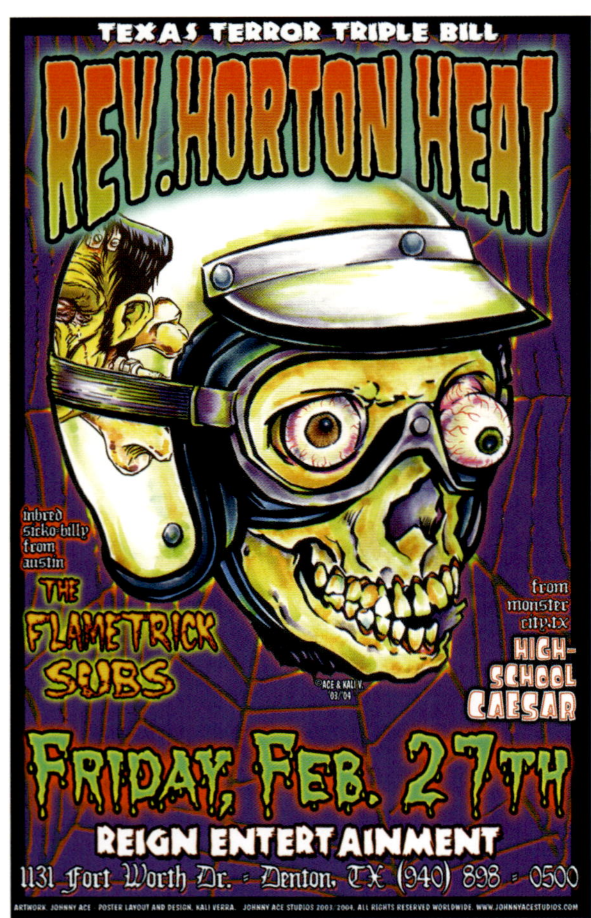

TEXAS TERROR TRIPLE BILL
REV. HORTON HEAT
inbred sicko billy from austin
THE FLAMETRICK SUBS
from monster city IX
HIGH-SCHOOL CAESAR
FRIDAY, FEB. 27TH
REIGN ENTERTAINMENT
1131 Fort Worth Dr. - Denton, TX (940) 898 - 0500
ARTWORK: JOHNNY ACE POSTER LAYOUT AND DESIGN: KALI VERRA. JOHNNY ACE STUDIOS 2004. ALL RIGHTS RESERVED WORLDWIDE. WWW.JOHNNYACESTUDIOS.COM

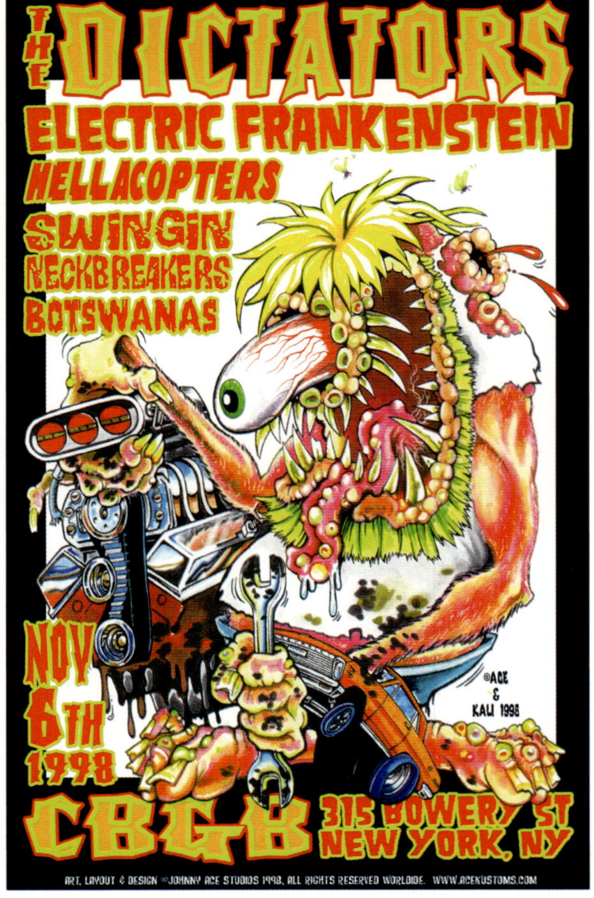

THE DICTATORS
ELECTRIC FRANKENSTEIN
HELLACOPTERS
SWIN'GIN' NECKBREAKERS
BOTSWANAS
NOV 6TH 1998
CBGB
315 BOWERY ST
NEW YORK, NY
ART, LAYOUT & DESIGN ©JOHNNY ACE STUDIOS 1998. ALL RIGHTS RESERVED WORLDWIDE. WWW.ACEKUSTOMS.COM

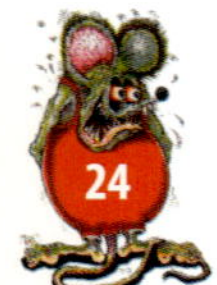

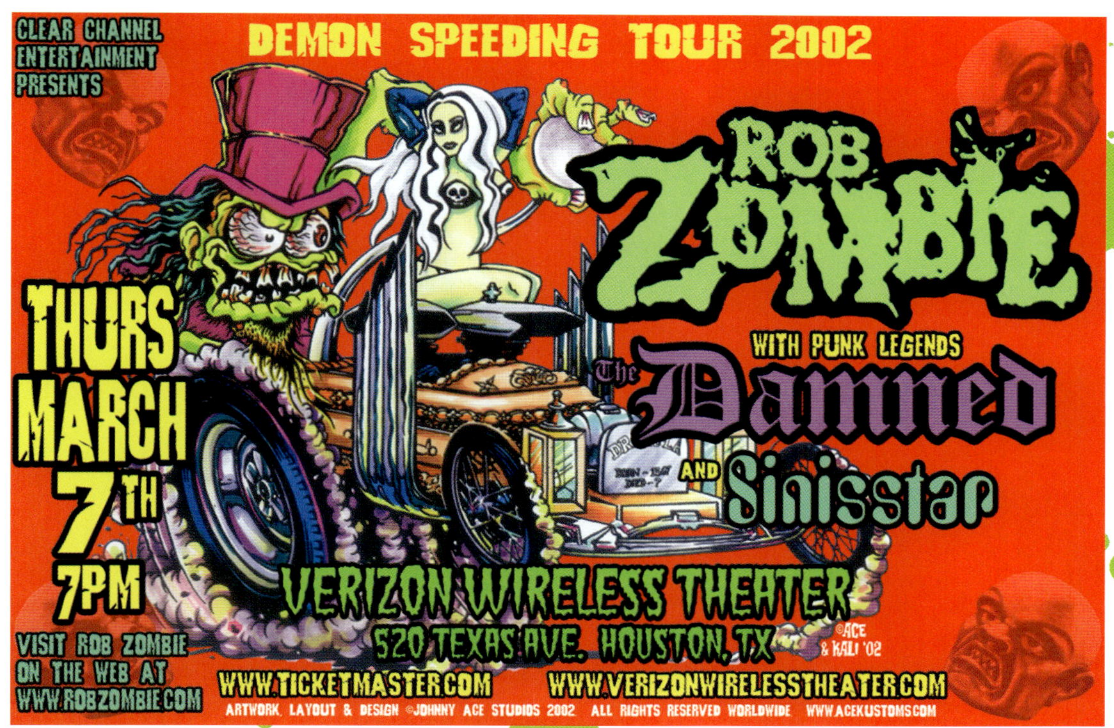

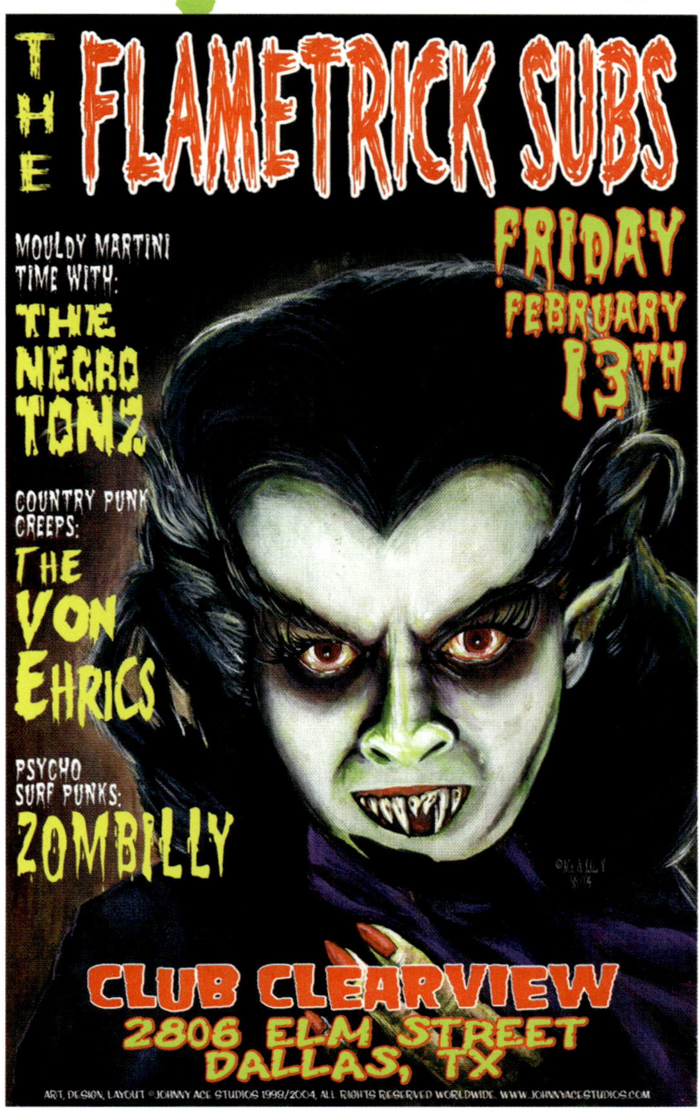

1. *Rob Zombie/The Damned, Demon Speeding Tour.* 2002.

2. *I Was a Teenage Ghoul-School Delinquent (Tribute to Sandra Harrison).* 1997.

3. *Von Klutch Meets Lady Luck.* 2003. "True American Punk Meets Inbred Texas Psychobilly in Jack Ruby's Back Yard!" This gig poster for punk legends X was dedicated to a personal cult hero of ours, Jack Starr.

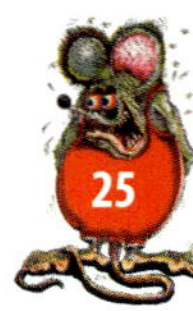

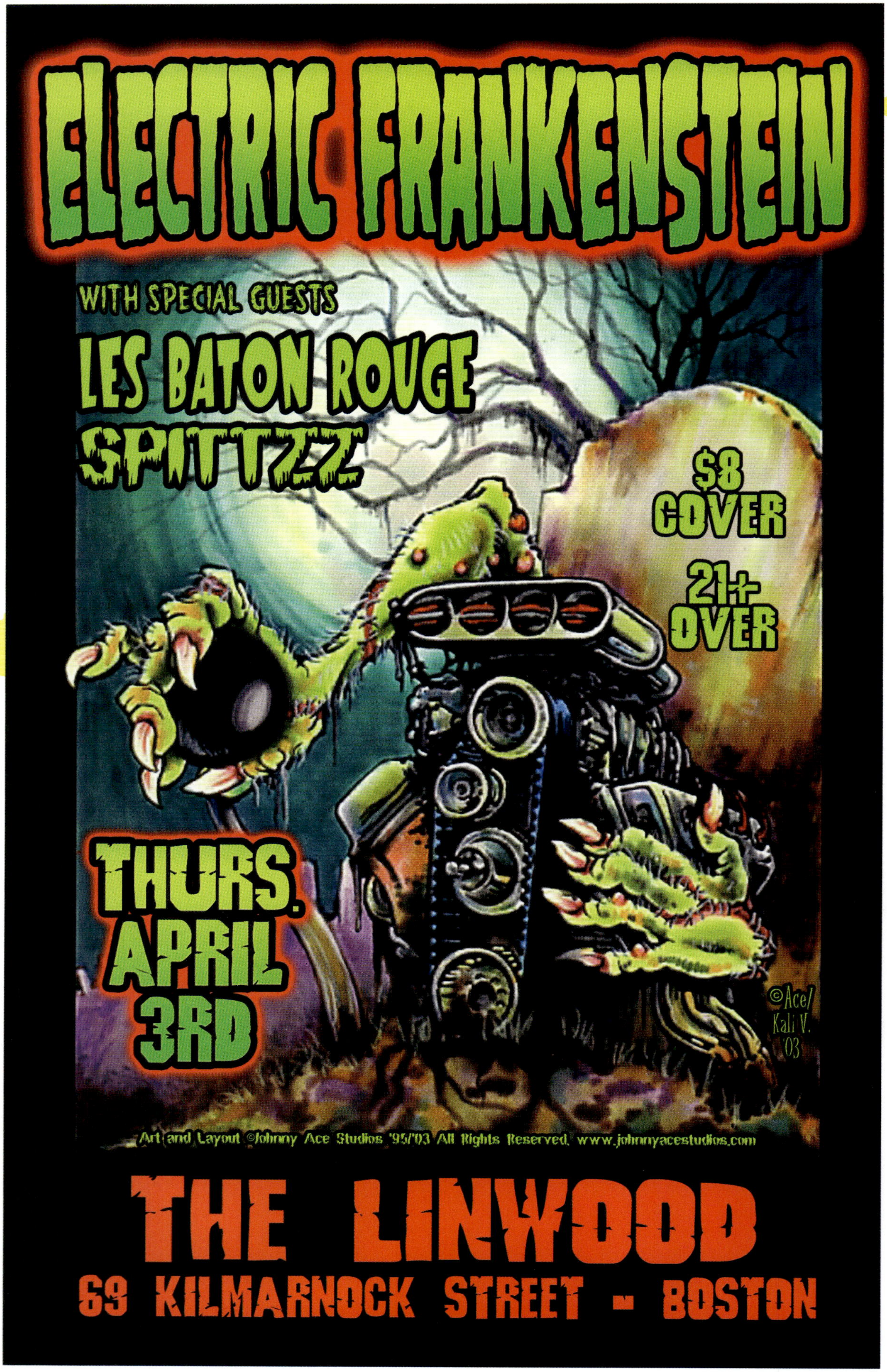

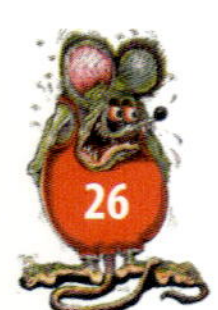

Hemi-Stein. 1995.

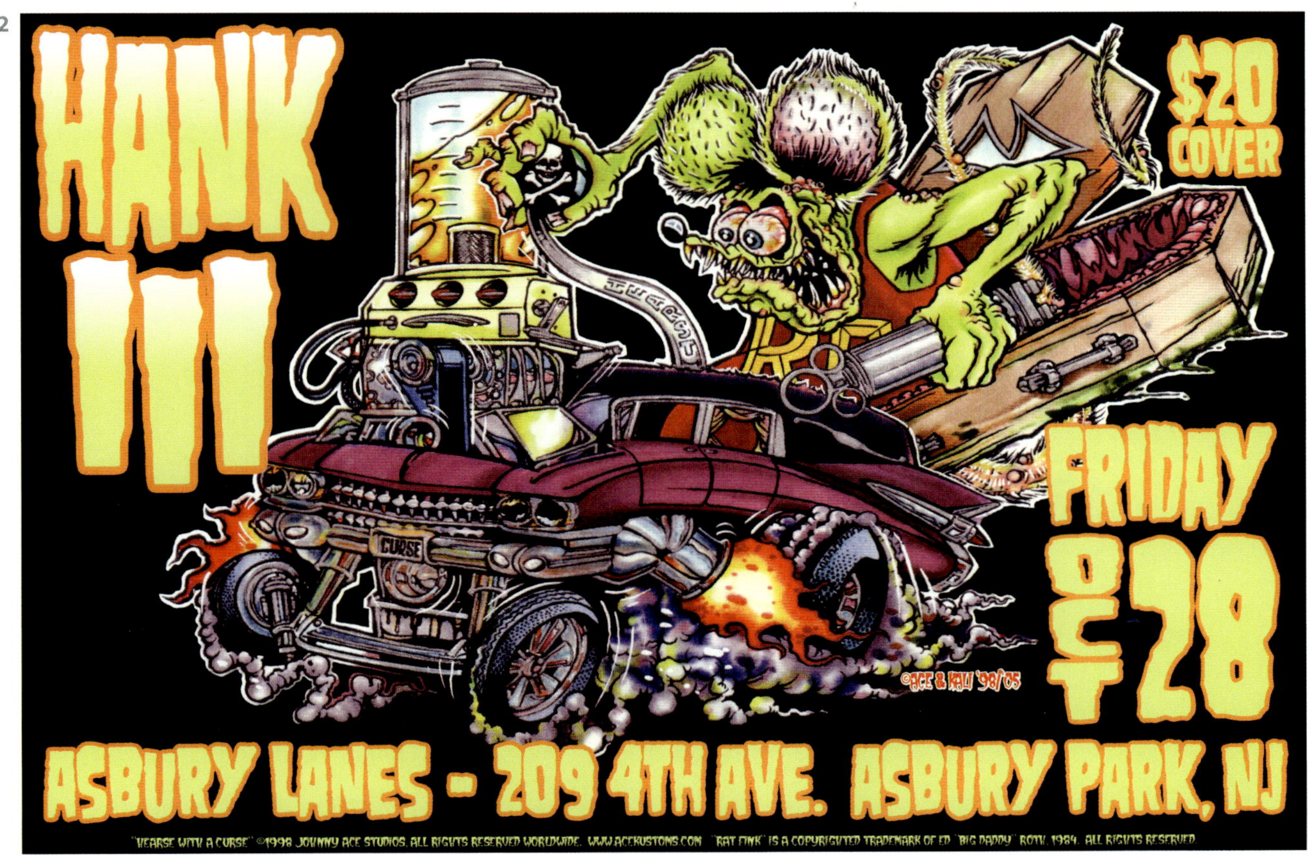

1. *Powered by Formaldehyde.* Character and artwork © 2004 by Johnny Ace Studios. "Gonna Take Your Daughter Out Tonight" design © 2005 by Felon Clothing.

2. *HearseFink (a.k.a. Hearse With a Curse, Part 1).* 1998. Inspired by a song from the infamous 1965 *Rods n' Rat Finks* LP by The Weirdos and Mr. Gasser (Ed Roth, hisself)! "There ain't nothin' worse than a hearse with a curse—don't buy it!"

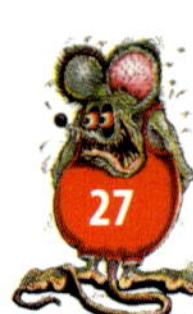

27

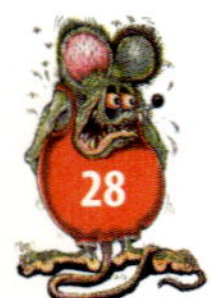

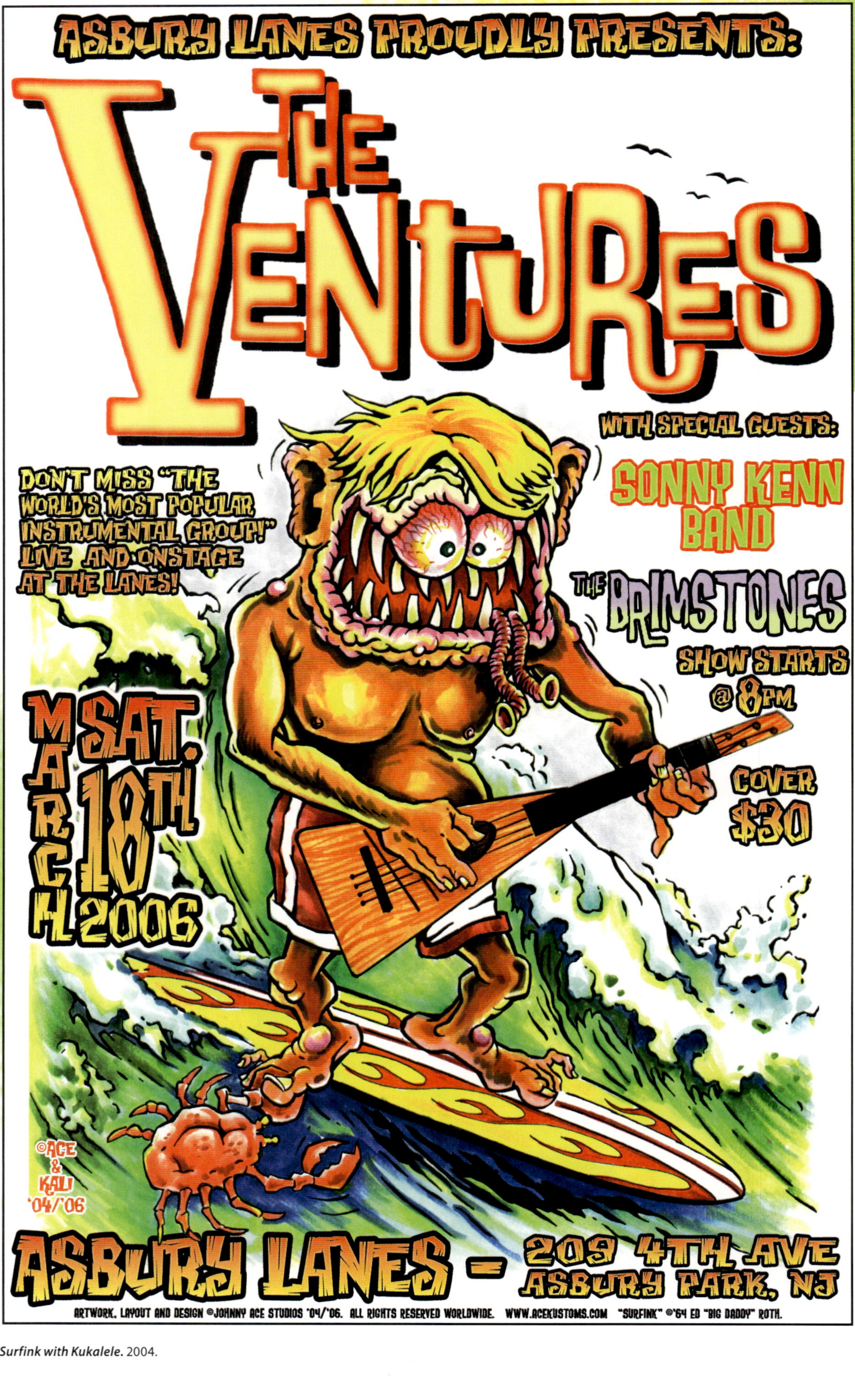

Surfink with Kukalele. 2004.

28

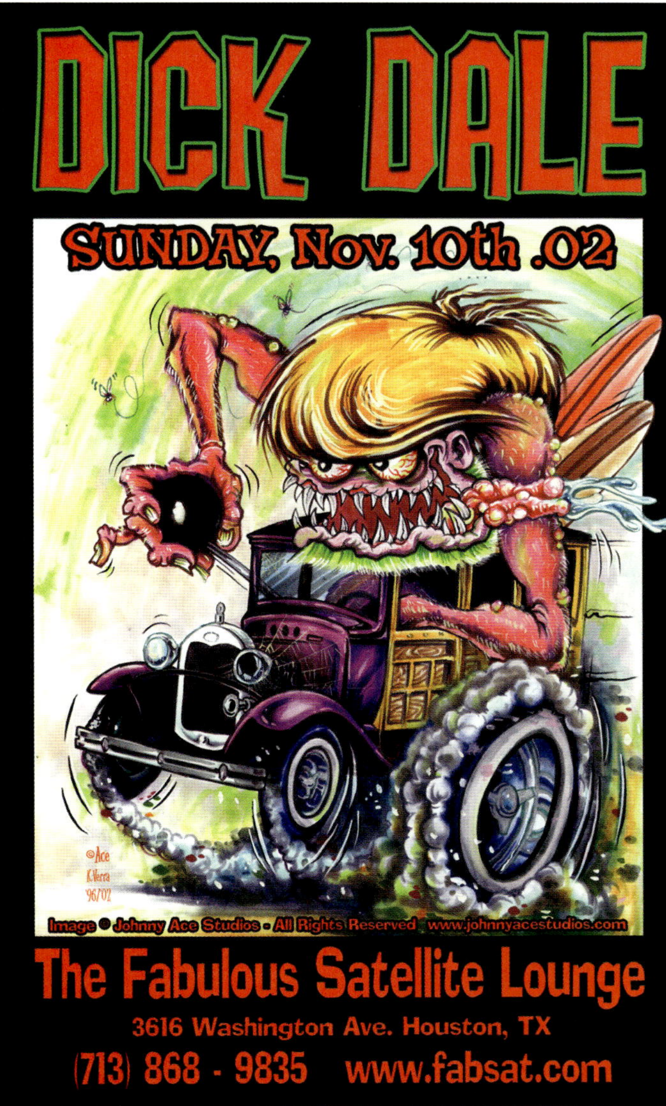

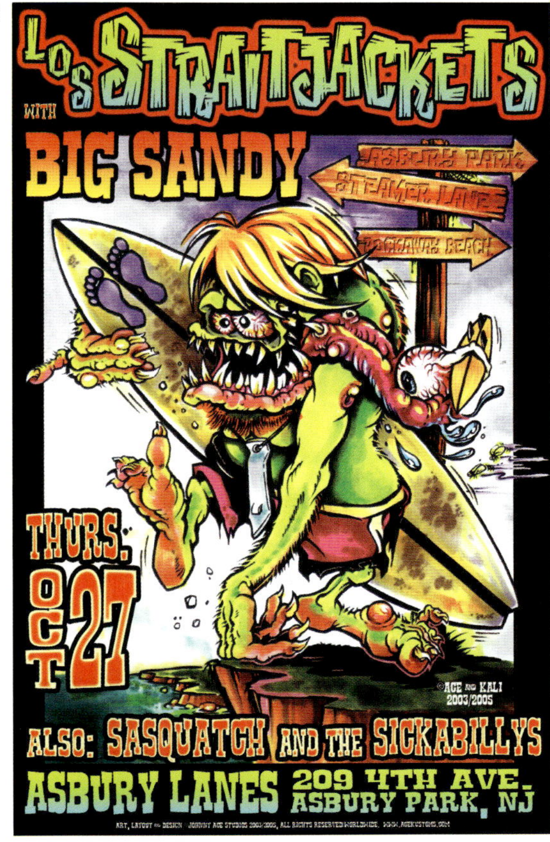

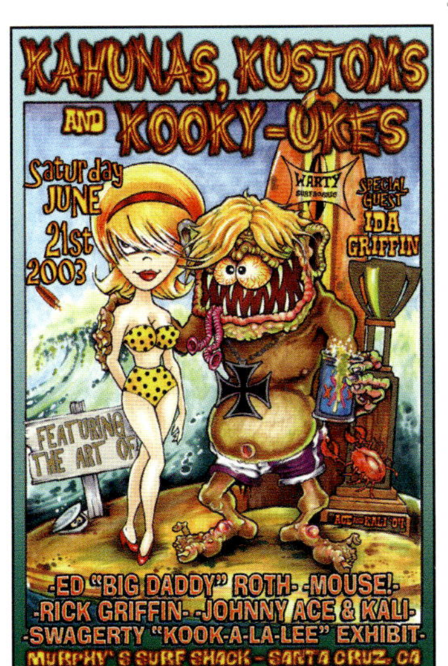

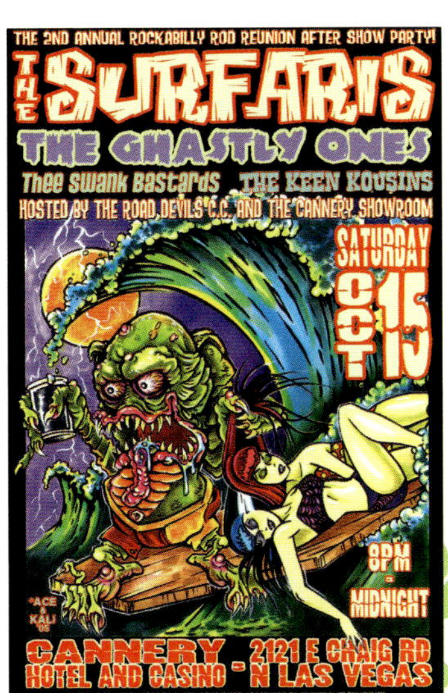

1. *Termites in My Woodie.* 1996.

2. *Church Key Fink (a.k.a. Steamer Lane).* 2003.
   This character was inspired by watching some locals surf at the infamous Steamer Lane Point located off the cliffs in Santa Cruz. We had been watching the seals and checking out the cliff overlook when three surfers behind us dropped into the cold water below. The line art version of this design also exists as an unreleased t-shirt graphic somewhere out there.

3. *Kahunas, Kustoms, and Kooky-Ukes Art Exhibit and Party.* 2003.
   This poster marks a very special occasion—we were honored to have had our art displayed with some true legends. Among the guests was Ida Griffin, who shared some special words with us regarding Rick Griffin and his work. In addition to original art by Griffin, there were original Roth and Mouse airbrushed monster shirts and a rare display of Swagerty Kooky-Ukes.

4. *CreatureFink (a.k.a. Two Ghouls for Every Boy!).* 2005.
   Full-color illustration © by Johnny Ace Studios.
   "Surf City" version © 2005 by Felon Clothing.

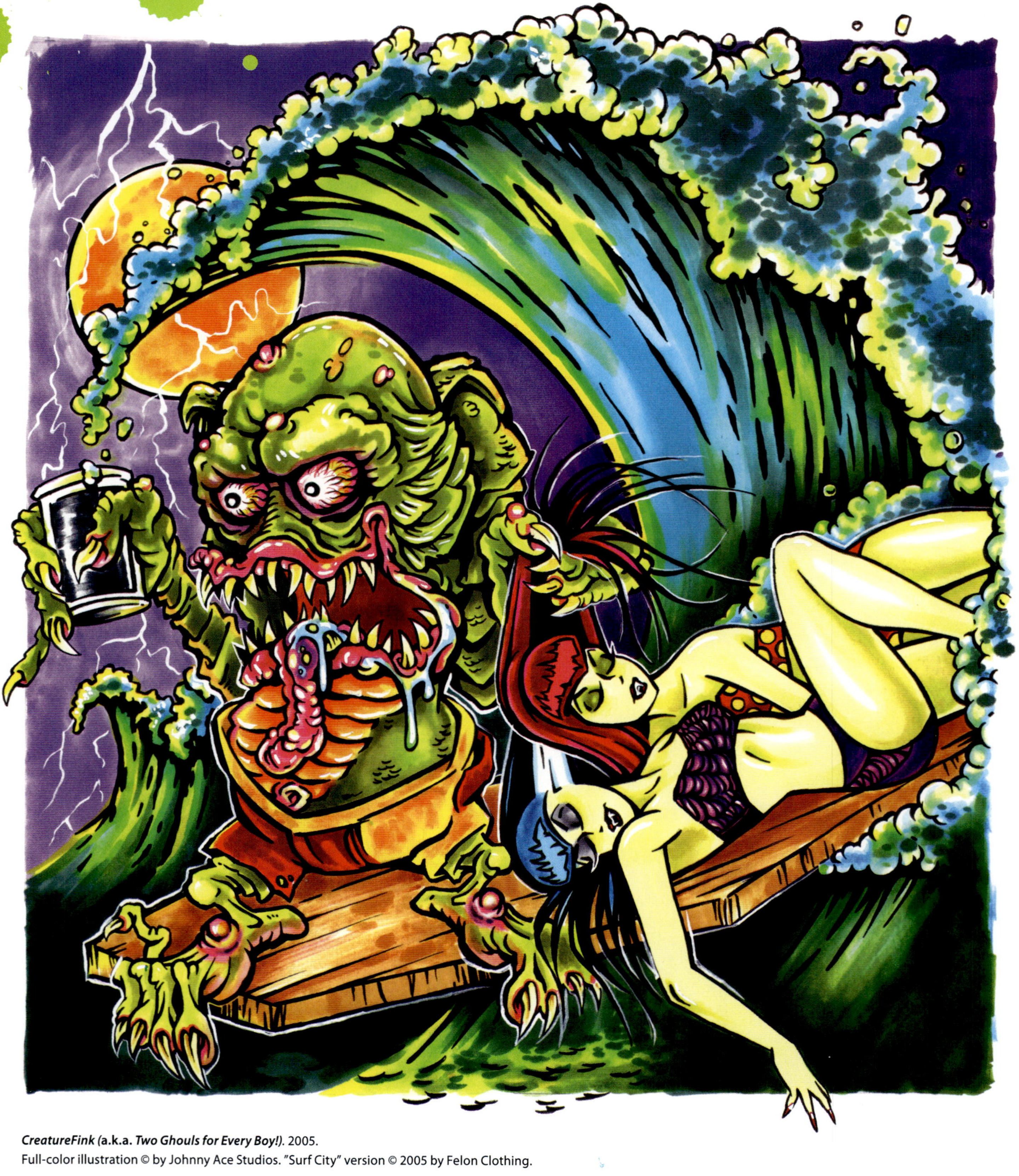

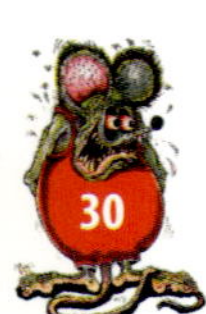

CreatureFink (a.k.a. Two Ghouls for Every Boy!). 2005.
Full-color illustration © by Johnny Ace Studios. "Surf City" version © 2005 by Felon Clothing.

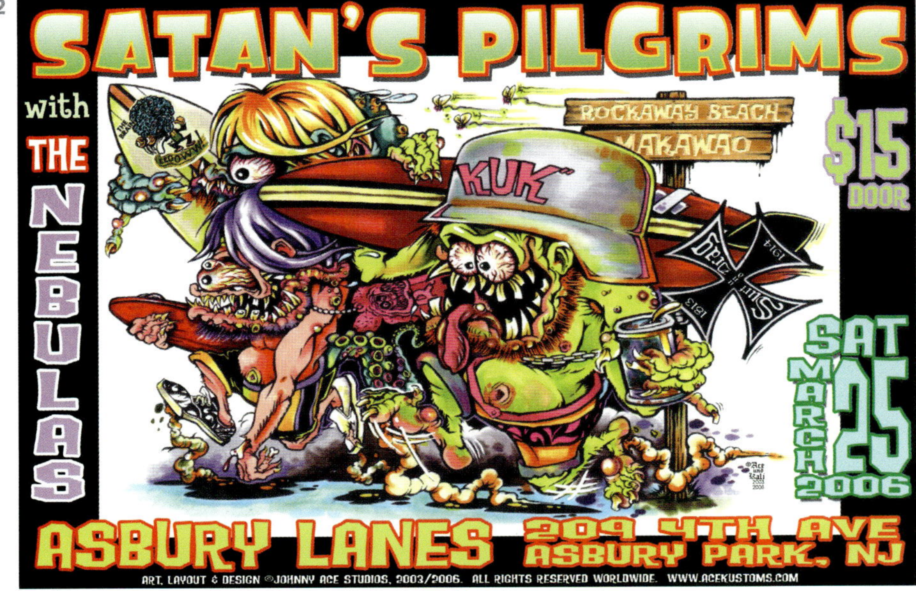

1. *Surfink Party Tonight!* 1998.
   Another tribute to Roth's Capitol three-LP series and the glory days of Revell models.

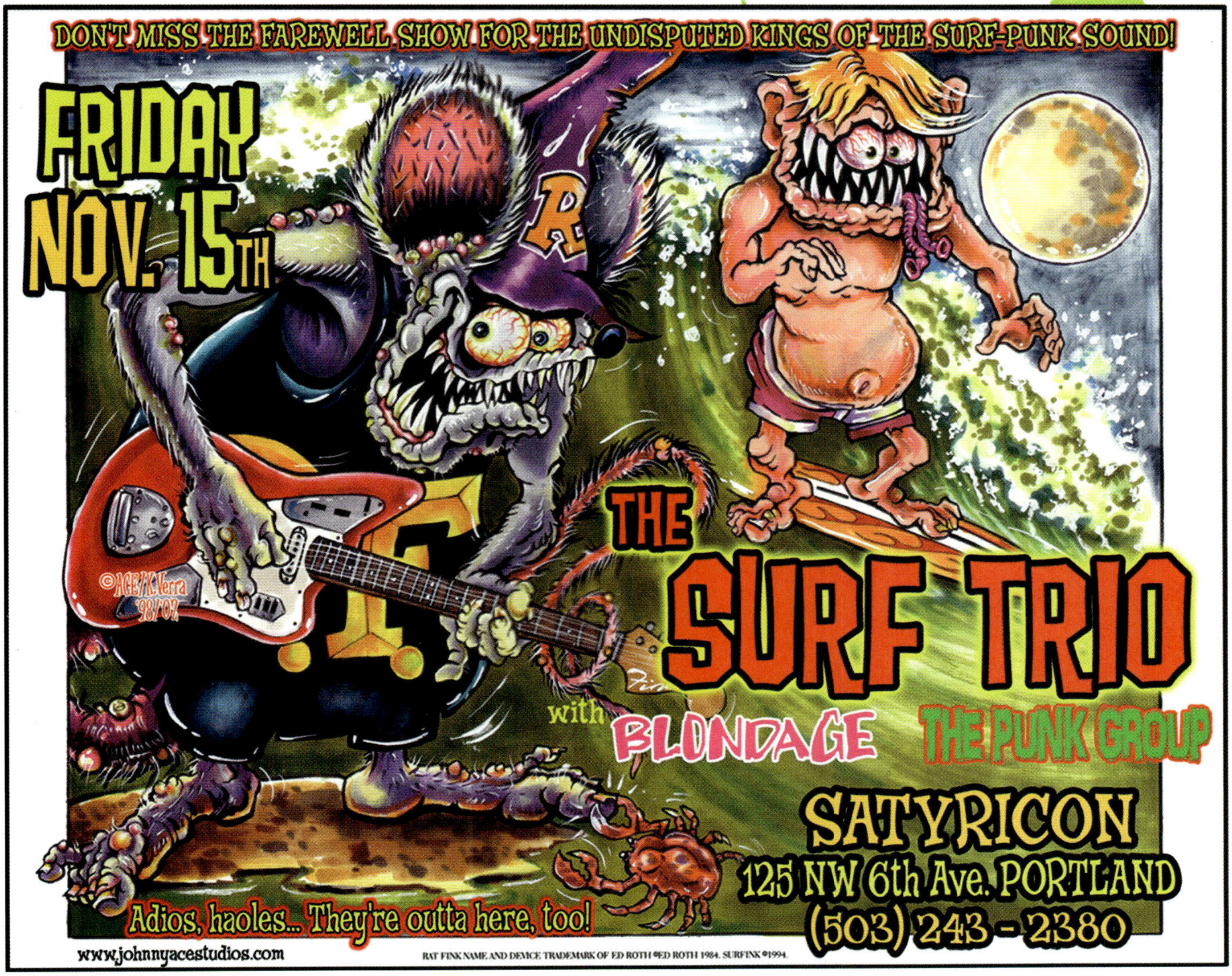

2. *Kuk Stampede.* 2003.
   We tried to incorporate as many sight gags into this scene as possible . . . "Kuk" in this case referring to a song title from a 1963 Astronauts LP. In tribute to Roth Studios, Kuk is sporting a genuine "Surfer Helmet" and "Surfer Cross." The fellow with the octopus coming out of his baggies is carrying a steel-wheeled Nash Duke Kahanamoku skateboard, one Duke shoe, and one slip-on. Makawao is home to Hawaii's biggest Ghoulardi fan.

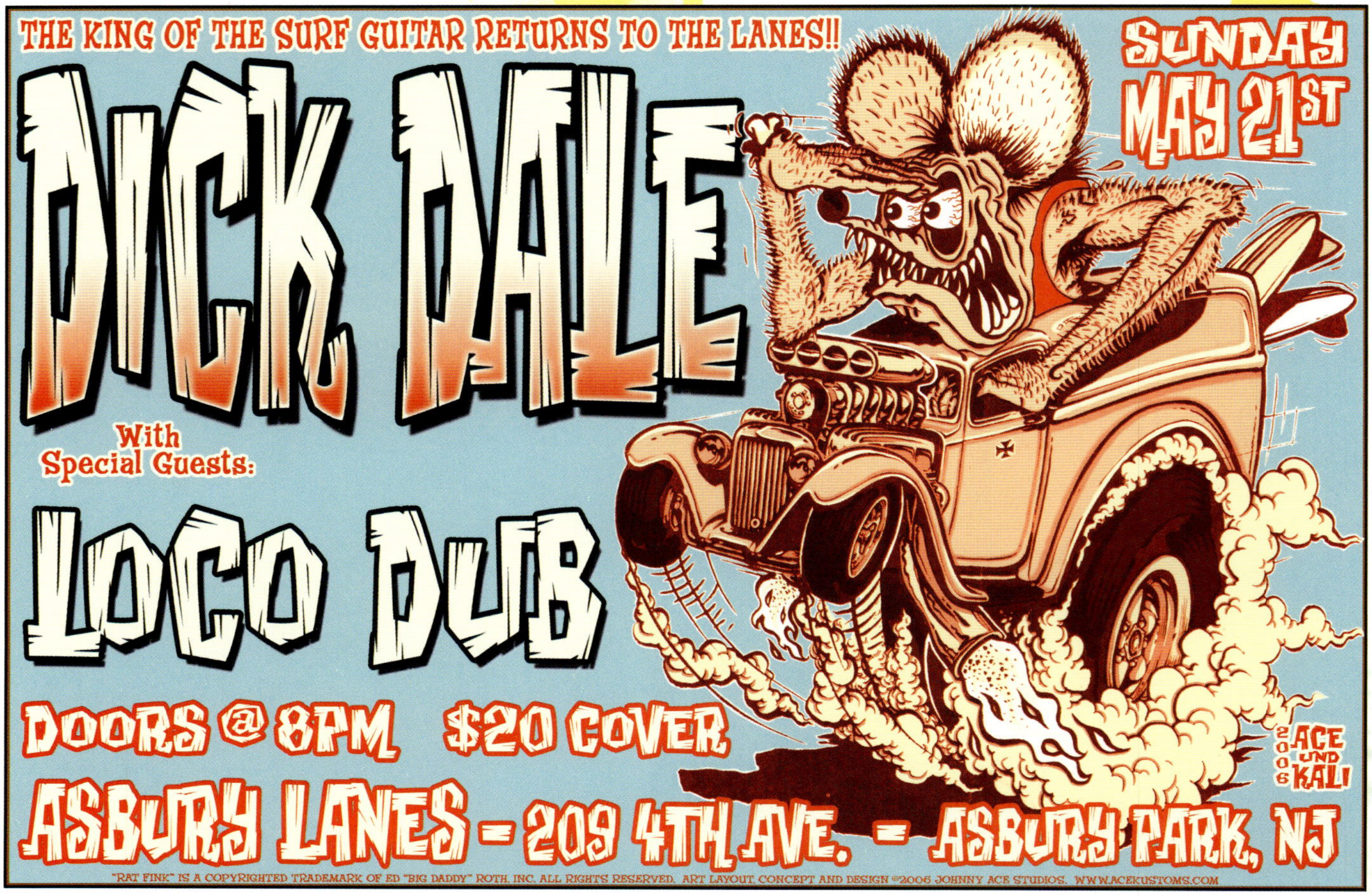

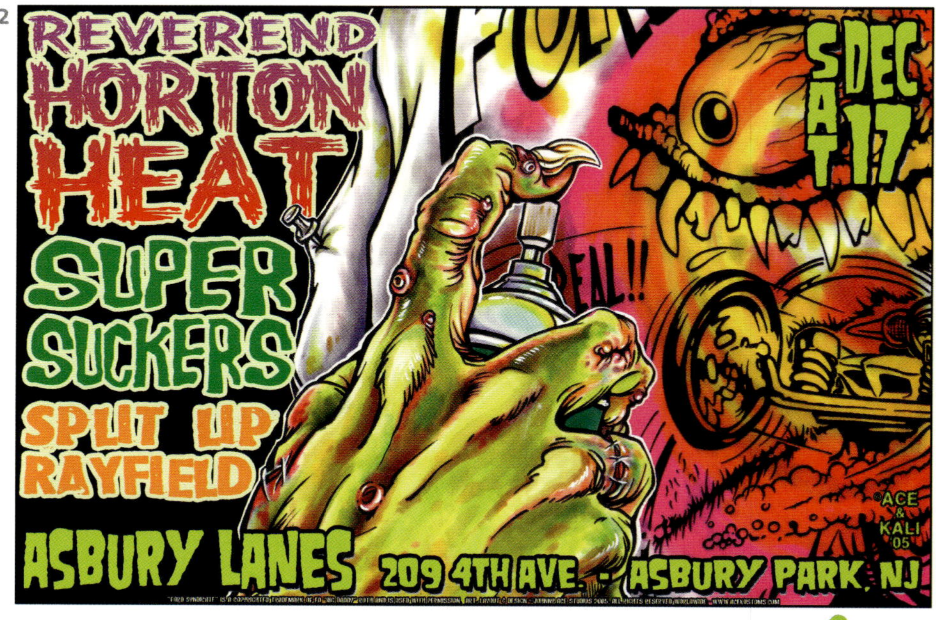

1. *Rat Fink as Hunter.* 2005.

The origins of this design go back to the early days of Roth Studios. When monster genius Ed Newton arrived on the scene, "Hunter" became a t-shirt classic. We decided that Rat Fink, along with the Ford panel truck (with Buick nailhead, cheater slicks, and American mags), would be the perfect image to commemorate this East Coast show by Dick Dale. We did our best to stay true to Newt's original brushwork as well as making the design look like a vintage waterslide decal.

2. *Join the Ford Syndicate!* 2005.

One of our many tributes to the world of early '60s custom monster shirts—a haze of fluorescent colors, lacquers, flakes, kandies, and highly flammable thinners!

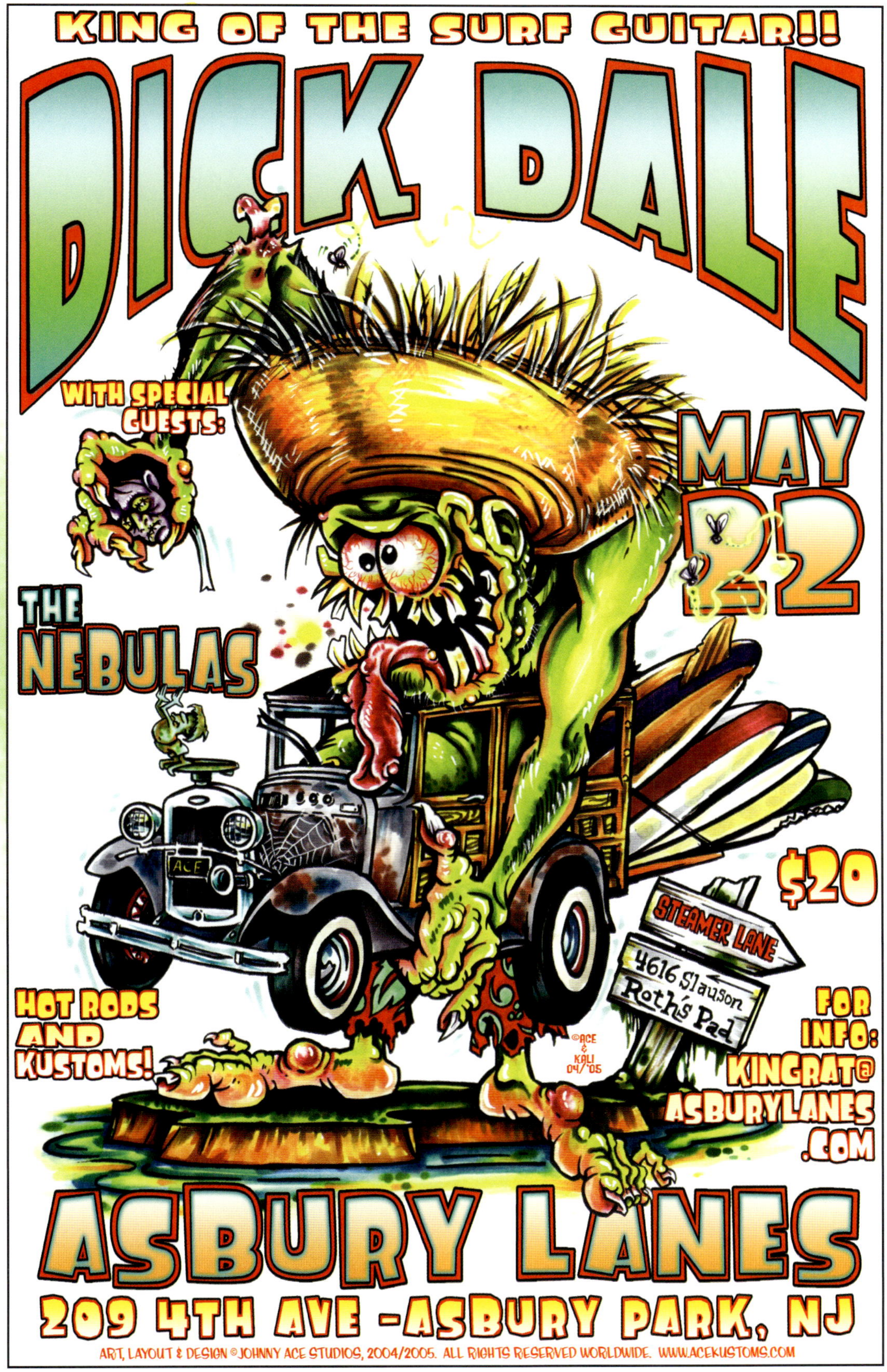

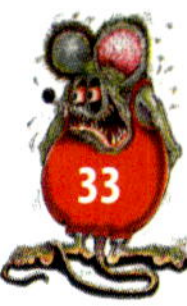

The Lonesome Surfer. 2005.
This Dick Dale gig poster features our own "Kuk" character making another appearance . . . Poster details include a tip of the hat to Roth's shop, Santa Cruz, and an early Rick Griffin character.

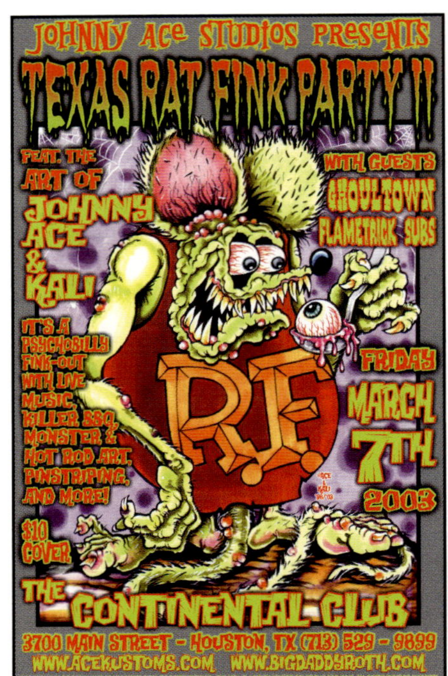

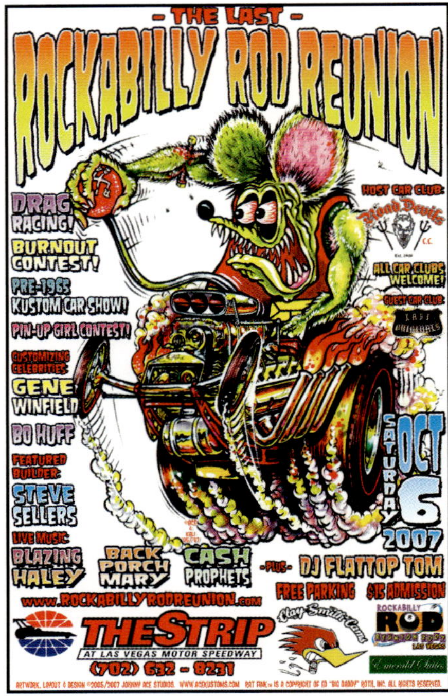

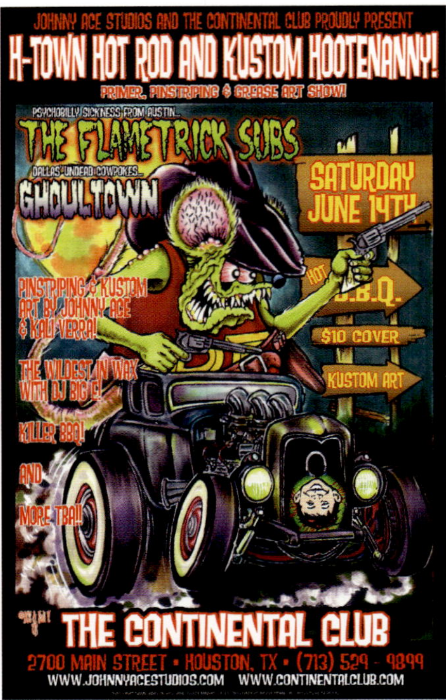

1. *Texas Rat Fink Party II.* 2003.
   We began hosting these parties in the Houston area in 2002 as the result of not being able to attend the official Rat Fink Reunion at Bonneville. We also wanted to create an event closer to home where cars, art, and music could be enjoyed while upholding our intense connection to Roth. We maintained that each event be designated to benefit a specific charity, in the tradition of Ed's practices.

2. *Rat Fink as Drag Lover.* 2005.
   We once again borrowed heavily from Newt's toolbox to put this one together. The event itself was presented by The Road Devils Car Club, which traditionally promotes hot rods, kustoms, drag racing, and sickles! Although the event name (now discarded) was "venue dictated," the Road Devils C.C. always puts on a QUALITY event, staying true to its roots . . . and the roots of hot rodding in general.

3. *H-Town Hot Rod and Kustom Hootenanny.* 2003.
   We also hosted this event, which was technically a Rat Fink Party, in spite of the title difference. With the same goals in mind, we successfully managed to blend displayed art, pinstriping, live music, and HOT BBQ! Our artwork for this poster features obscure in-jokes atop esoterica: the inverted image of Melvin Koznowski is in reference to the famous Yeakel Brothers-sponsored '29 Ford roadster of the mid-'50s. The grille shell insert was painted by the legendary Von Dutch, which he rendered inverted. The '29 sported the image as it was and was famous for that characteristic at shows and for its formidable record on both the salt and strip. On a side note, Melvin the K. was featured prominently on the plaque for the So-Cal Veeblefetzers car club of the '50s.

4. *Monster Rally.* 1999.
   Yet another of our events/Rat Fink Parties where we got together to pinstripe, do monster shirts, etc. in the spirit of the original Rat Fink Reunions. This particular show took place in 2003 on a freezing December night at Hans' Rod & Cycle, a huge custom garage where we worked for hours (despite the temperature) surrounded by the smell of 1-Shot, pizza, and beer and the presence of a very impressive '42 Caddy flathead-powered '27 roadster project.

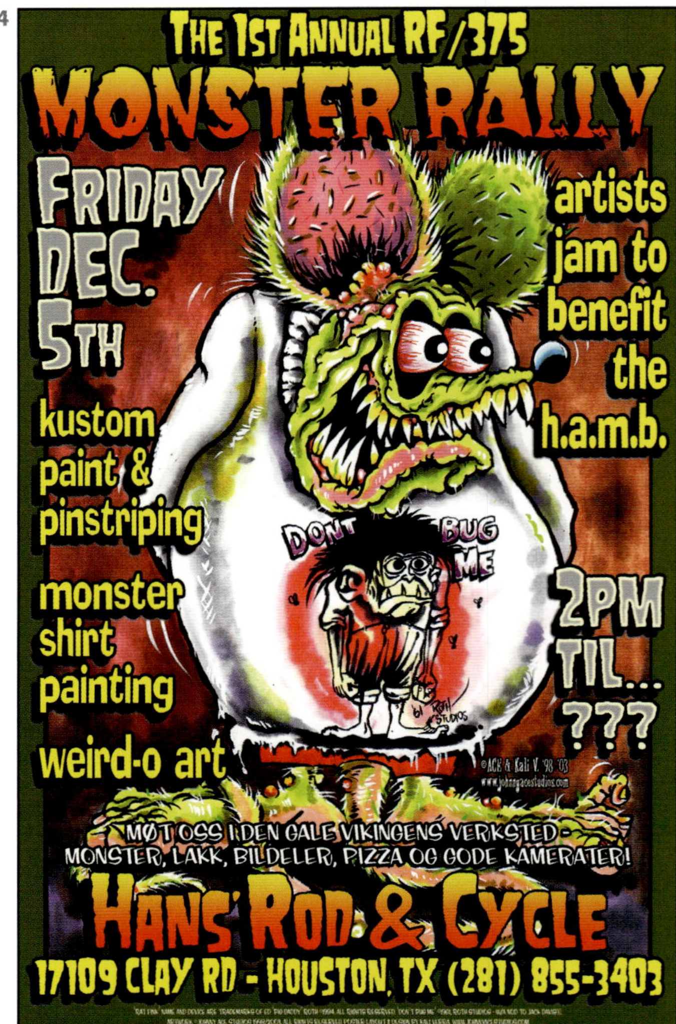

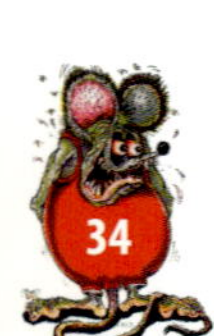

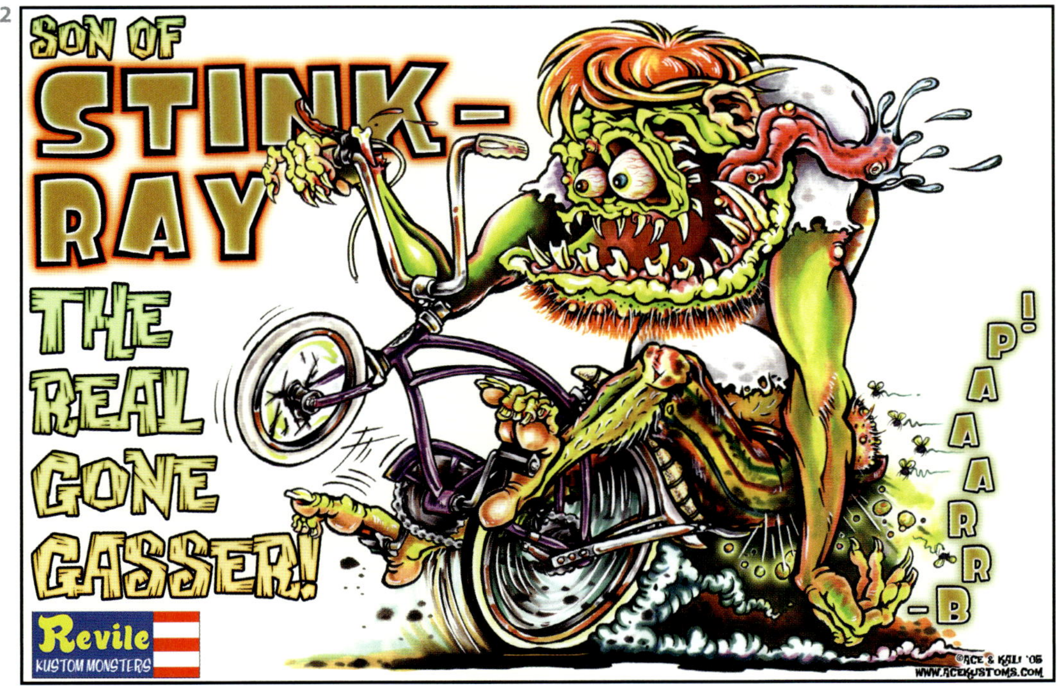

1. *Brother Rat Fink with Chopper Fink.* 2006.

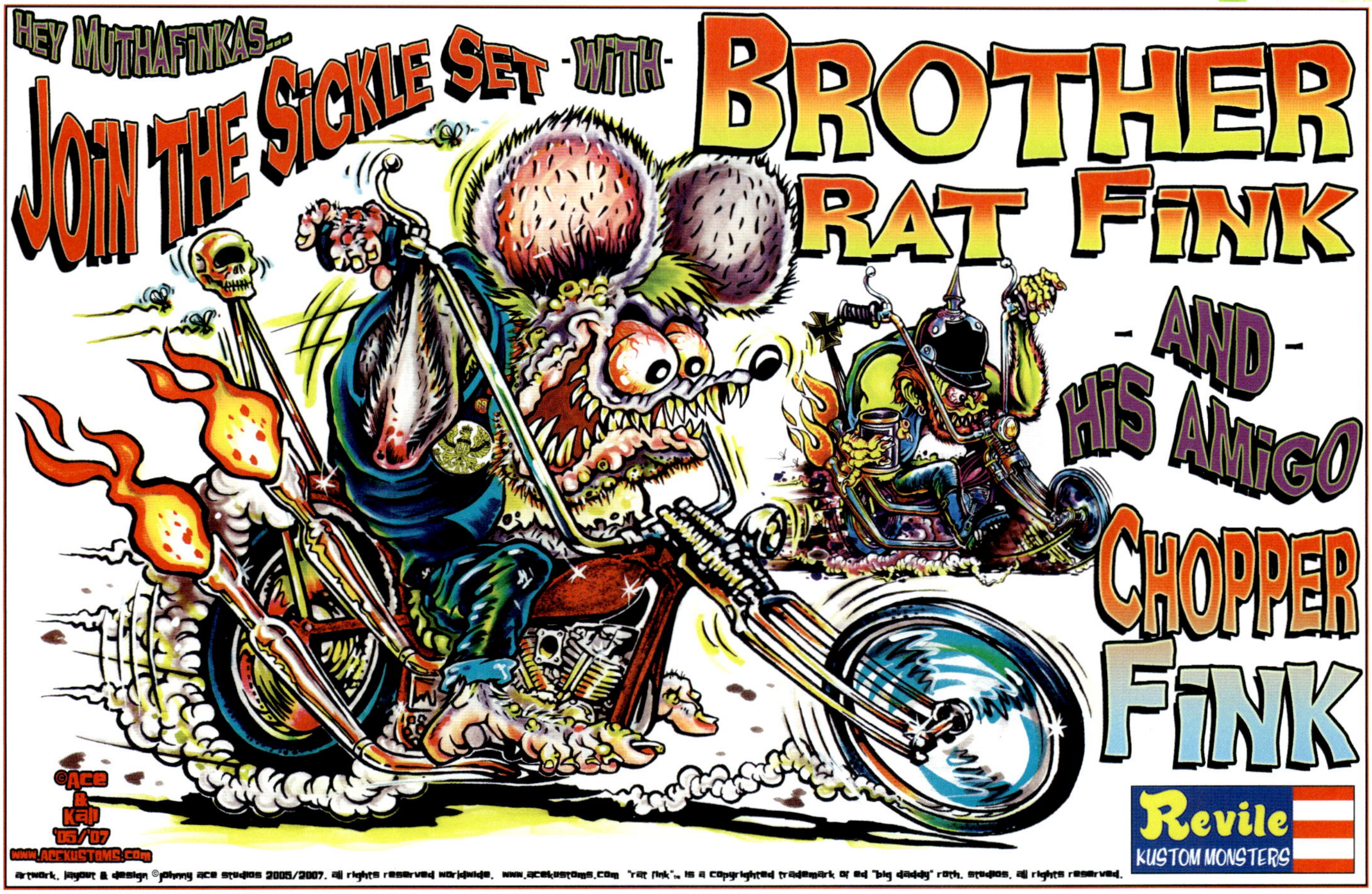

2. *Son of Stink-Ray, the Real Gone Gasser.* 2005.

These examples of non-existent model kit box art were done in tribute and in fond memory of the classic Revell kit series based on Roth Studios' characters and show cars. Look closely to see details based on Roth merchandising and products of the time: the Wham-O Wheelie Bar from 1966, Newt's monster shirt art, Roth novelty buttons, etc. Imagine if Revell had produced kits like these!

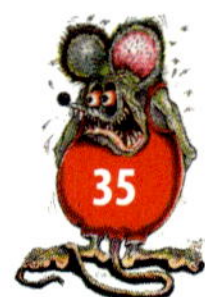

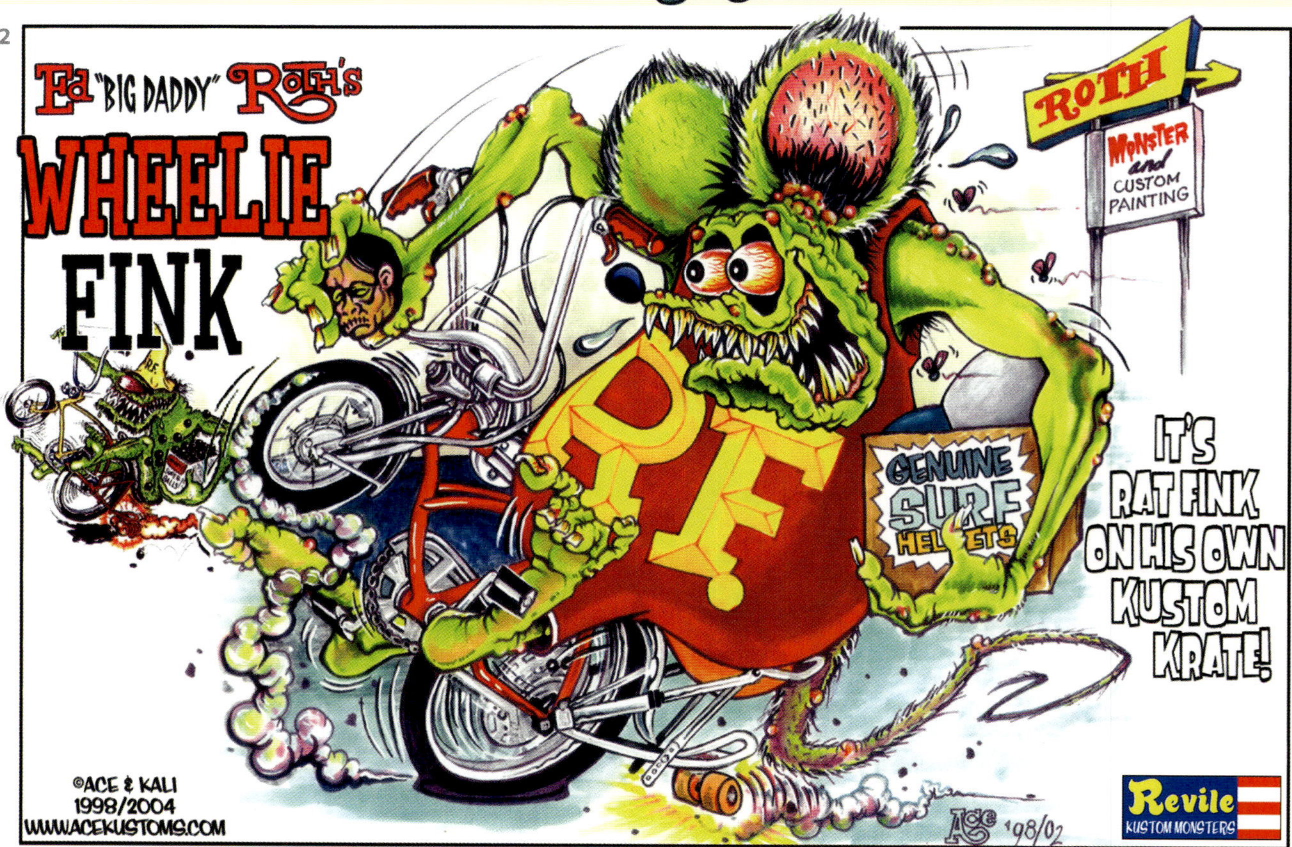

1. *Stink-Ray Fink with Swet-Fink.* 1998.

2. *Wheelie Fink.* 1998.

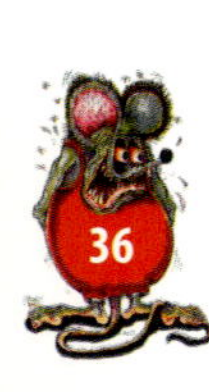

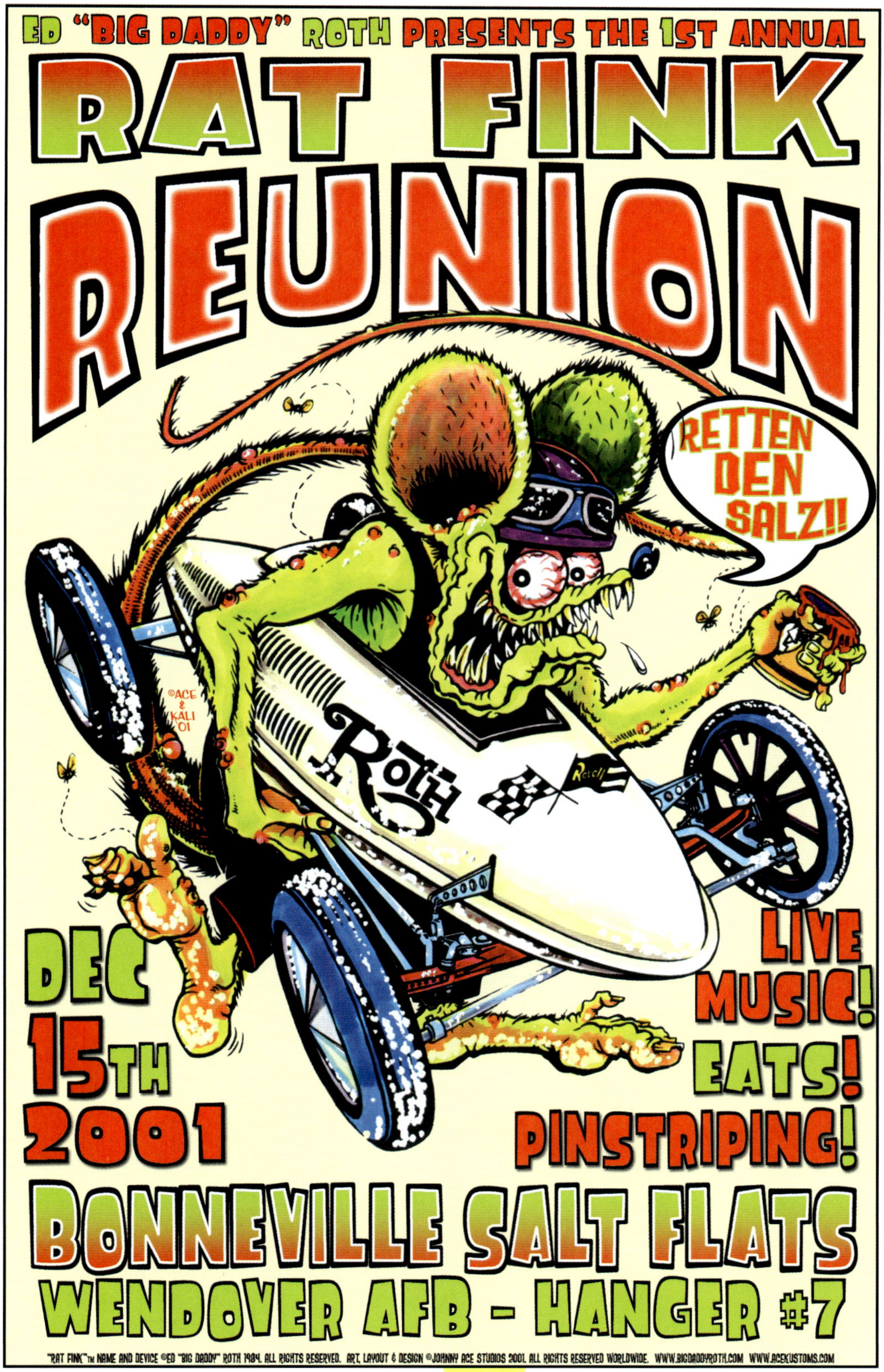

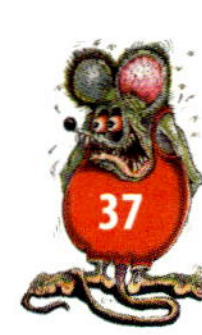

Rat Fink Reunion 2001.

This event poster marks a very important turning point in Ed's history of presiding over the annual Rat Fink Reunion parties in So-Cal. The original Rat Fink Reunion gatherings were started by Robert and Suzanne Williams in 1977 out of fondness for the annual Roth Studios Christmas parties, which ceased in 1970 when Roth Studios closed its doors. At first, Roth was hesitant to attend due to his religious convictions but ultimately began to make the event his own by introducing the "paint party" element by inviting his pinstriping and sign-painter friends. These parties continued to grow over the years and ultimately ended up being hosted by the resurrected Mooneyes company until the final event in December 2000.

We received a phone call the afternoon of the party, from a very agitated Roth, who informed us that the cops had shut down the event. Ed had become increasingly unhappy with the infiltration of certain artists and individuals into what was supposed to be his traditional and spiritual gathering. The Rat Fink Reunion, which came to serve as a charity function and gathering of former Roth employees and Roth Studios devotees, often became populated by artists and vendors who had no respect for Ed's wishes, often selling offensive and unlicensed work and products right under his nose.

Ed had been provoked to the breaking point and instructed us to immediately begin working on an event poster that would mark the return of his control over his own events. "We're going to have these parties in the middle of NOWHERE from now on . . . We'll paint, eat, and hang out, and if none of these people want to show up, that's THEIR problem . . . Who needs 'em?!?"

Needless to say, we are extremely proud to have been chosen by Ed to mark this event.

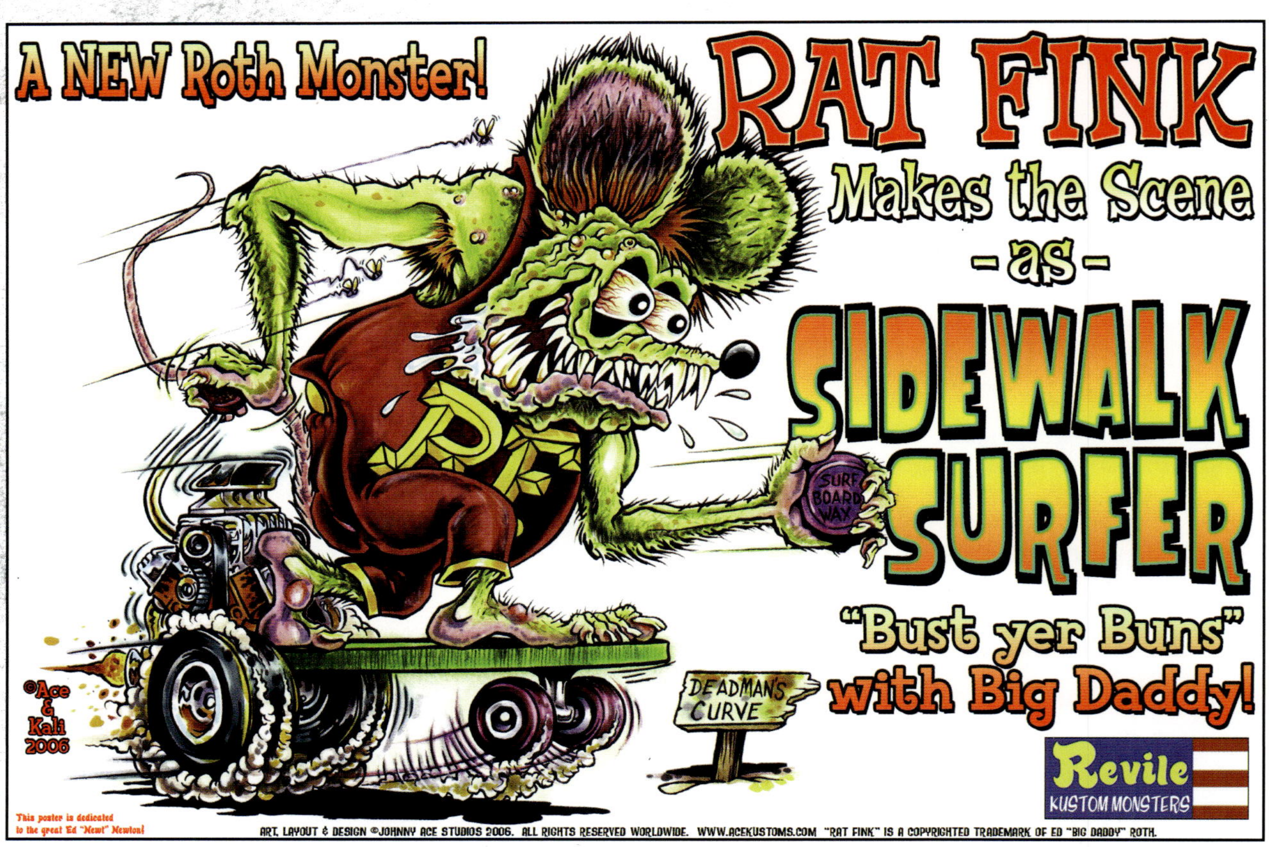

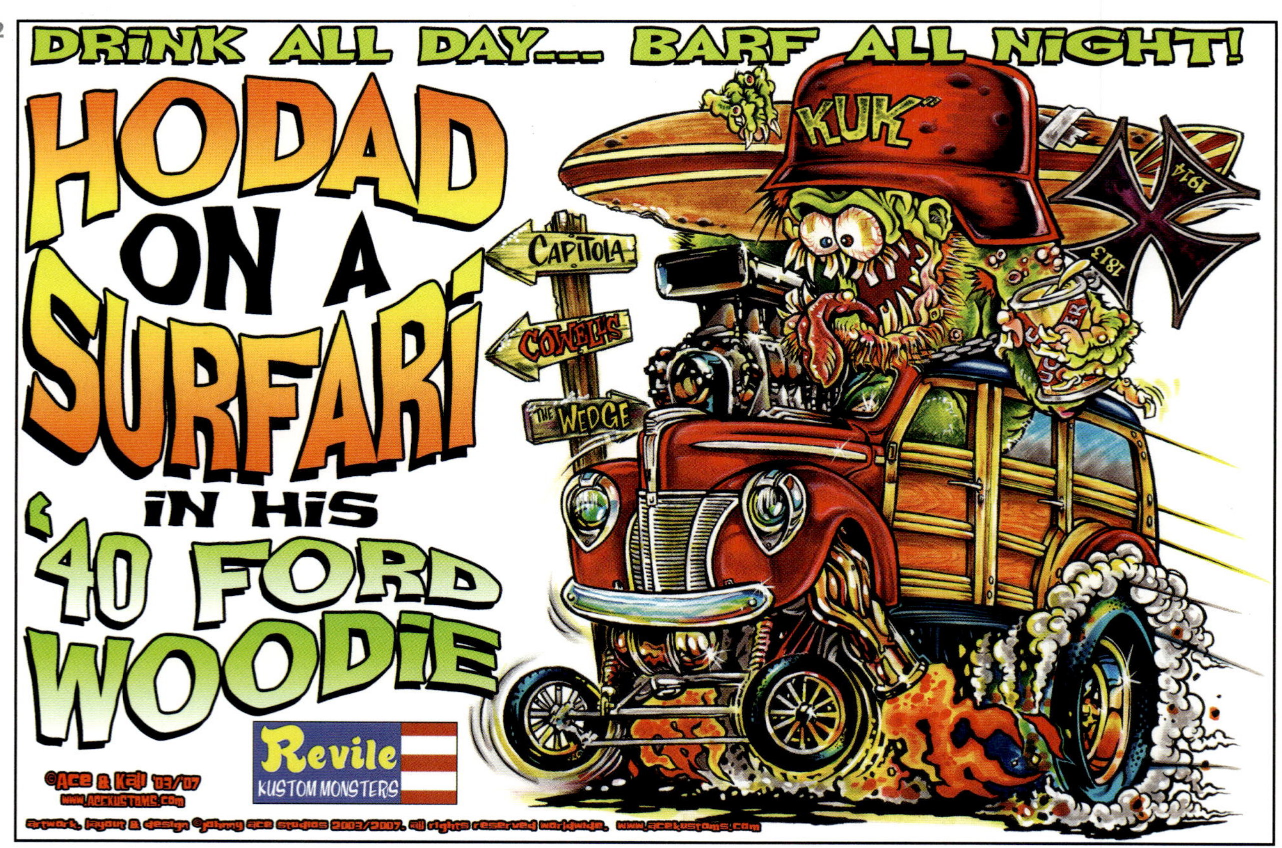

1. *Rat Fink as Sidewalk Surfer.* 2006.

2. *Hodad on a Surfari.* 2006.

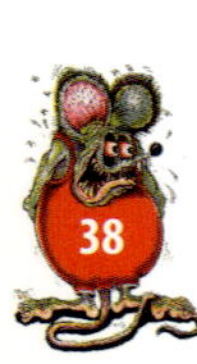

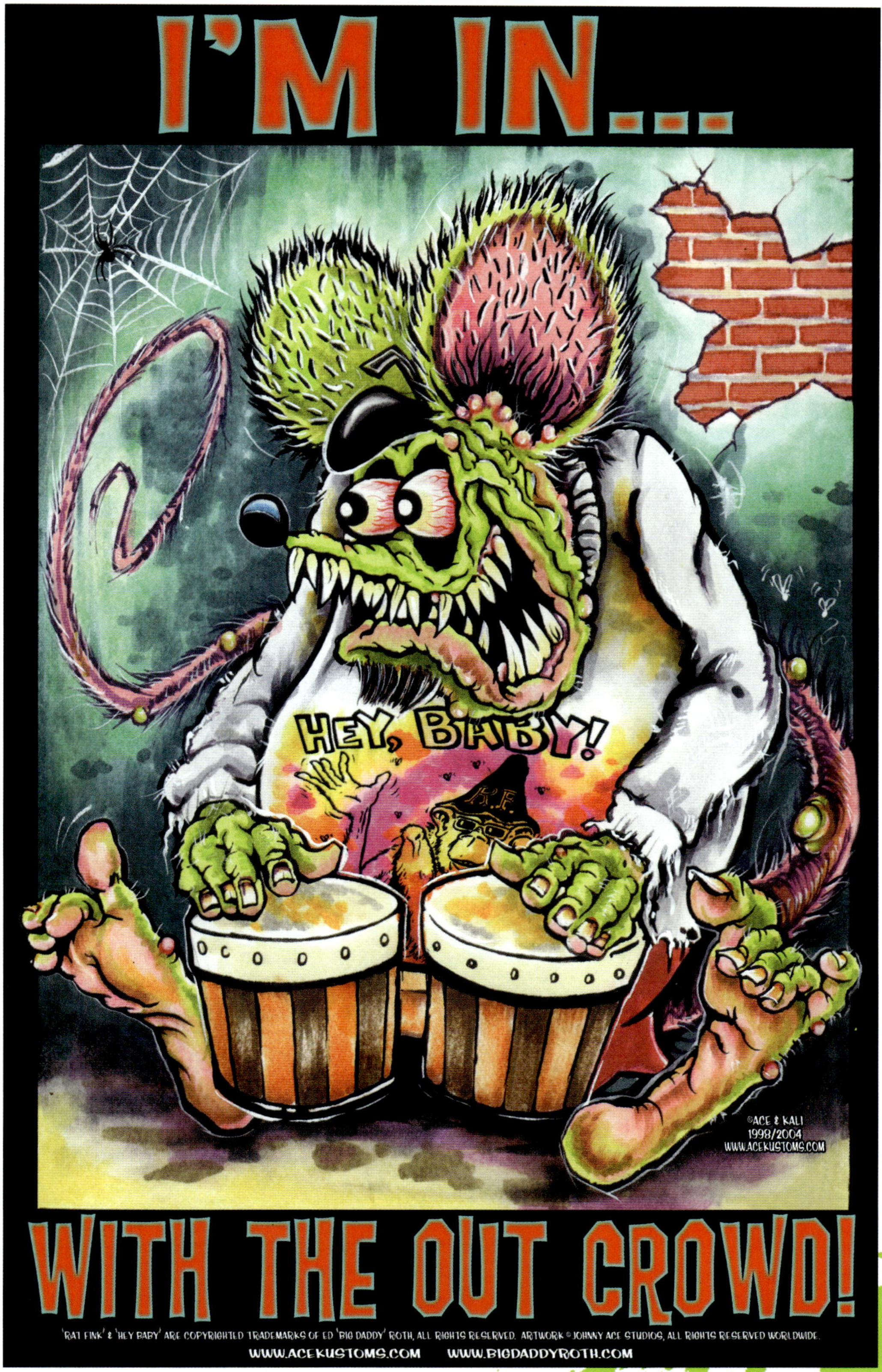

Beat Fink (a.k.a. I'm IN With the OUT Crowd!). 1998. One of Ed's fondest memories of working with Von Dutch was that Dutch could do a great impersonation of Beat humorist Lord Buckley, which would crack Ed up each time. Ed thought Lord Buckley was really British, and when relating this recollection to us, Ed asked, "What was the name of that British guy again?? The beatnik??" Ed and Dutch were considered original hot-rodding beatniks themselves . . . Car magazines and Ed's contracts with companies like Revell Models readily exploited this image. This artwork (named after a classic Sam the Sham and The Pharoahs tune) pays tribute to Roth and Dutch, as well as Newt, Pete Millar, Tom Kelly, Dean Jeffries, Monte, and Larry Watson.

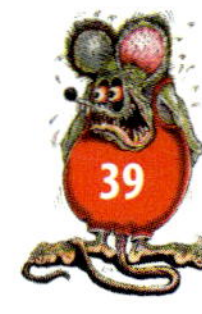

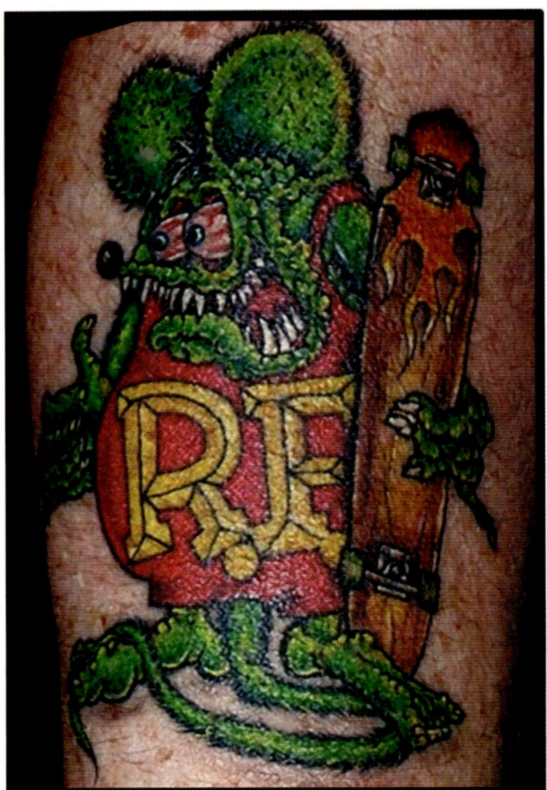

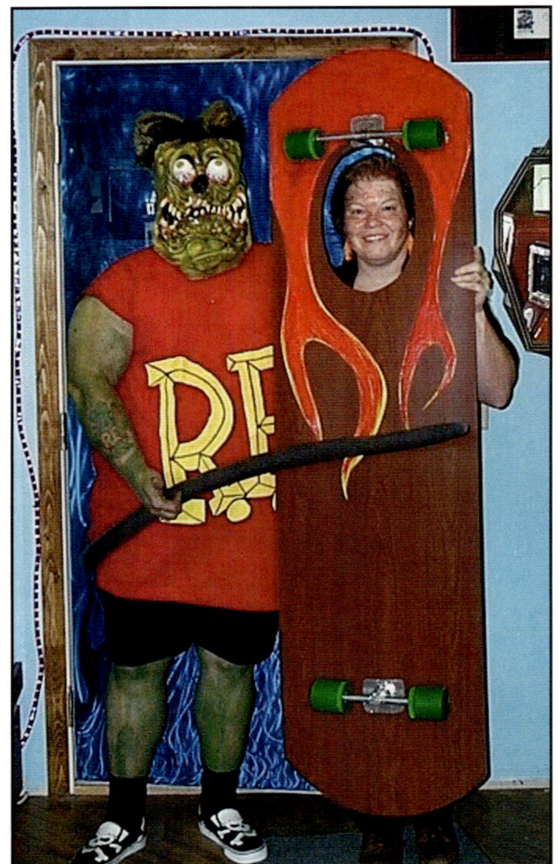

1. SkateFink came about as a request to us for an original artwork by super-Fink fan Pat "SkateFink" Maphis of Maryland. The original illustration features a reference to Ed "Big Daddy" Roth's flamed '57 Chevy Bel-Aire. The image quickly became his next tattoo, done by "Nate" at Mouse & Poncho's in Edgewood, MD.

2. Life imitates art as the owner of both the tattoo and the artwork (with skateboard/wife Erin) brings Rat Fink and his longboard into 3D form as a tandem Halloween costume!

3. *SkateFink.* 2003.

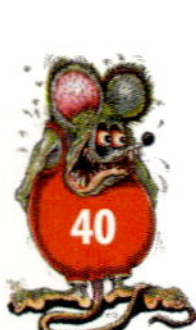

D-D-D-DEAD AND BURIED

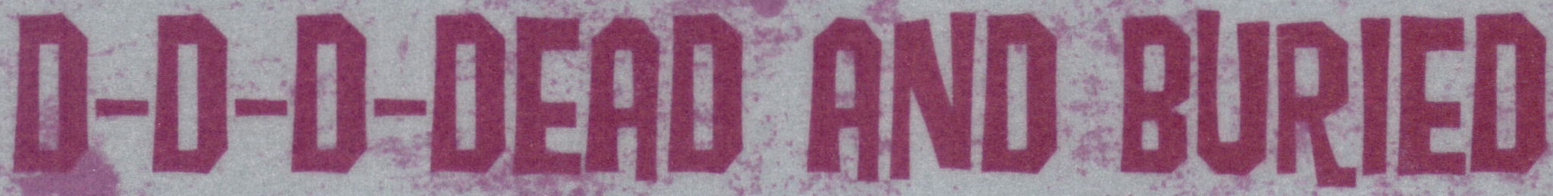

"...but I could not tear my thoughts from my employment,
loathsome in itself, but which had taken an irresistible hold of my imagination."

D-D-D-DEAD AND BURIED

*...but I could not tear my thoughts from my employment,
loathsome in itself, but which had taken an irresistible hold of my imagination.*

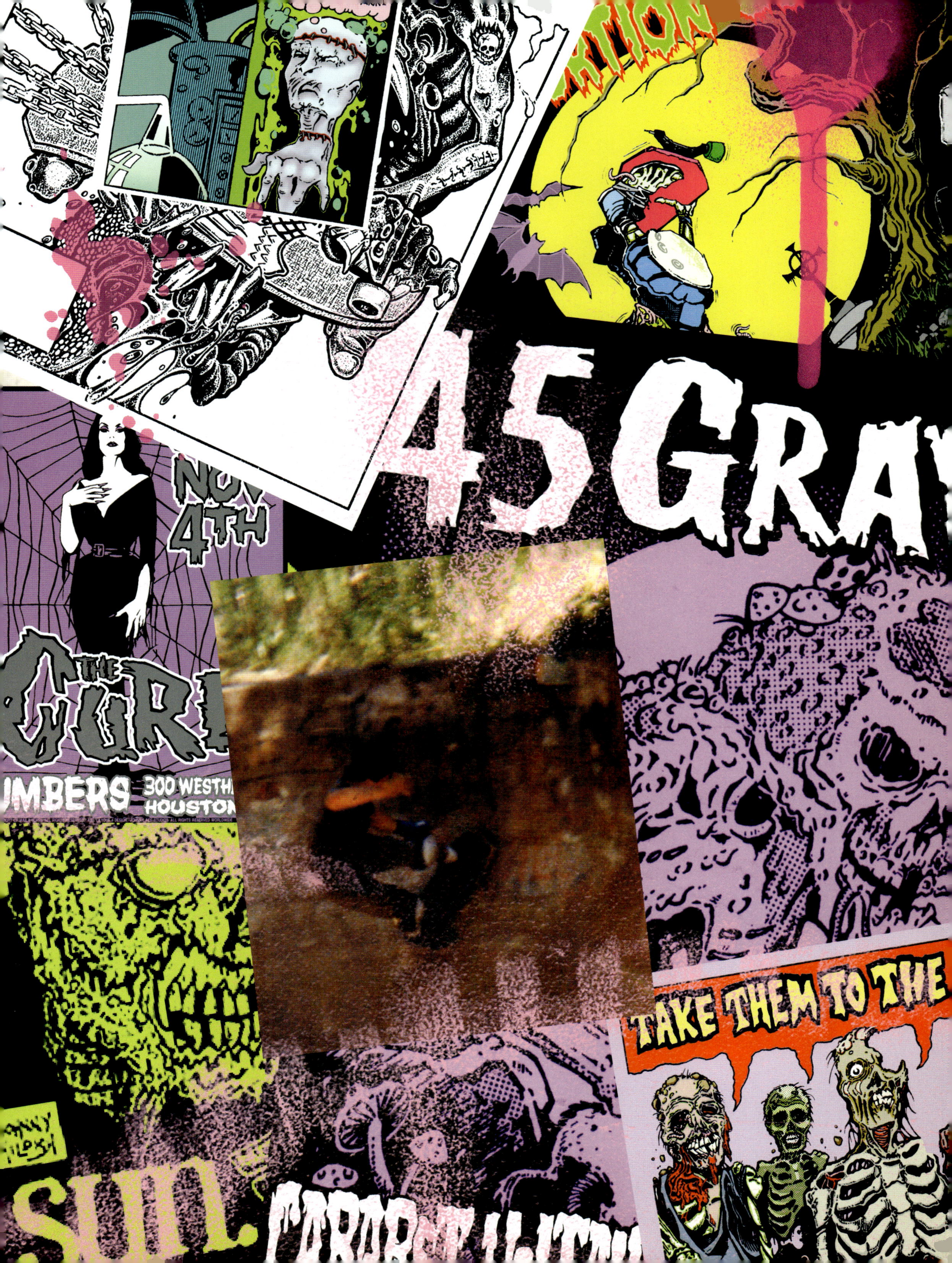

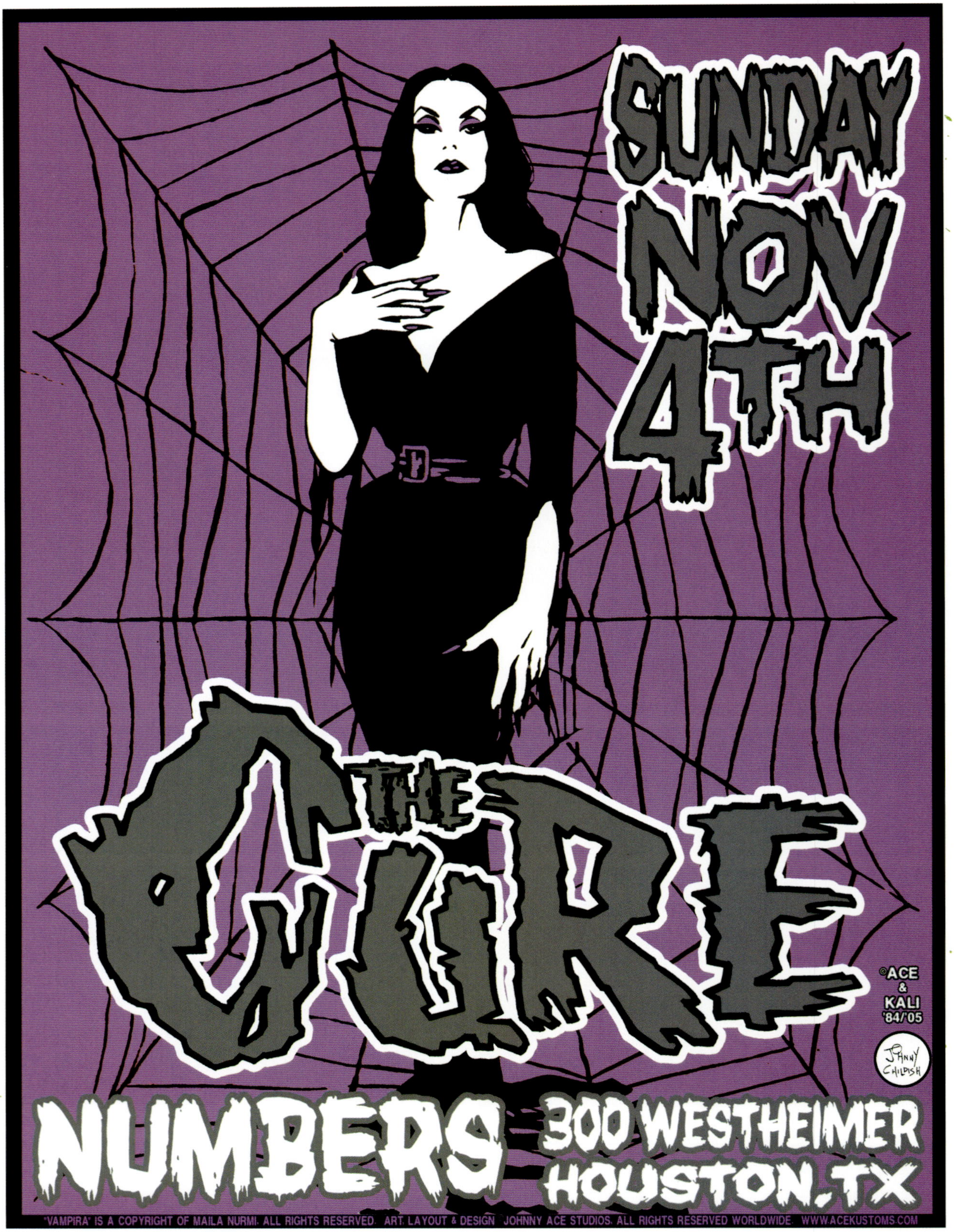

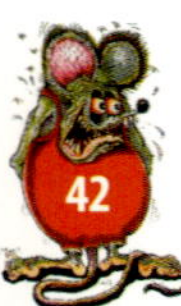

The Cure. 1984.

A long, long show . . . I recall a sea of big hair, clove smoke, fog machines, and black clothes. The fans definitely received a show to remember. The choice to use an illustration of Vampira reflects more of a hope that the Misfits would have gotten back together and toured than an attempt to relate this poster to The Cure. I created numerous images preparing for this scenario, but it never came to pass in the '80s. Even so, this artwork is a good example of the freedom I enjoyed in coming up with event posters for venues such as Numbers, Cabaret Voltaire, etc. These posters reflected my personal interests and obsessions, and the power to work this way overcame many of the negative factors involved in the business of dealing with some clubs and promoters. I never had trouble with Numbers—and I'm thankful to then-owner Bill for giving me the opportunity to see many of these bands and hone my craft as a poster artist.

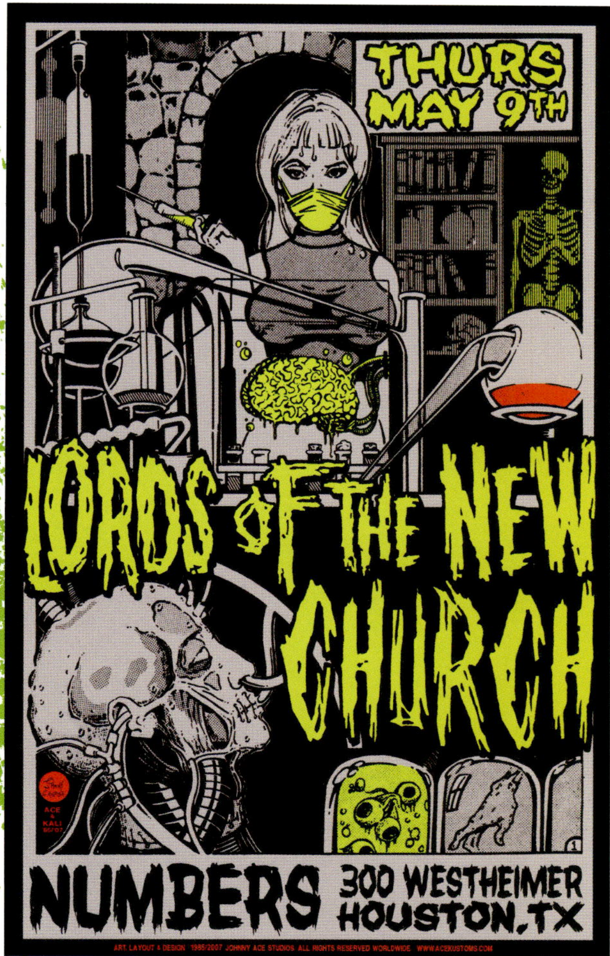

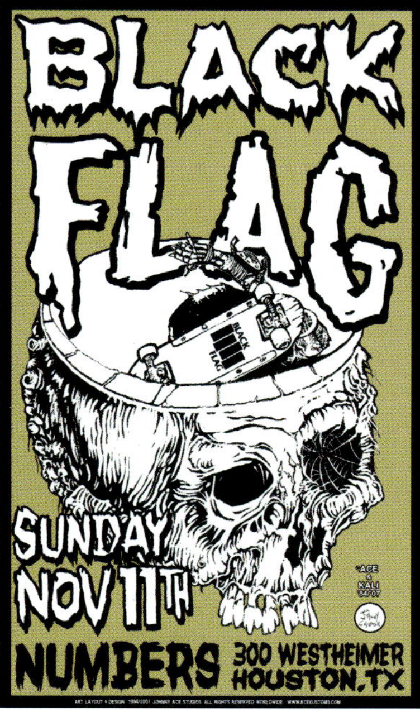

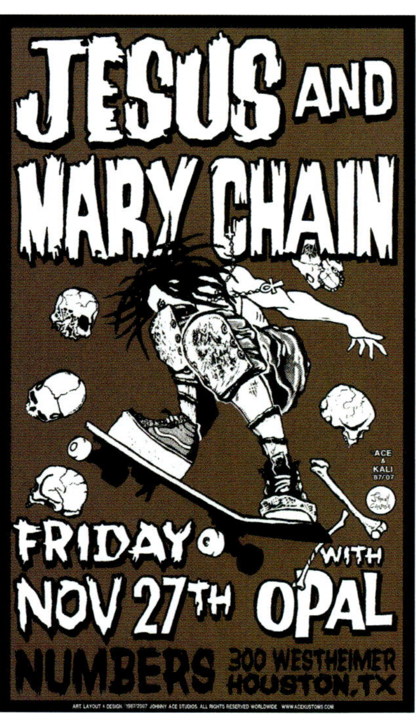

1. *Lords of the New Church.* 1985.
   The show? Brian James and Dave Tregunna powering out Lords anthems while Stiv Bator swayed about in thigh-high boots, insulting their keyboard player, kissing anyone he could grab, and showering potato chips on the crowd . . . The Lords always gave you your money's worth . . .

   Another example of the use of comic pages as poster images. Having been very influenced by *Cruisin'* 1960–67 (Mike Royer), Neal Adams, Crumb, and other artists' illustrations on album covers, the possibilities seemed endless—a comic story could serve as a great source for gig flyers and posters; individual panels and splashes could promote your characters and stories while promoting the show. This particular splash was from "Behold! The Head!", the origin story for a series that saw print later in *Thrasher Comics* in 1989 as well.

2. *Black Flag.* 1984. Image used again in alternate version in *Thrasher Comics.*
   This was an awesome show. I have a vivid image of Greg Ginn grinding out power chords with Henry Rollins belting out "Rise Above" to a packed venue. The crowd consisted mostly of skate punks . . . at that time, metal-heads seemed eager to come to hardcore punk shows, but I recall seeing only one at this gig. I consistently used skate-related imagery in punk and other shows, regardless of musical styles, mostly because we (skate punks) thrived on both high-energy and variety in our lives. I also recall helping Rollins search out ZZ Top and John Lee Hooker albums pre-show. Black Flag came through Houston fairly often . . . the next spring, they played directly across the street from Numbers (a showcase venue and club) in what was for all purposes a large two-story house—packed to the rafters upstairs, a sweatbox ready to collapse from the immense weight of the crowd.

3. *Jesus and Mary Chain with Opal.* 1987. This image was used and re-used many times during the '80s, including in an unpublished comic story.
   Despite a very high level of anticipation for this show, the actual event suffered from a very bad sound and mix—turning the already infamous fuzz-laden sound of JAMC into almost pure white noise with very drunken vocals. Not that this live performance detracted from our enjoyment of Psycho Candy, etc.; there were many hours spent skating to JAMC. The choice to include skate-related imagery here was not as intentional as might appear at first glance—it was an honest reflection of elements in my environment at the time. Also included is my good-natured observation on '80s skateboarding hairstyles. The early years saw minimalist hair, but somehow long hair and dreadlocks took over many a skater as the decade wore on. Prime examples were the Zorlac and Alva teams, the latter being composed of 97% natty heads!

   This particular character is also my personal tribute to a close childhood friend who was responsible for introducing me to *Famous Monsters, Vampirella, Creepy, Eerie,* and so much of the mid-'60s culture that inspires me, and now Kali, too, to this day. His affliction of polio as a child is the prime characteristic of my tribute character.

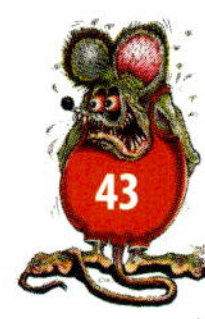

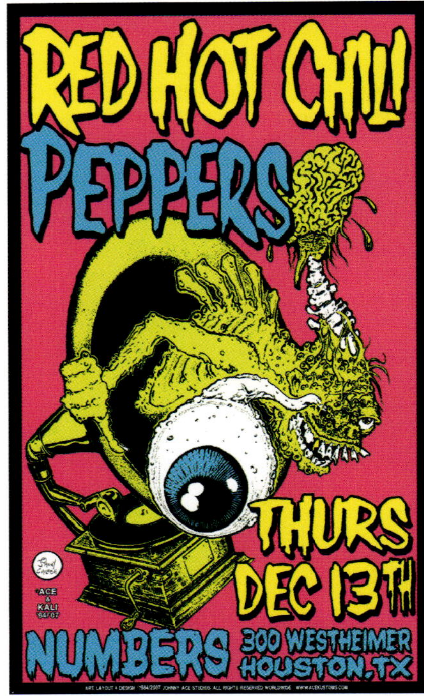

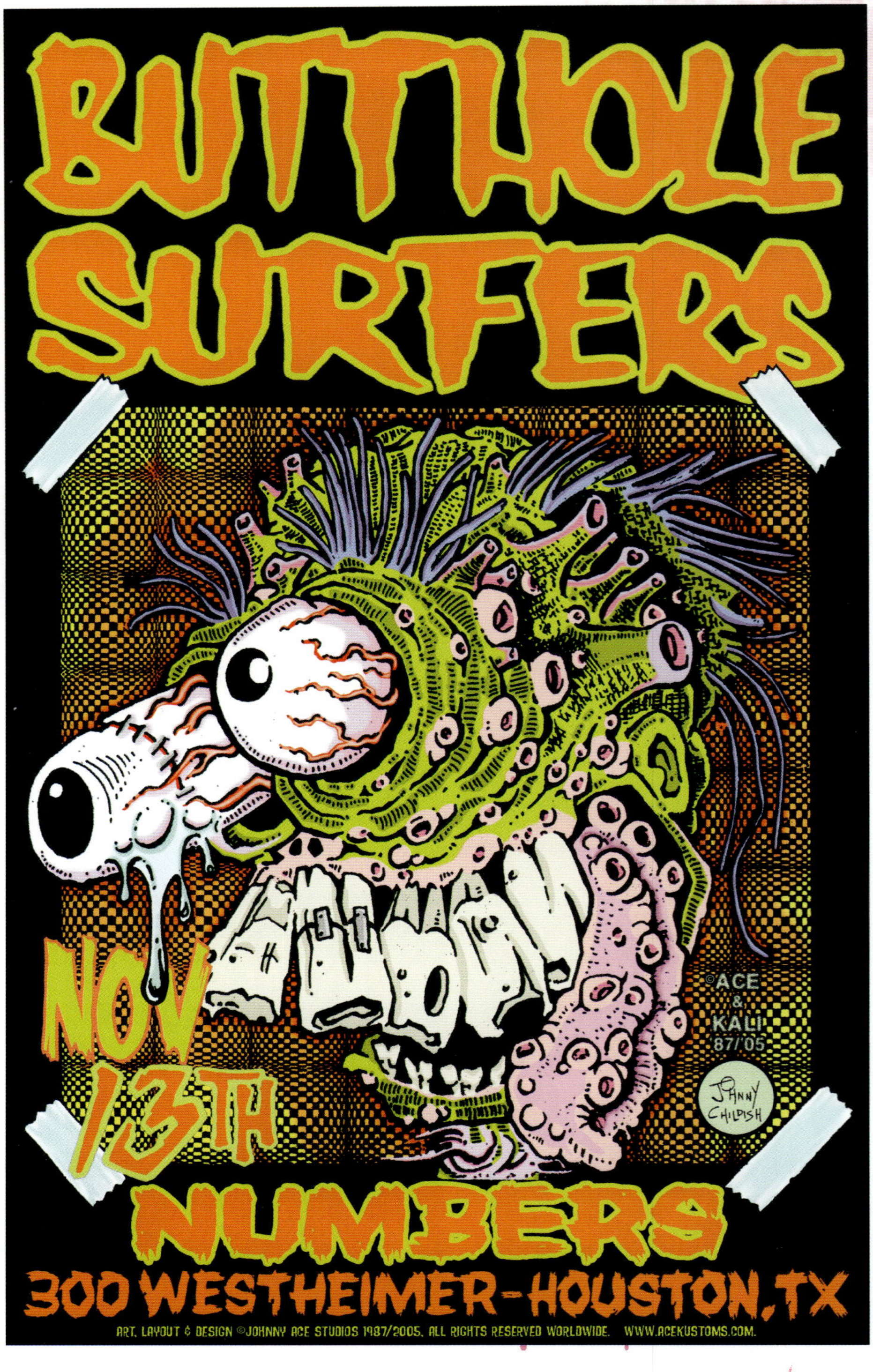

1. *Red Hot Chili Peppers.* 1984. This image was used again in *Thrasher Comics* #8, 1990.

This may have been the first RHCP tour outside of California. In any case, it was a great time to be doing gig posters and seeing many different bands early on in their careers. Of course, this show was monumental—Flea totally manic, Kiedis posturing as the consummate frontman, resplendent in brown miniskirt and Mickey Mouse ears. Texas always did enjoy a good punk-funk workout (a la The Big Boys!) and we enjoyed the sucker-punching this show treated us to . . . and yes, the boys treated us to a genuine "sock man," added as a nervous encore!

2. *Butthole Surfers.* 1987. This image was used again as part of a Basil Wolverton/Jack Davis tribute card series and comic called "Ughly Chicks" and published in *Thrasher Comics*.

To attempt a complete description of this show would indeed be considered folly . . . Rather, flashing images appear when I reflect upon the insanity that was and is a Butthole Surfers show. Their album *Locust Abortion Technician* had been released, and we were subjected to much of this material in a live setting, complete with a background projection screen showing some sort of penile surgical procedure . . . I remember the screaming in the audience . . . and Gibby echoing, "Raisins . . . Raisins . . . Raisins . . ."

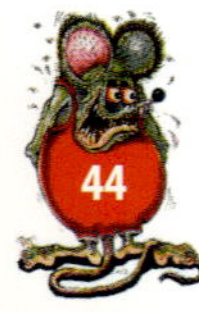

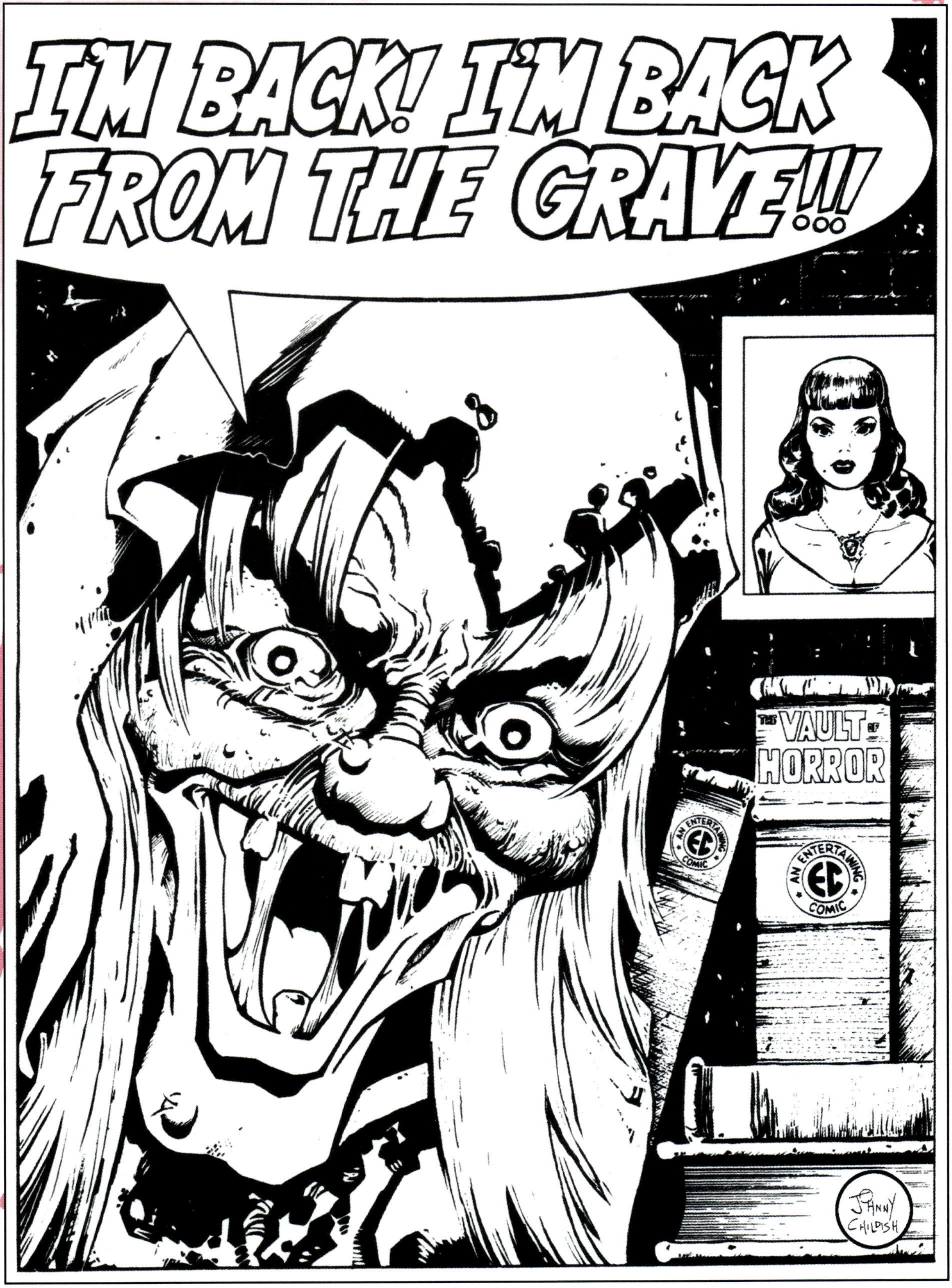

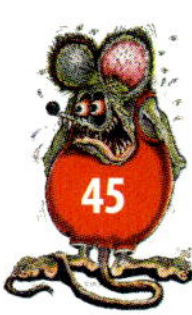

I'm Back! I'm Back from the Grave!! (**A Tribute to Johnny Craig**). 1990. Vault Keeper and Drusilla © William M. Gaines.

This was my very best attempt to imitate Johnny Craig's style, and I was extremely gratified with his kind comments upon receiving a copy of the artwork. Having been a lifelong fan of his work, as well as the other EC legends, I considered this a career highpoint. Originally, the illustration had no caption—upon reading an interview with EC fan-addict Gary Arlington, I decided to present it to him as a surprise. Gary was a longtime fixture of the San Francisco comics underground and had always hoped for a resurgence of EC-style comics.

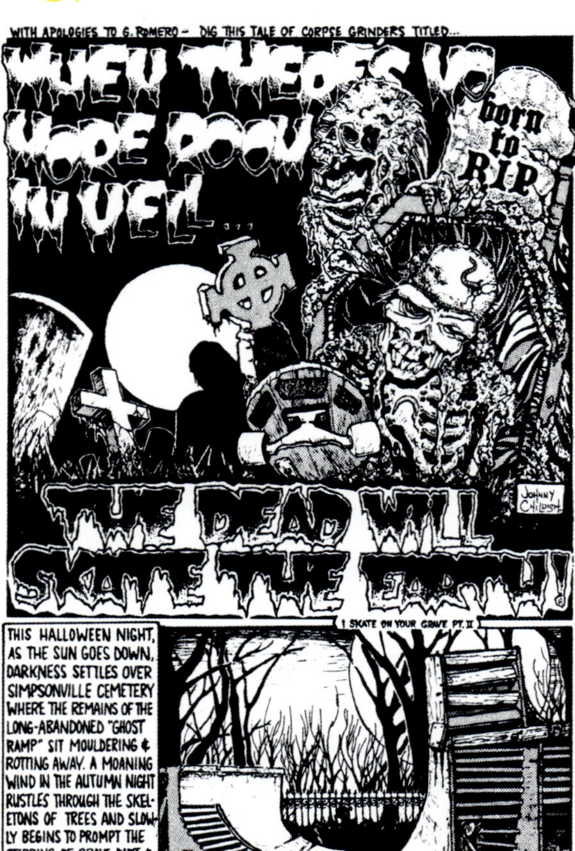

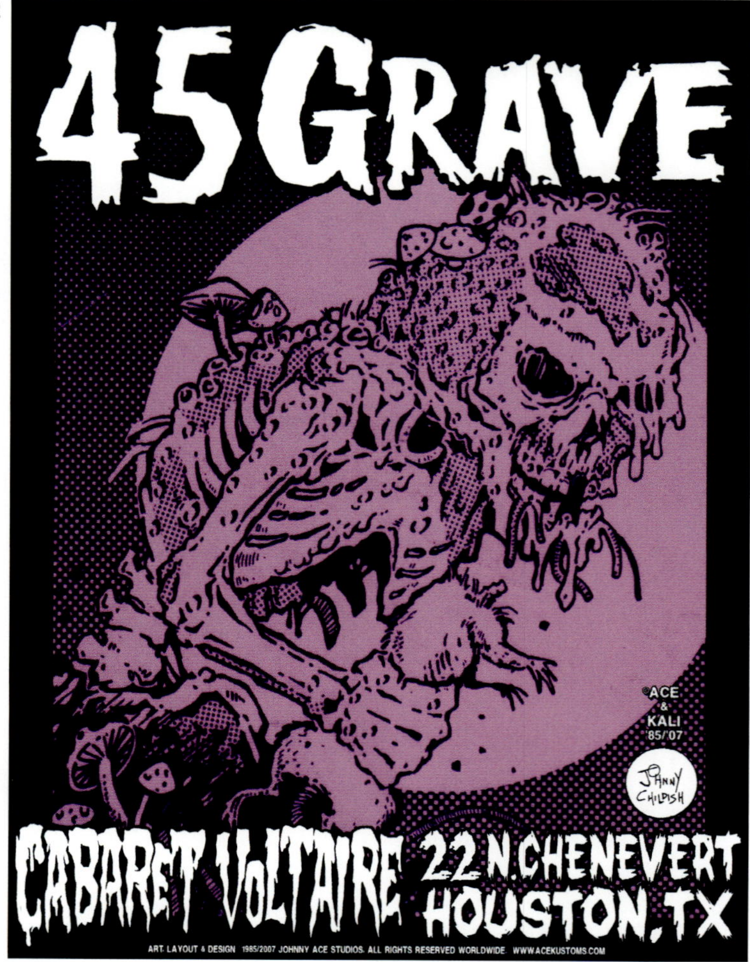

1. *When There's No More Room In Hell . . . The Dead Will Skate The Earth!! (I Skate on Your Grave Pt. II).* **Comic splash page. 1988.** First published in *Thrasher Comics* #4.
   This six-pager was yet another of many EC Comics-meets-skate-punk scenarios. I made no apologies for combining my horror and punk backgrounds and took every opportunity to utilize both. Much of my work during this decade is a mixture of well-planned panels, but also hastily finished segments at times. Often, the best results came from work done without dealing with editors or half-interested art directors. If I sensed any attitude or indifference regarding my work, I often made the deadline but saved the effort for another time or place.

2. *45 Grave.* **Unreleased flyer art. 1985.**
   There had been a lot of talk about Dinah and the guys coming to Houston sometime in early summer of '85 . . . The show date, however, was never confirmed or related to me by the club owner. Unfortunately, if they did come through town, I missed the show. This artwork was brought back from the dead and used again as a comic panel five or six years later in *Thrasher Comics.*

3. *Thrasher Comics* #4. **Cover Illustration. 1988.** Artwork was also released as a t-shirt by *Thrasher Comics.*

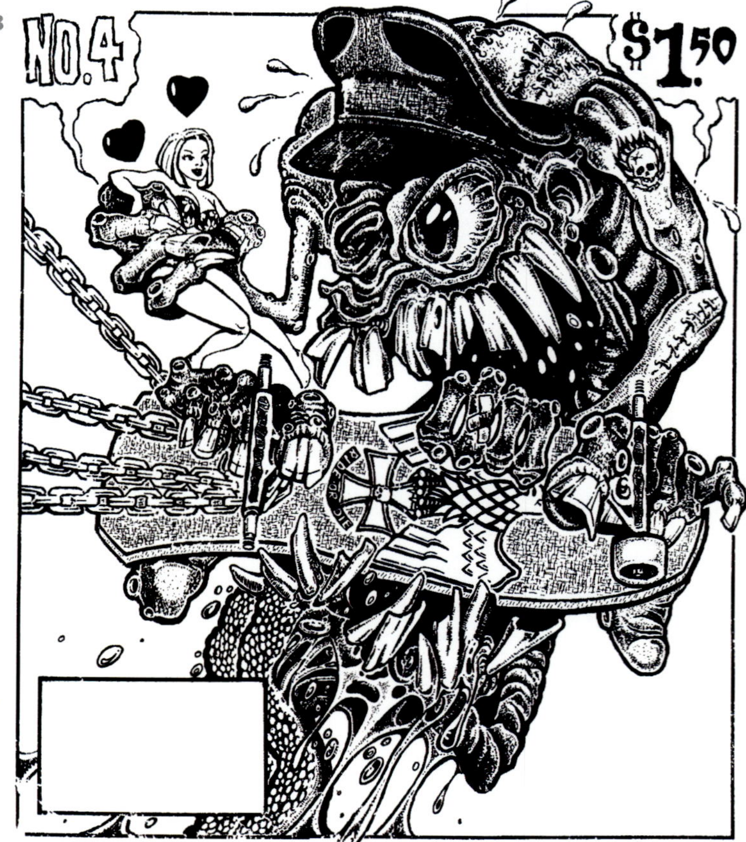

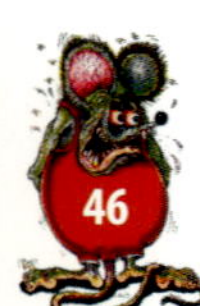

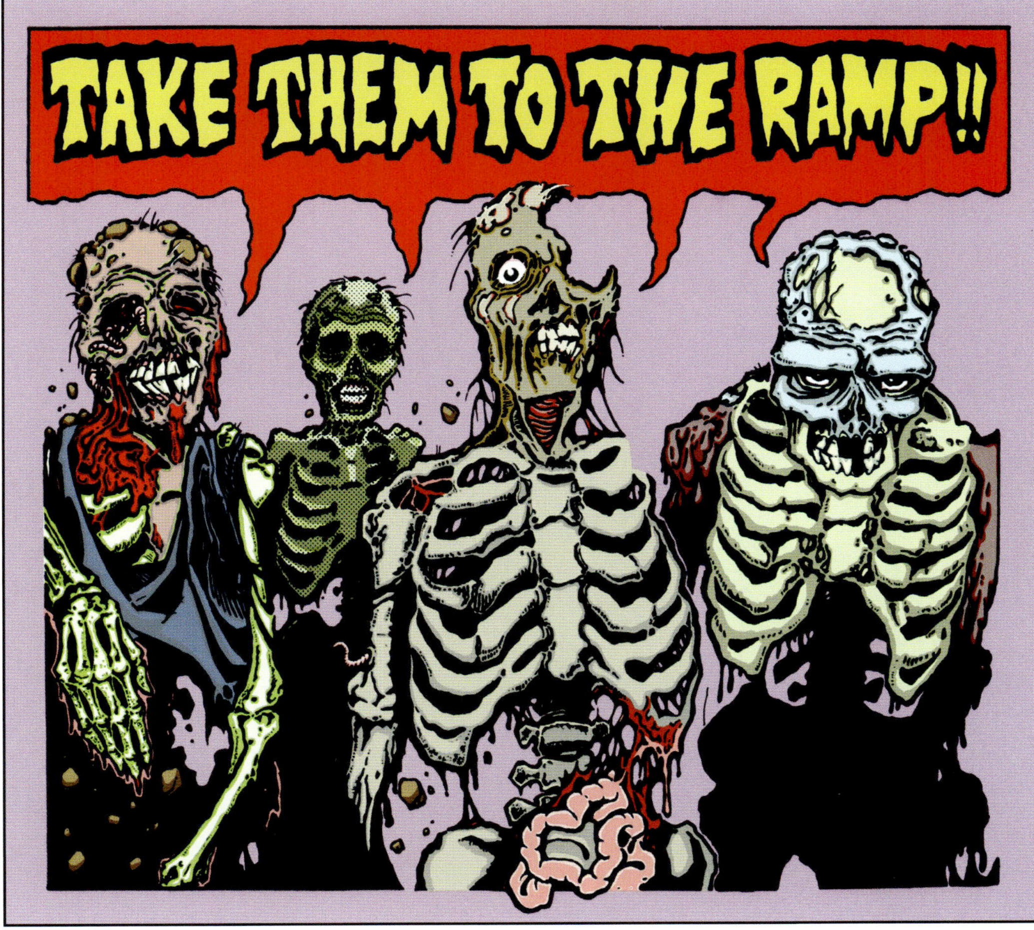

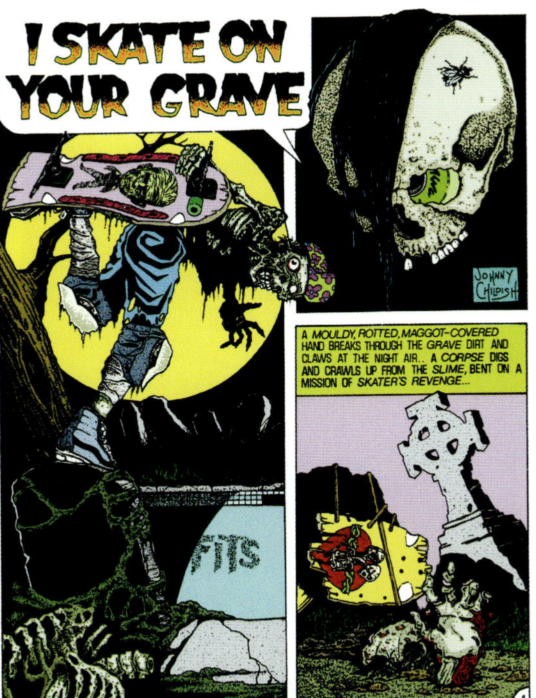

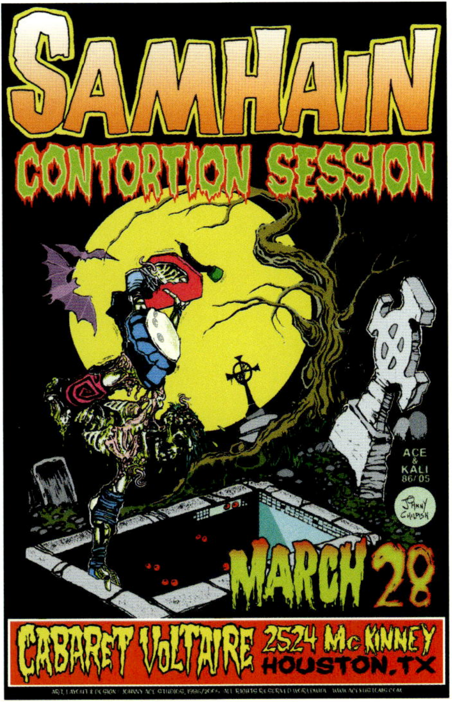

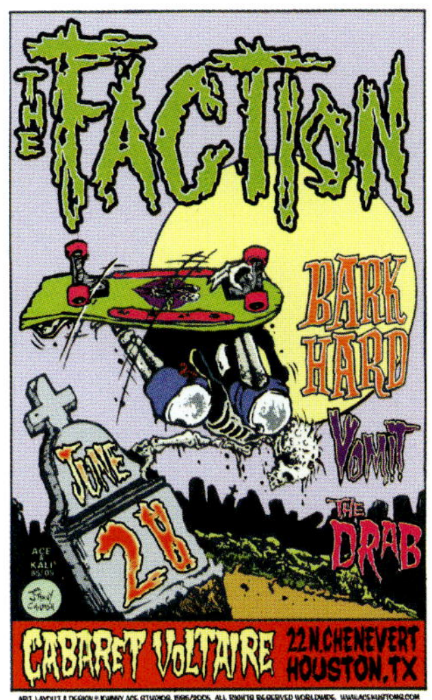

1. *Take Them to the Ramp!!* Comic panel. 1988. From *I Skate on Your Grave Pt. II*.

2. *I Skate on Your Grave Pt. I.* Comic splash page. 1986.
Horror/skate punk meets traditional EC Comics layout. This appeared in *Thrasher Magazine*, December '87 issue.

3. *Samhain—Contortion Session.* 1986. This artwork, in addition to use as a poster illustration, was an unpublished comic cover. Prior to the days of those wonderful House Industries font packages, if you wanted poster lettering, you had to chisel it out of stone yourself! I was particularly fond of emulating the styles used on '60s Aurora model kit boxes, *Famous Monsters of Filmland* magazines, Captain Company ads, and horror movie press books, among other random materials. This method often provided great sources for band names, venues and dates—as well as one's own creativity in coming up with any missing letters or numbers!

4. *The Faction—Bark Hard.* 1985. I discovered early on in the game that comic panels made excellent poster art. I also learned how to recycle art while working for Roth Studios. I often pulled random panels from in-progress comic stories, and it wasn't unusual to see examples of art done years earlier, but sometimes not published definitively until years later. The practice of doing alternate artwork and variations on Xerox copies was also a tip I learned from Roth . . . it saved the original art, but provided multi-uses as the need arose.

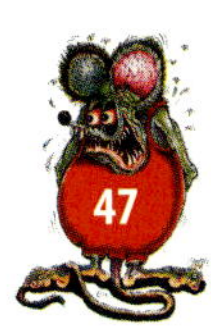

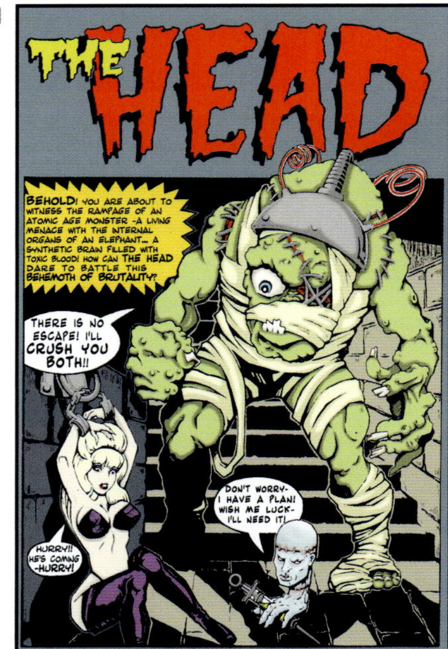

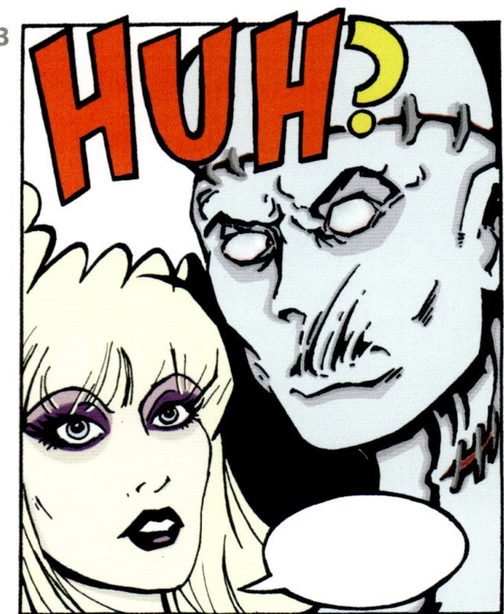

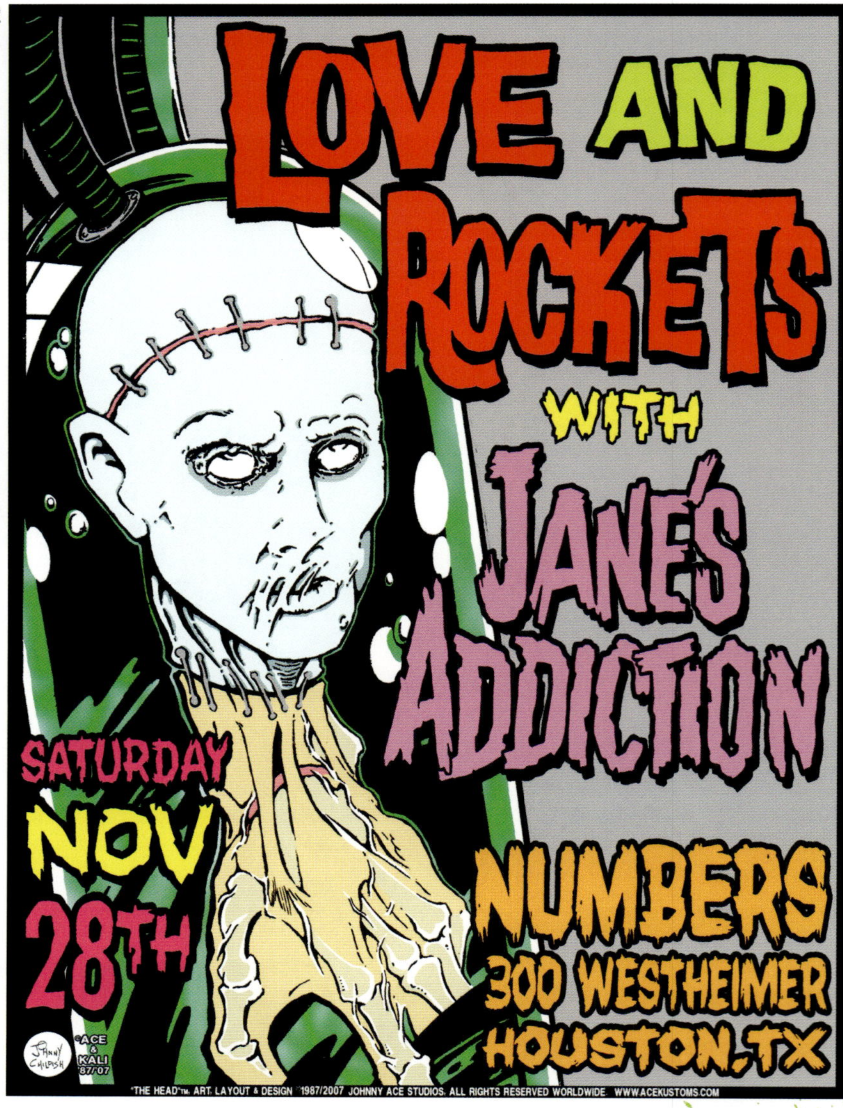

1. *The Head, Pt.II.* **Comic splash page.** 1989.

2. *Love and Rockets with Jane's Addiction.* 1987.
"The Head" © 1987, 2007 by Johnny Ace Studios.
All Rights Reserved.

3. *The Head.* **Comic splash panel.** 1989.

4. *The Head.* **Tattoo owned by Greg Wheeler,**
Houston, TX.

5. *The Head.* **Comic splash panel.** 1989.
"The Head" first appeared in the '80s on various
gig posters, then as sequential comic art in
Thrasher Comics for a couple of published
episodes. This character was based on several
other head/hand concepts from such disparate
sources as *Big Daddy Roth Magazine* ("Flanges"),
Ghastly Graham Ingels, and Berni Wrightson
(most likely in tribute to Ingels).

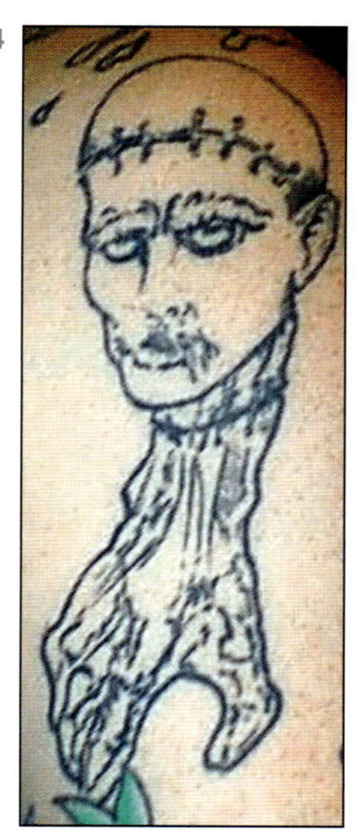

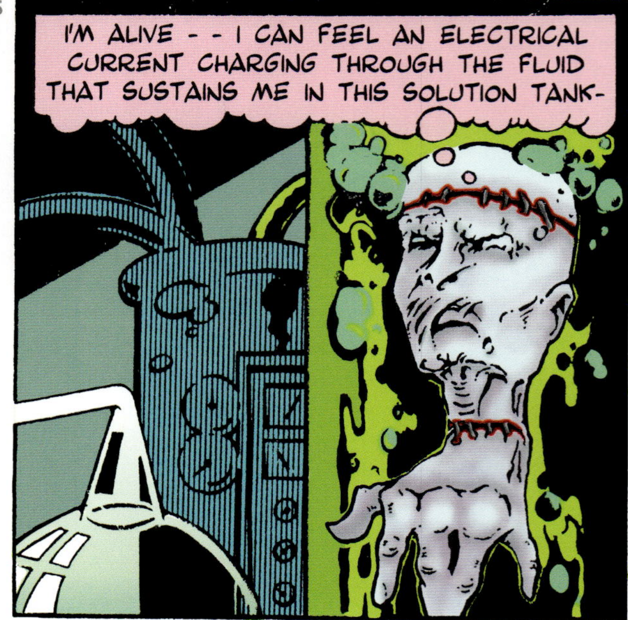

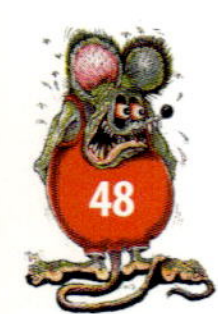

MAN-MADE MONSTERS & RE-ANIMATED RESIN

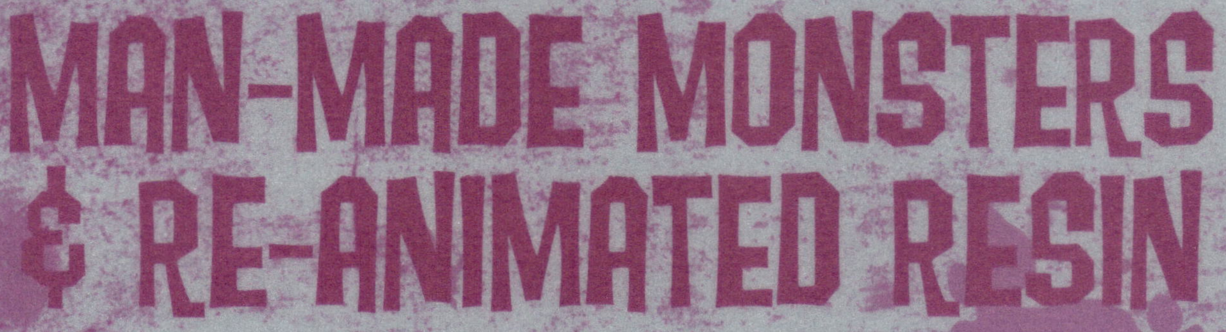

" . . . often did my human nature turn with loathing from my occupation, whilst, still urged on by an eagerness which perpetually increased, I brought my work to a near conclusion."

MAN-MADE MONSTERS
& RE-ANIMATED RESIN

"...often did my human nature turn with loathing from my occupation, whilst, still urged on by an eagerness which perpetually increased, I brought my work to a near conclusion."

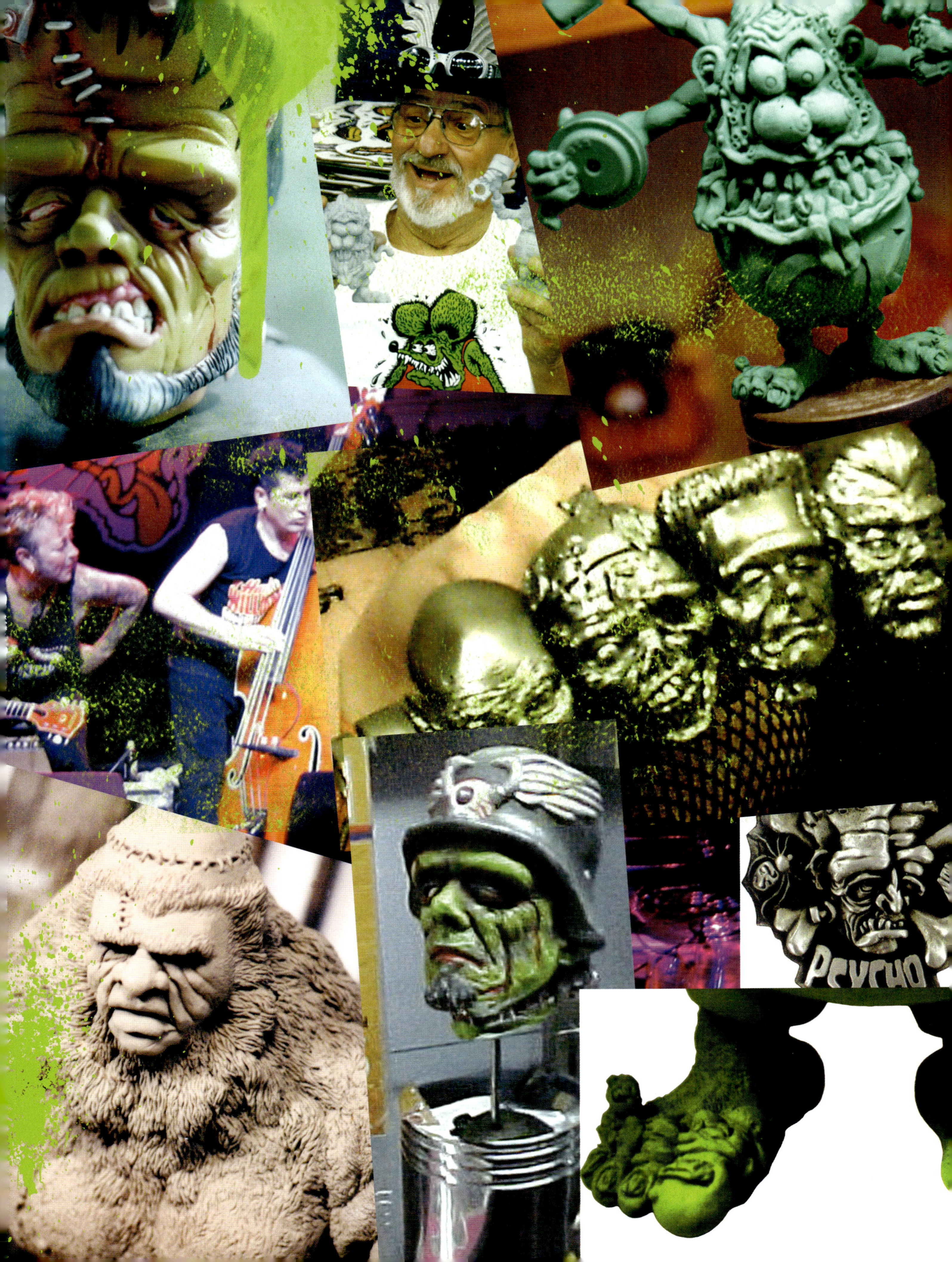
Psycho

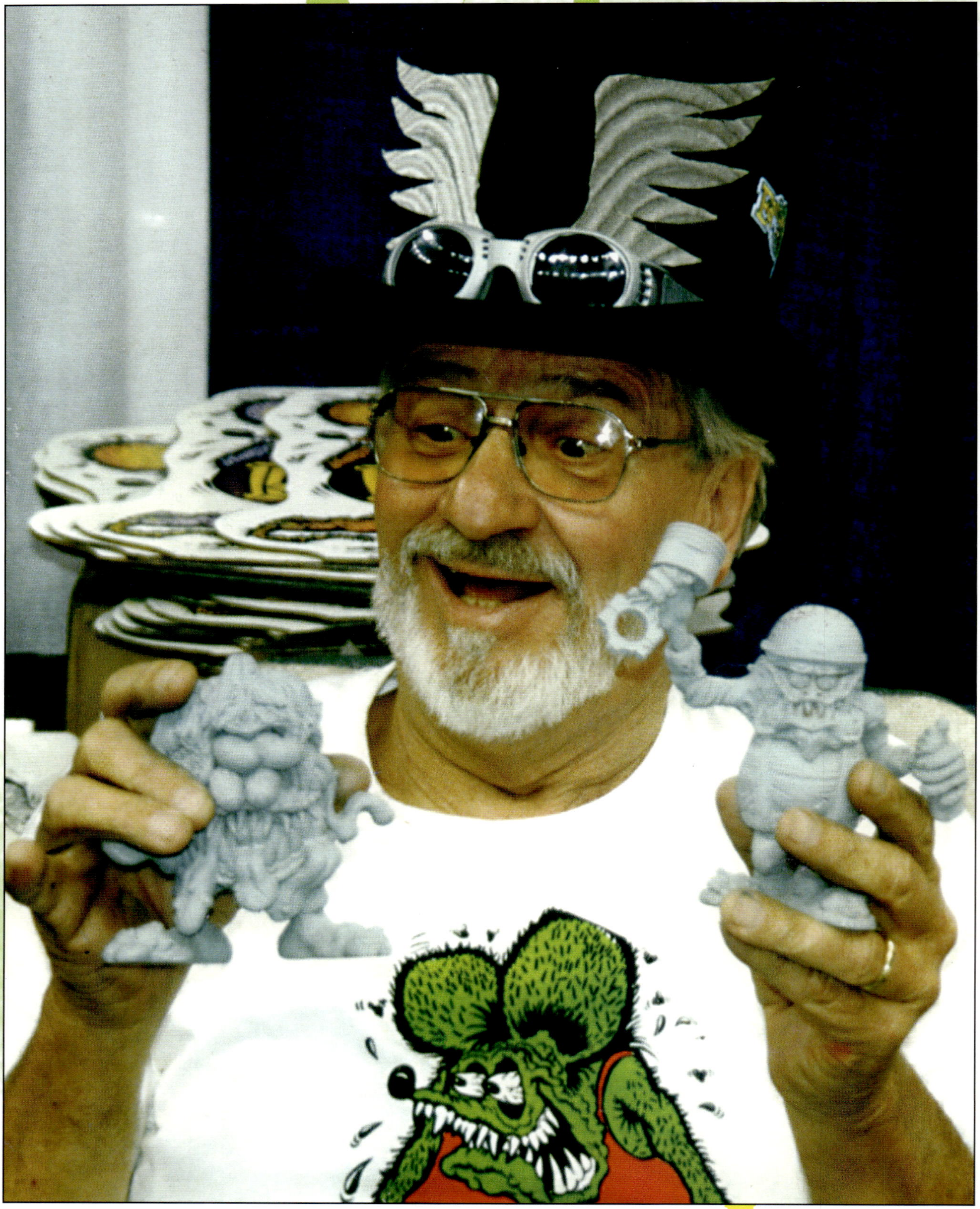

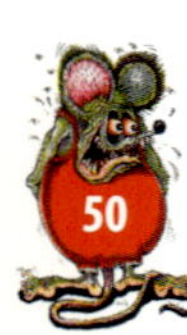

Big Daddy doing a promo shot for two of our sculpts. Ed would sometimes do very exaggerated faces and comical expressions for photos, depending on his mood . . . this was taken early in the day at a car show; later on he would be all business.

Roth would sometimes call us over from merch duties to share a profound thought, creative idea, or often whatever was on his mind . . . this photo perfectly captured Ed's ability to shift from friendly crowd-pleaser to two-fisted ass-kicker when need be.

"Hey, check this out . . . " as he discreetly motioned toward his gear. "This is in case anyone tries to get cute, heh heh . . . " He pulled out a Heckler & Koch .40 Universal SelbstladePistole (USP) semi-automatic with laser sight (given to him by son Darryl Roth). "Let's see anyone start somethin'!"

Roth had a long reputation of TCB if trouble started, and he carried protection on the road due to his economical habit of sleeping in his trailer, next to his show-cars. The majority of problems were handled with his fists—and that very often fixed the problem for good!

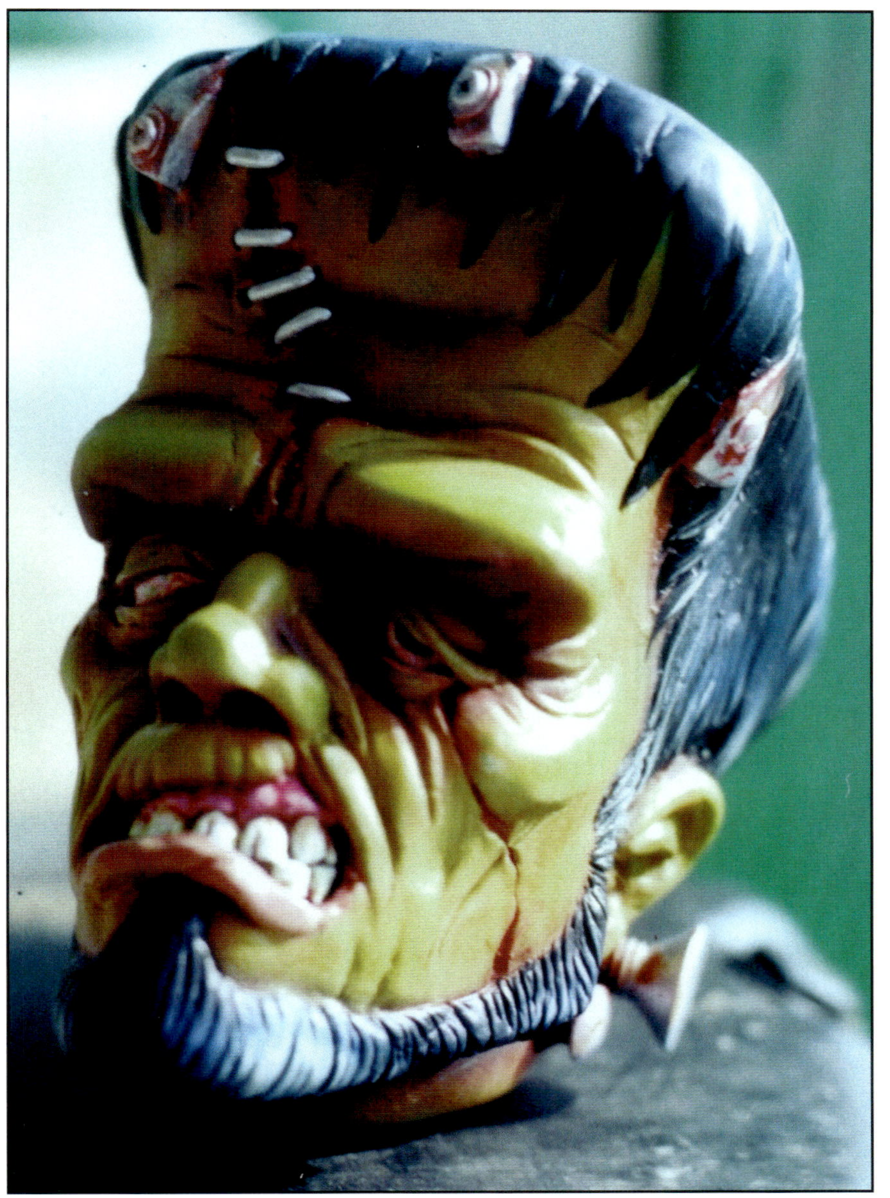

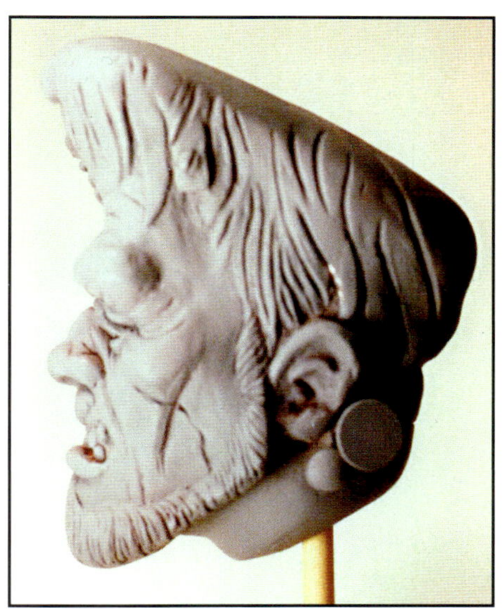

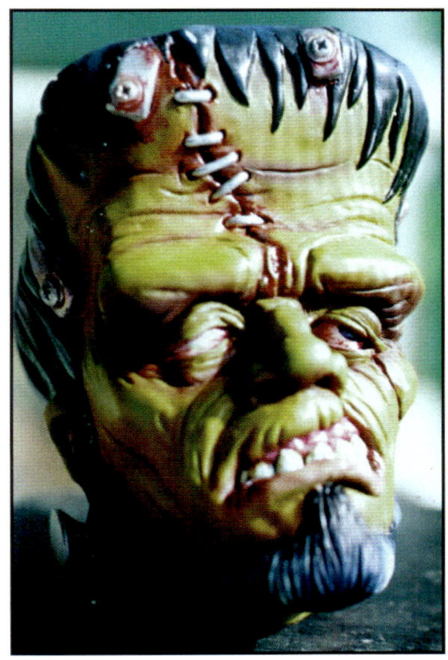

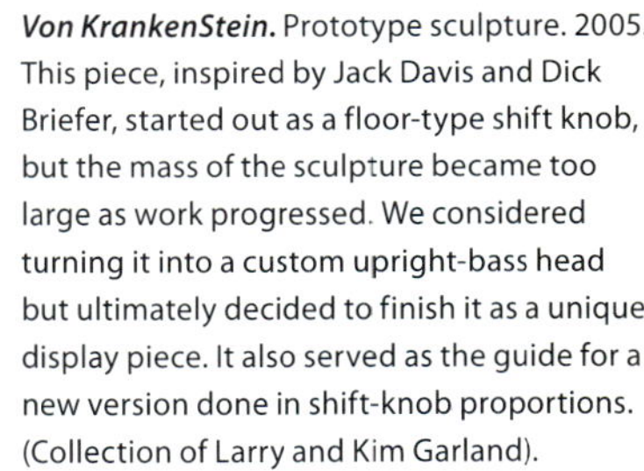

Von KrankenStein. Prototype sculpture. 2005. This piece, inspired by Jack Davis and Dick Briefer, started out as a floor-type shift knob, but the mass of the sculpture became too large as work progressed. We considered turning it into a custom upright-bass head but ultimately decided to finish it as a unique display piece. It also served as the guide for a new version done in shift-knob proportions. (Collection of Larry and Kim Garland).

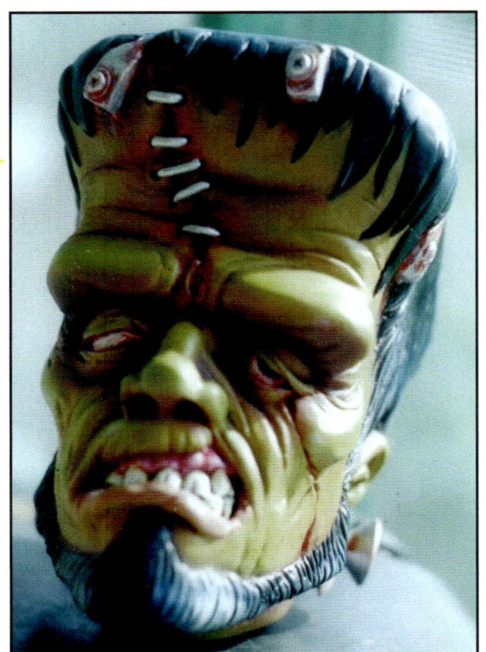

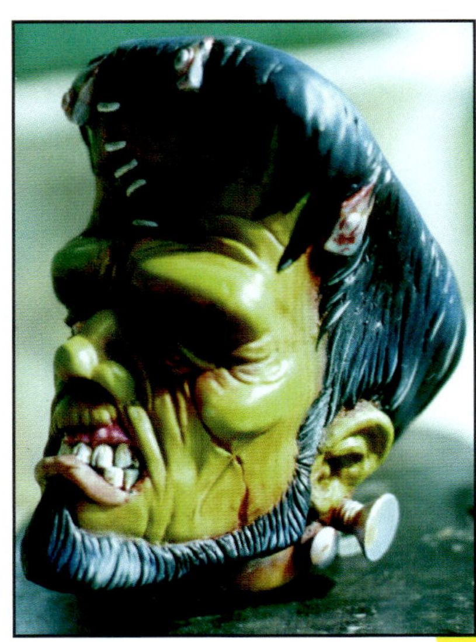

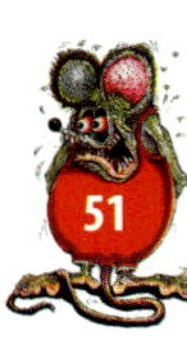

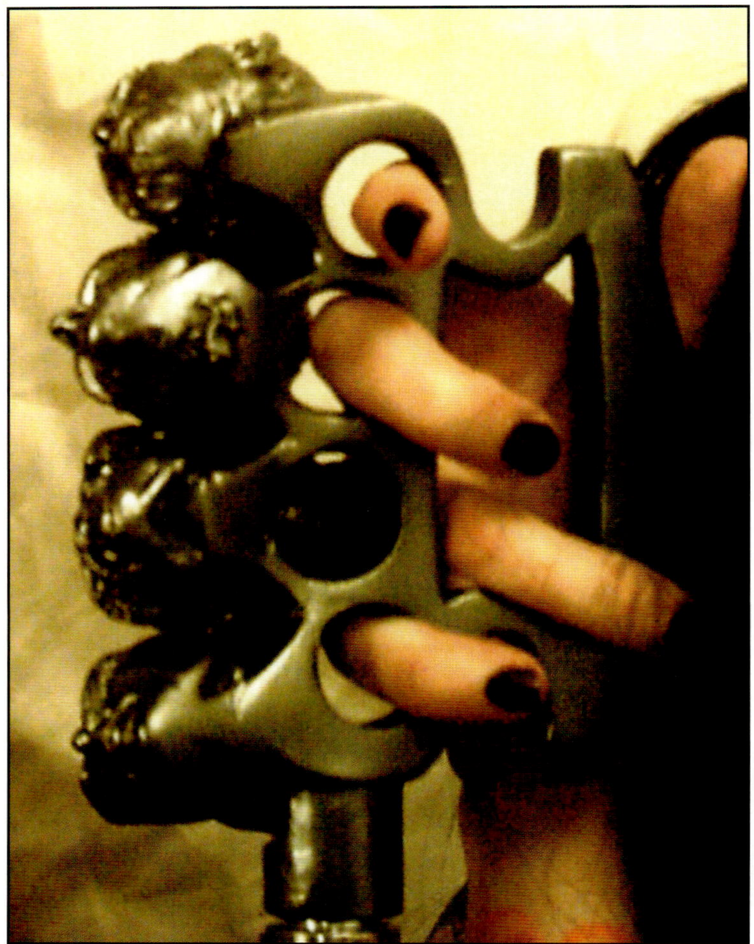

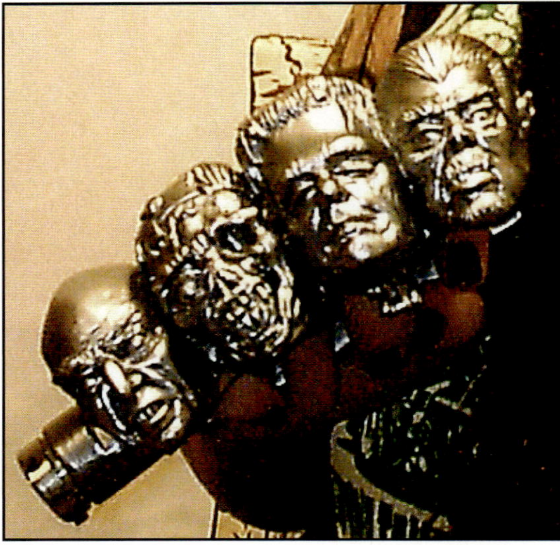

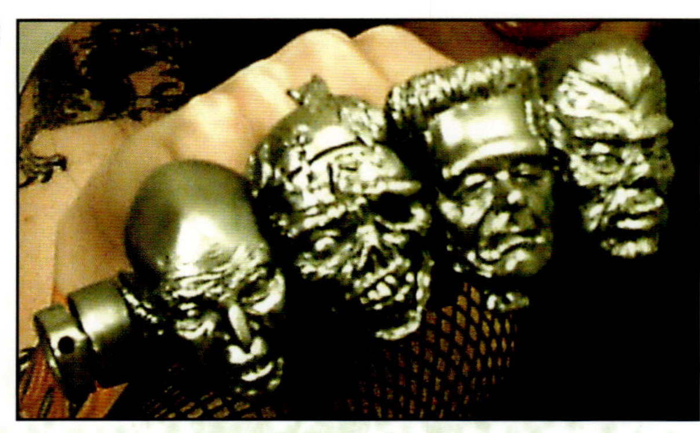

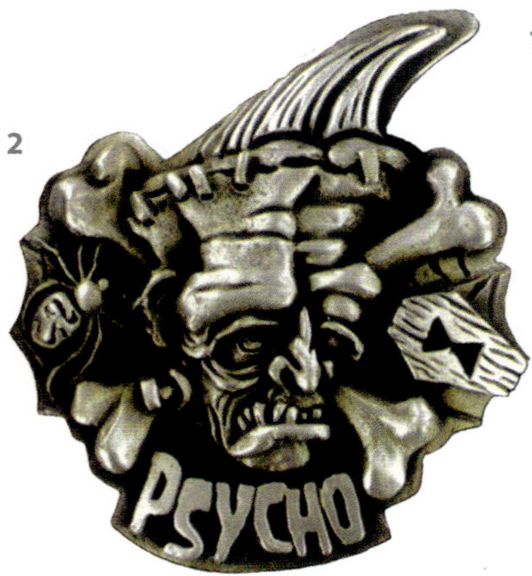

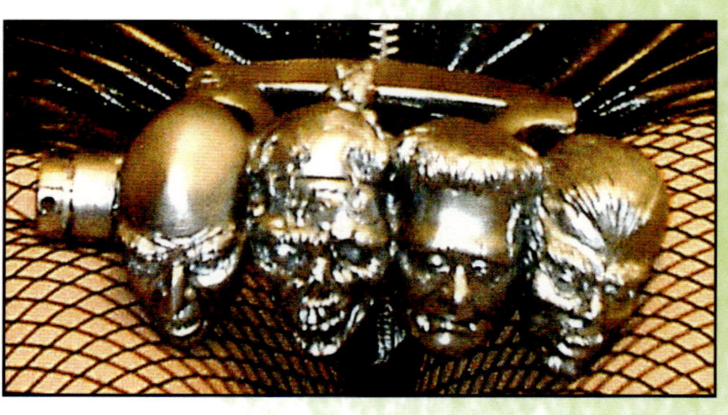

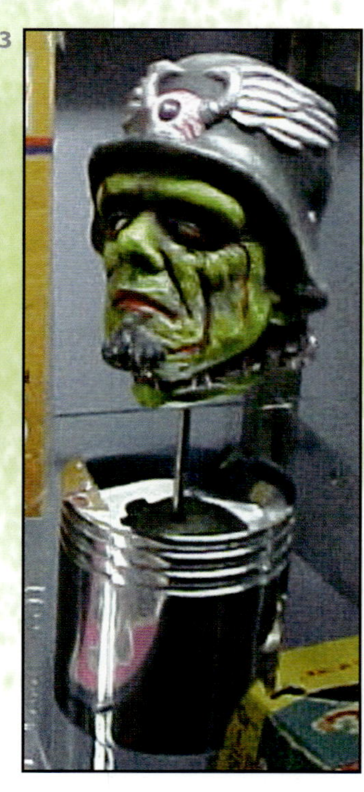

1. *Monster Brass Knuckles/A Face Full of Monsters!* Shift-knob prototype. 2006.
This piece featured four classic monster characters (Max Shreck/Nosferatu, EC zombie, Frankenstein monster, werewolf, and a brain-eating rat as an extra) built into a brass knuckle-type hand/floor shifter that was designed both as a collectible solid metal display piece or as an actual shifter. This version was purchased by Felon Clothing.

2. *Psycho Pewter Belt Buckle.* 2005. © by Felon Clothing.

3. *Son of KrankenStein.* Painted polymer clay prototype shift knob. 1997.
Approx. 1/6 scale. Unreleased. Collection of and photo by Larry and Kim Garland.

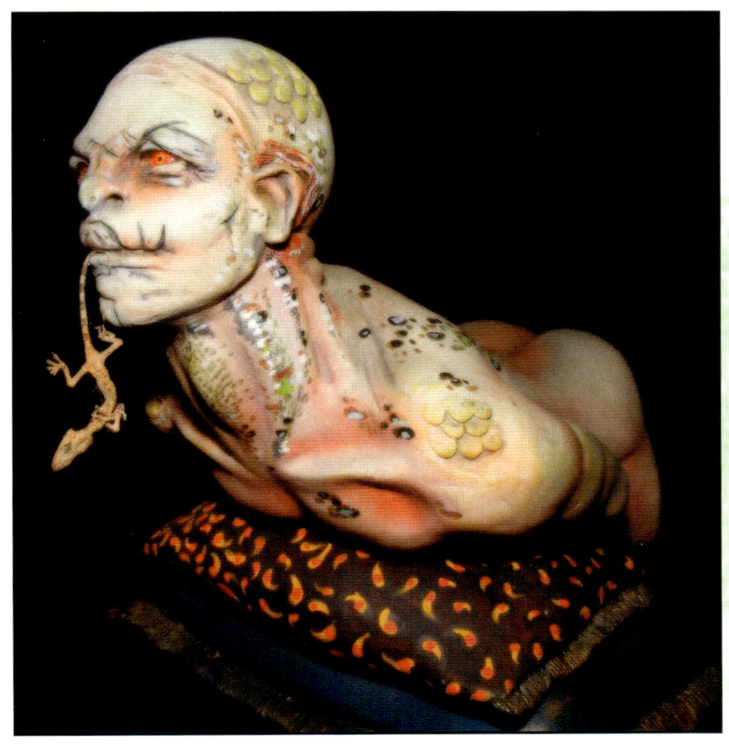

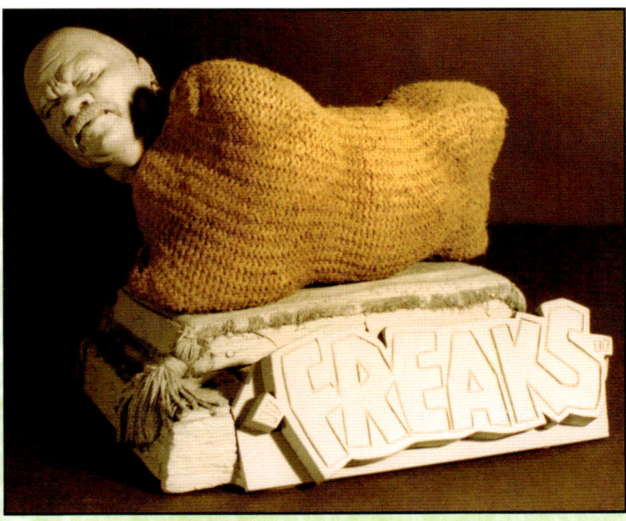

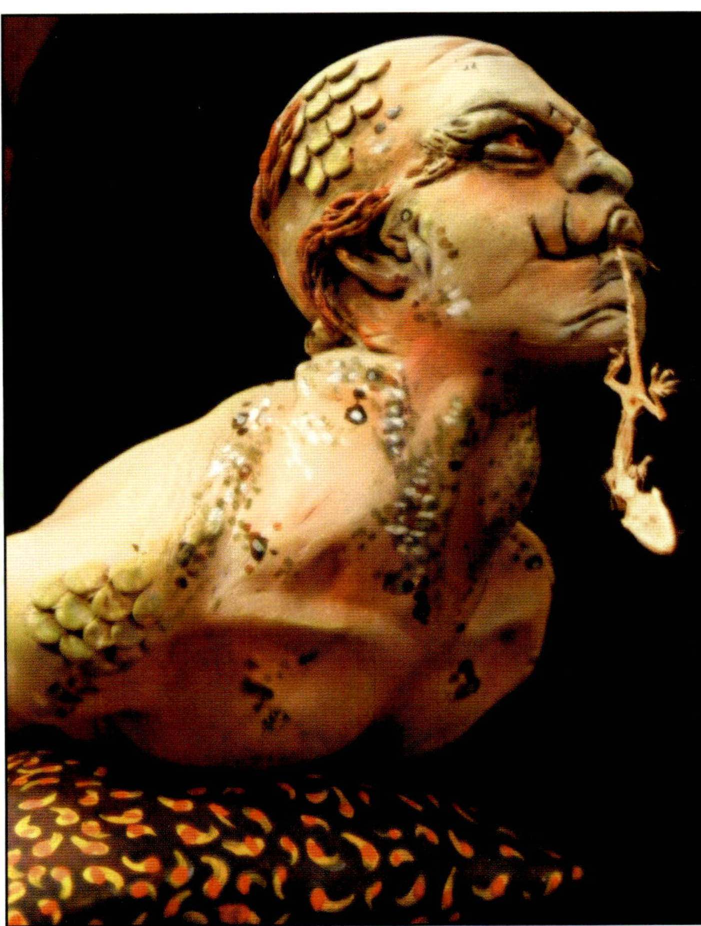

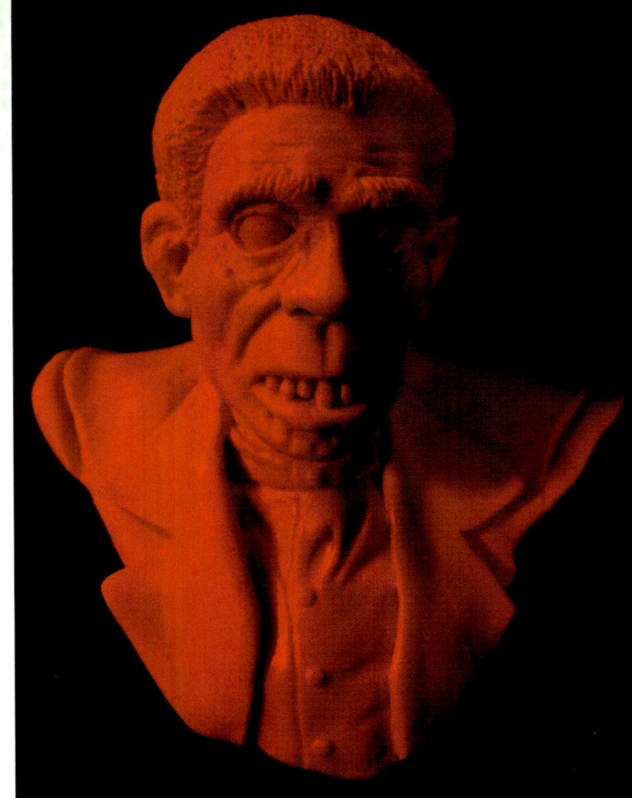

1. *Sssnake Boy.* 1997.
   Approx. 1/6 scale. Largely based on the actor who portrayed a reptilian/human circus sideshow exhibit in a cult 1970s movie.

2. *Tribute to Prince Randian.* Original prototype for resin kit. 1998.
   Approx. 1/4 scale.

3. *Jake.* Bust study. 1998.
   Approx. 1/6 scale. This character from the 1939 film *Dark Eyes of London* was always a familiar sight to those of us who read *Famous Monsters of Filmland* religiously . . . We have always been partial to the artwork on the U.S. one-sheet poster for the film *The Human Monster.*

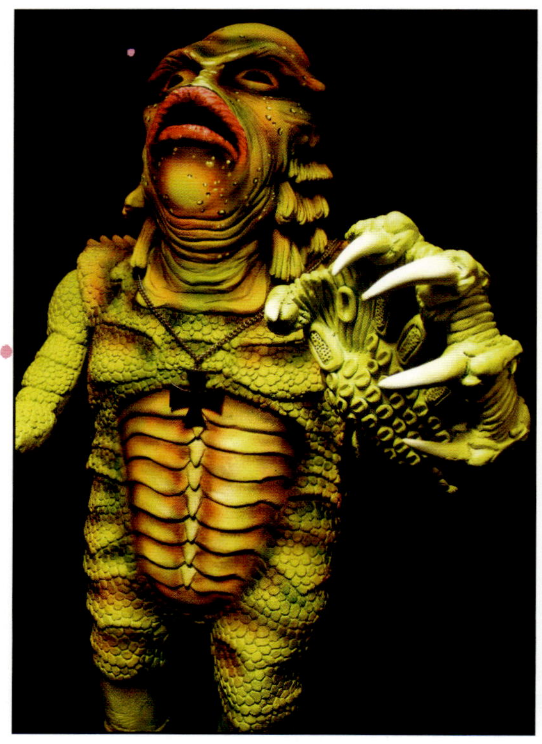

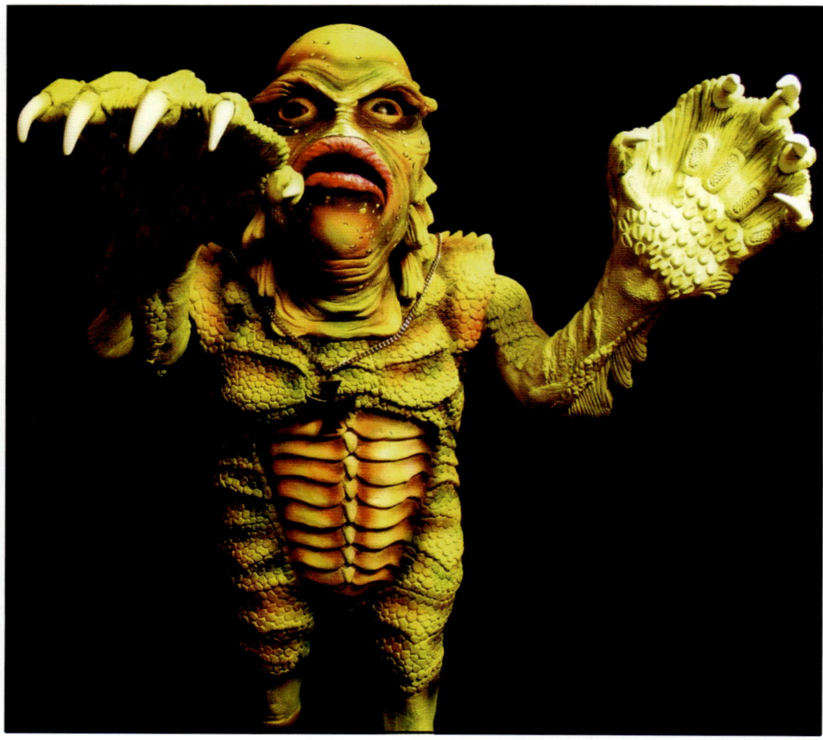

Big Creature. Paint in progress/ mock-up. 1996. Ace & Kali. Standing at almost two feet tall, this "Gigantic Creature" was the first in a tribute series we started to accompany the dearly departed Aurora "Gigantic Frankenstein"/"Big Frankie" released in 1964. It was also partially influenced by the *It's Monster Surfing Time* album by The Deadly Ones—specifically the cut "There's a Creature in the Surfer's Lagoon." This series of large monsters, created to be showcased in our portfolio, also included a Wolfman, Phantom, and Dracula. This huge project came to a screeching halt shortly after sending the first sculpture to be cast. Not only did it disappear without any explanation, we later found copies of our sculpture being sold to collectors and attributed to ANOTHER SCULPTOR, to add insult to injury. Nevertheless, despite the disreputable practices of certain areas of the garage kit hobby, we greatly enjoyed creating the concept and prototype of the Big Creature.

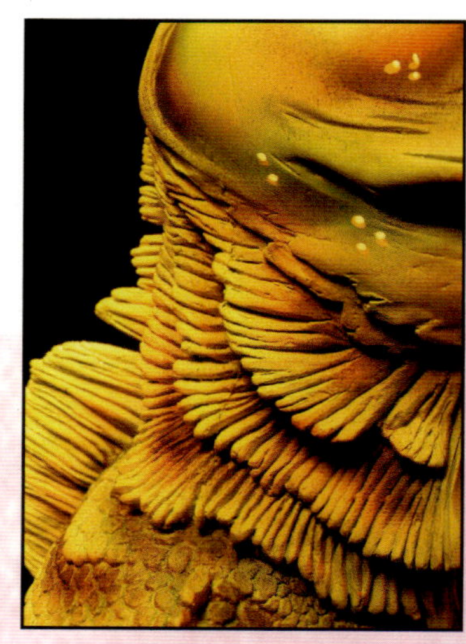

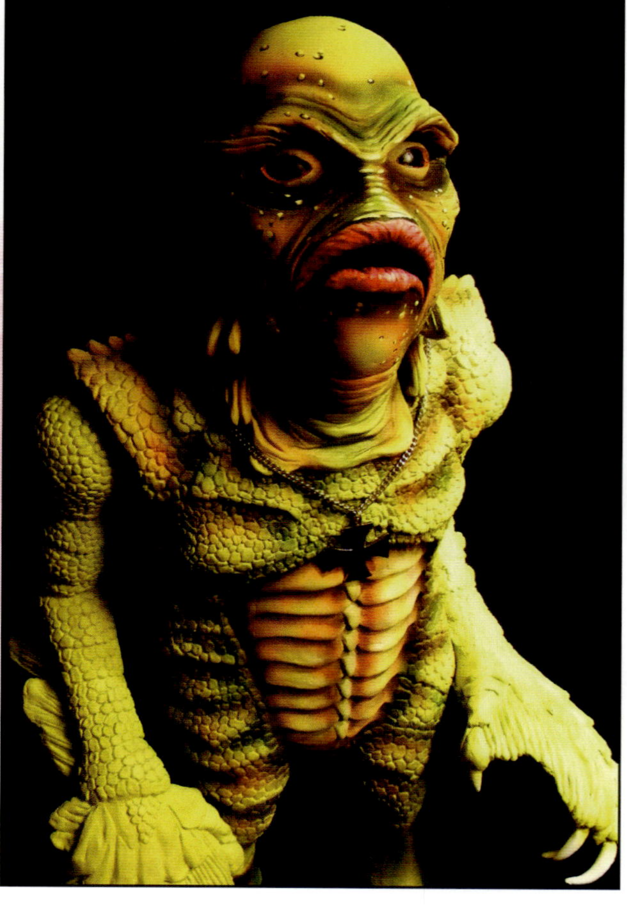

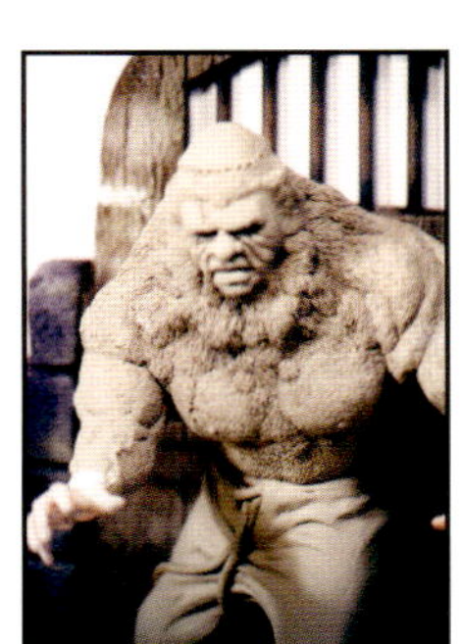

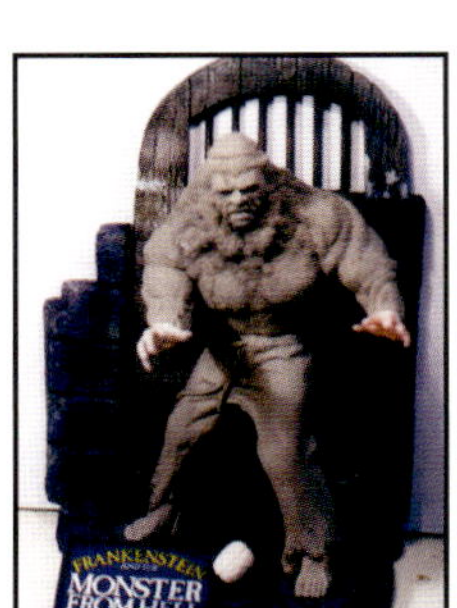

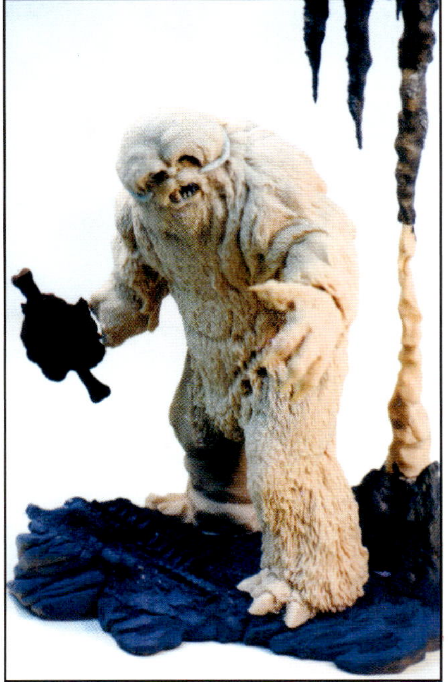

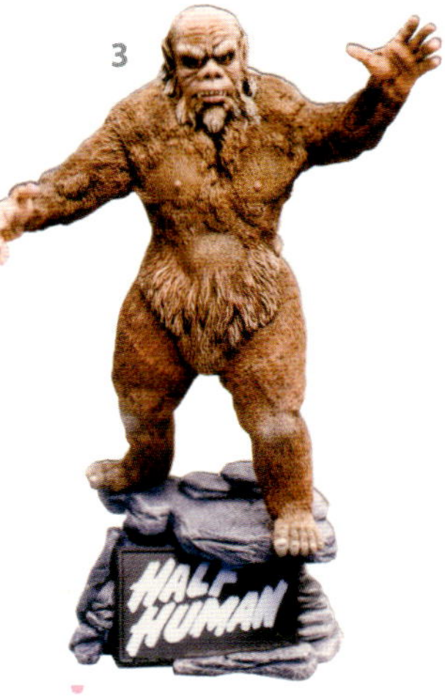

1. *Hammer Frankenstein.* 1996. 1/6 scale. This private collector's piece was done as a character study of David Prowse's bulky but very unique and memorable monster suit in one of our favorite Peter Cushing Hammer *Frankenstein* series. Current whereabouts unknown.

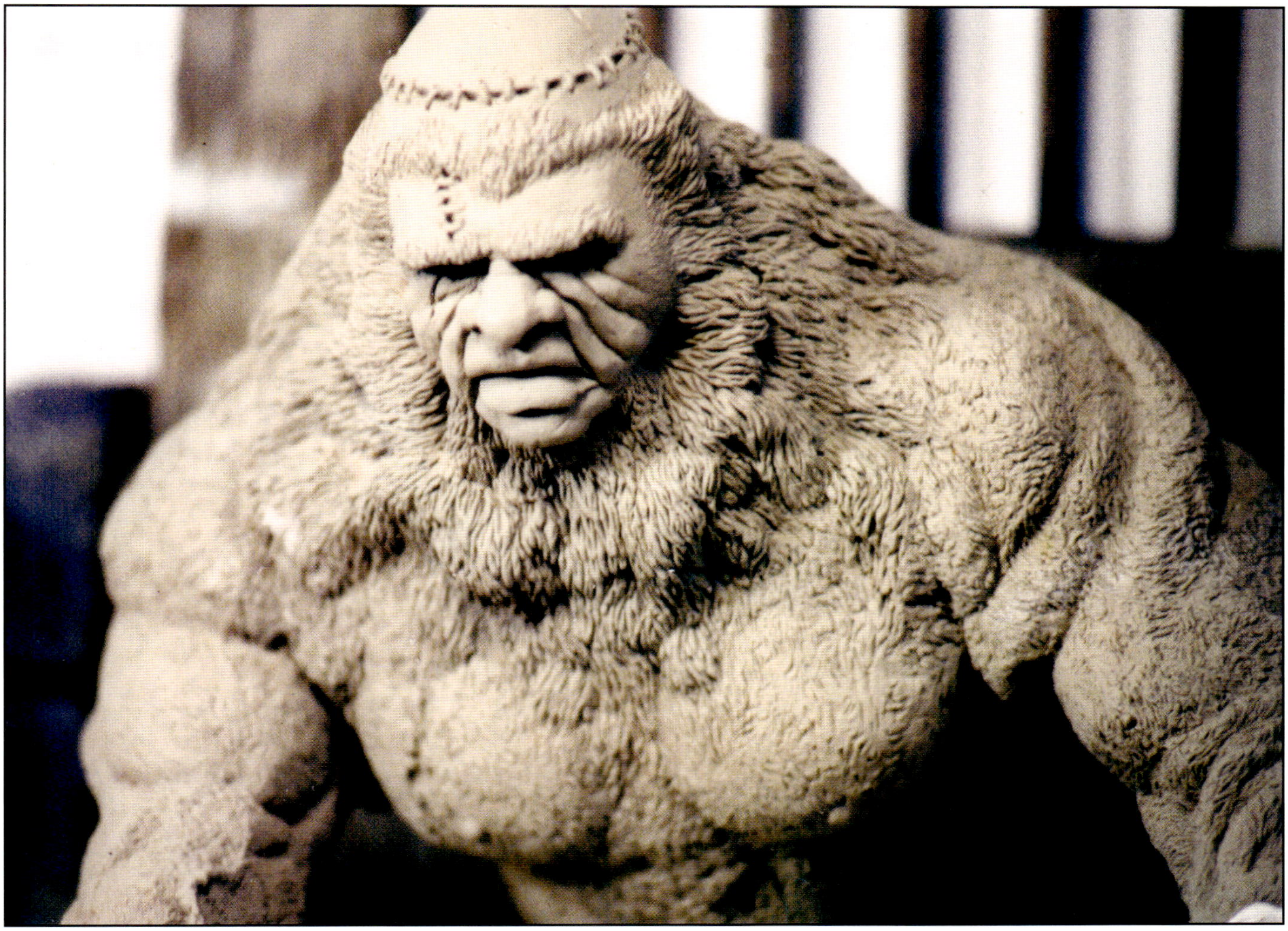

2. *Wampa.* 1997. Approx. 1/8 scale. This piece was done as another sculptural study of monster fur and was intended to serve as a sample for portfolio purposes. It was acquired by a private collector and never seen again by us.

3. *Half-Human.* 1996. 1/8 scale. Yet another monster-suit favorite. This was released in resin kit form for a number of years before we lost track of it. The American version of the original Japanese film *Jujin Yukio Takeo* ("Half-Human") remains a '50s creature-feature classic.

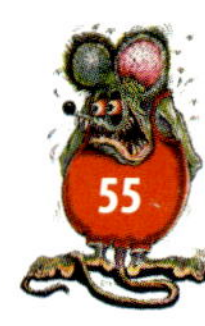

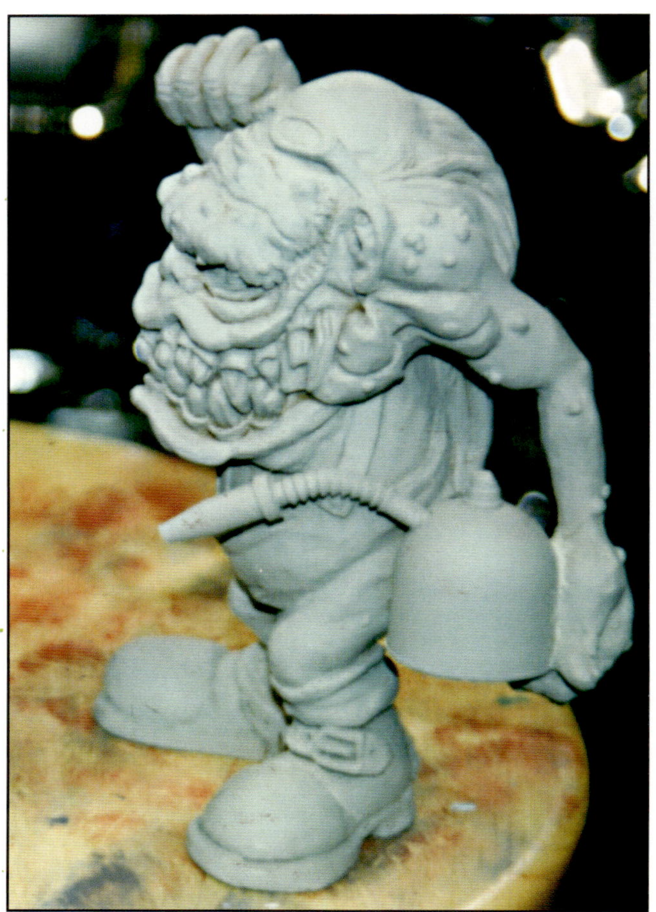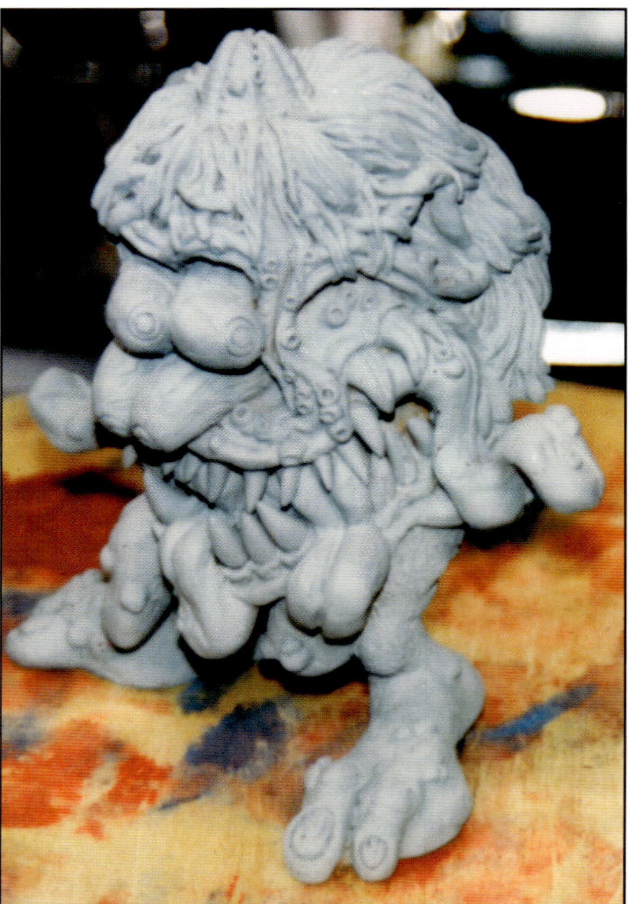

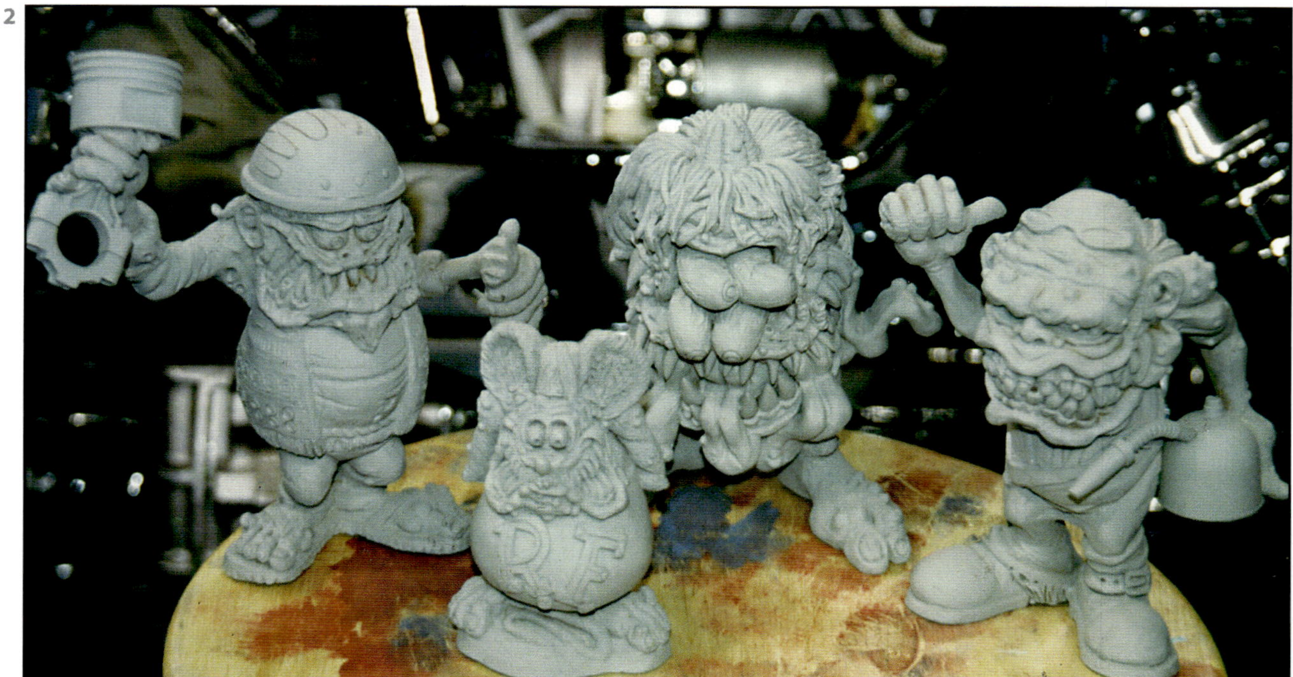

1. *Junkyard Kid* and *Irresistible Beast.* Polyclay prototypes. 1999.

2. *DragNut, Rat Fink with Fez, Irresistible Beast,* and *Junkyard Kid.* Polyclay prototypes. 1999.

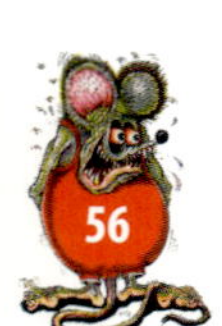

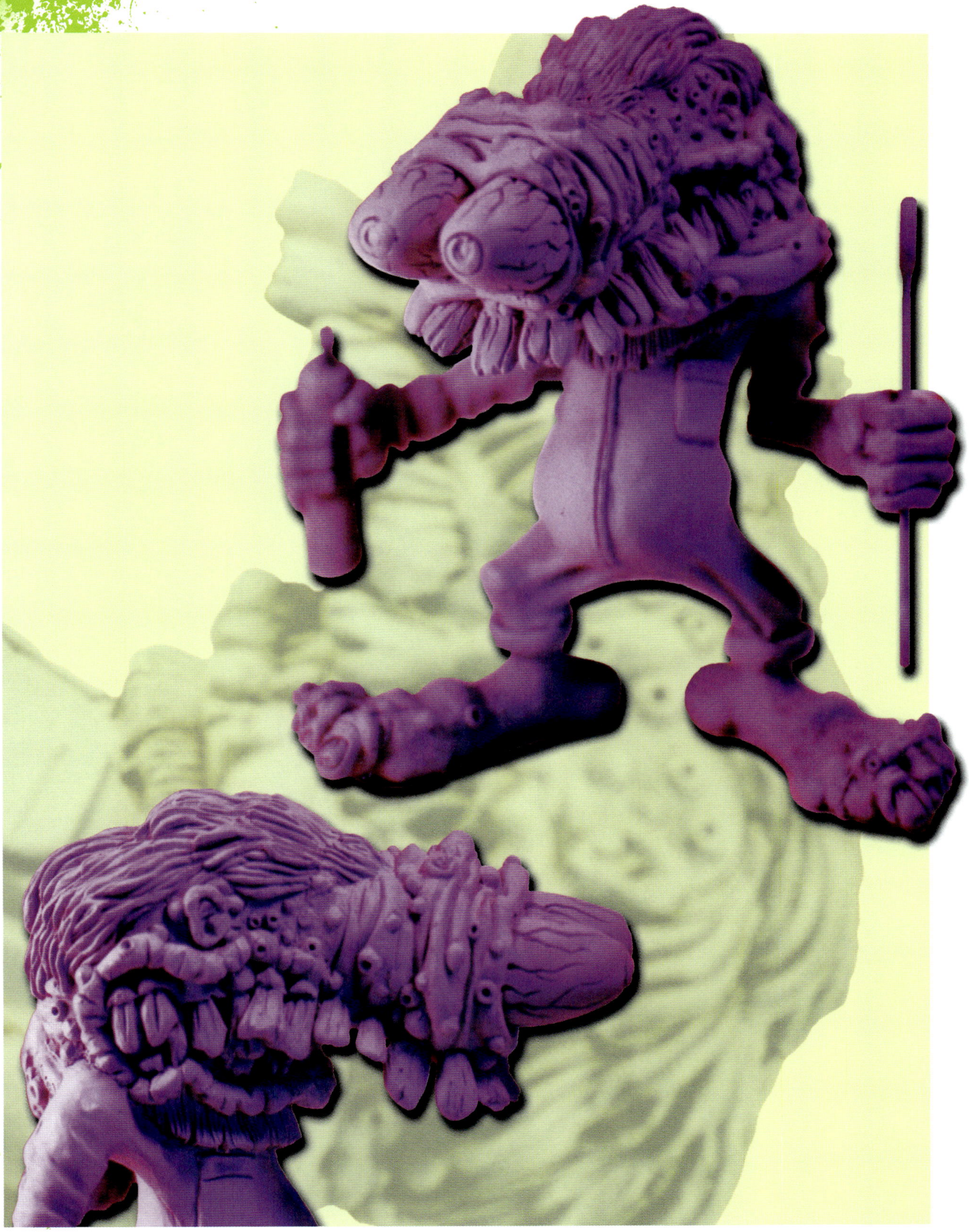

Speedo Fink. Polyclay prototype. 2000.
While many of the figures that were destined for glove molds required less detail and particular attention to undercuts, more articulated prototypes such as this version of Speedo Fink allowed us to render the character with much more personality. This figure was not intended to be cast, but rather served as yet another model for digital scanning. We embellished upon the t-shirt artwork version of Speedo Fink by riffing on two of our personal inspirations—Basil Wolverton and his Topps "Ugly Stickers" partner in crime, the great Wally Wood. We also included a nod to the classic "Nutty Mads" series by Marx and the Hawk Model Company's "Weird-Ohs" kits, which seems fitting because they clearly based their successful lines on territory that Roth Studios blazed first, subject-wise!

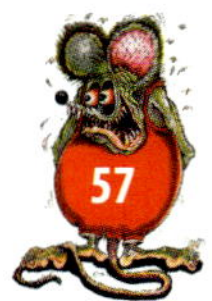

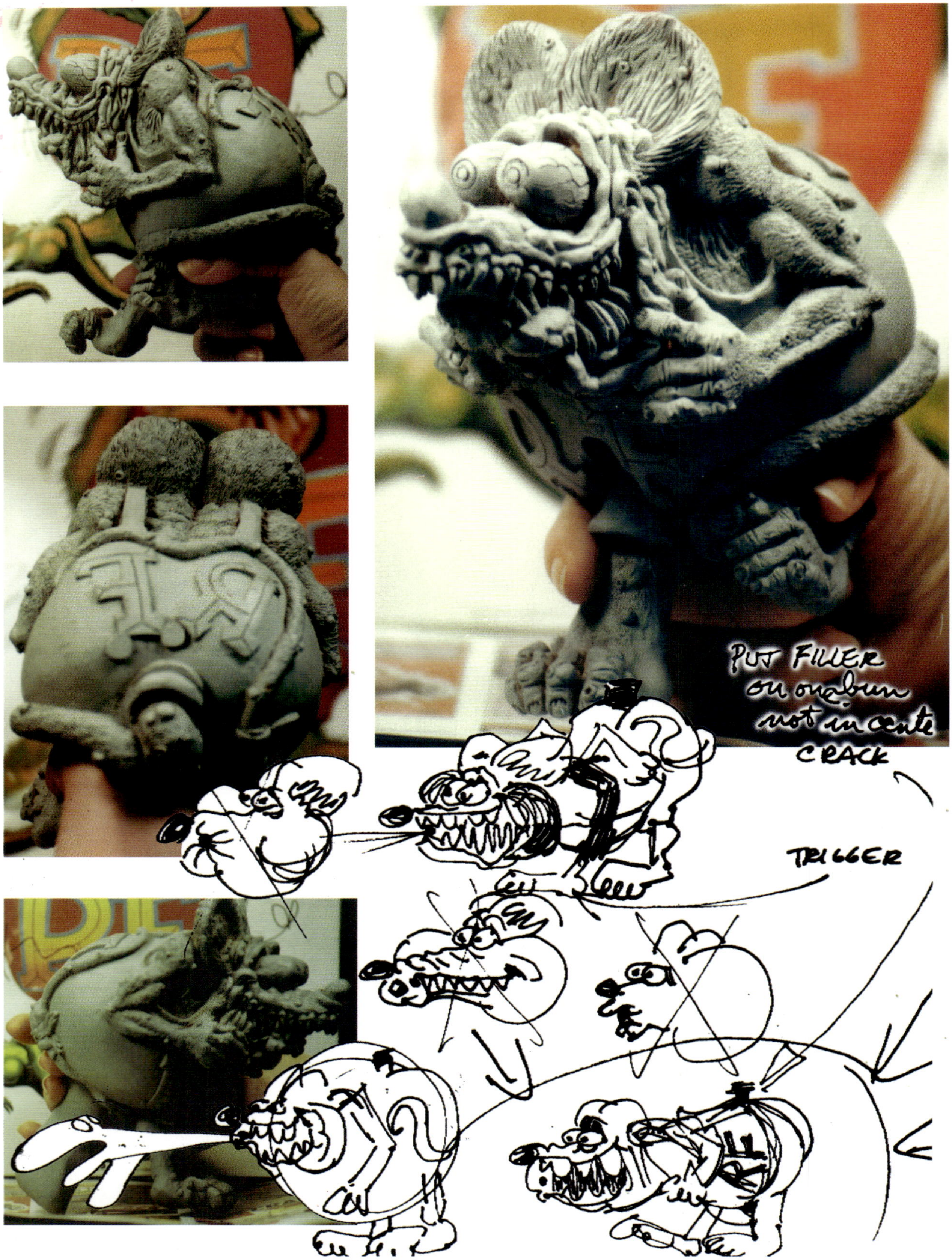

Rat Fink Water Gun. Polyclay prototype. 2000.
These turnaround photos show how large the Fink squirt gun actually
was. Rat Fink's foot served as the trigger, and the squirt hole was placed
between his two front fangs. Note Ed's original concept art and instructions
not to place the filler plug in Finky's butt-crack!

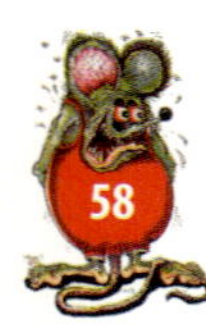

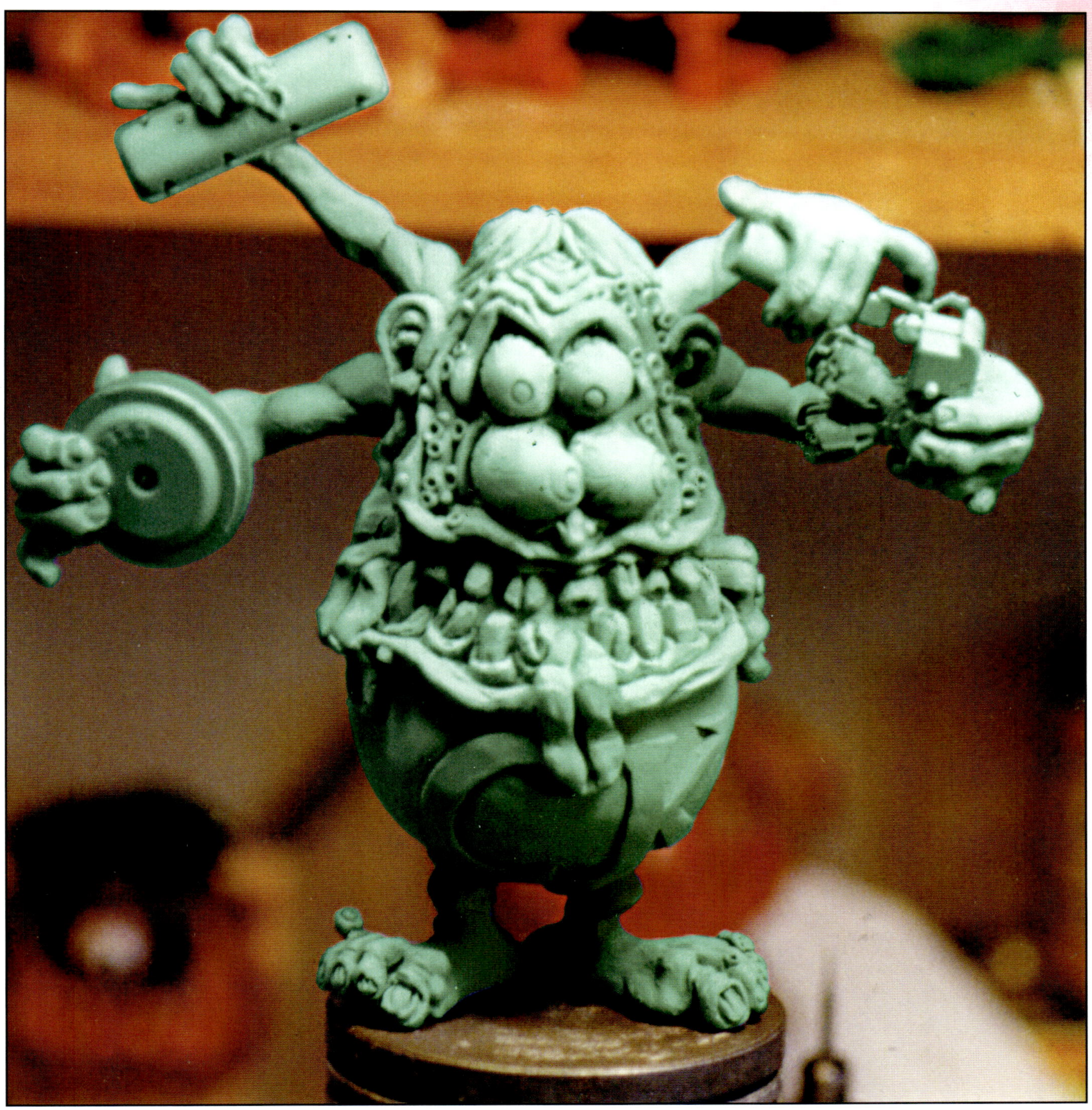

Chrome Shop Kid. Polyclay prototype. Date unknown.
This larger figure is another example of the many sculptures we created for Roth Studios that
were intended for digital scanning.

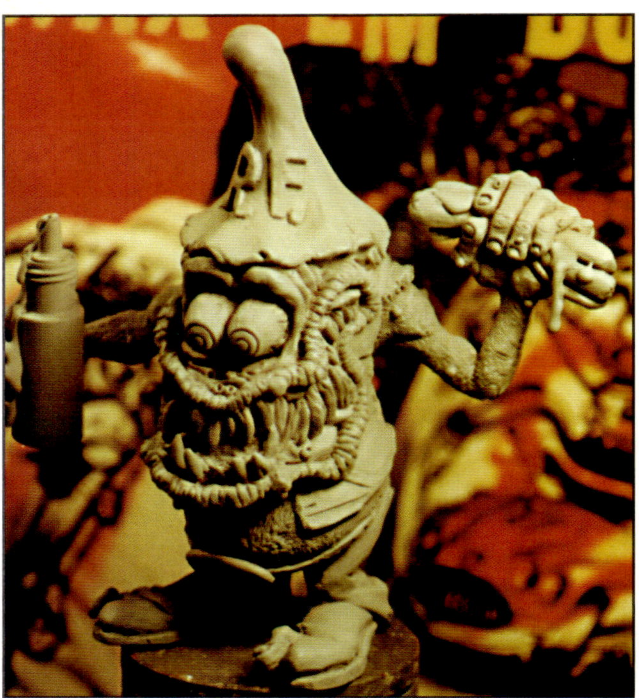 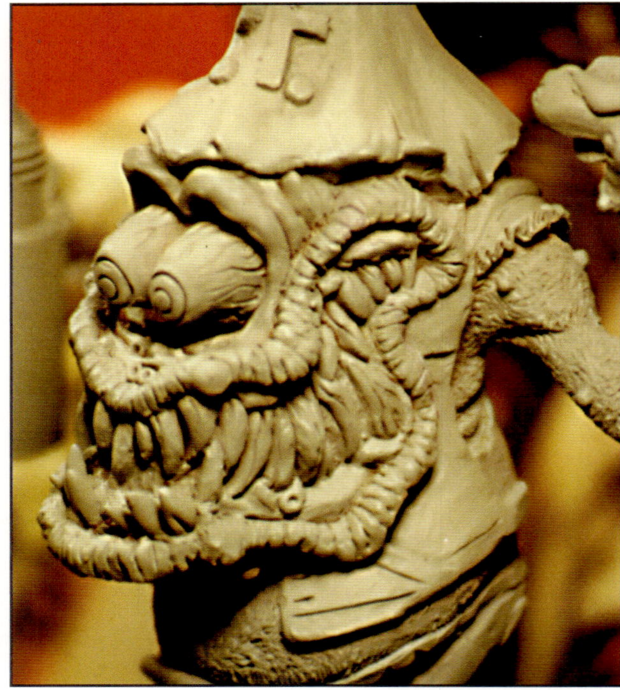

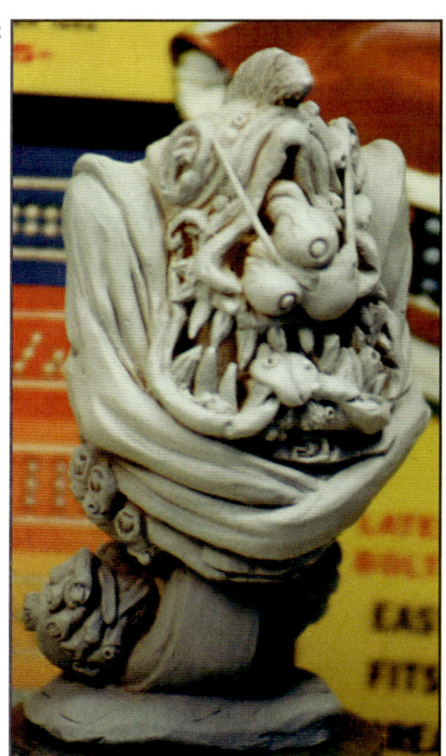 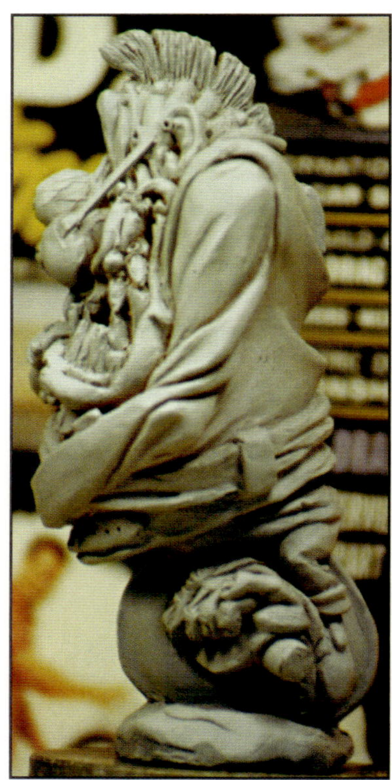 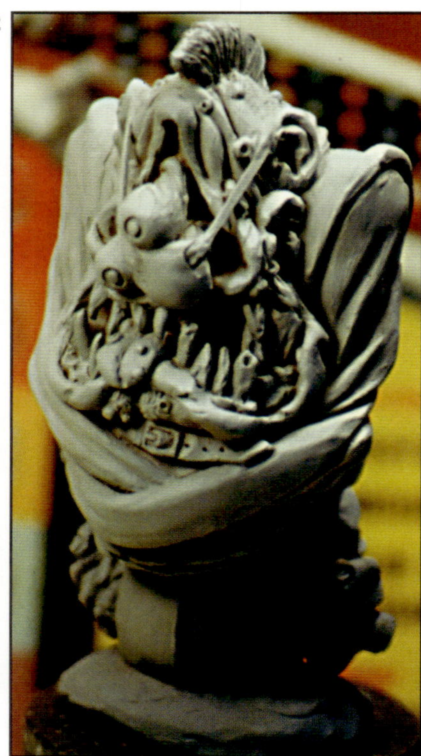

1. *Wild Child (with Hot Dog & Mustard Bottle).* Polyclay prototype. 2000. Although Wild Child's character details remain the same over the years, Ed decided to lose the original's bloody axe, straight razor, and knuckles in latter-day depictions.

2. **Unnamed character.** Polyclay prototype. 5.5". 2000.
This three-eyed, straitjacketed, racing slick-riding monster with an eye patch was the product of Ed's doodling in church. It was not uncommon for Ed to provide us with these types of characters on a Monday morning after one of his "inspired" Sundays. The Lord works in mysterious ways?!?

Actually, the roots of many of these Roth Studios characters go back to the earliest years ('60–'62) and began as some of Roth's earliest airbrushed t-shirts. The world of Roth has many multi-eyed and slick-riding characters, such as Irresistible Beast, Cluster Buster, Chrome Shop Kid, Nervous Brothers I & II, and the infamous Chicken Shift. (Done for Roth Studios by Don "Monte" Monteverde, who inked some of Roth's earliest decal/shirt designs, including the original Rat Fink archetype!)

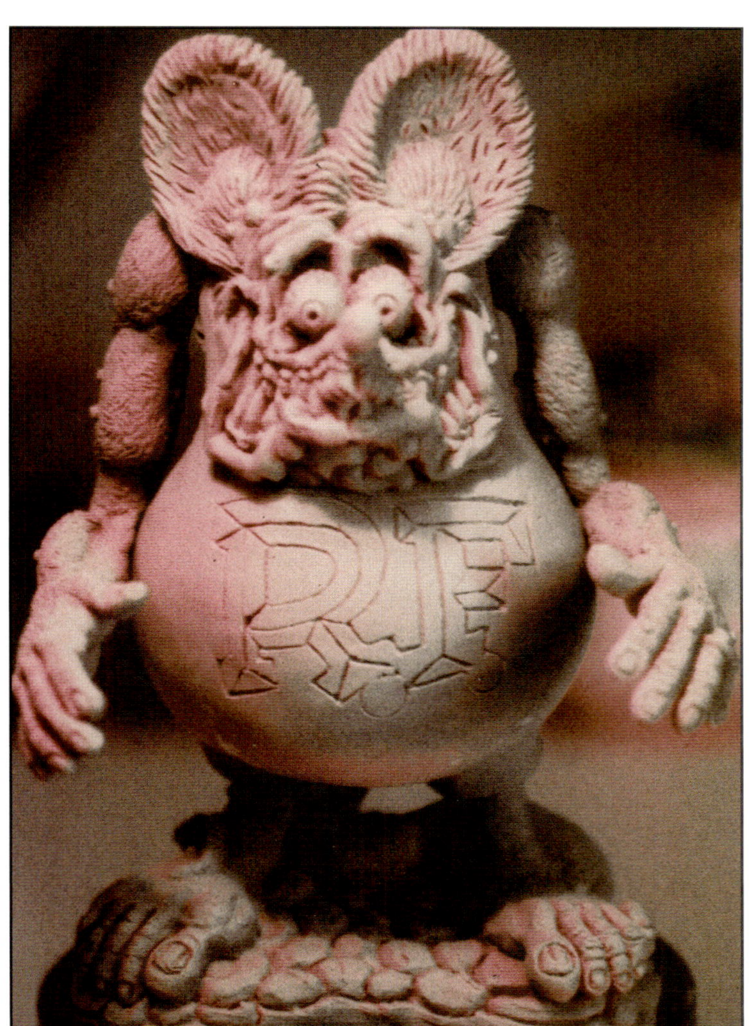

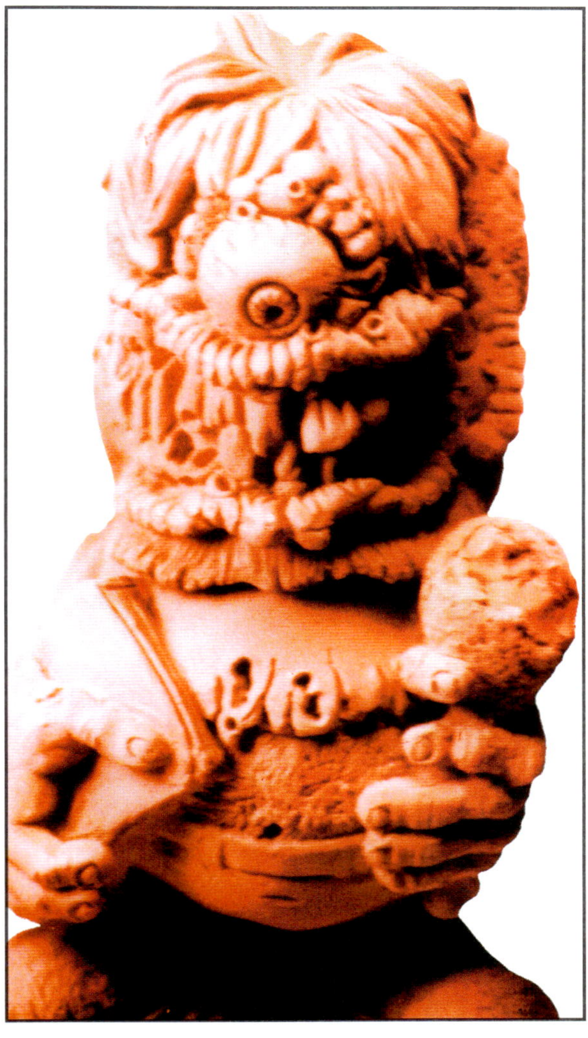

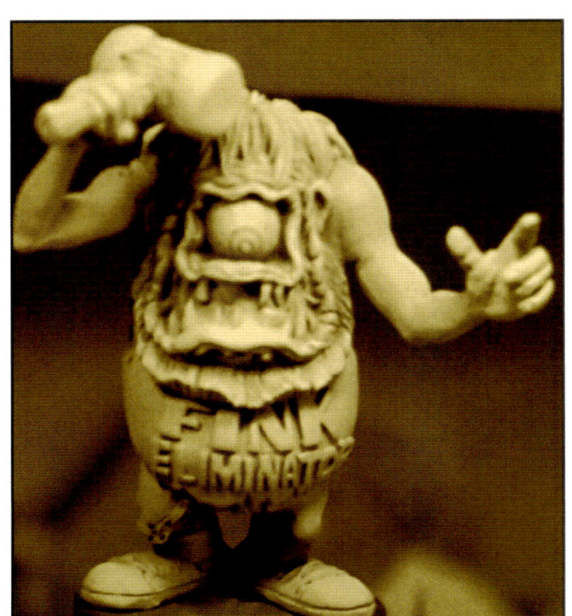

1. ***Rat Fink Poseable.*** Polyclay prototype. 8". 1999.
   This figure featured movable arms and was most likely destined to serve as a proportion guide for animators and house sculptors at various toy design companies. Despite our attempts to catalog the details of all the work we did for Roth Studios over the years, many times pressing deadlines, malfunctioning cameras, Ed's scheduling, and good old Murphy's Law made it difficult to keep track of what we did and where it went.

2. ***Drag Lover/Hermie.*** Polyclay prototype. Approx. 5.75". 1999.
   Classic Roth Studios character holding copy of Pete Millar's *Big Daddy Roth Magazine* and fried chicken leg.

3. ***Fink Eliminator.*** Polyclay prototype. Date unknown.

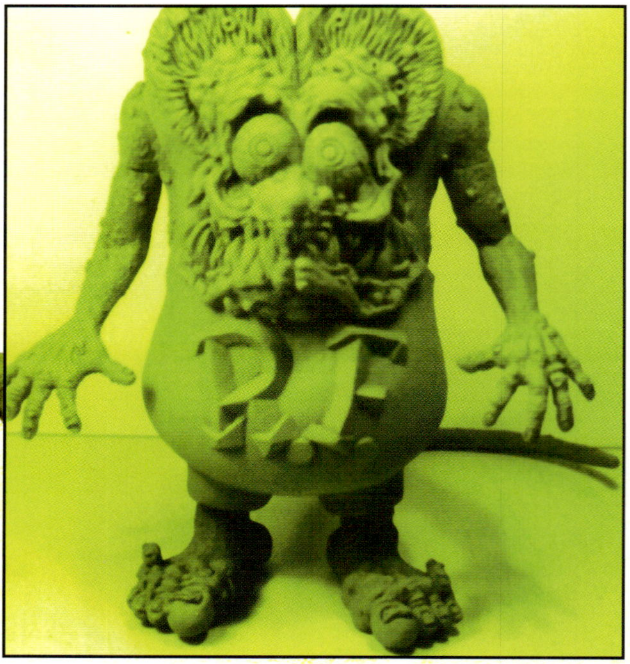

1. *Big Finkie guide model.* Polyclay prototype. 1999.
This 11" figure with moveable arms and tail was done to serve as a digitally scan-able model for possible CGI and/or animation projects by studios and companies that frequently approached Roth.

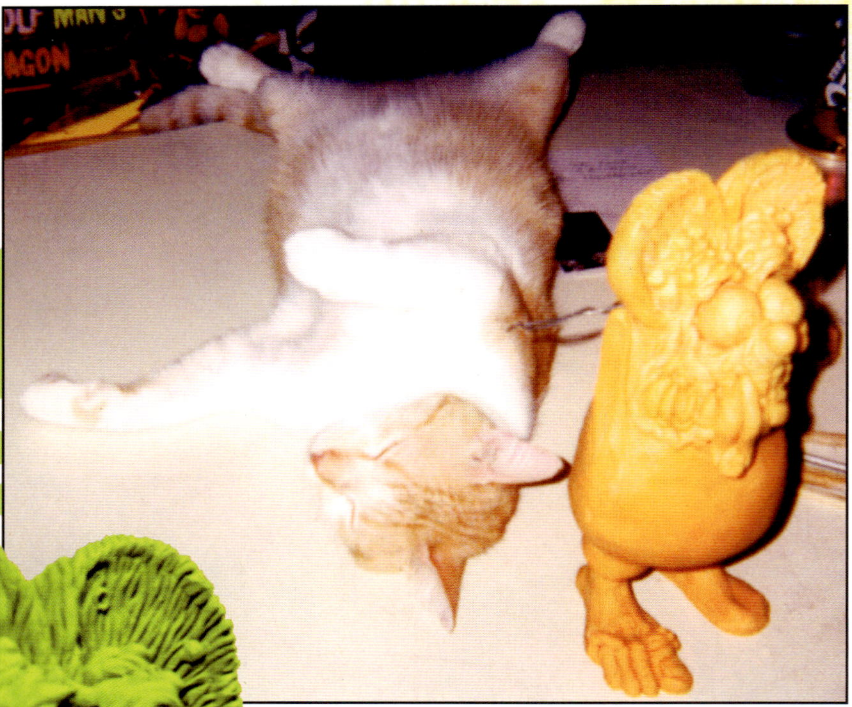

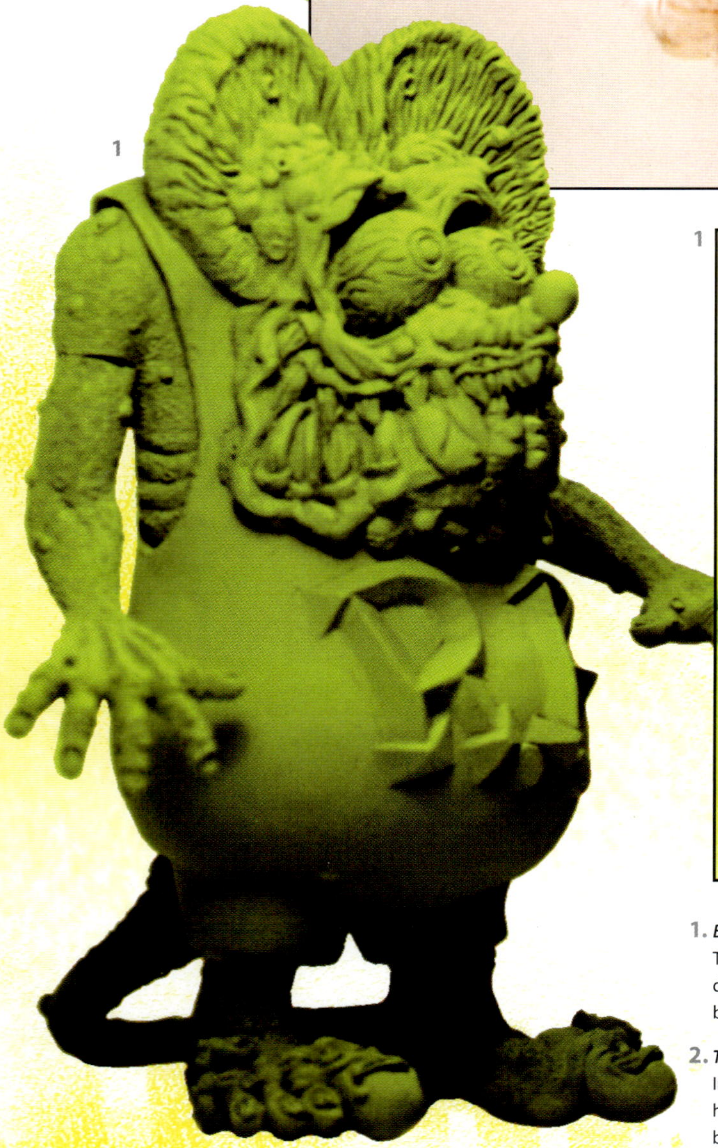

2. *The studio model in repose . . .*
In this case, our resident Fink model and Wooly Bully, Biscuit, shows how life as the perfect Rat Fink model can be an exhausting job. In between posing for the Big Finky project, our boy grabs a few winks whenever possible.

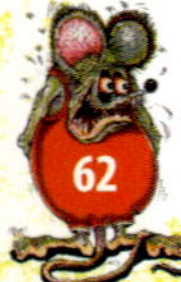

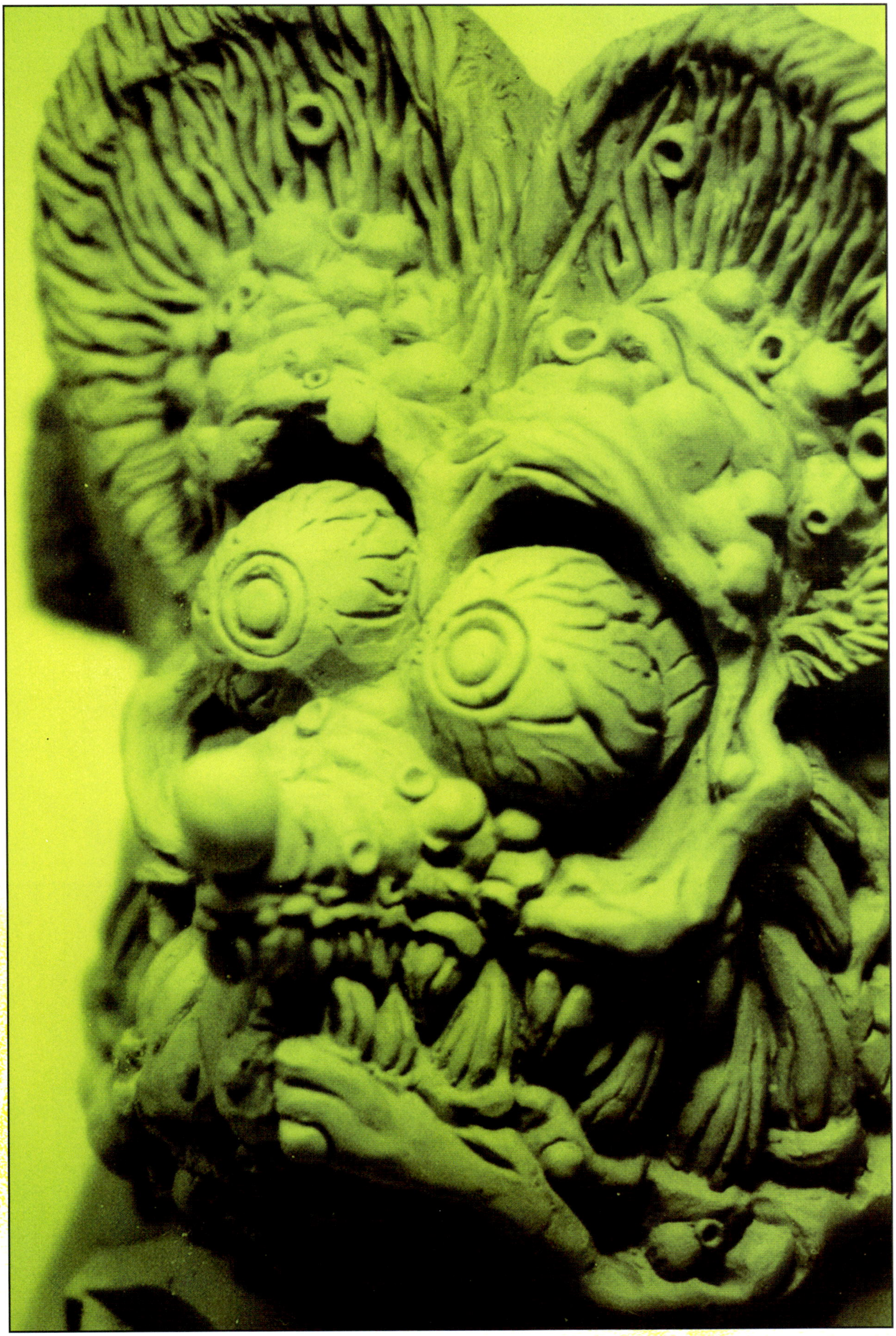

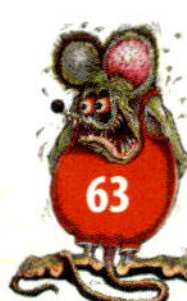

Big Finkie guide model detail. Polyclay prototype. August 1999.

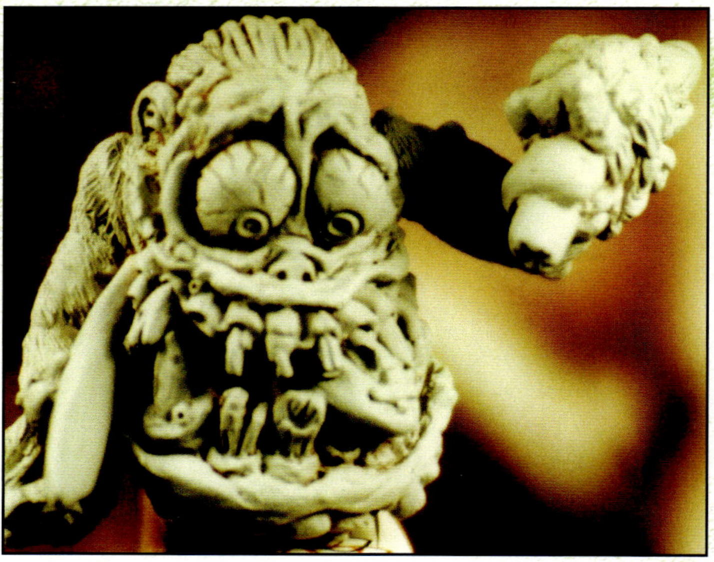

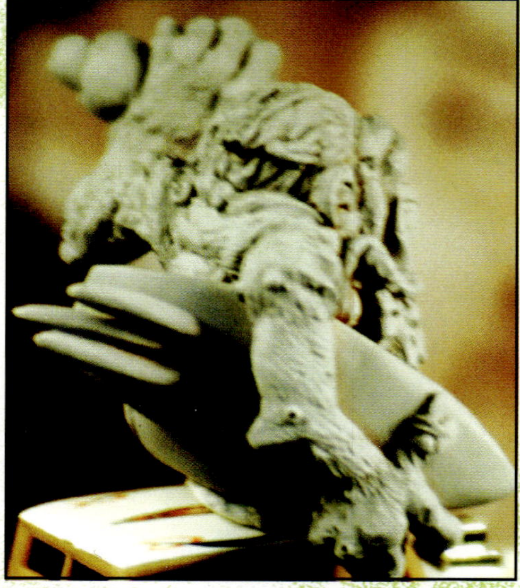

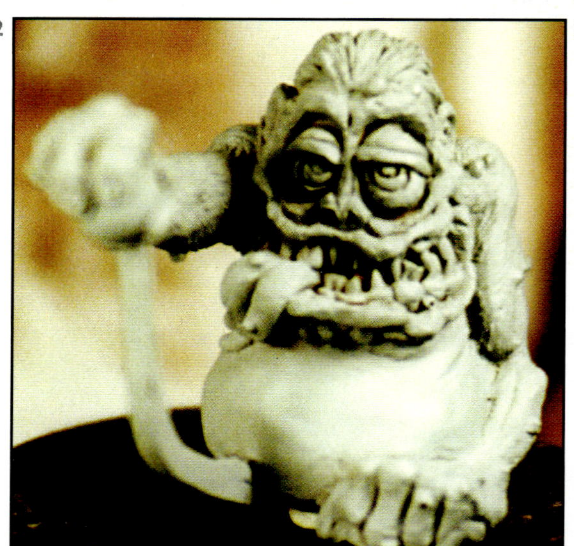

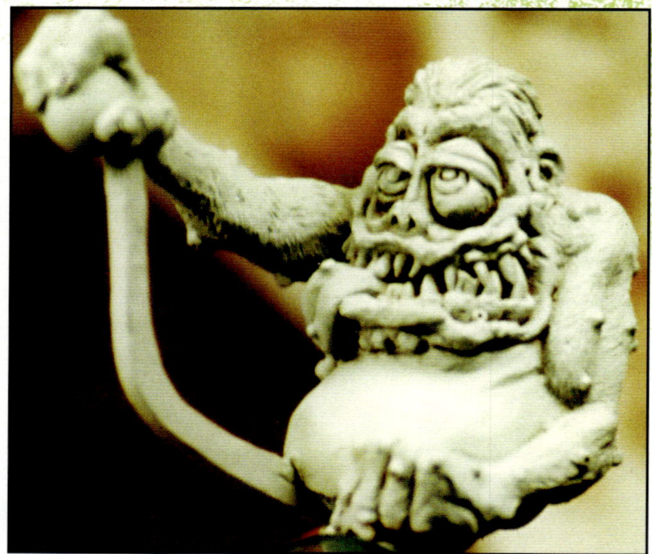

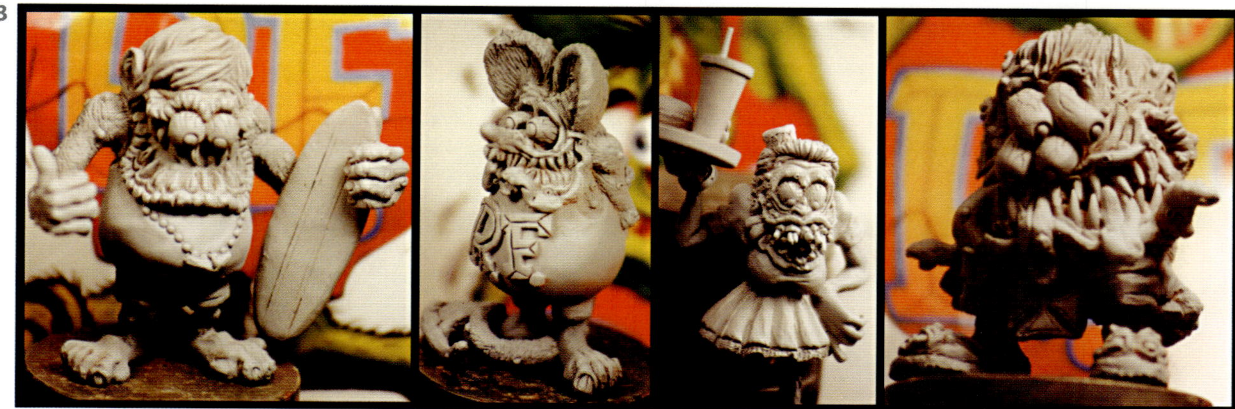

1. **Total Craziness.** Polyclay prototype. 2" x 2.5". 2000.
   This figure was part of a series Ed was planning with Ertl and was done in 1:64 scale to fit with their vehicles.

2. **Mother's Worry.** Polyclay prototype. 2" x 2.5". 2000.
   Another in the Ertl series . . . as far as we are aware, these never went into production.

3. **Surfink, Rat Fink, Crazy Girl, Irresistible Beast.** Polyclay prototypes. 2000.
   This set of four figures was originally sculpted in early summer 2000, but not released until 2002 by Fewture/Artstorm of Japan.

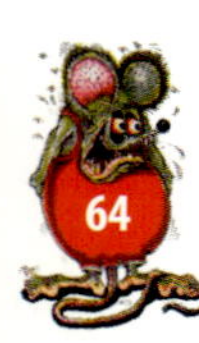

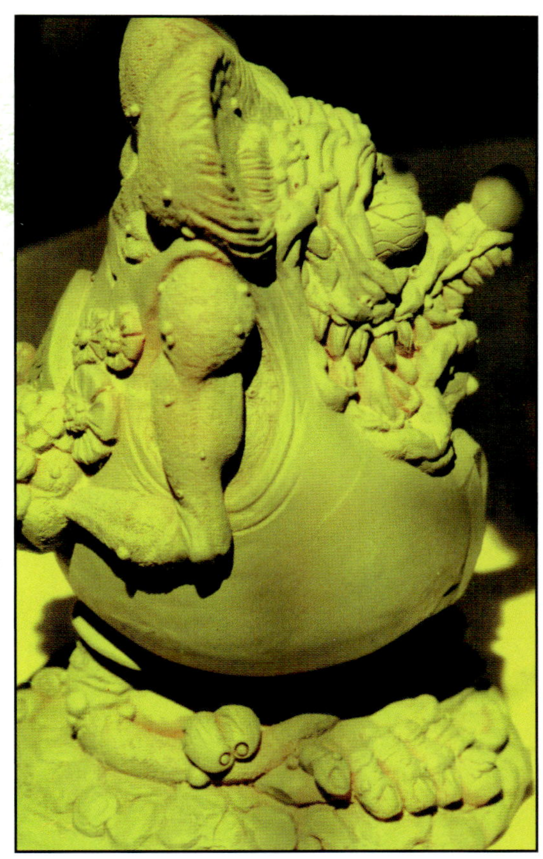

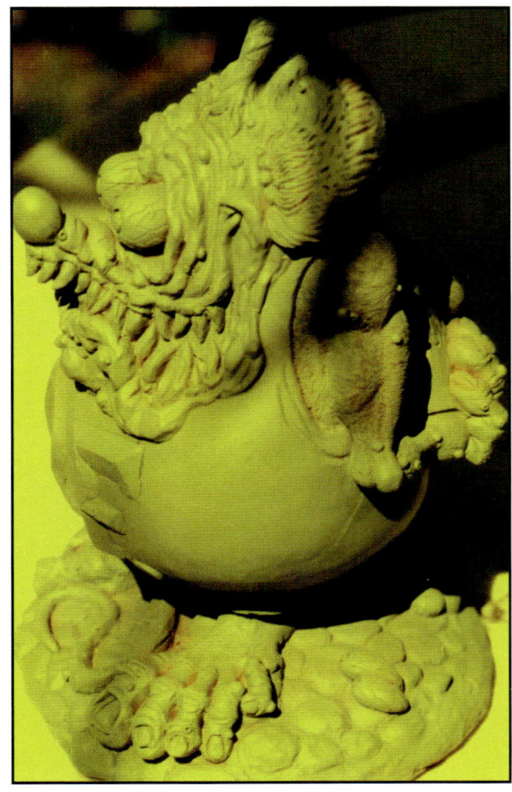

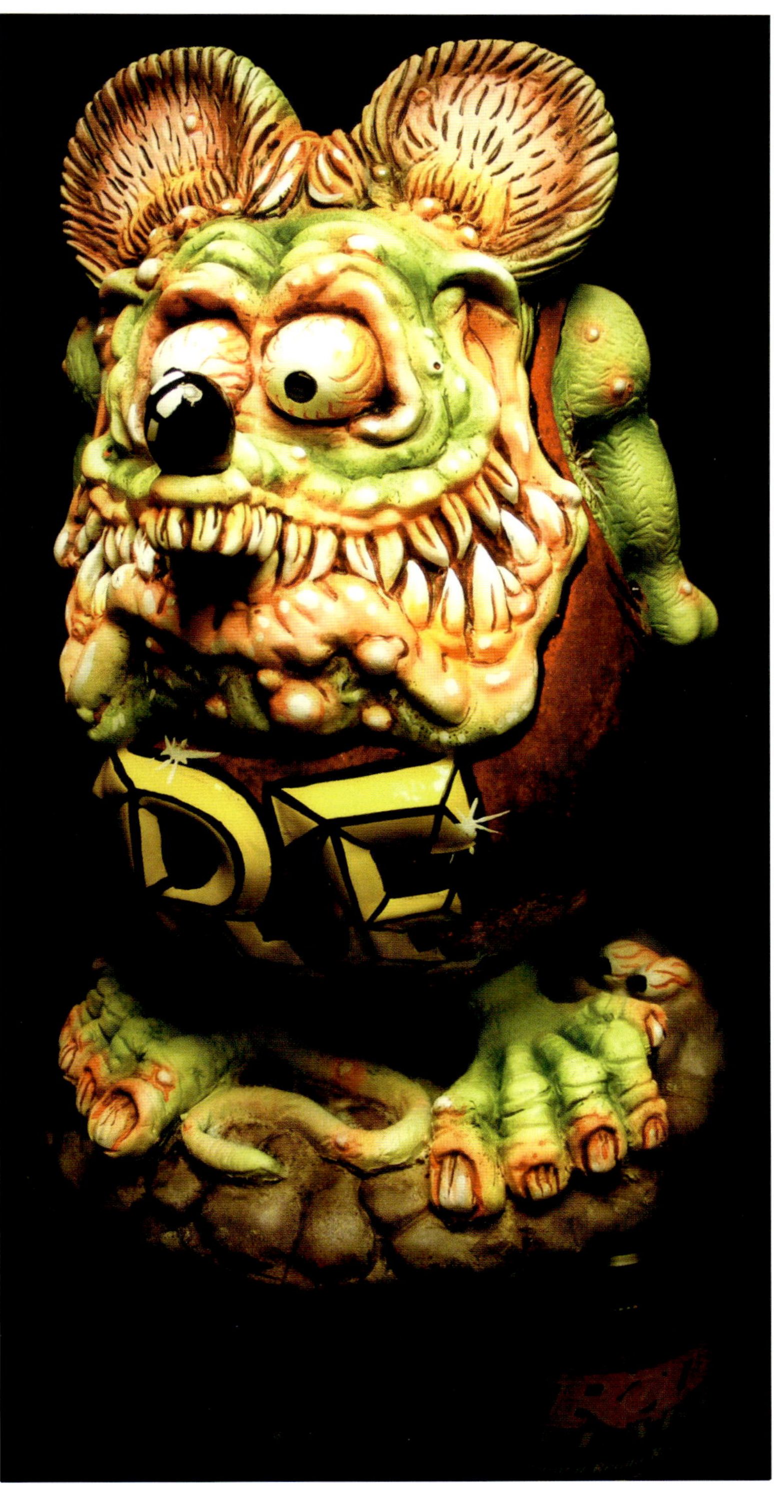

Rat Fink coin bank. Custom painted version by Johnny Ace & Kali, 2007. Lil' Daddy Roth Flake in Ruined Retina Red, 1-Shot, Createx Auto Air. Filled with expanding foam to make RF even fatter!

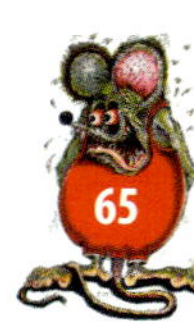

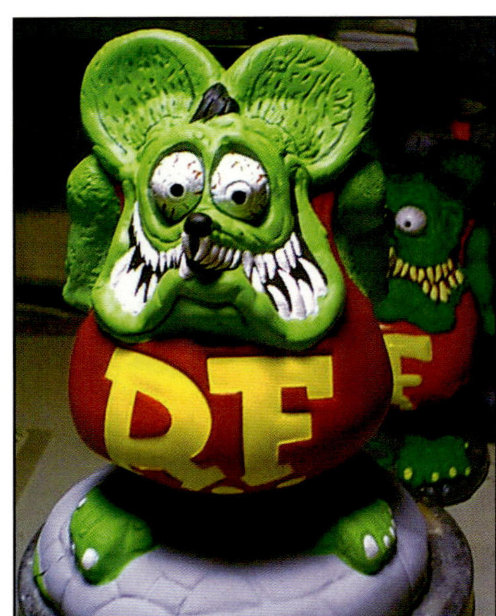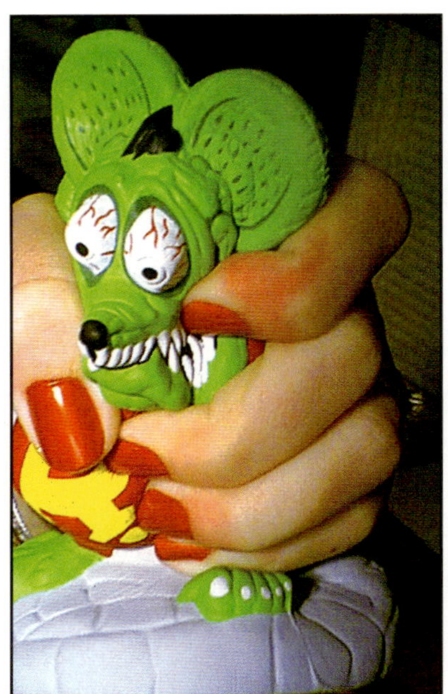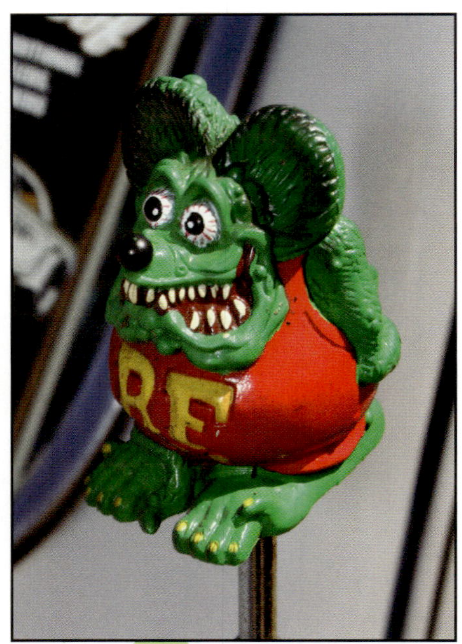

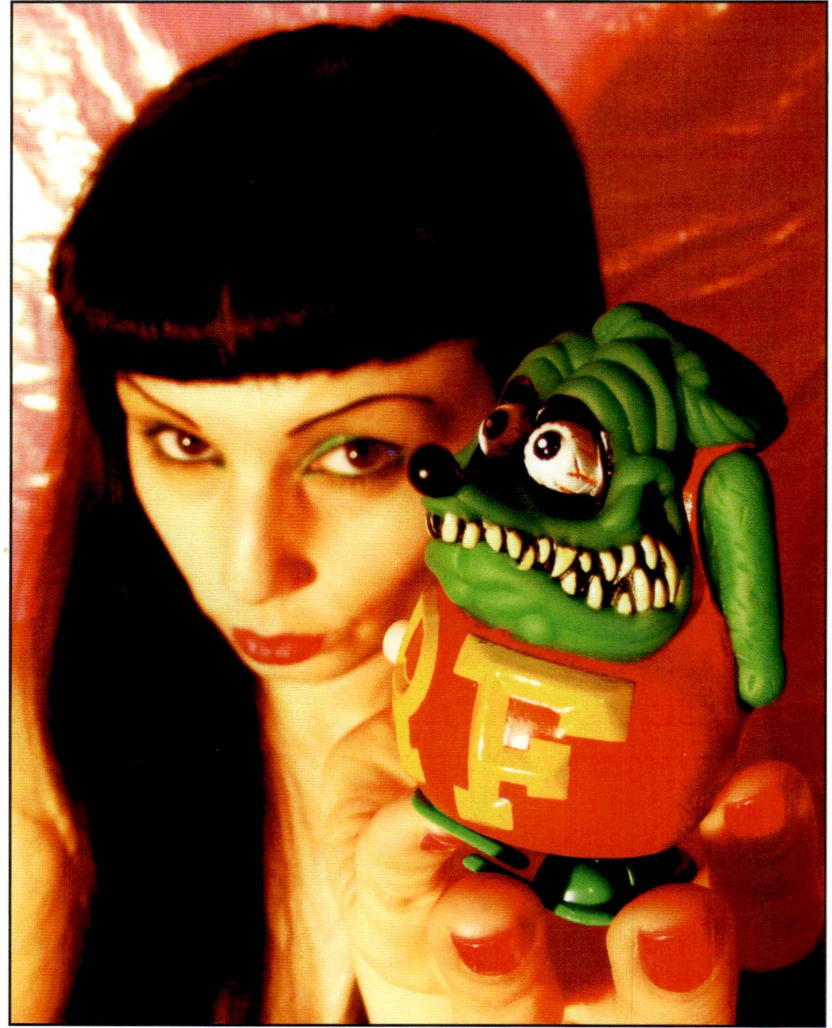

1. *Rat Fink Foam Squeezie.* Test press. 5". 2000.
Pictured is the final product based on the prototype we sculpted. This was part of a group of Rat Fink figures we did that included an antenna ball (which was ultimately released as a wind-up walking toy), a 2" PVC Rat Fink figure (pictured here as an antenna ball, oddly enough), and a 10" hollow vinyl Rat Fink bank. The company responsible for producing these toys ended up altering our work somewhat for the final release and product.

2. *Rat Fink PVC Figure.* 2". 2000.
Photo © 2006 by Dave Molloy, Pro Photo Photography.

3. *Rat Fink wind-up walking toy.* Released by American Leo, Inc. 2001. Model, Patti Waggin. Photo by Johnny Ace, 2007.

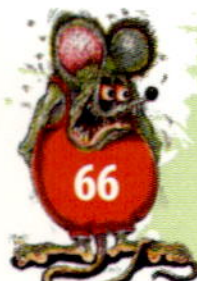

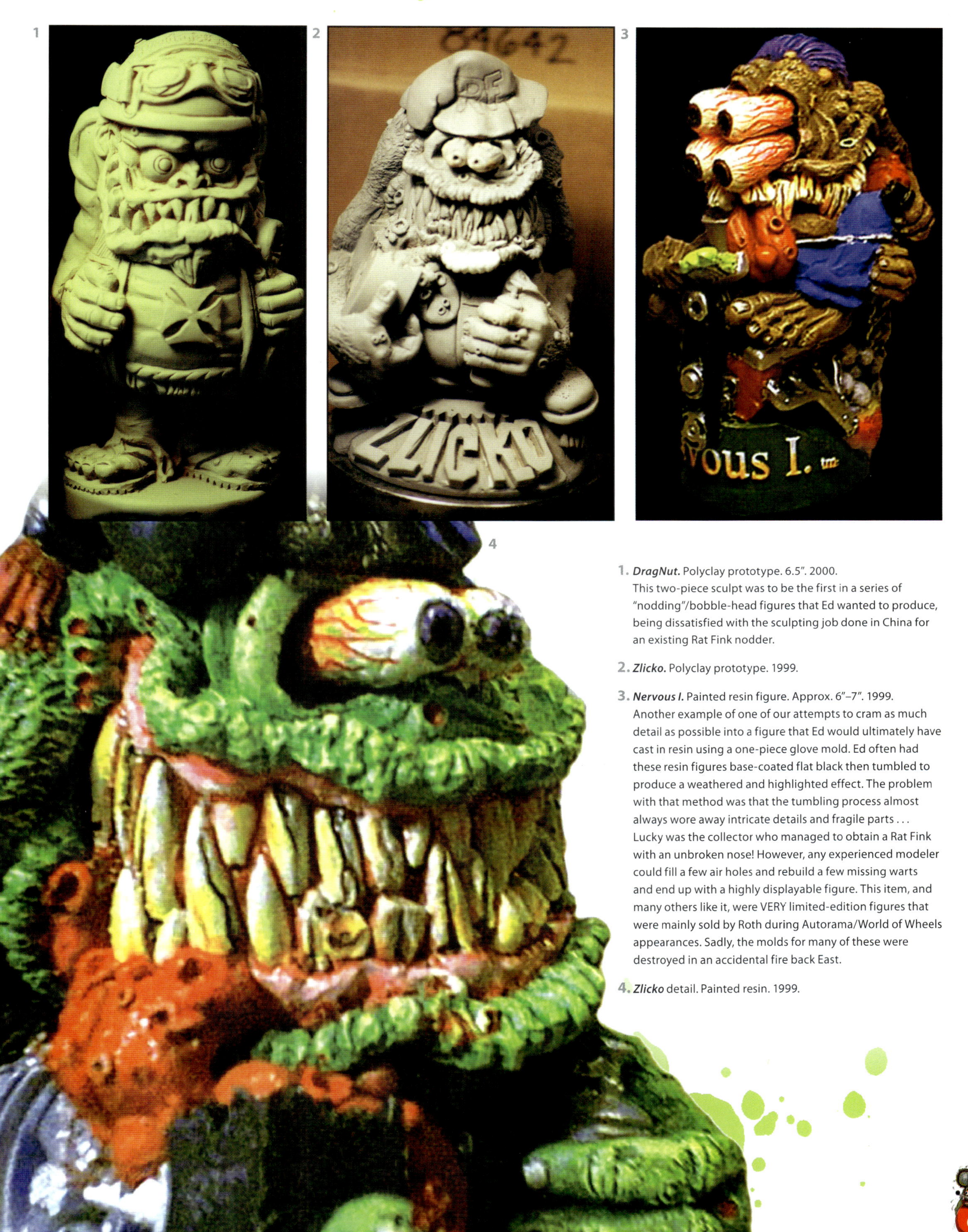

1. *DragNut.* Polyclay prototype. 6.5". 2000.
This two-piece sculpt was to be the first in a series of "nodding"/bobble-head figures that Ed wanted to produce, being dissatisfied with the sculpting job done in China for an existing Rat Fink nodder.

2. *Zlicko.* Polyclay prototype. 1999.

3. *Nervous I.* Painted resin figure. Approx. 6"–7". 1999.
Another example of one of our attempts to cram as much detail as possible into a figure that Ed would ultimately have cast in resin using a one-piece glove mold. Ed often had these resin figures base-coated flat black then tumbled to produce a weathered and highlighted effect. The problem with that method was that the tumbling process almost always wore away intricate details and fragile parts . . . Lucky was the collector who managed to obtain a Rat Fink with an unbroken nose! However, any experienced modeler could fill a few air holes and rebuild a few missing warts and end up with a highly displayable figure. This item, and many others like it, were VERY limited-edition figures that were mainly sold by Roth during Autorama/World of Wheels appearances. Sadly, the molds for many of these were destroyed in an accidental fire back East.

4. *Zlicko* detail. Painted resin. 1999.

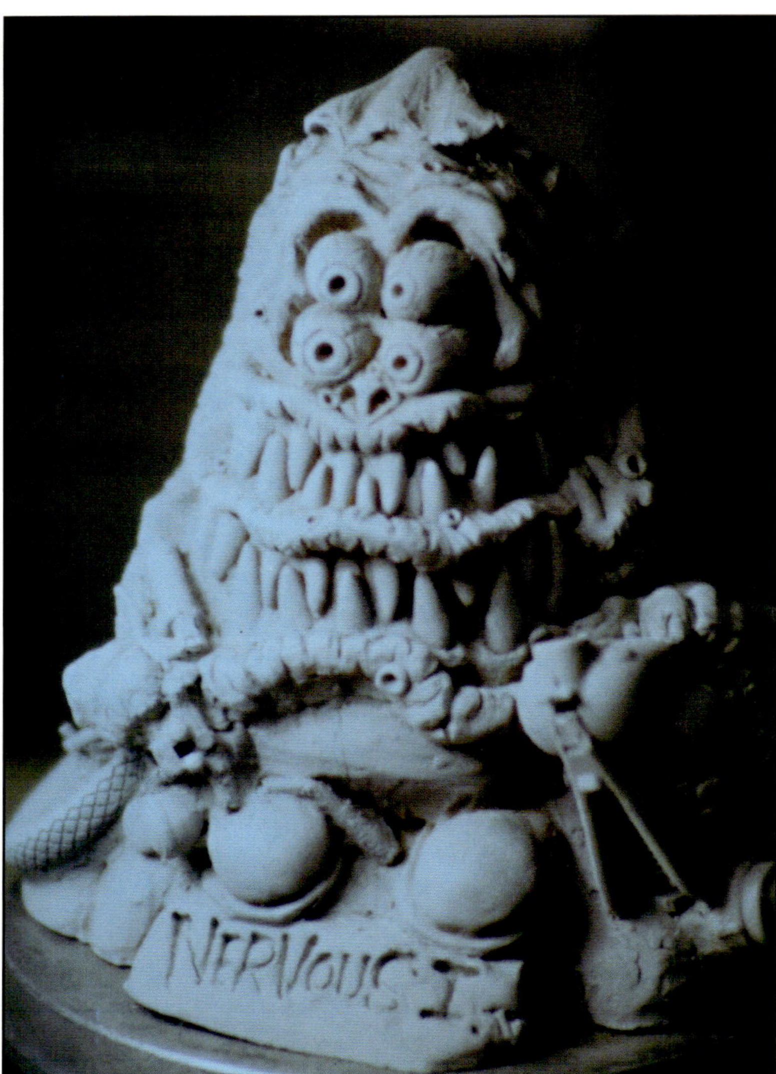

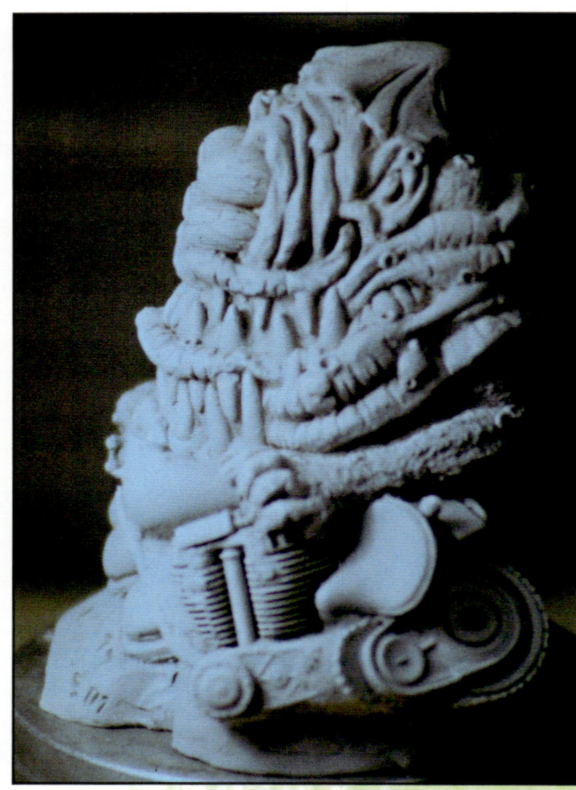

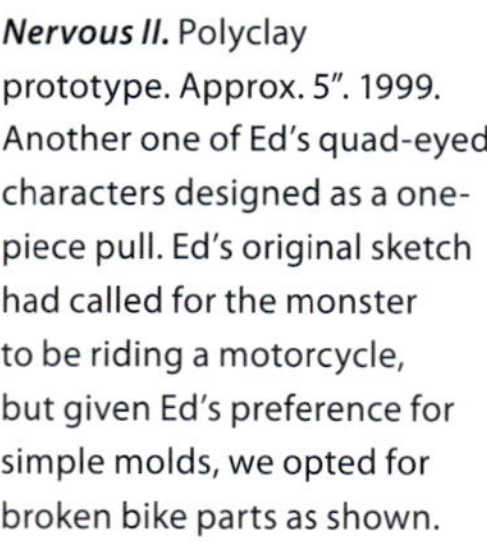

Nervous II. Polyclay prototype. Approx. 5". 1999. Another one of Ed's quad-eyed characters designed as a one-piece pull. Ed's original sketch had called for the monster to be riding a motorcycle, but given Ed's preference for simple molds, we opted for broken bike parts as shown.

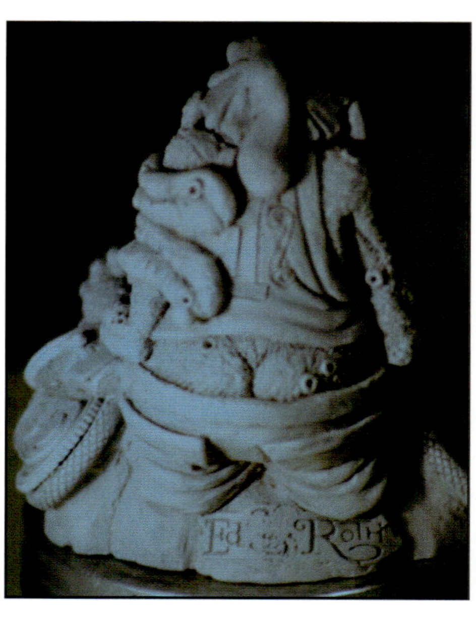

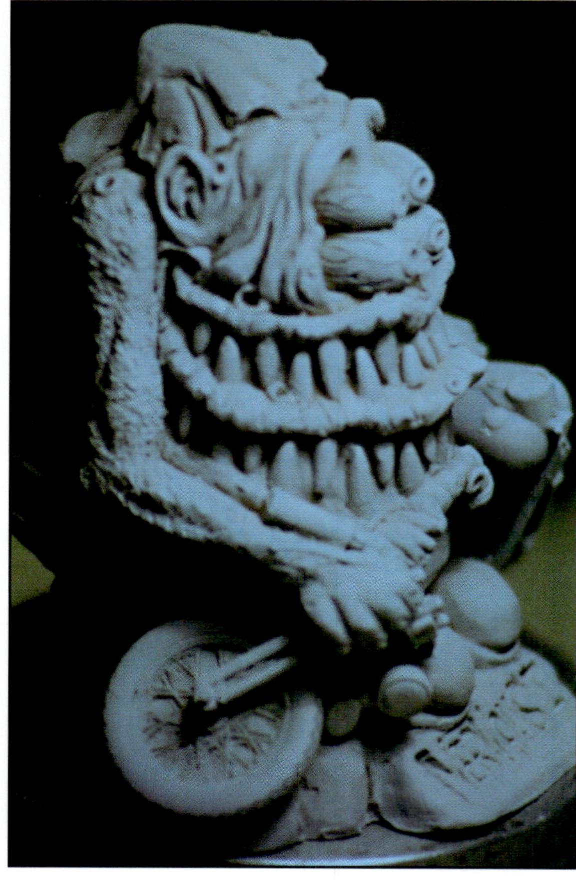

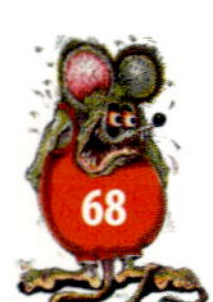

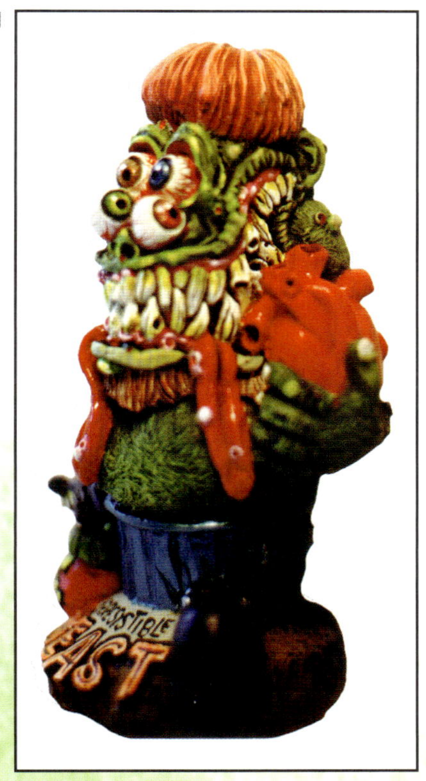

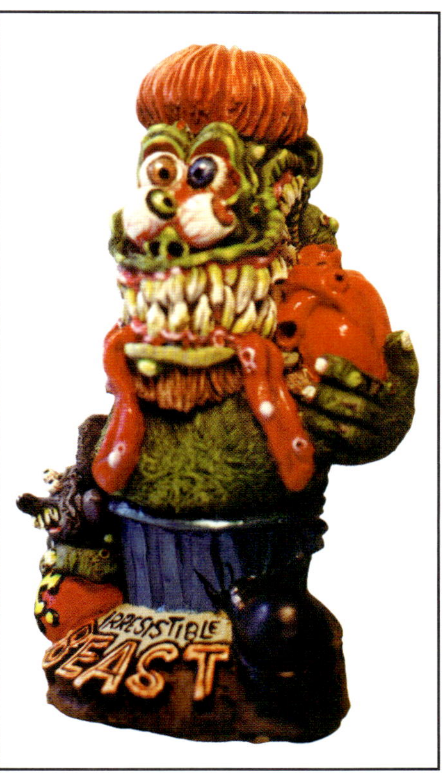

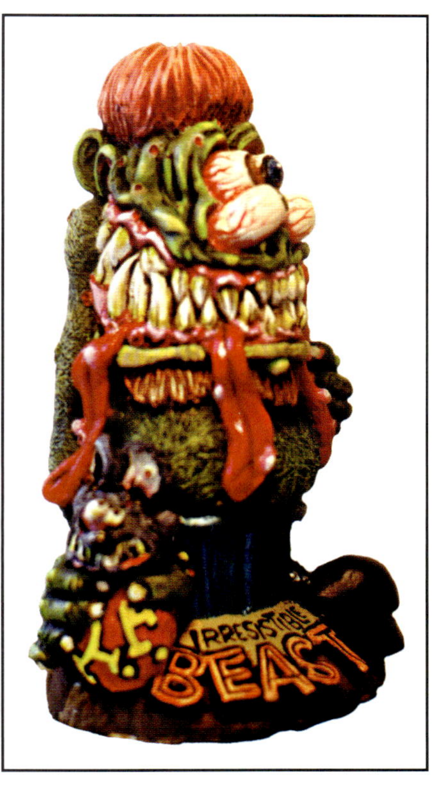

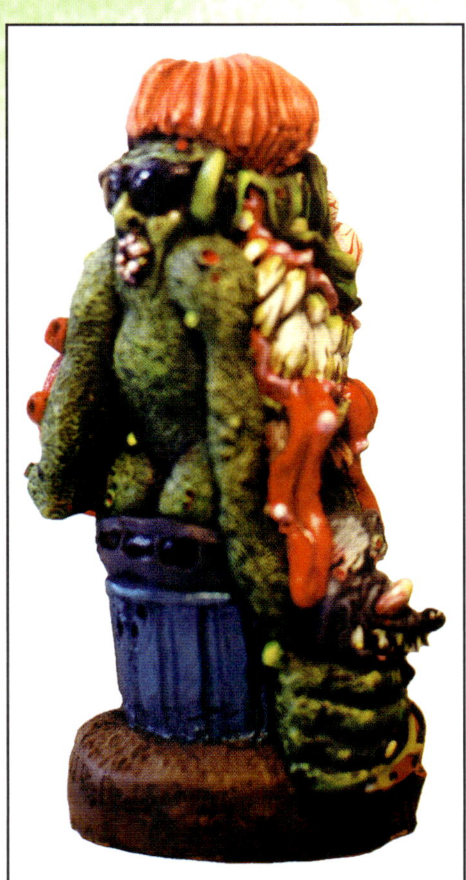

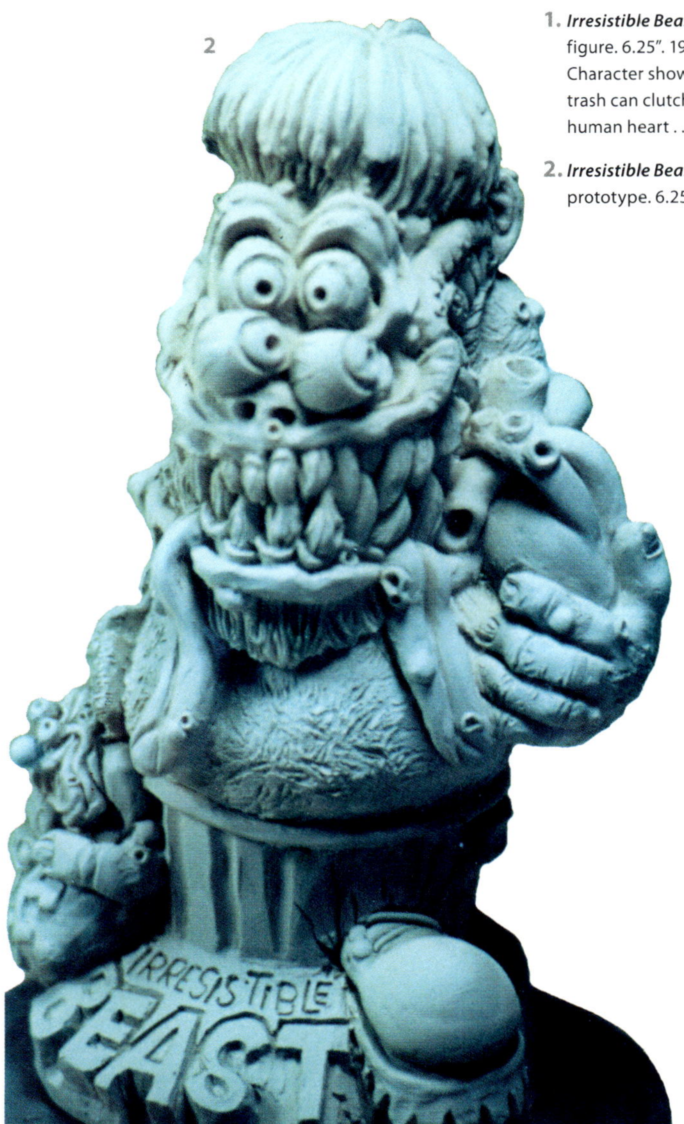

1. *Irresistible Beast.* Painted resin figure. 6.25". 1999. Character shown bulging out of a trash can clutching mini-R.F. and a human heart . . .

2. *Irresistible Beast.* Original polyclay prototype. 6.25". 1999.

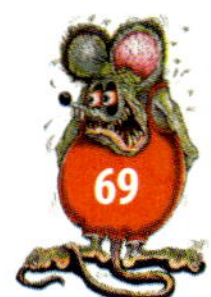

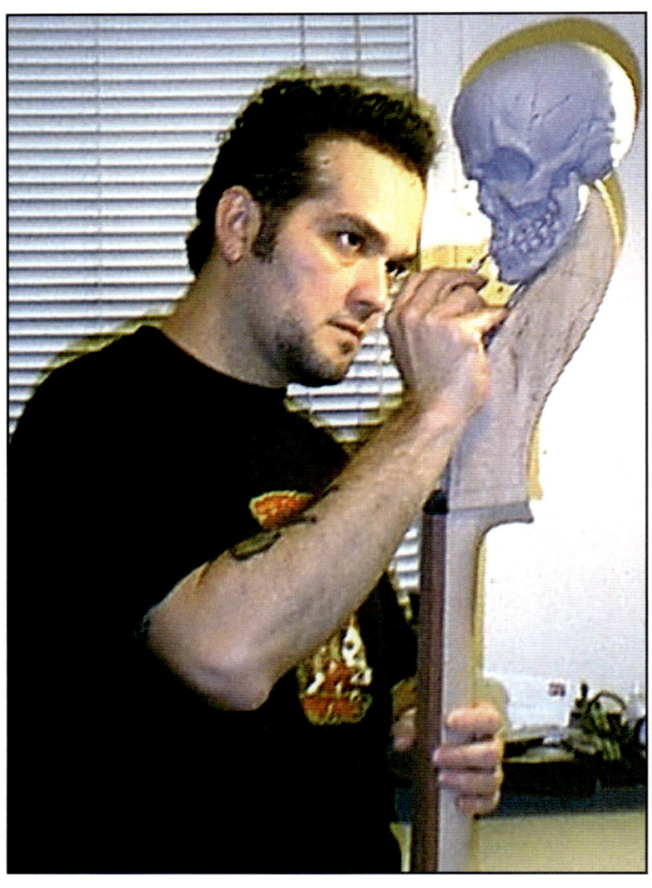

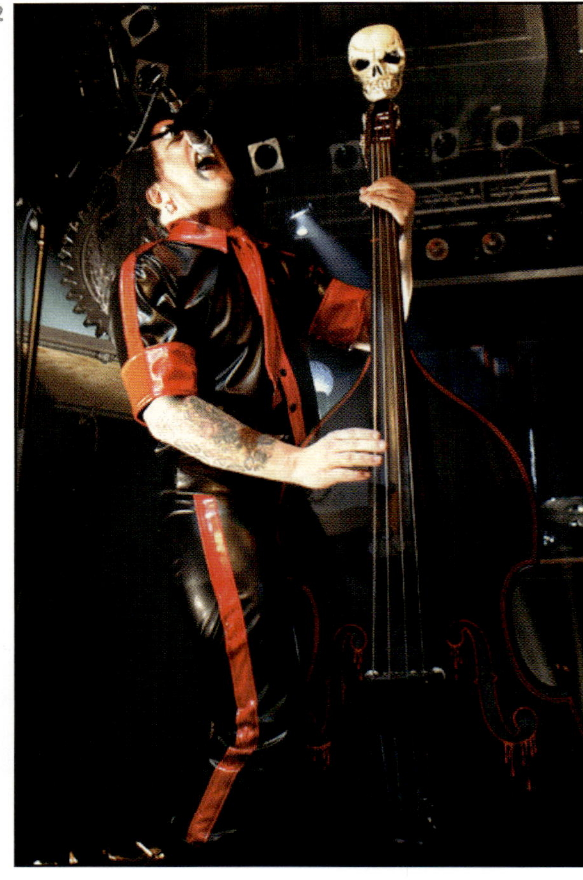

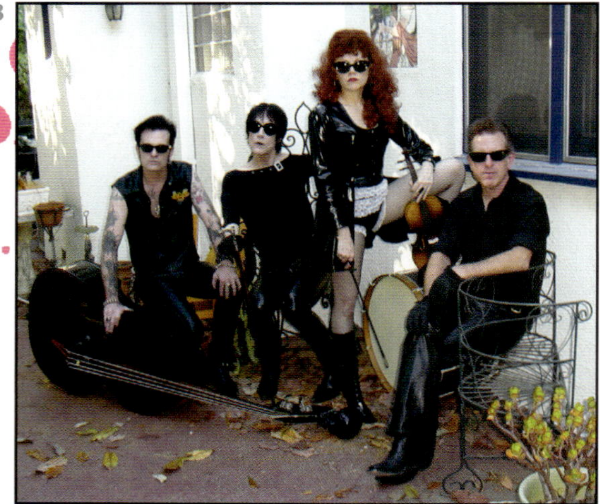

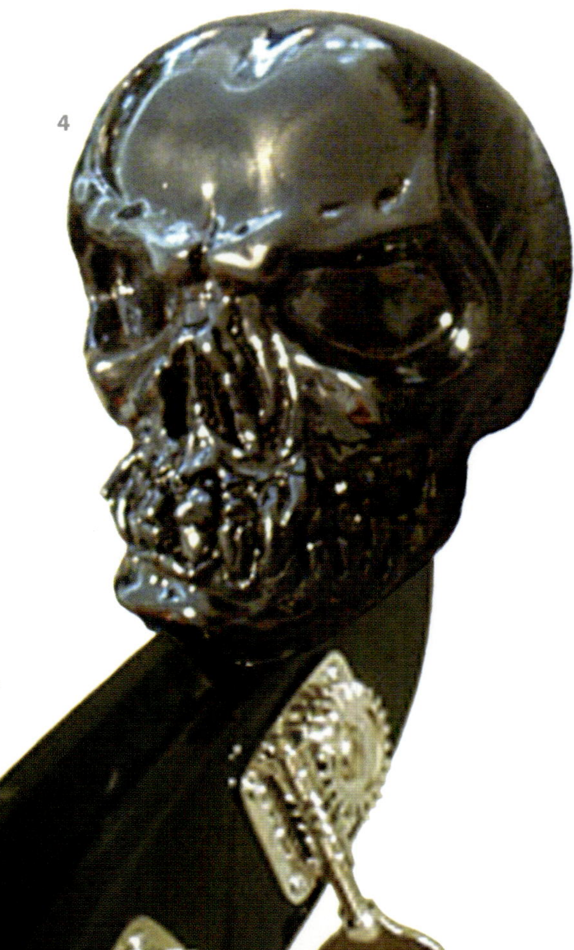

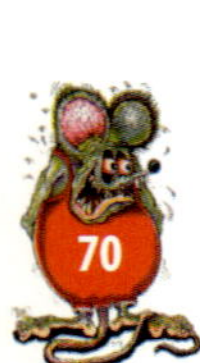

1. Ace sculpting the Death King prototype. 2002. Photo by Kali.
   We began working with King Doublebass in 2001 and produced a total of four projects together. To our way of thinking, sculpting these almost 1:1 scale bass headstock pieces was no different than sculpting a very oversized floor-shifter knob.

2. Evil D. of the Genitorturers and Morbid Angel shown here with his Death King. Photo © by Colin Davis.

3. This Cramps promotional photo shows bassist Chopper Von Frankenstein posing with his Death King. Photo © www.cramps.com.

4. *Death King.*
   Finished bass in black lacquer.

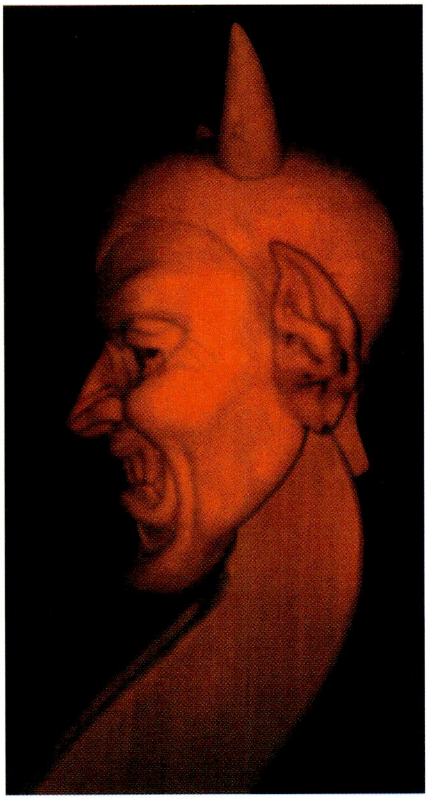

1. *FormaldeHead.*
   Finished, painted headstock. Photo © www.kingdoublebass.com.

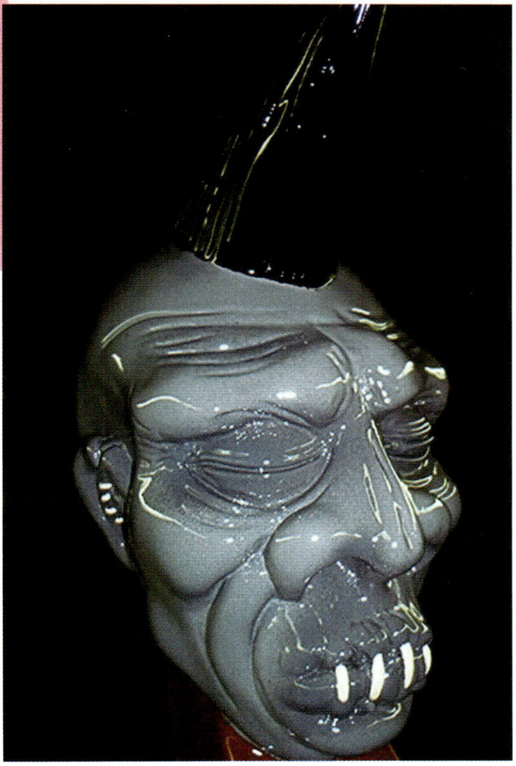

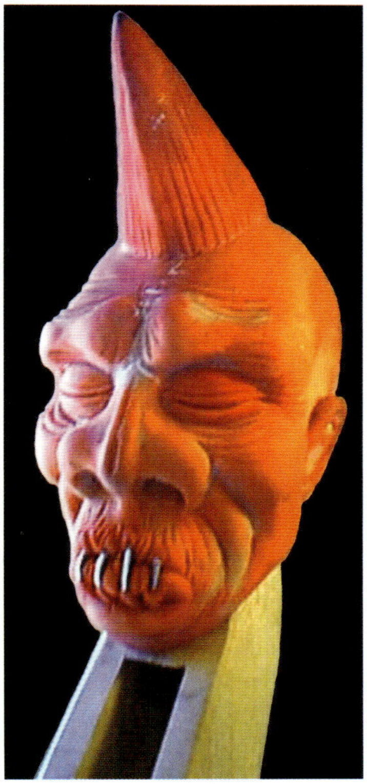

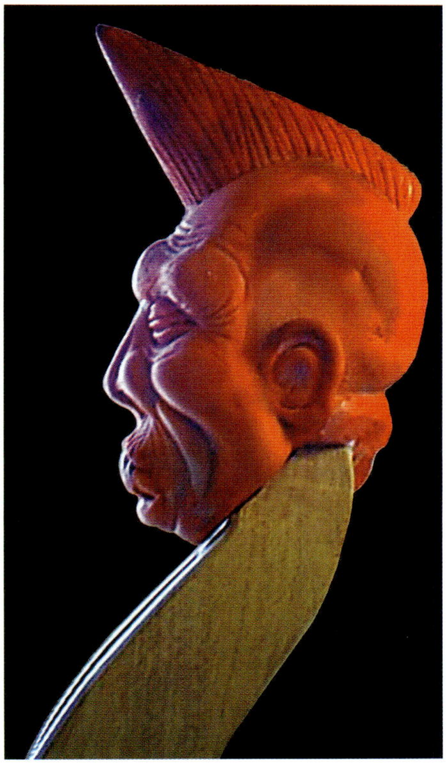

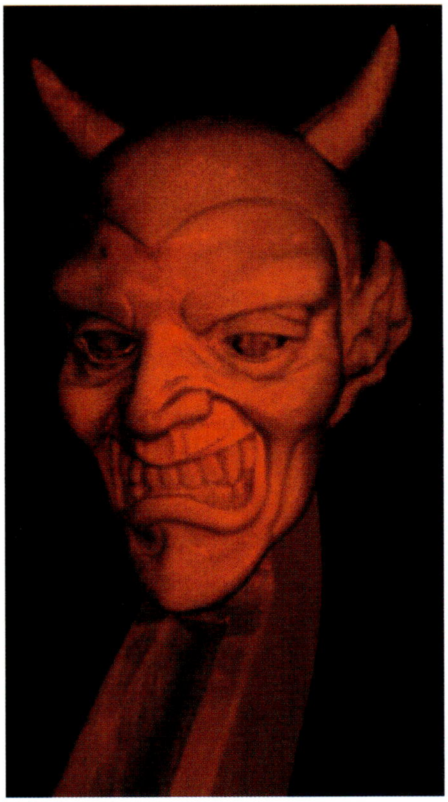

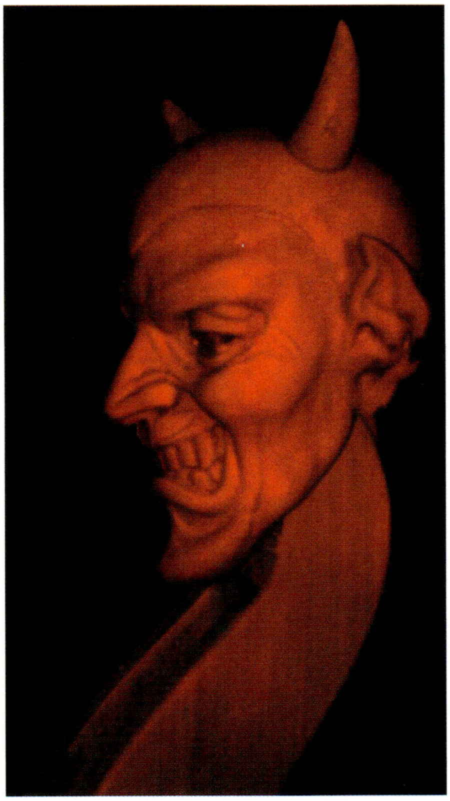

2. *FormaldeHead.* 1:1 scale polyclay prototype.
   This Psychobilly-style shrunken head was done as a one-of-a-kind bass project.

3. *Devil Head.* Another 1:1 scale bass headstock polyclay prototype done as a one-of-a-kind
   edition, this Devil Head character was based on '50s horror comic and decal imagery.

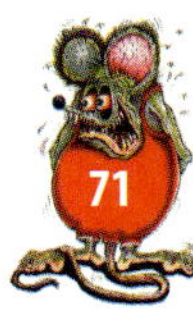

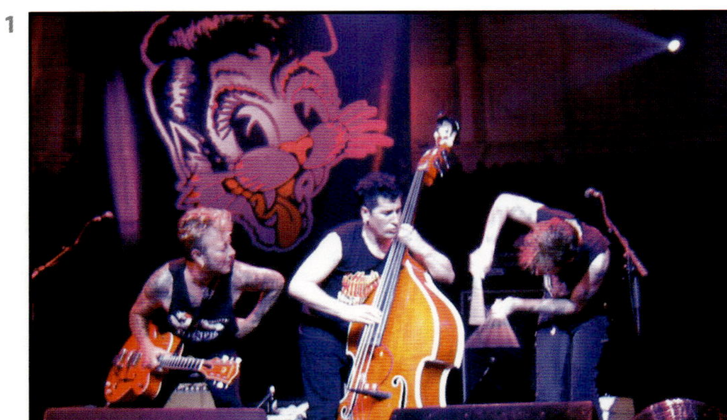

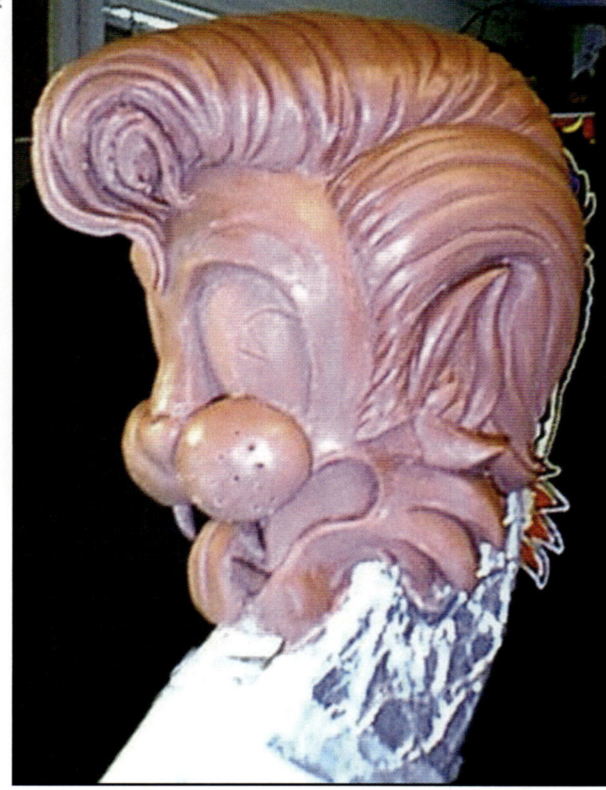

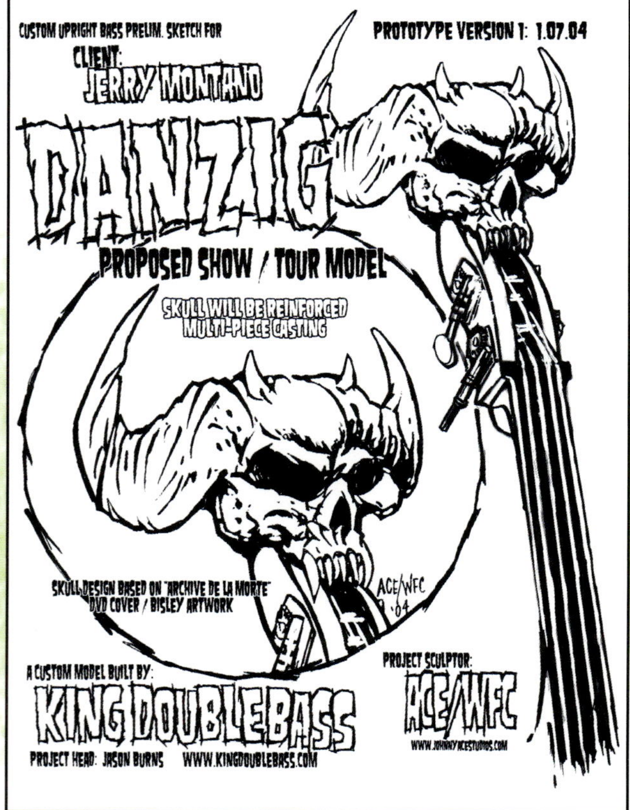

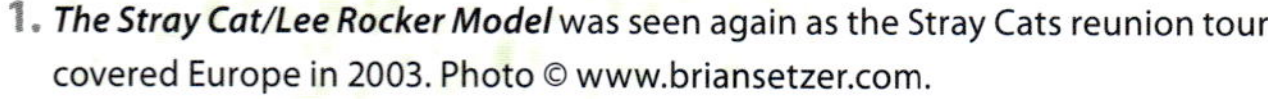

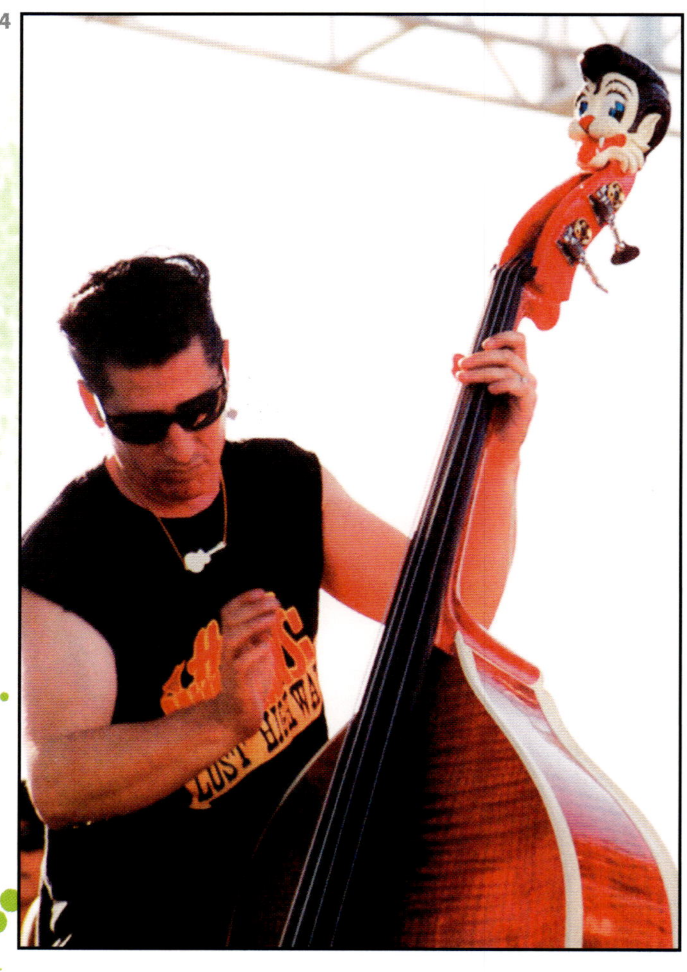

1. *The Stray Cat/Lee Rocker Model* was seen again as the Stray Cats reunion tour covered Europe in 2003. Photo © www.briansetzer.com.

2. *The Stray Cat/Lee Rocker Model.* Polyclay prototype in progress. 2003.

3. This concept artwork was intended as the basis for a King Doublebass custom model for the bass player of Danzig, but the project never saw fruition.

4. Lee Rocker shown here playing the bass in its finished state at the 2003 Hootenanny/Stray Cats Reunion show. Photo © Gloria Uberdelli.

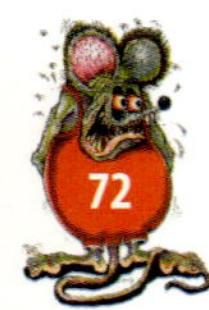

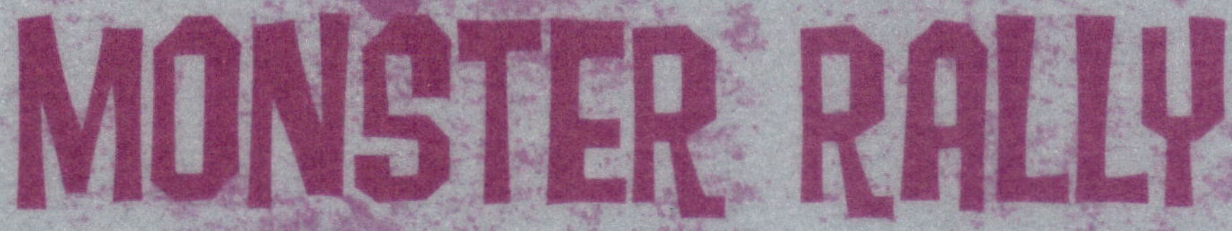

MONSTER RALLY

" . . . my enthusiasm was checked by my anxiety, and I appeared rather like one doomed by slavery to toil in the mines, or any other unwholesome trade, than an artist occupied by his favorite employment."

MONSTER RALLY

"...my enthusiasm was checked by my anxiety, and I appeared rather like one doomed by slavery to toil in the mines, or any other unwholesome trade, than an artist occupied by his favorite employment."

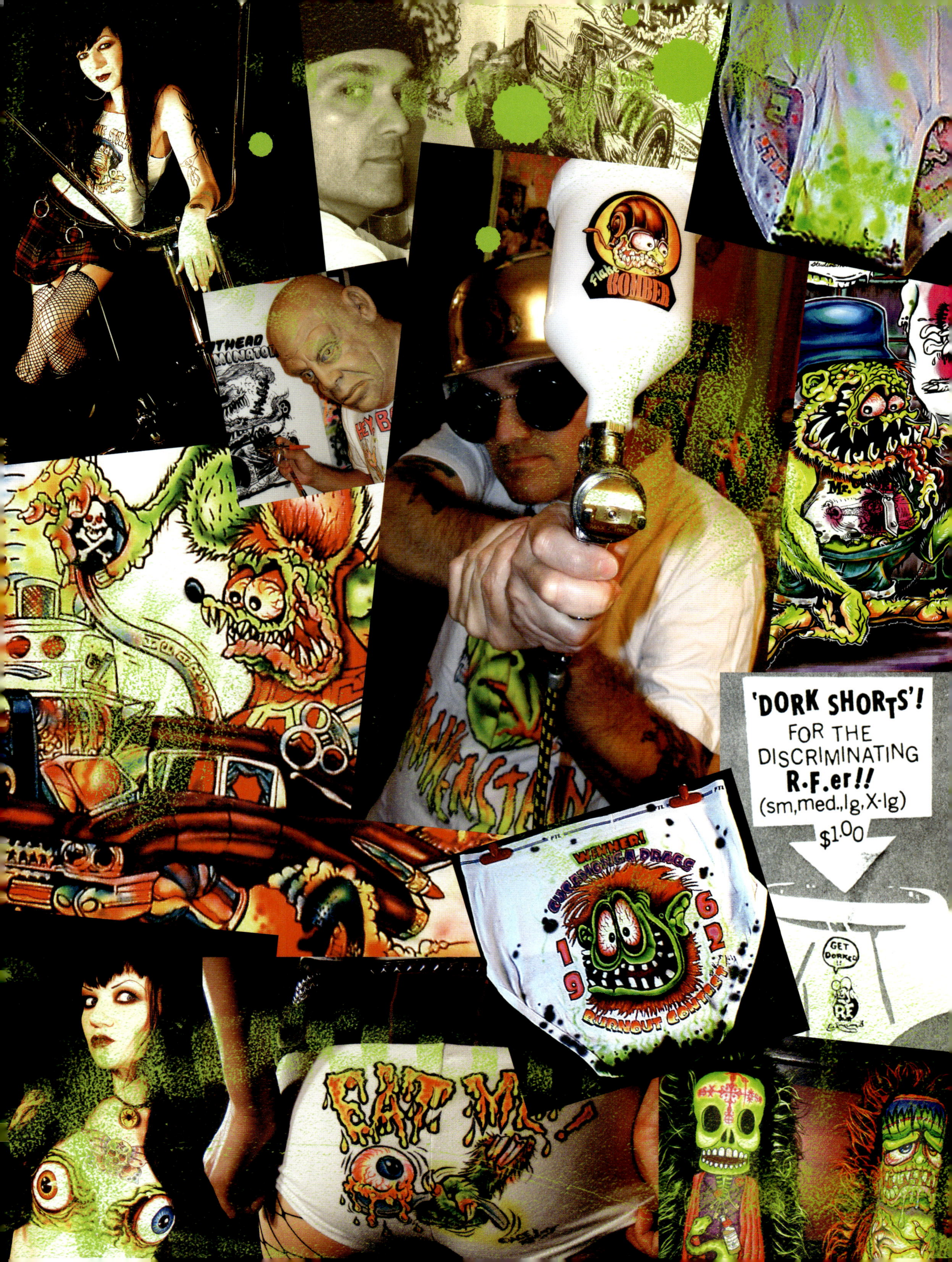
Flake BOMBER
'DORK SHORTS'!
FOR THE DISCRIMINATING
R.F.er!!
(sm, med., lg, X-lg)
$1.00
GET DORKED!!
WINNER!
CUCAMONGA DRAGS
1962
BURNOUT CONTEST
EAT ME!

Drag? Airbrushed t-shirt. Kali is shown here rendering a classic Roth Studios image with this popular Frankenstein-like character. Along with the favorite "Untouchables" (also known as "Frankie Boy"), these designs appeared in Roth Studios ads and catalogs from approx. 1960–62. These catalogs, over time, carried the titles *Weerdo, Weirdo, Weirdo Pad*, and *Wierd*, but never "Weird-Oh," which was a Hawk Models line. The original artist who created "Drag" is unknown. This is our version—complete with grille bullets.

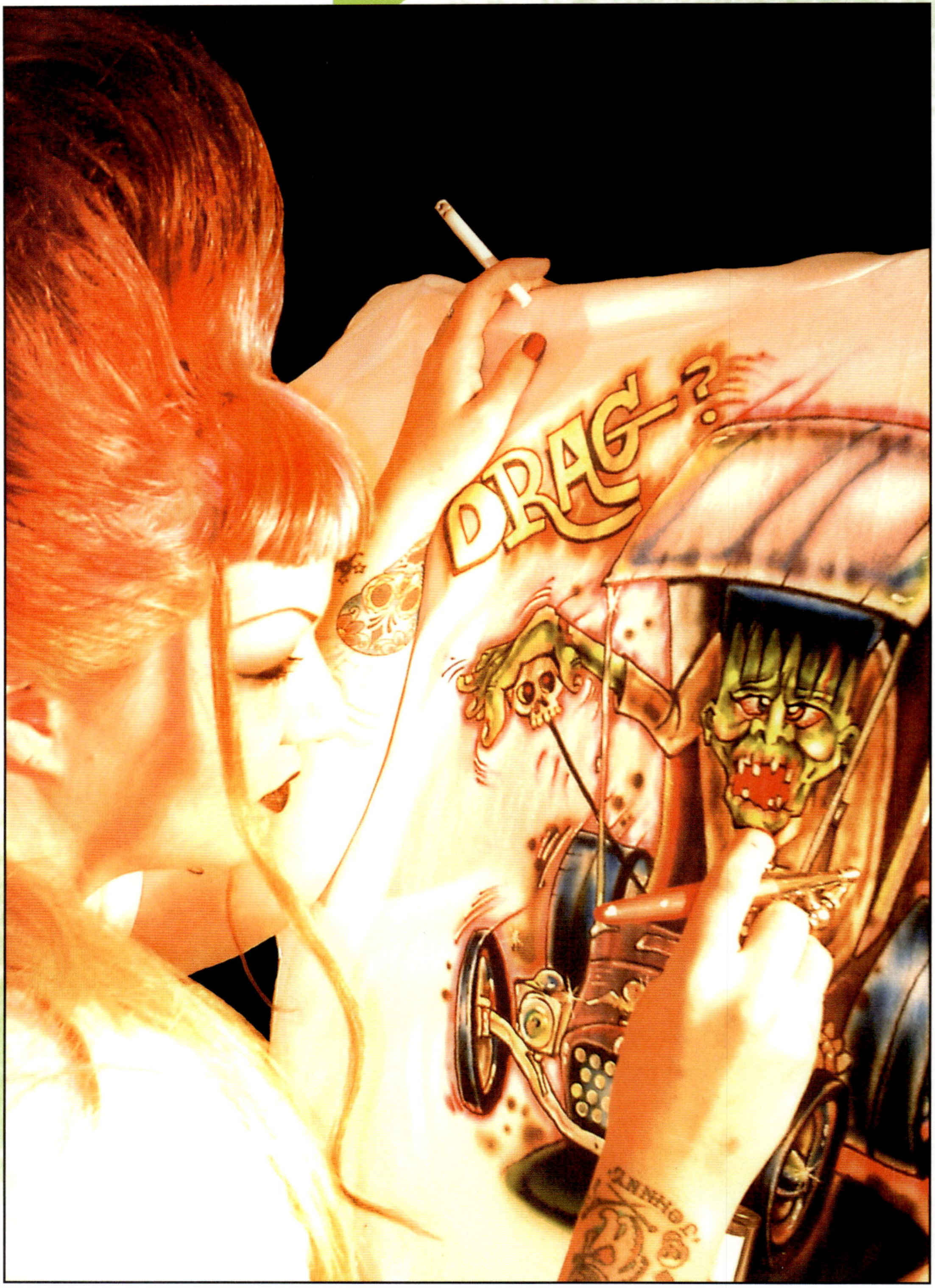

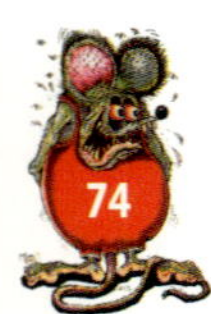

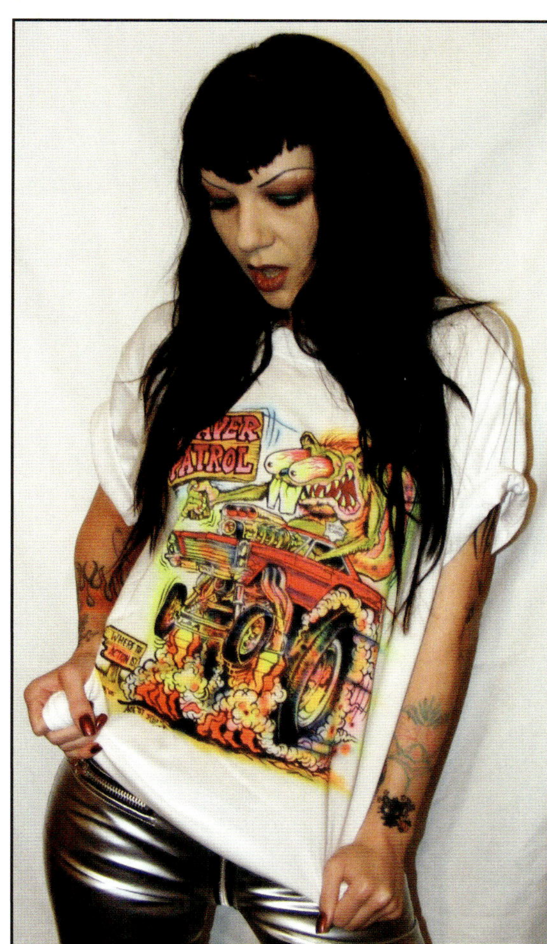

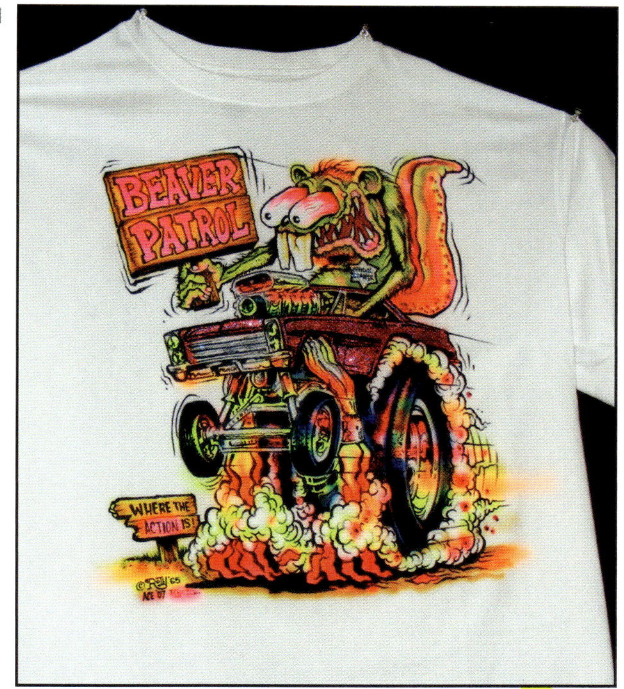

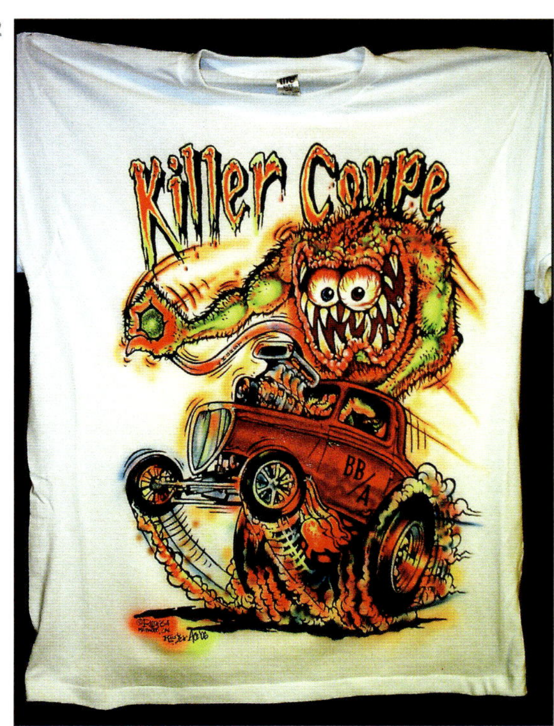

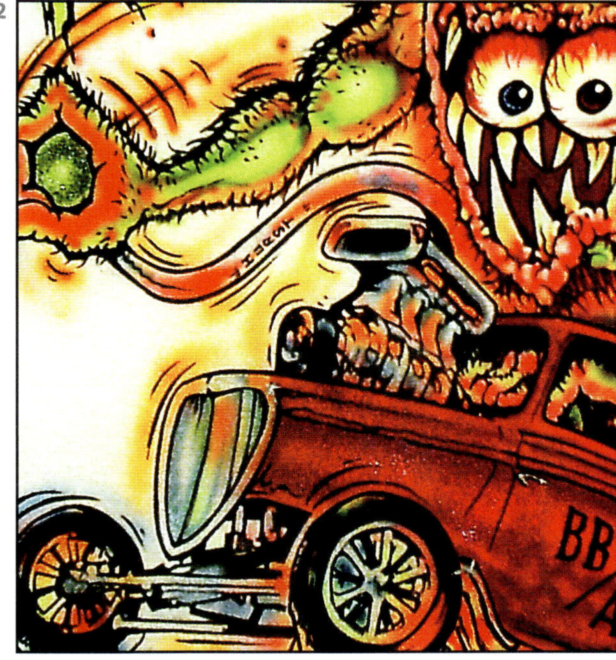

1. *Beaver Patrol.* Airbrushed t-shirt. Model: Kali.

2. *Killer Coupe.* Airbrushed t-shirt.

These two designs were originally created by Ed "Newt" Newton, who was responsible for illustrating hundreds of masterpieces of monster and hot-rod art during his almost seven-year reign at Roth Studios. Newt is considered by many, including us, to be the artist who took Roth's oftimes crude early graphics and refined them, elevating the monster art genre to its ultimate level in the process. Newt's designs each contain balances and combinations of extremely well-conceived imagery and a masterful use of blacks, whites, composition, layout and visual humor.

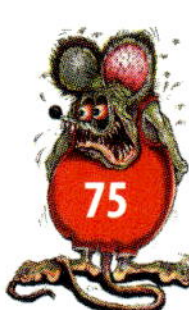

Welcome to Roth Studios. 1996. Original illustration with digital composition (Boss Fink artwork originally created by Newt). From his earliest appearances in the Roth Studios catalogs, Rat Fink stood out as Big Daddy's most popular-selling character. Much like the Frankenstein Monster, R.F. contains bits and pieces of parts from such mad geniuses as *Mad* magazine's Don Martin, Stanley "Mouse!" Miller, Don "Monte" Monteverde, and other influences lost to time and memory at present . . . Earlier Roth Studios artists, specifically Wes Bennett and Newt, were the first to provide different views and sight gags using R.F., followed in the '80s by Dave Christensen, The Pizz, R.K. Sloane, and more. We took things even further during our employment with Roth Studios, rendering countless 2D and 3D versions of our beloved rabid rodent. The "standard" 1963 Rat Fink quickly became as easily recognizable with Ed Roth as an alter-ego/company icon as Alfred E. Neuman is to *Mad* or Spider-Man is to Marvel!

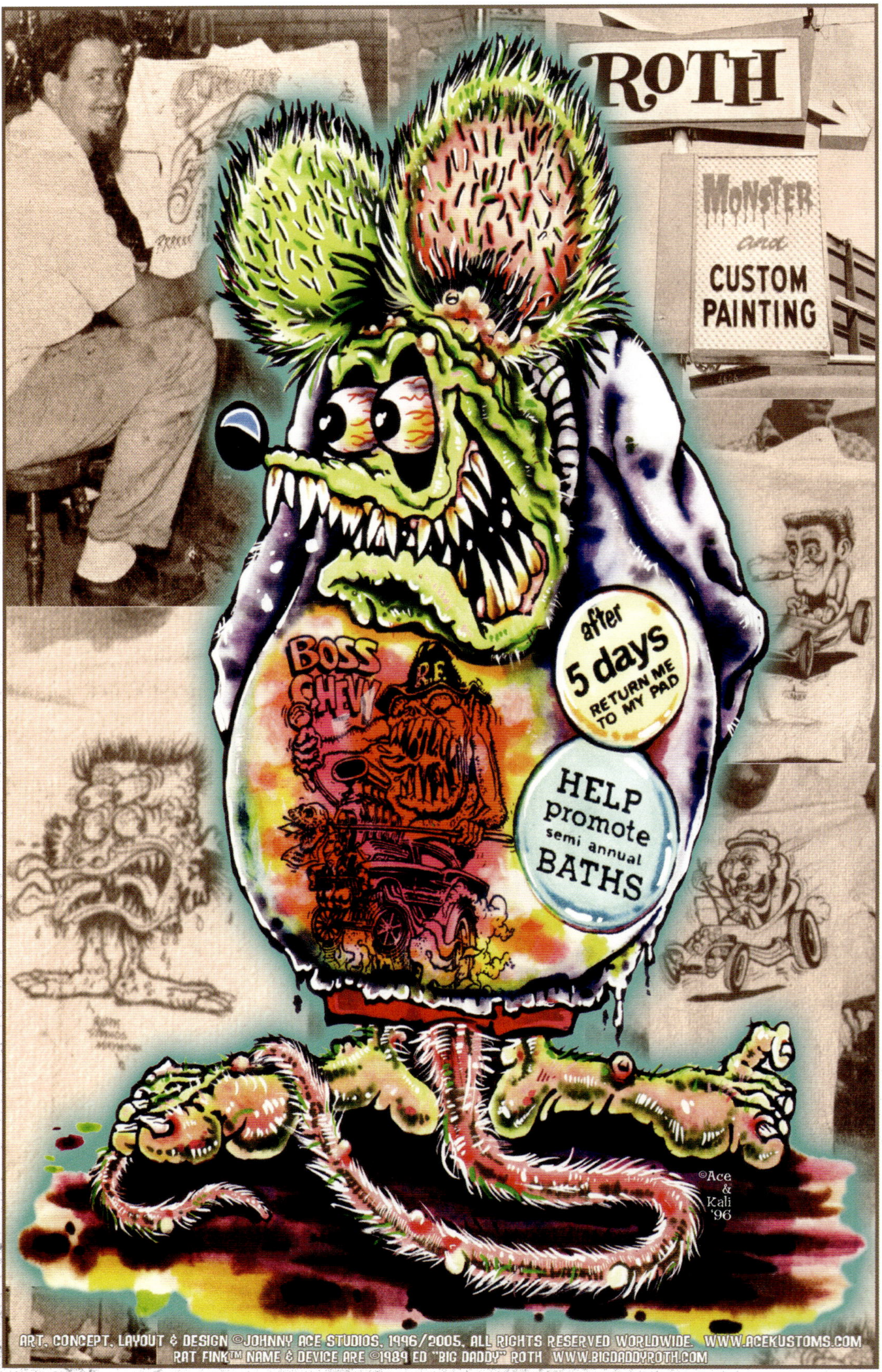

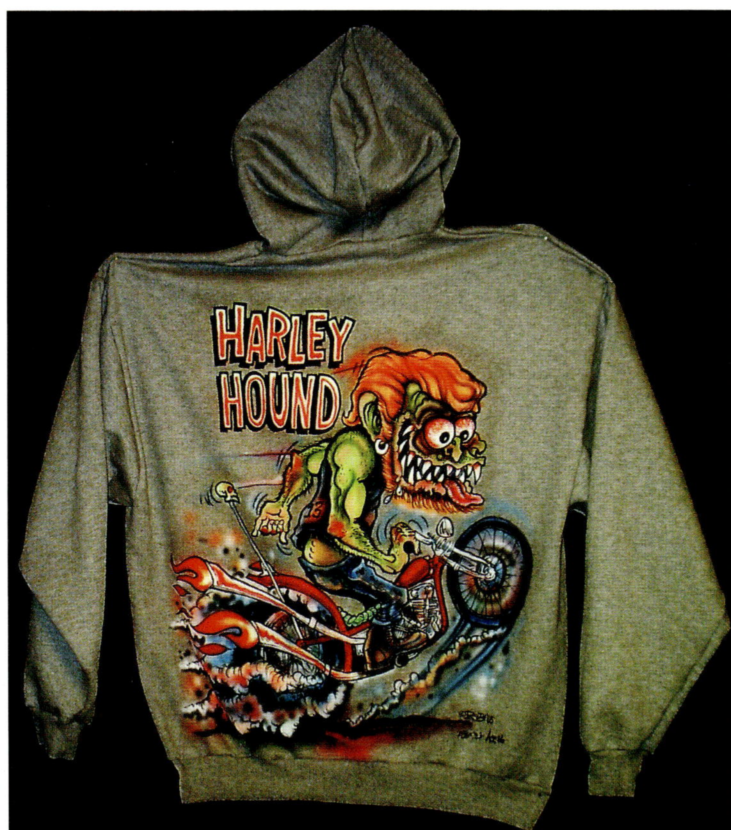

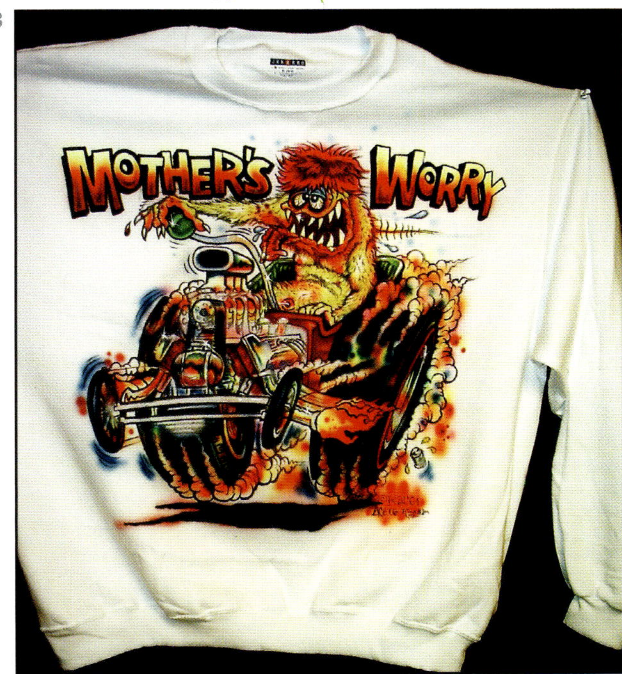

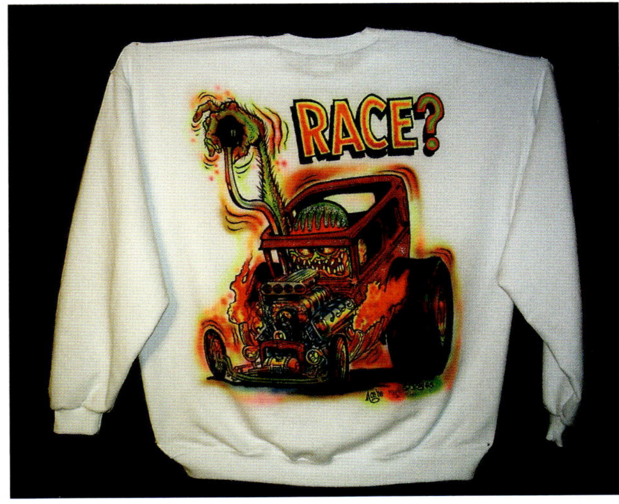

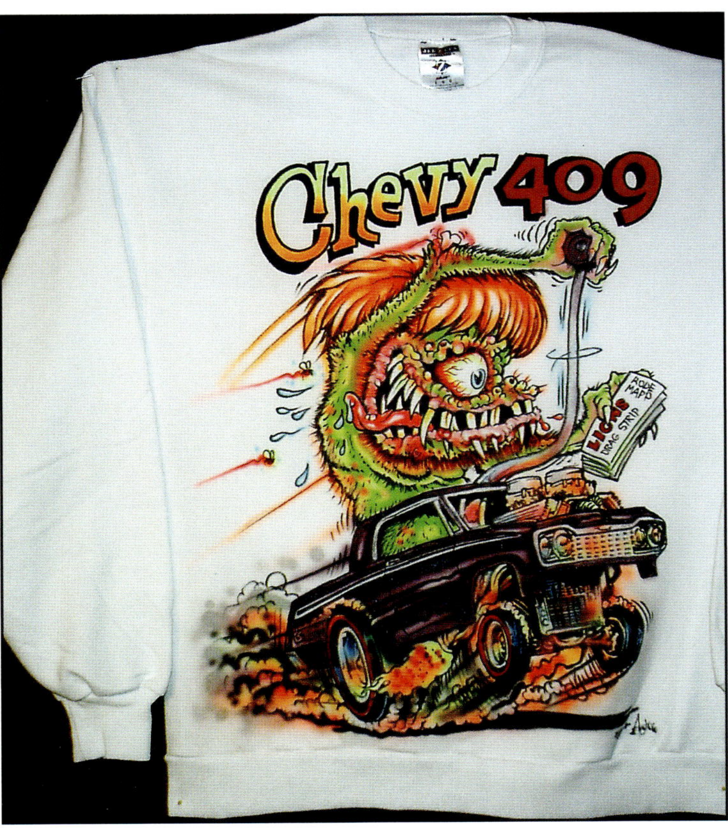

1. *Harley Hound.* Airbrushed hooded sweatshirt. 2006.

2. *Chevy 409.* Airbrushed sweatshirt. 2006.

3. *Mother's Worry.* Airbrushed sweatshirt. 2006.

4. *Race?* Airbrushed sweatshirt. 2006.

Harley Hound and Chevy 409 were created by Newt for Roth, while Mother's Worry and Race? were both in Studio catalogs prior to Newt's arrival as Ed's art director and chief artist in 1964. Pictured here are our take on Newt's versions of these. Roth referred to these two designs in *Confessions of a Rat Fink*: "In every town that I invaded, I painted up a Mother's Worry and a Race? and hung 'em up to get sales rollin' in my booth. As soon as people spotted these wild wearable 'sicko' art statements, it was like a feeding frenzy! They sold as fast as I could paint 'em . . ." It is interesting to note that these versions described by Roth are even earlier airbrushed designs done individually, while the artwork by Newt, Wes Bennett, and others saw production as Roth's earliest silkscreened shirts.

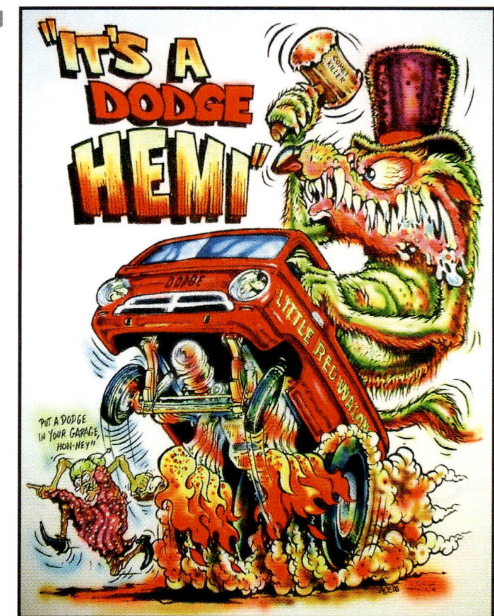

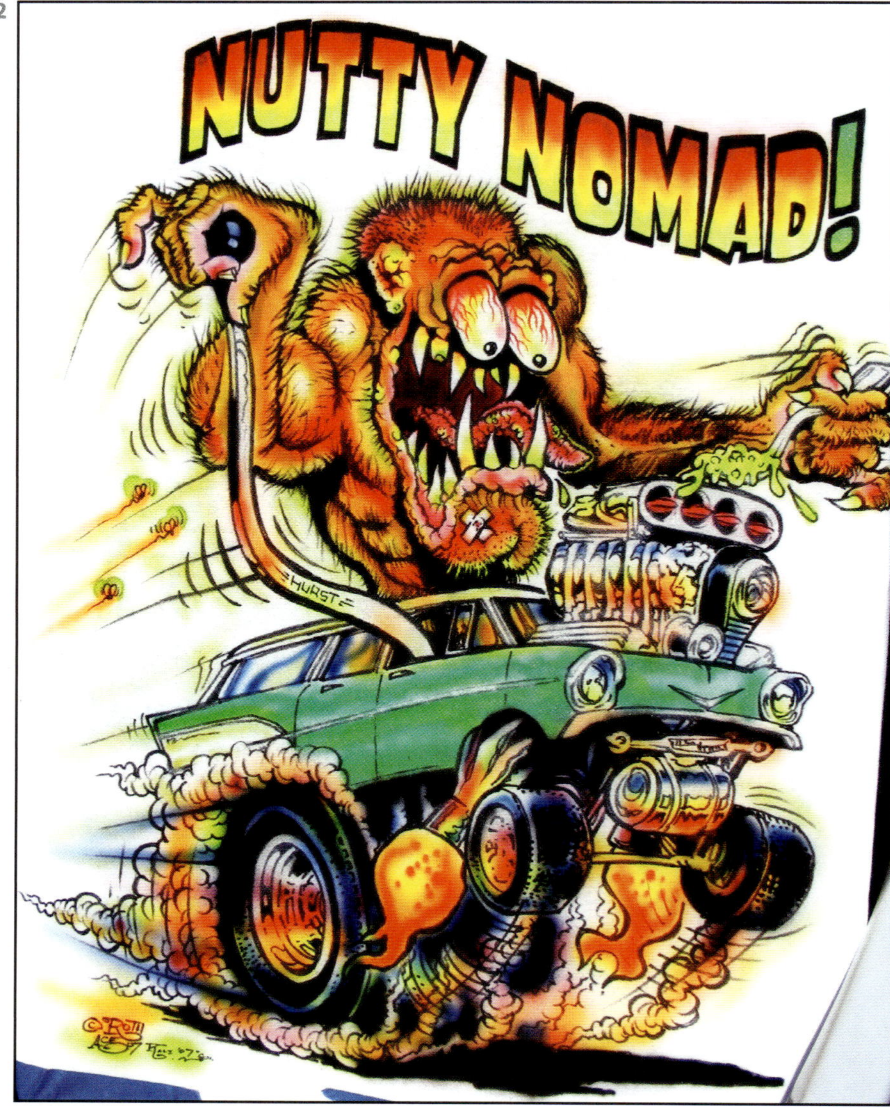

1. *It's a Dodge Hemi!* Airbrushed t-shirt. 2006.

2. *Nutty Nomad.* Airbrushed t-shirt. 2006. Collection of John Evans.

3. *Brother Rat Fink.* Airbrushed t-shirt. 2005.

The Nomad shirt was cobbled together from two different Newt designs, while the Dodge Hemi and BRF are excellent examples from the highly sought-after and cherished *Ed "Big Daddy" Roth Monster Coloring Book* from 1965. While the contents are comprised mostly of Newt's artwork, the cover was painted by Bud Moore.

4. *Chicken Shift.* Airbrushed t-shirt. 2005.
Our take on Don Monteverde's hilarious companion piece to Rat Fink, Bad News, and a few other designs for Roth Studios in 1963. This image remains a cult favorite, but did not attain the popularity of Rat Fink . . . C.S. was released, however, as a popular waterslide decal along with the aforementioned Monte designs.

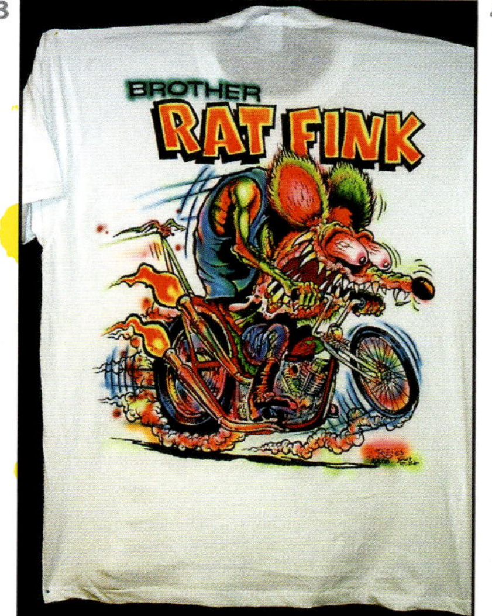

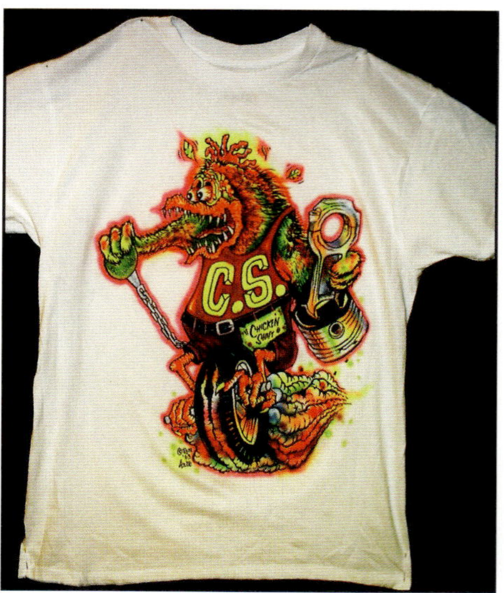

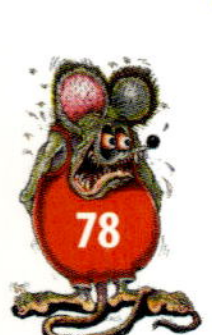

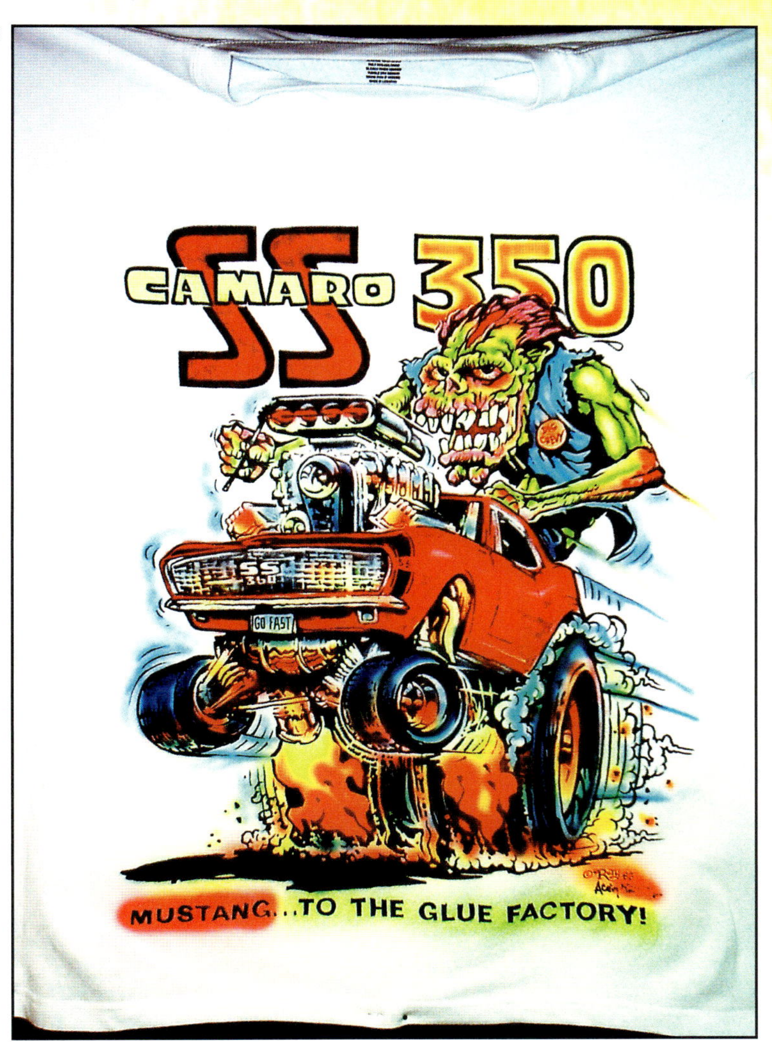

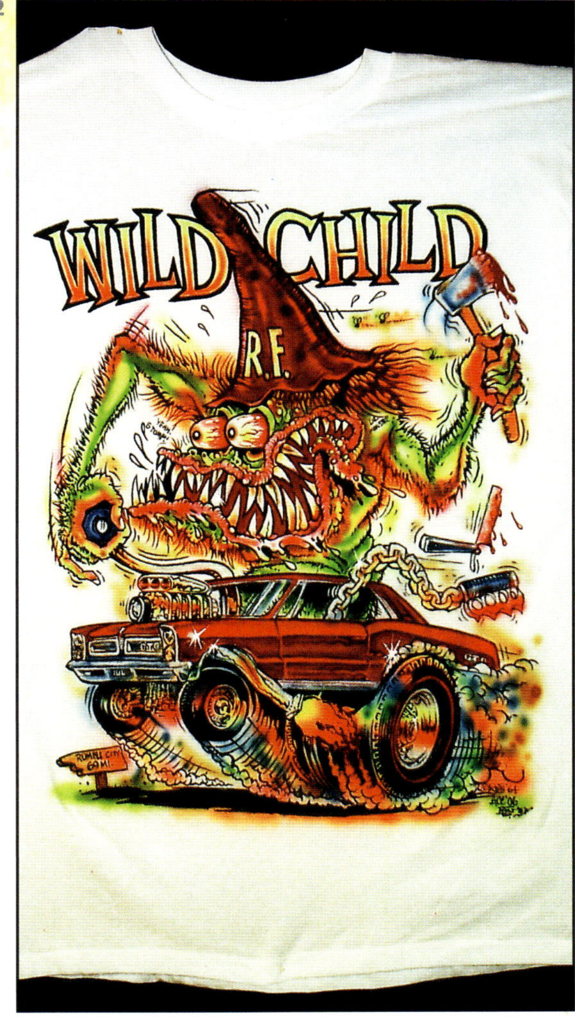

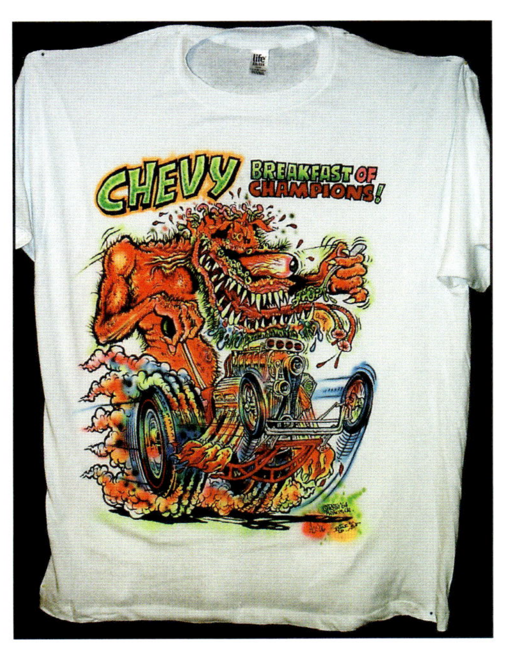

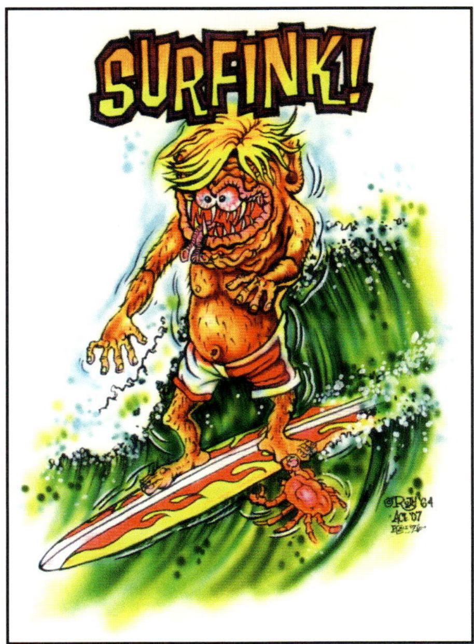

1. *Camaro SS 350.* Airbrushed t-shirt. 2007. Based on an original illustration created by Ed "Newt" Newton, 1966.

2. *Wild Child.* Airbrushed t-shirt. 2005. Based on a Newt design, 1965.

3. *Chevy, Breakfast of Champions.* Airbrushed t-shirt. 2005. From Newt's 1965 design.

4. *Surfink.* Airbrushed t-shirt. 2006. Based on Revell's Surfink box art and promo materials.

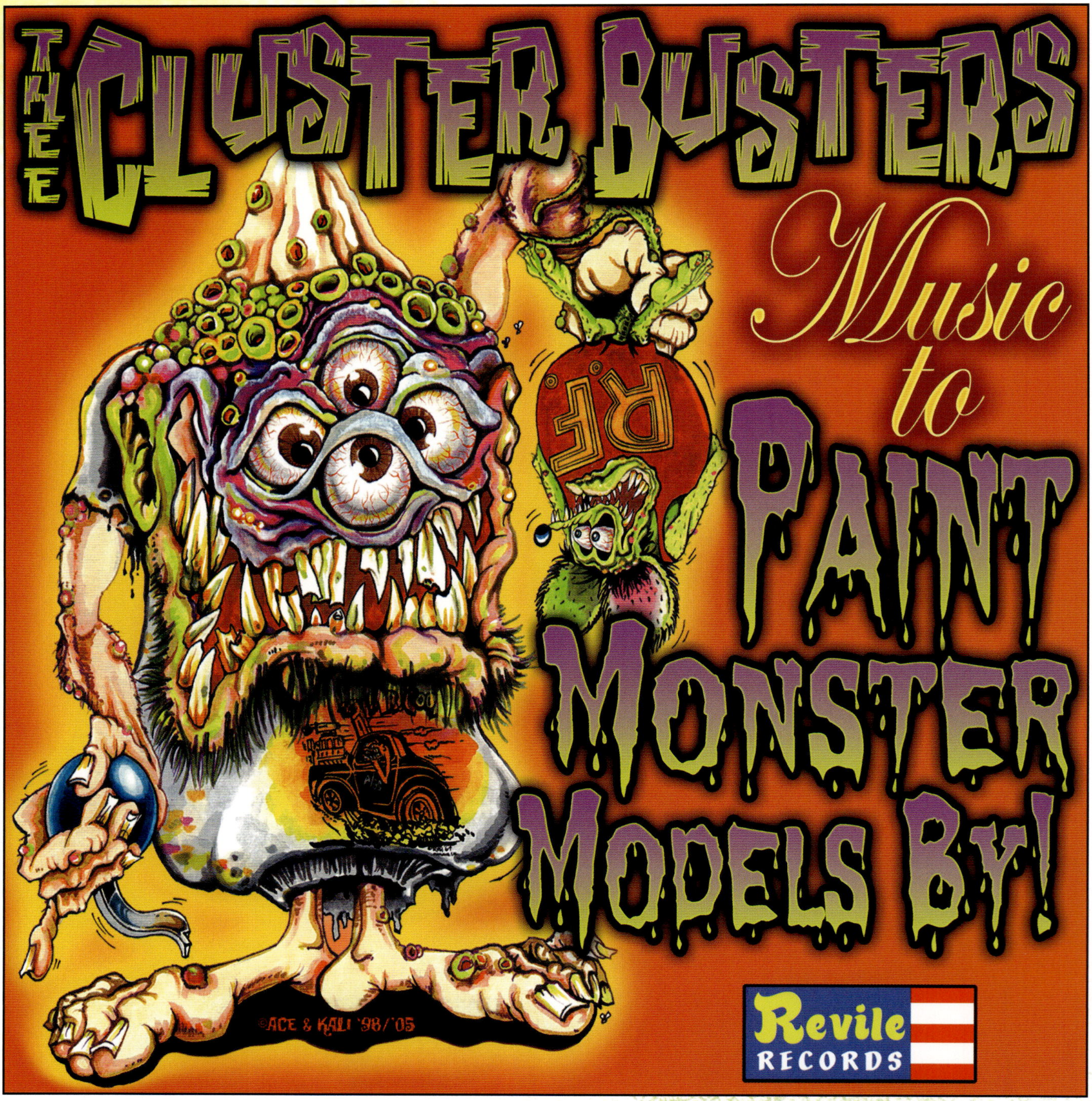

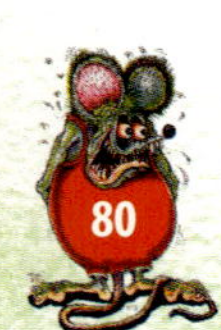

Thee Cluster Busters—Music to Paint Monster Models By! 2005.
Even though we did these mock album covers as parodies, they are sincere tributes
to certain elements we hold very dear . . . At first glance, these pieces should trigger
certain responses in the viewer—the smell of model glue and a freshly unwrapped
styrene kit, the garish colors of an airbrushed monster shirt, the music and lyrics
of Gary Usher and Roger Christian, and the knowledge that once that record was
wobbling on your cheap player and the Testors cement had dripped onto the kit
instructions, you would soon be leaving the "real world" behind.

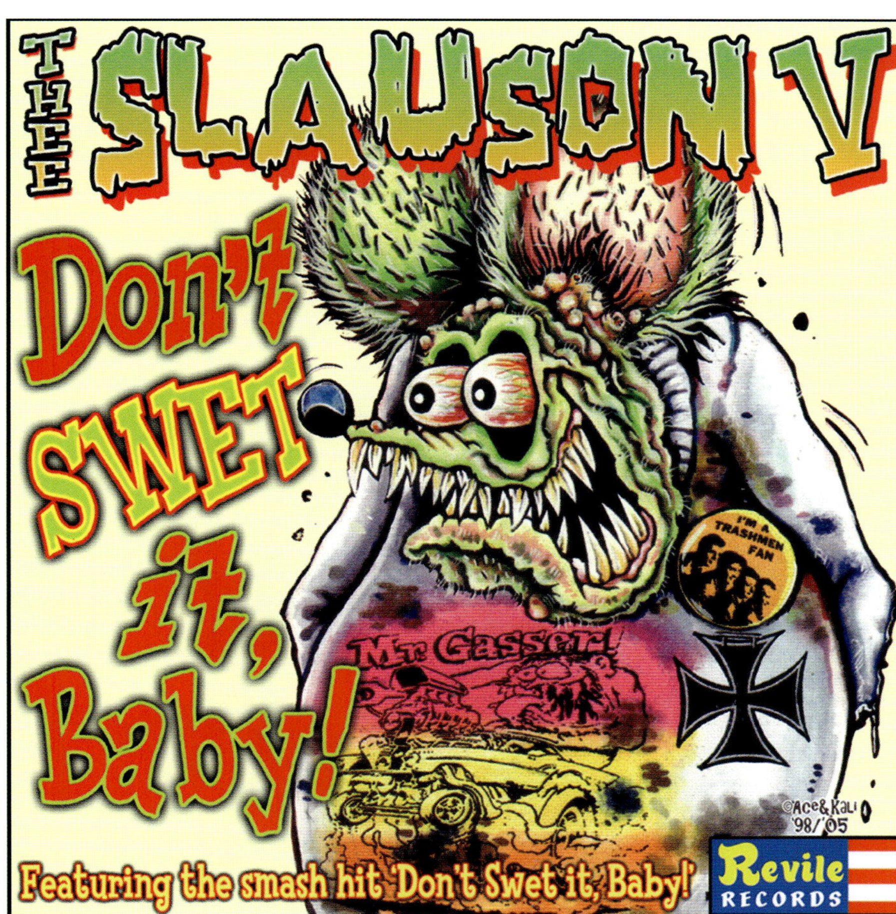

1. *Thee Slauson V—Don't Swet it, Baby! (a.k.a. I'm a Trashmen Fan.)* 2005. These mock album covers were especially fun to do and are meant to capture the feeling of monster and music styles represented in the classic Capitol LPs Roth was involved in during the early '60s.

2. *Thee Slauson V—Don't Swet it, Baby!* back cover. Those of you familiar with Roth Studios' early catalogs will recognize most of these song titles as being actual t-shirt slogans. Long before art galleries in So-Cal got around to displaying the work of Roth, Newt, and others, the walls of that infamous shop on Slauson served as the first functional display of monster art.

"There was a slang expression, 'Don't sweat it,' that I wanted to use on my airbrushed t-shirts for the shows. The problem was that kids didn't know how to spell sweat . . . They kept reading it aloud as 'SWEET!' Like, 'Don't SWEET it.' I just figured I'd forget the established system of traditional spelling and spell it 'SWET' . . . Now there was no mistakin' it. 'Don't SWET it' had some jazz to it . . ."
—Ed "Big Daddy" Roth, *Confessions of a Rat Fink*

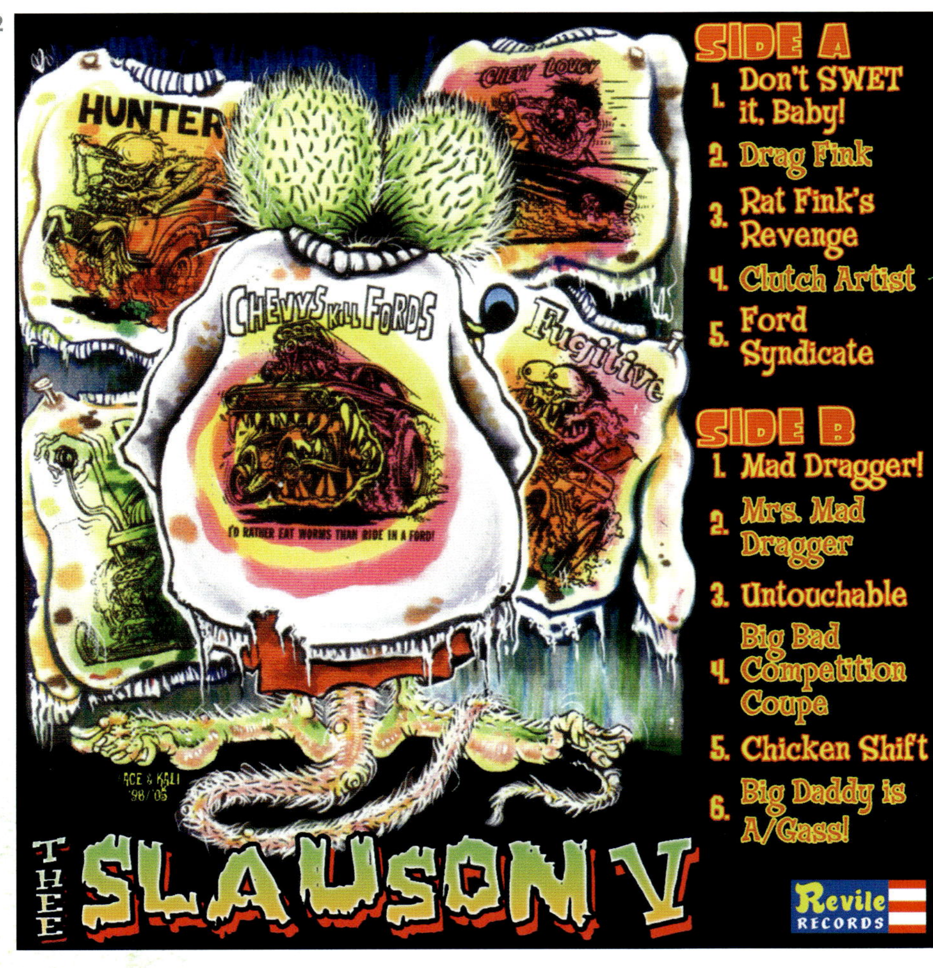

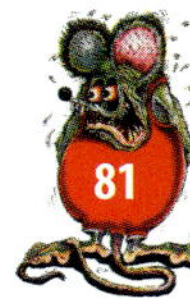

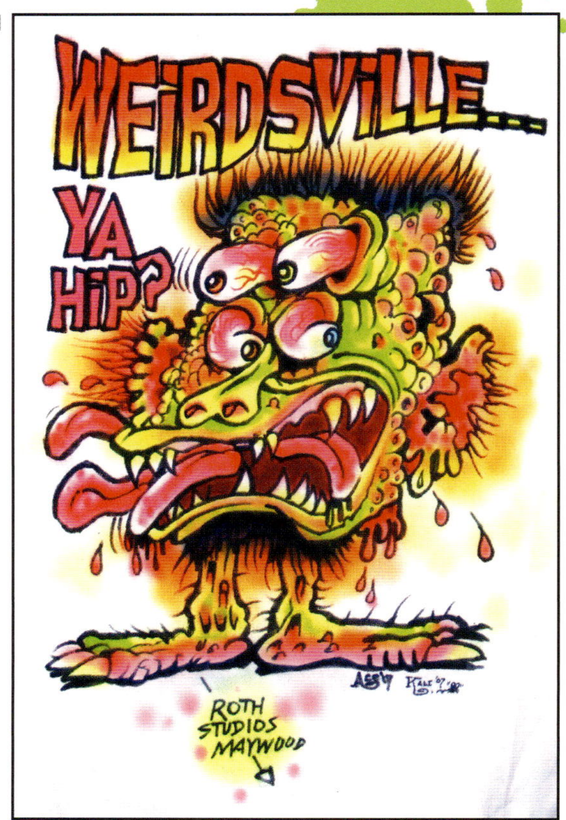

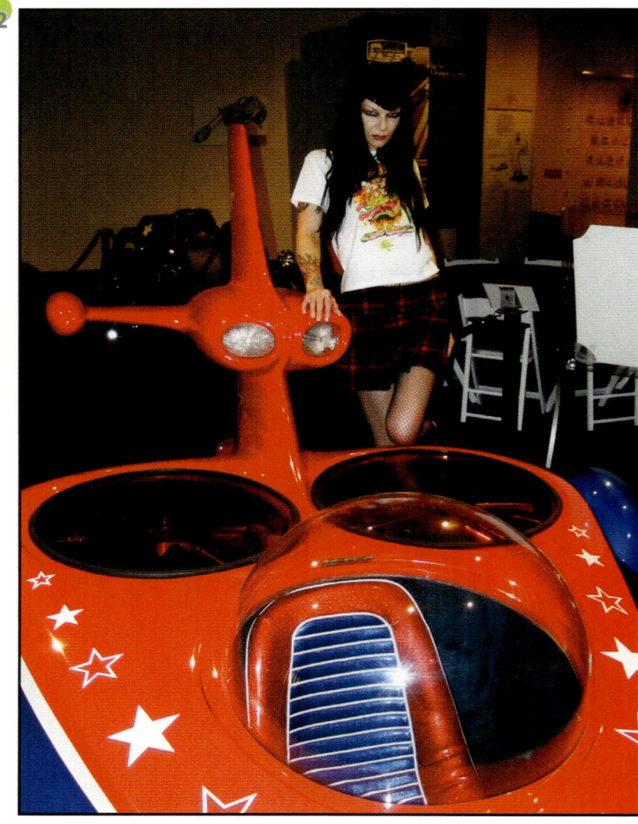

Upon learning we were privileged to have the opportunity (courtesy of America's Car Collection) to do a last-minute photo shoot with the Roth Showcar Exhibit at the Petersen Automotive Museum, we quickly rendered some appropriate airbrushed tees for Kali to sport with some of the vehicles.

1. *Weirdsville . . . Ya Hip?* Airbrushed t-shirt. 2007. This shirt, featuring the Irresistible Beast, was inspired by an early Roth Studios Rod & Custom ad from 1961.

2. Kali is shown here next to Roth's Rotar, restored by Mark Moriarity in 1996.

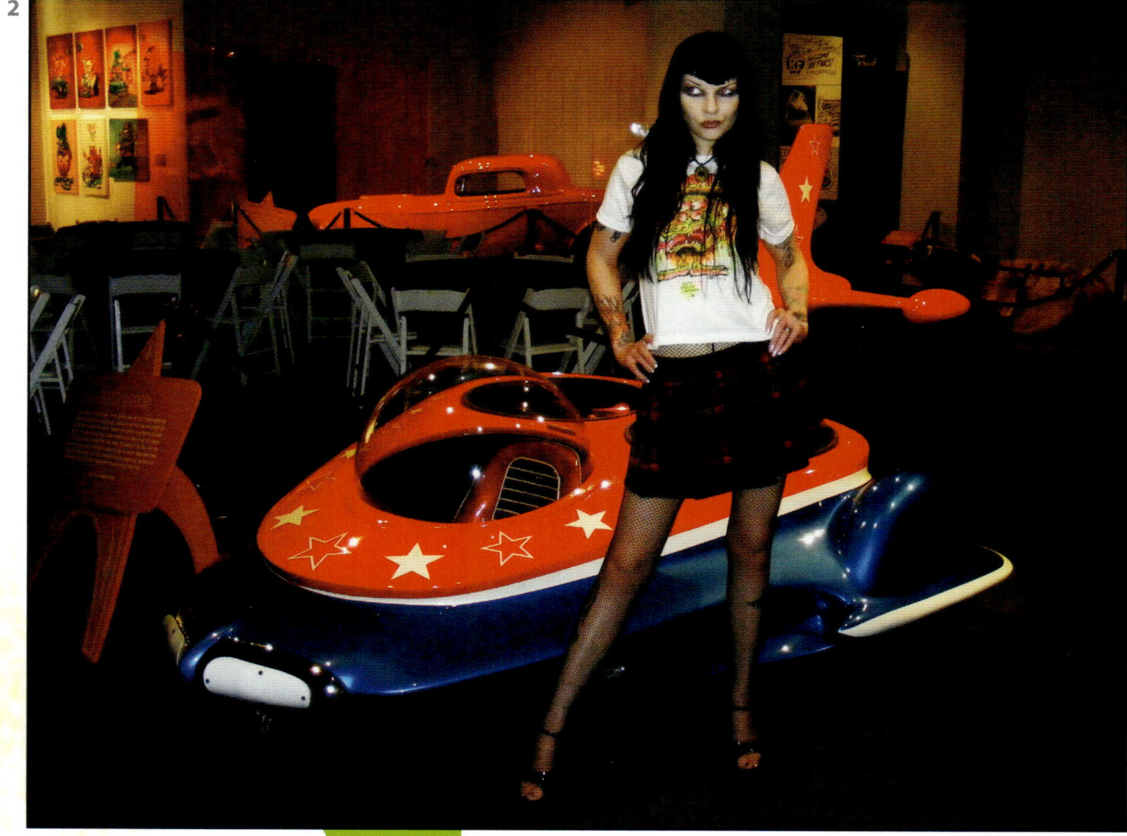

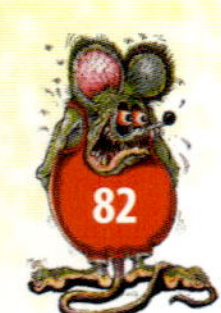

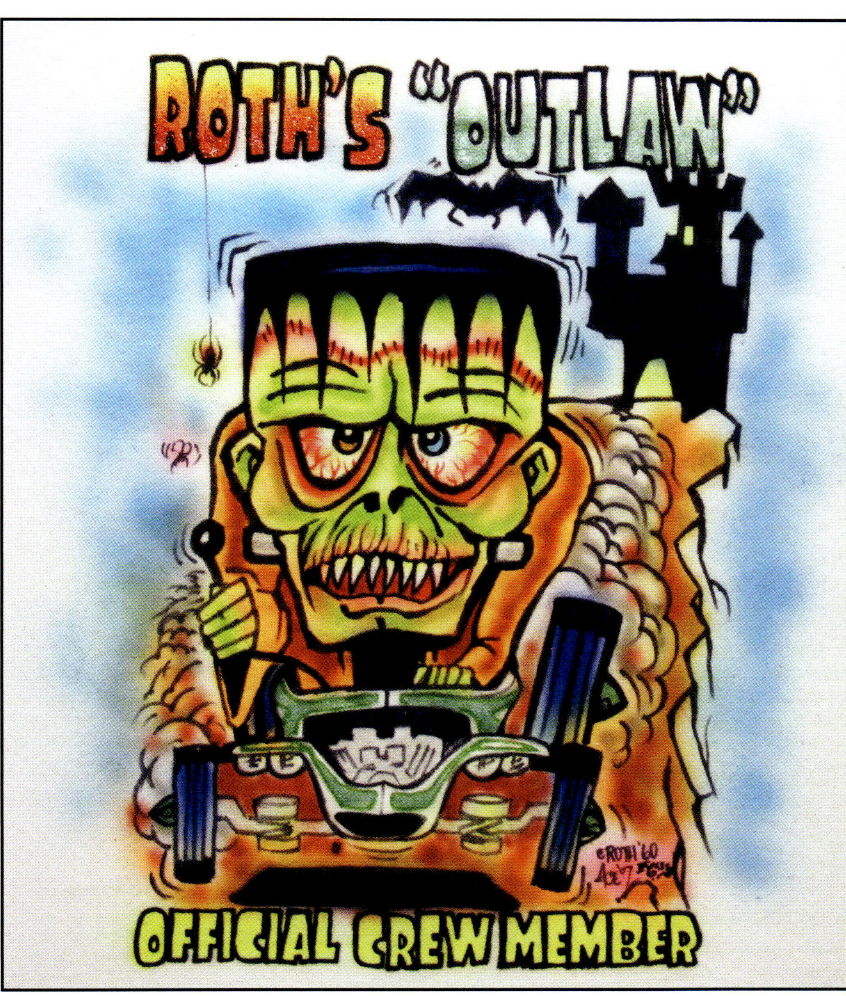

1. *The Untouchables/Roth's Outlaw—Official Crew Member*. Airbrushed t-shirt. 2007.
This infamous Roth Studios classic dates back to about 1960 and was riffed on by everyone from Roth himself to Dick Ash to "Al" over at Barris Kustom City.

2. *Johnny Ace—The Weirdo Painter.* Airbrushed t-shirt. 2003.
We did this one for show appearances, and it features our character Orville Eye, The Way-Out Wigger. Personalized monster shirts have always served as attention-getting, walking advertisements. This promotional gimmick was created by the originators of monster shirts, pinstriping, and weirdo art—Von Dutch, Roth, Dean Jeffries, Pete Millar, Tom Kelly, Mouse!, and others . . . The ultimate example of art, advertisement, and practical use.

3. Kali with Untouchables shirt and Roth's original Outlaw.

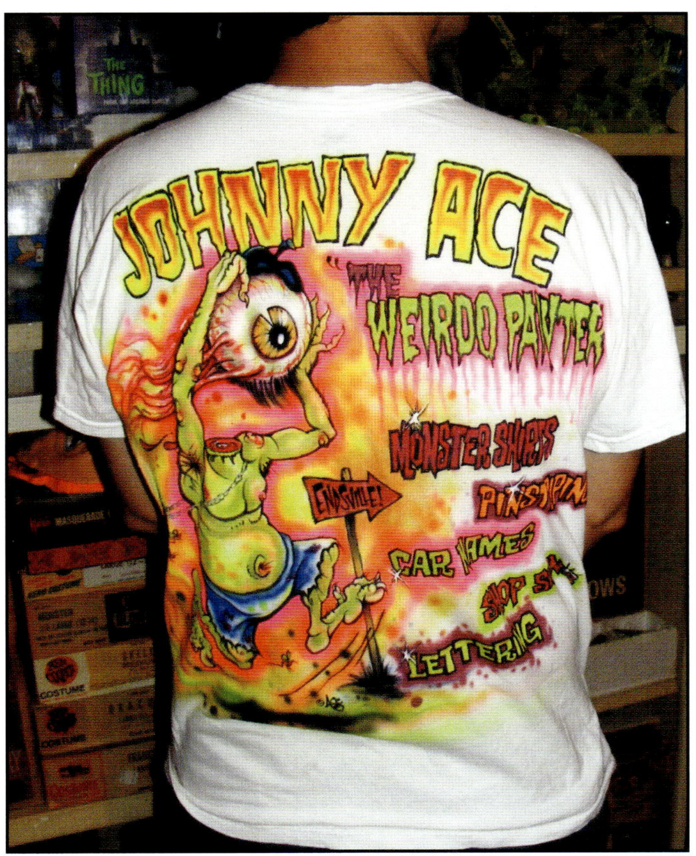

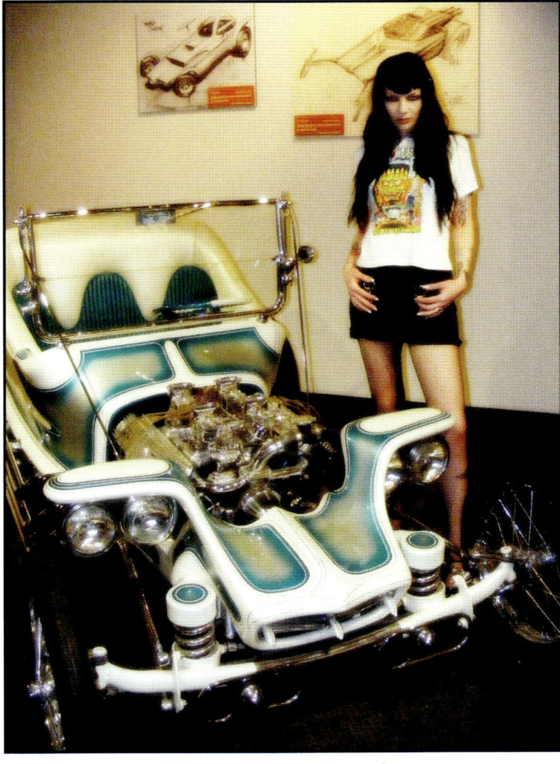

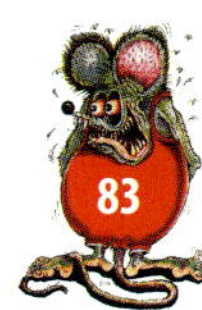

1. *Drag Fink*. Airbrushed t-shirt. 2004. From a Newt design, 1965.

2. Kali with Roth's Road Agent, restored by Mark Moriarity in 1998.

3. *I Work Hard for Big Daddy!* Airbrushed t-shirt. Auto-Air acrylic & Roth Metalflake. 2007. Based on a Newt design, 1965.

4. The Moriarity-restored Road Agent, with airbrushed Drag Fink t-shirt by Ace & Kali, 2004. Photo © by Mark Moriarity, 2005.

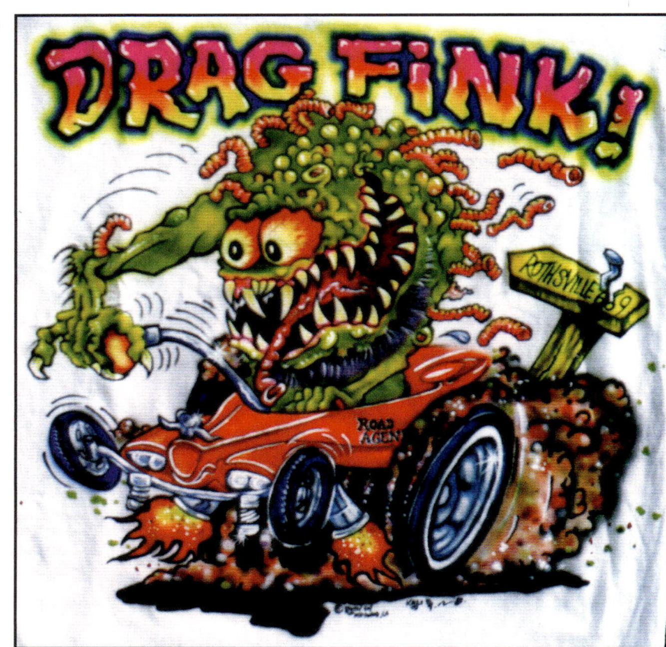

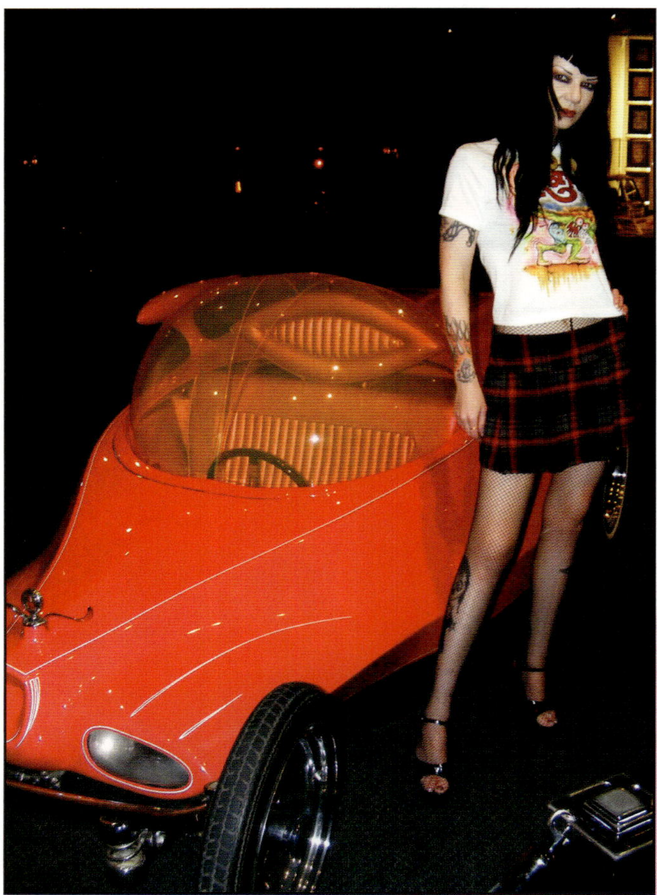

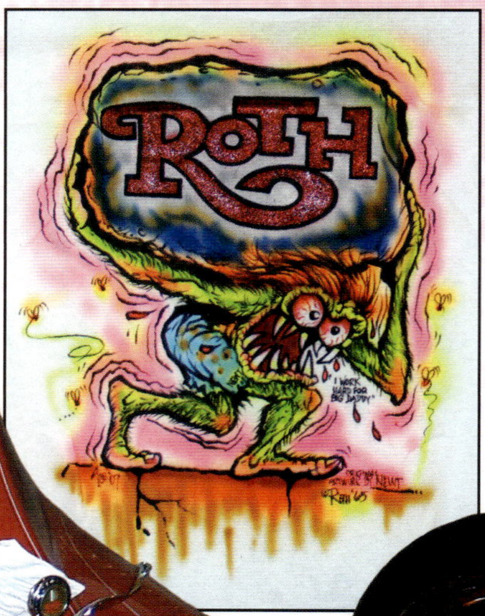

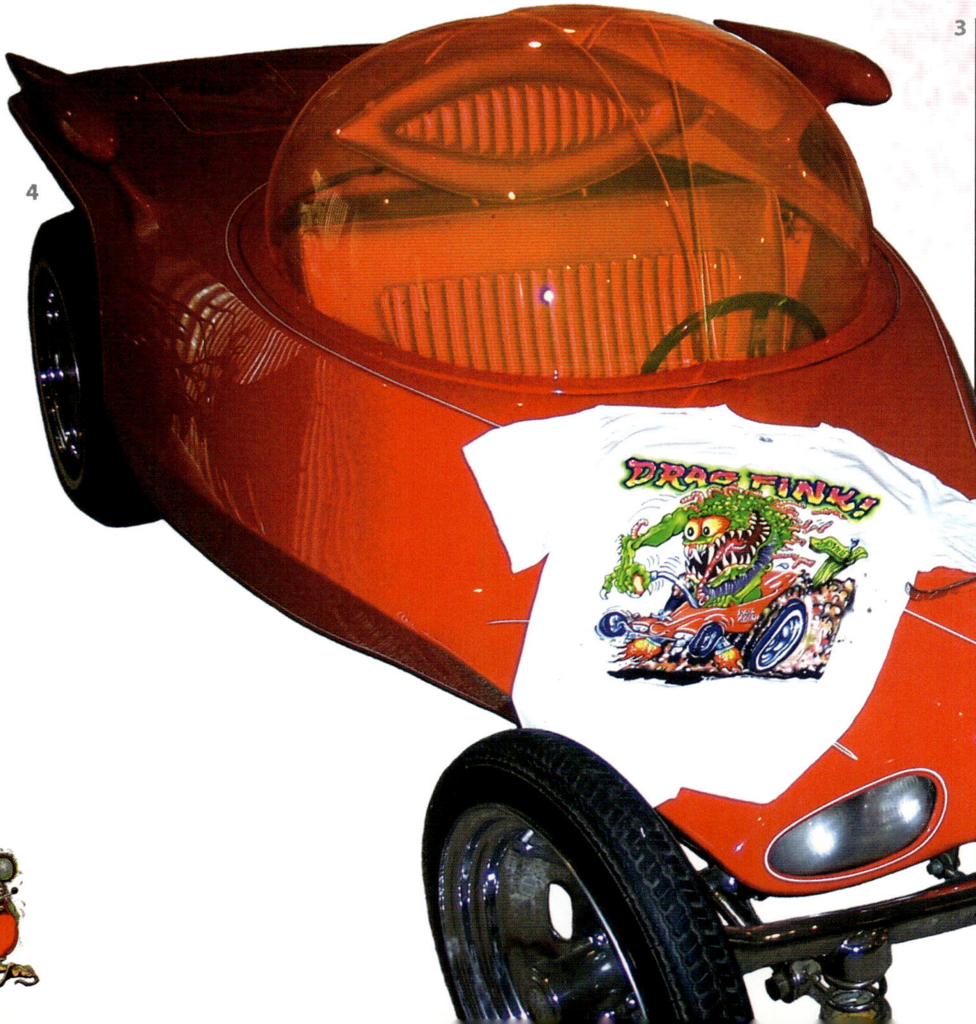

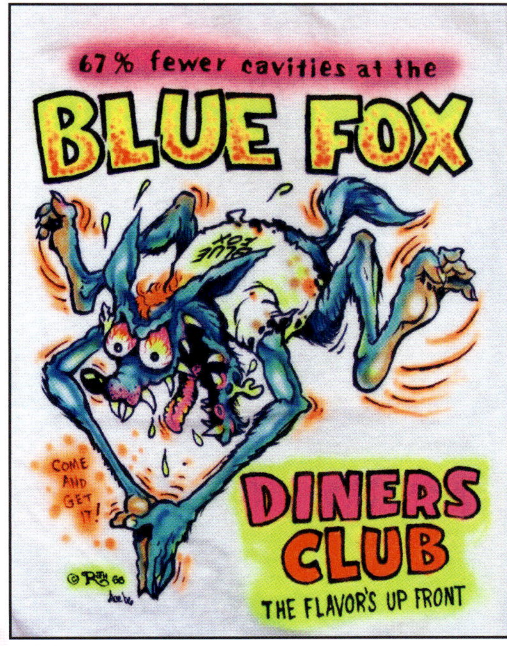

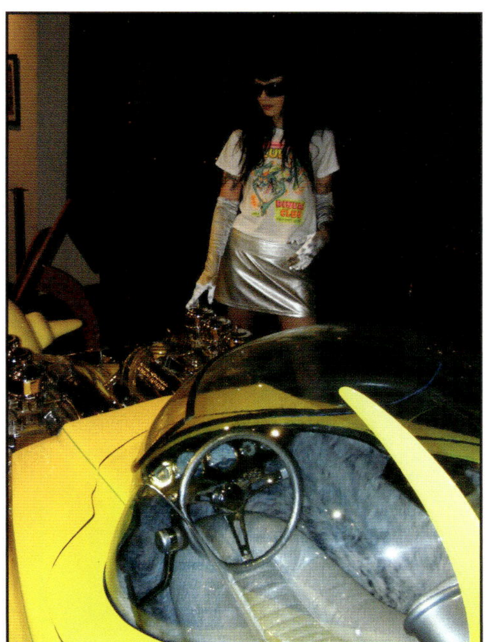

"The artists that scrawled these images on vehicle body work and working man's clothing were influenced by everything from beatniks to banned books. Their *Mad* humor was in a jugular vein, while rods & customs were their drug of choice . . . and their art was a series of twisted in-jokes which were never meant to please the eye or be understood by their elders . . ."
—Ed "Newt" Newton

1. *67% Fewer Cavities at the Blue Fox Diner's Club! (The Flavor's Up Front!).* Airbrushed t-shirt. 2005. Newt design, 1966.

2. Kali with Mysterion (restored by Dave Schuten).

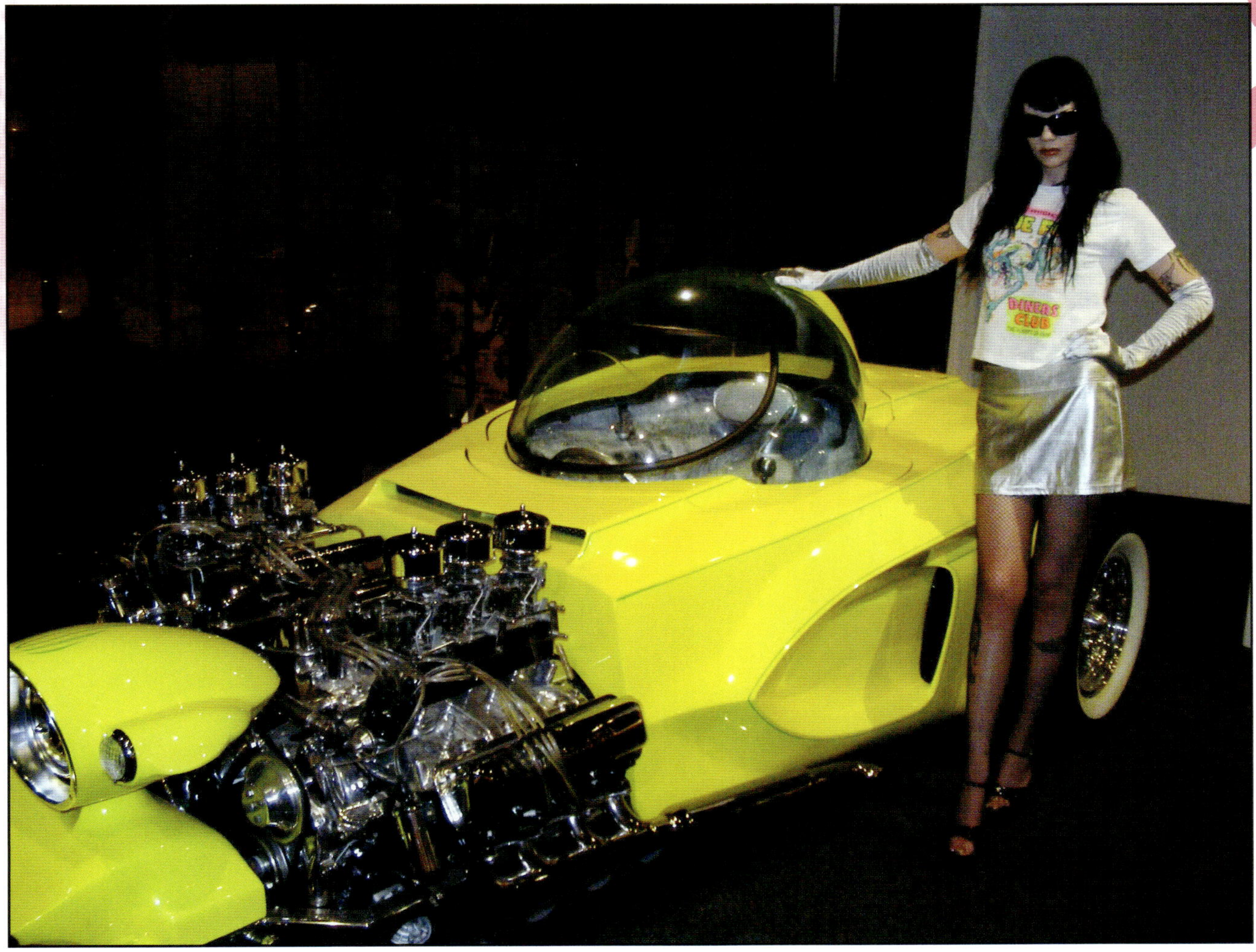

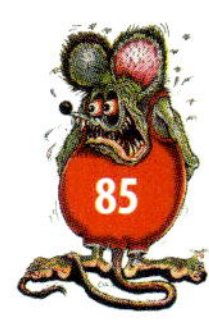

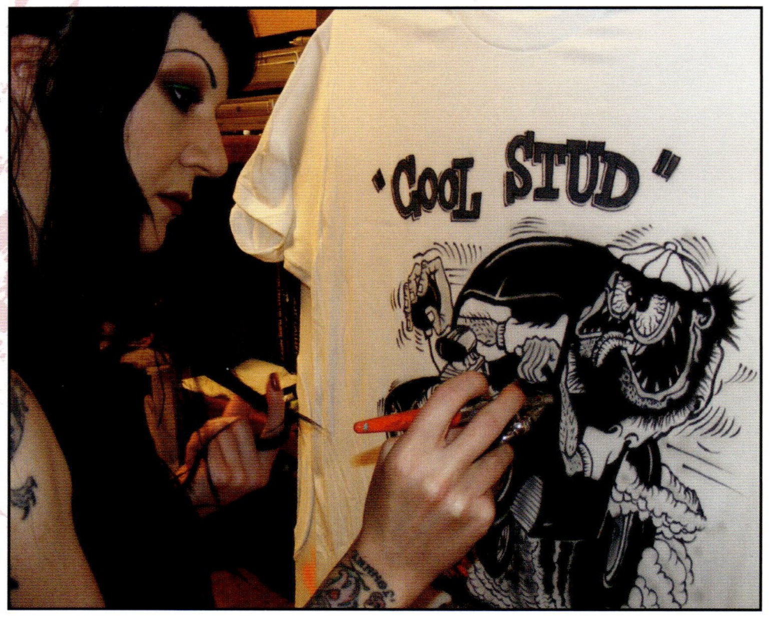

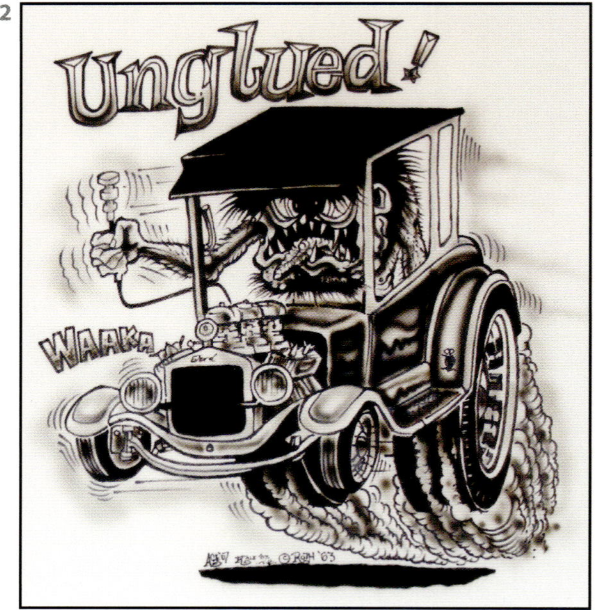

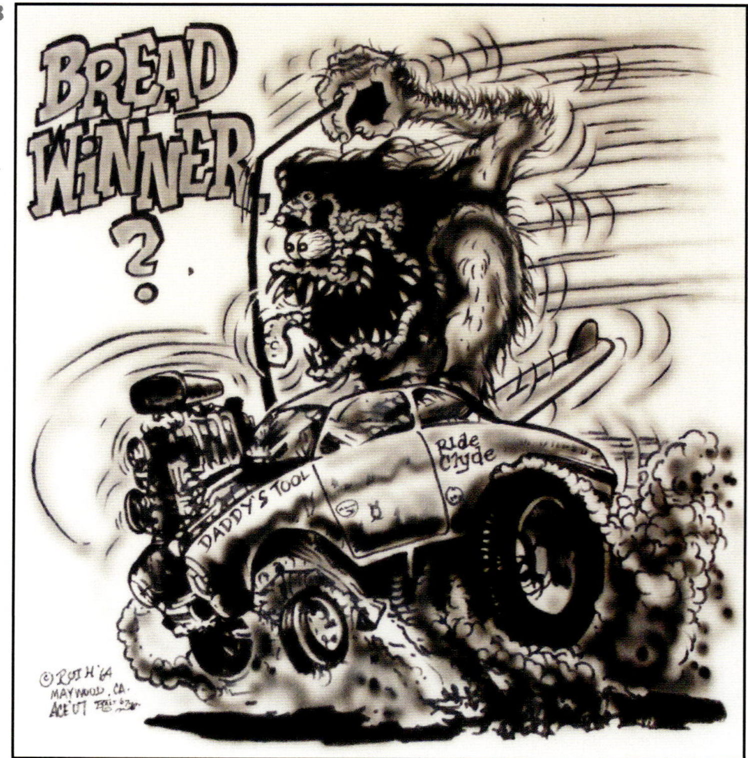

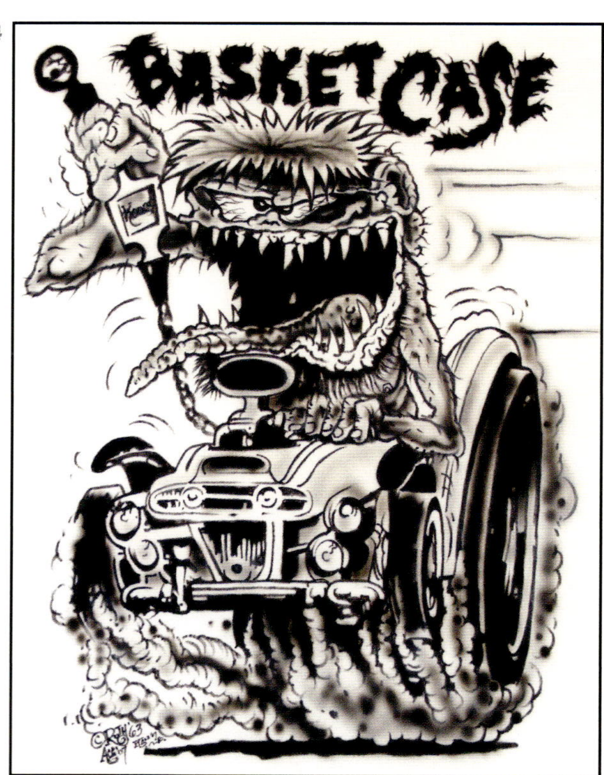

1. Kali airbrushing *"Cool Stud."* 2007. Collection of Mark Braccio.

2. *Unglued!* Airbrushed t-shirt. 2007. Collection of Mark Braccio.

3. *Bread Winner?* Airbrushed t-shirt. 2007. Collection of Mark Braccio.

4. *Basket Case.* Airbrushed t-shirt. 2007.
While many of Roth's pre-'64 shirt artists and designs remain uncredited (such as the other designs on this page), we know that Monte did Basket Case and that it was released both as a screened shirt and a waterslide decal. Collection of Mark Braccio.

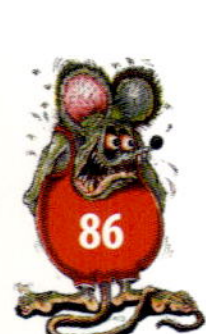

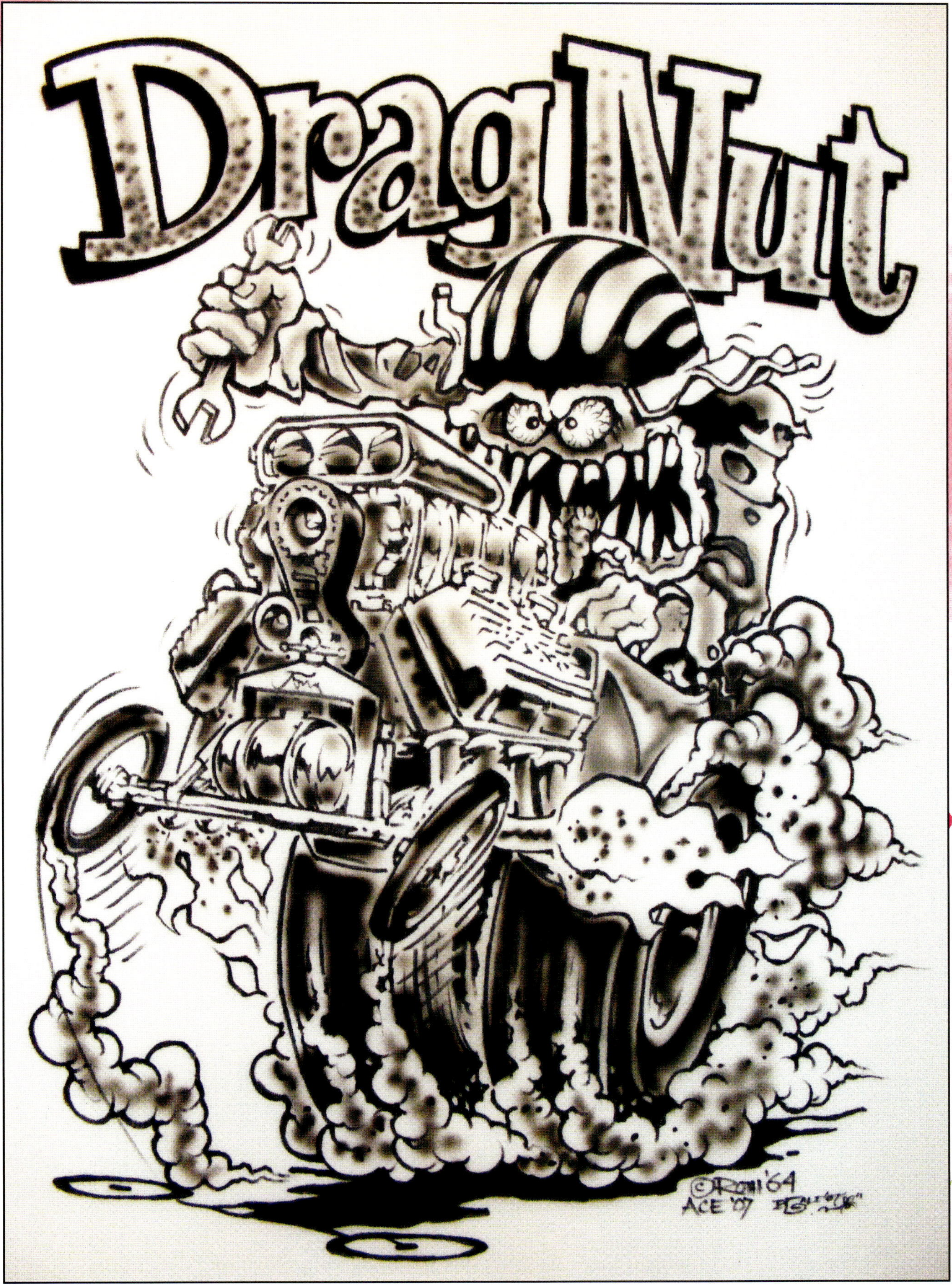

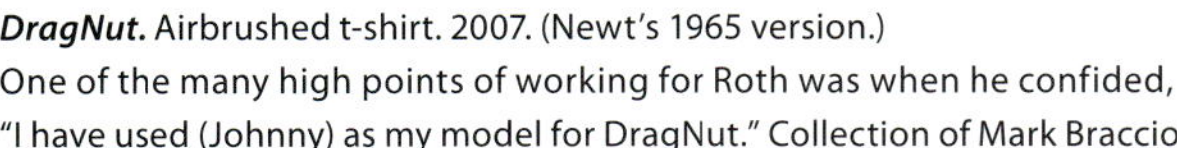

DragNut. Airbrushed t-shirt. 2007. (Newt's 1965 version.)
One of the many high points of working for Roth was when he confided,
"I have used (Johnny) as my model for DragNut." Collection of Mark Braccio.

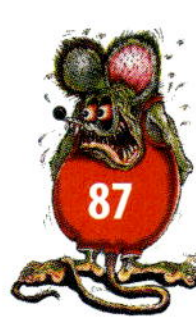

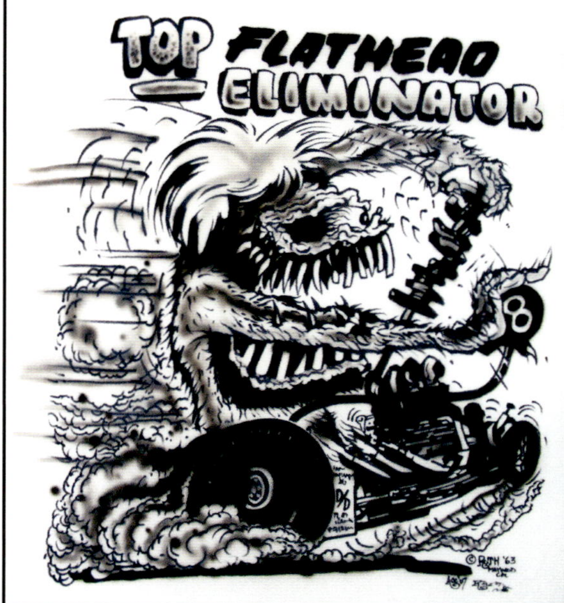

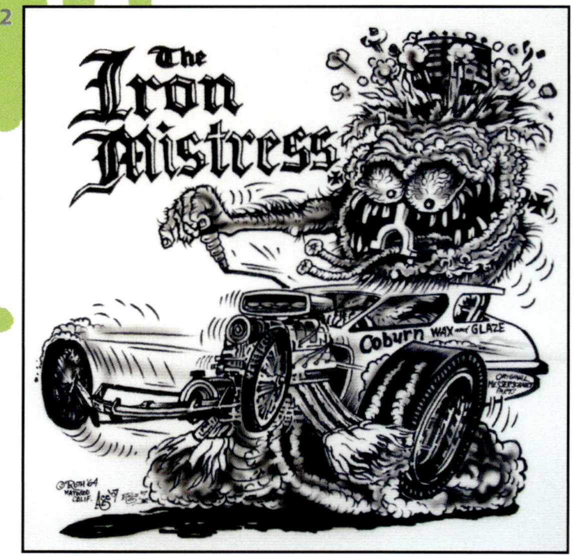

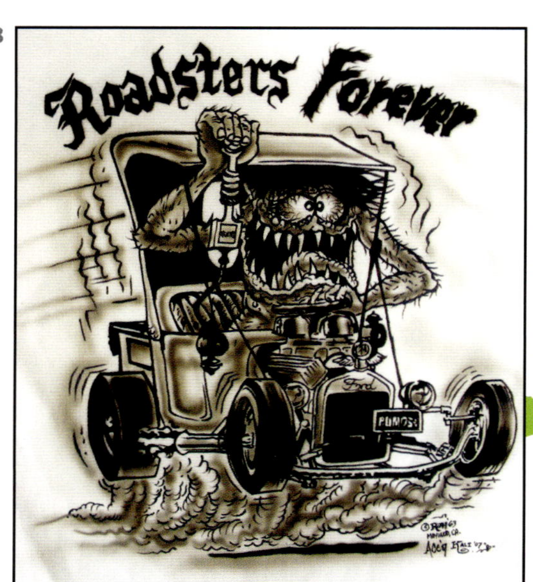

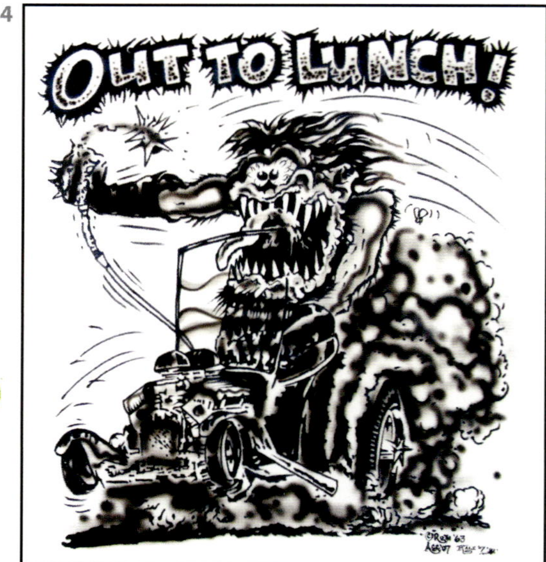

1. *Top Flathead Eliminator.* Airbrushed t-shirt. 2007.
Collection of Mark Braccio.

2. *The Iron Mistress.* Airbrushed t-shirt. 2007.
Collection of Mark Braccio.

3. *Roadsters Forever.* Airbrushed t-shirt. 2007.
Collection of Mark Braccio.

4. *Out to Lunch!* Airbrushed t-shirt. 2007.
Collection of Mark Braccio.

5. Ace at work, 2007.
In the early days of custom monster shirts, felt-tip markers
and an early form of airbrush, the air pencil, were utilized.
Many artists, especially Roth, did much of their renderings
in blacks, whites, and grays. When we were commissioned
by Roth friend and contributor Mark Braccio to do a series of
monochromatic designs, we saw it as a great opportunity to
rediscover and research Roth Studios' earliest imagery.

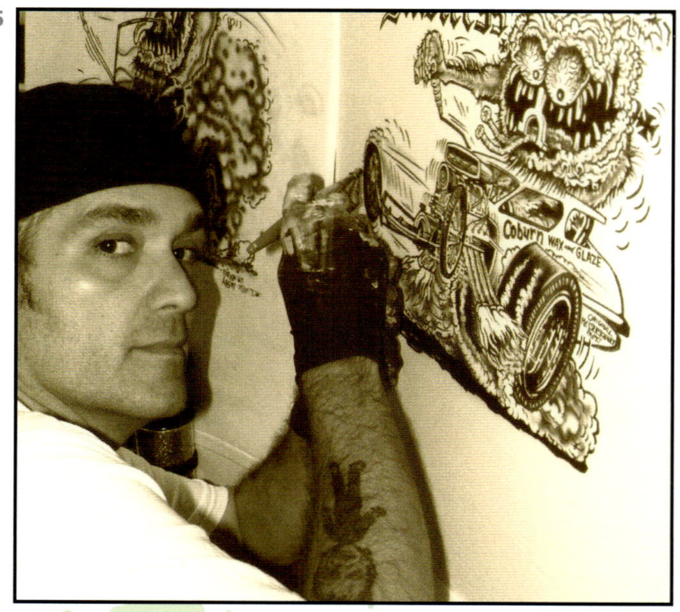

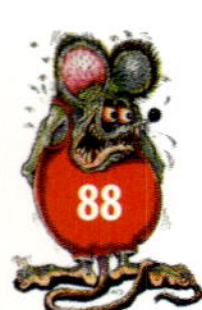

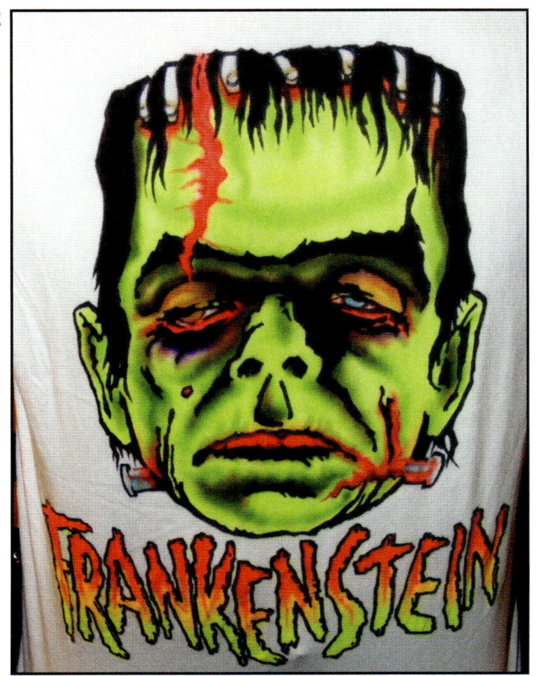

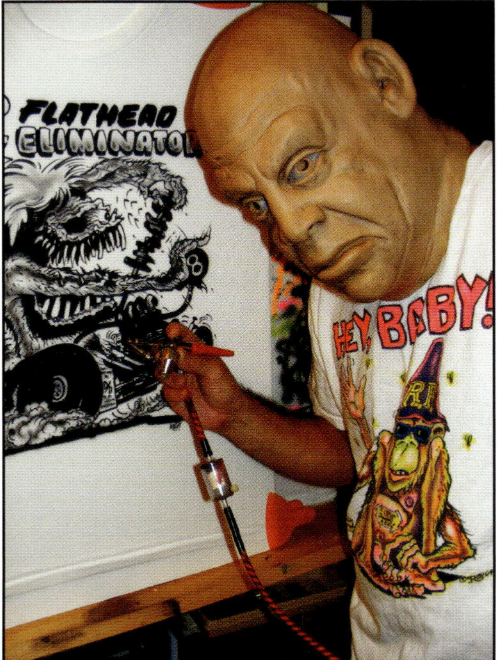

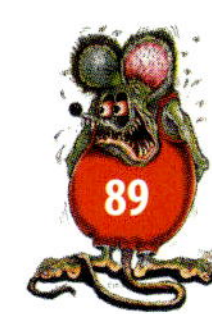

1. Ace filling in color on yet another custom shirt with Newt's version of *Race?* 2007. R.D.F.L.!

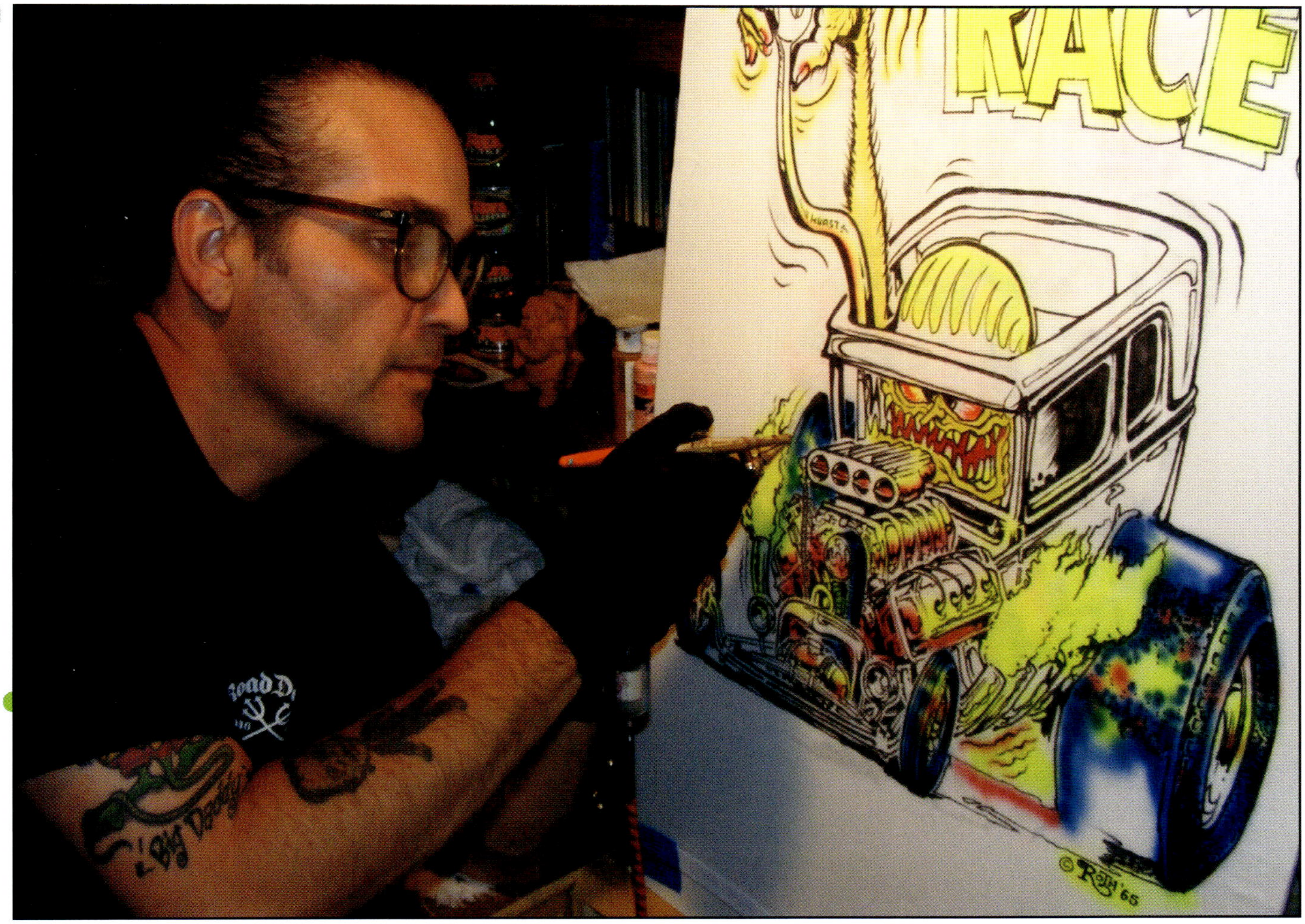

2. *Frankenstein.*
This was our rendition of one of the fondly remembered Mani-Yack monster transfers from the early '60s. A perfect example of monster shirts done for personal enjoyment and use.

3. Tor Like Monster Shirts . . . Tor Model *Hey, Baby!* Famous design by Newt. Tor airbrushing *Top Flathead Eliminator*, then Tor say, "Time for go to bed."

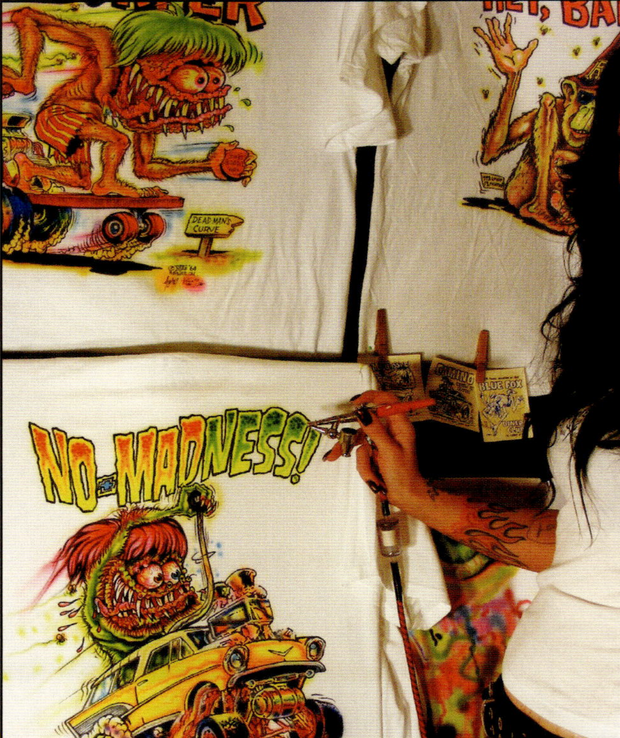

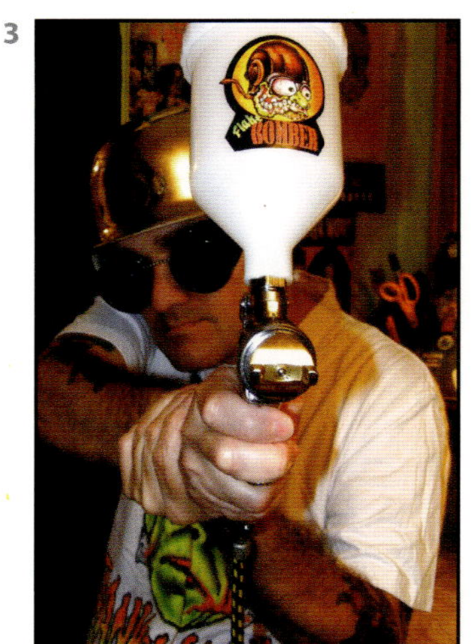

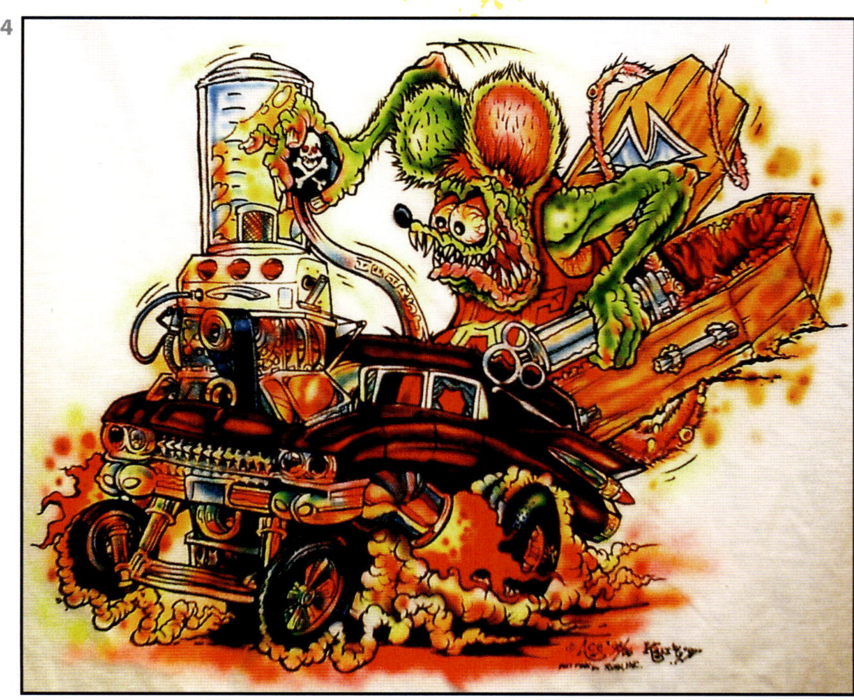

1. *Who Gives a CRAP?!?* Airbrushed t-shirt. 2007. This design, based on a rubber mask sold in *Horror Monsters* magazine in the '60s, might well be our studio motto . . .

2. *No-Madness!* Airbrushed t-shirt. 2007. Collection of Nick Solovtzoff.
Kali shown here working on a Newt-inspired shirt for yet another Nomad enthusiast. Note Newt's *Sidewalk Surfer* and *Hey, Baby!* in the background . . .

3. Hands up, muthaFinkahs!! Ace brandishing a fresh out of the box Roth Flake Bomber featuring Ace Studios artwork . . . The chrome "surfer's helmet" is genuine Roth Studios issue from the '60s (courtesy of Darryl Roth).

4. *HearseFink/Hearse with a Curse.* Airbrushed t-shirt. 2005. Ace original artwork inspired by Newt.

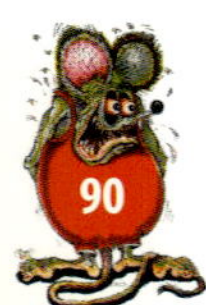

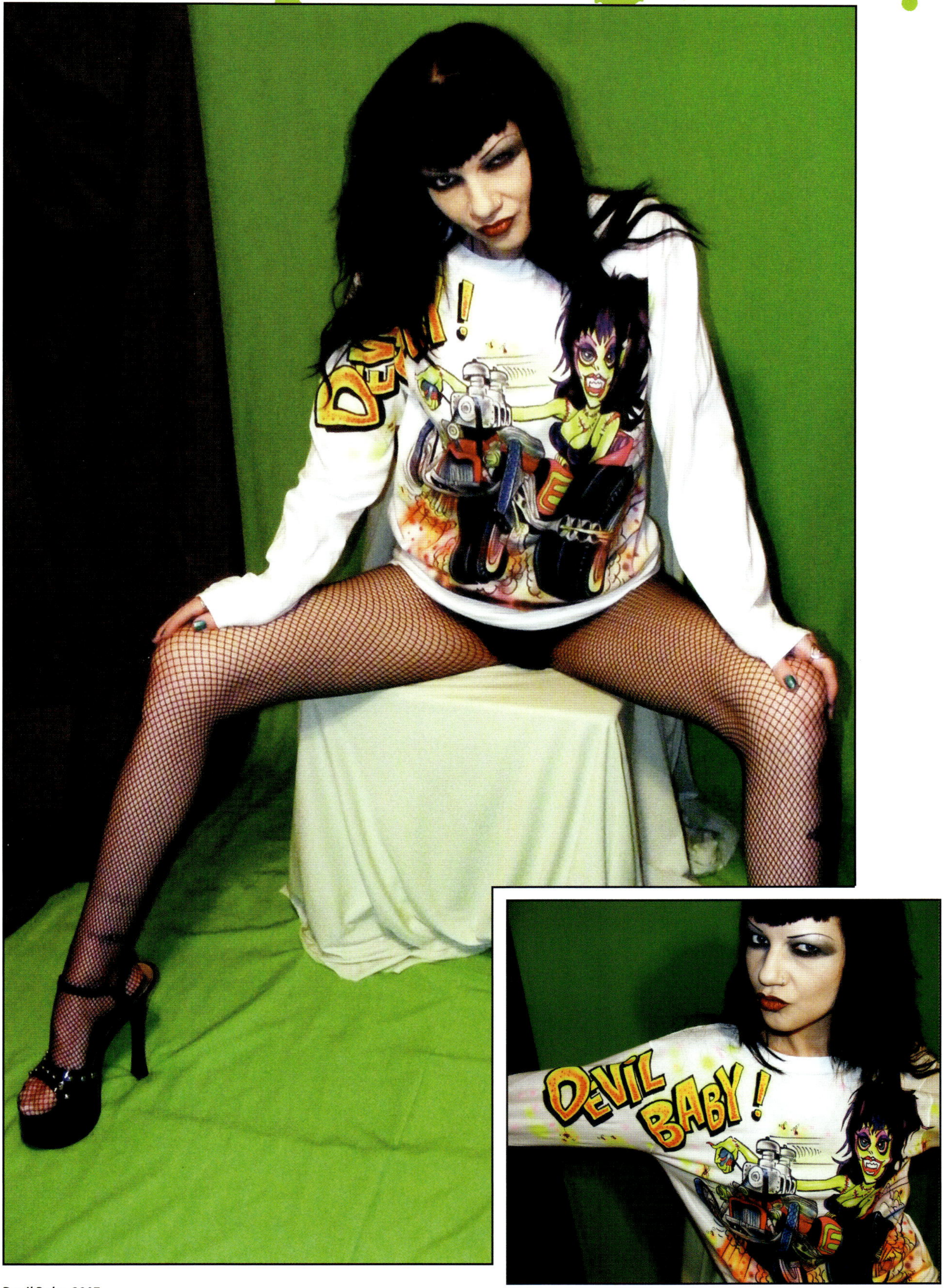

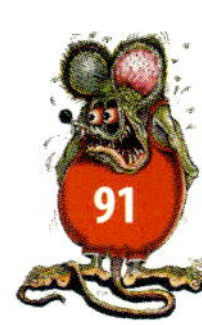

Devil Baby. 2007.
Model: Kali. Photos by Johnny Ace, 2007.

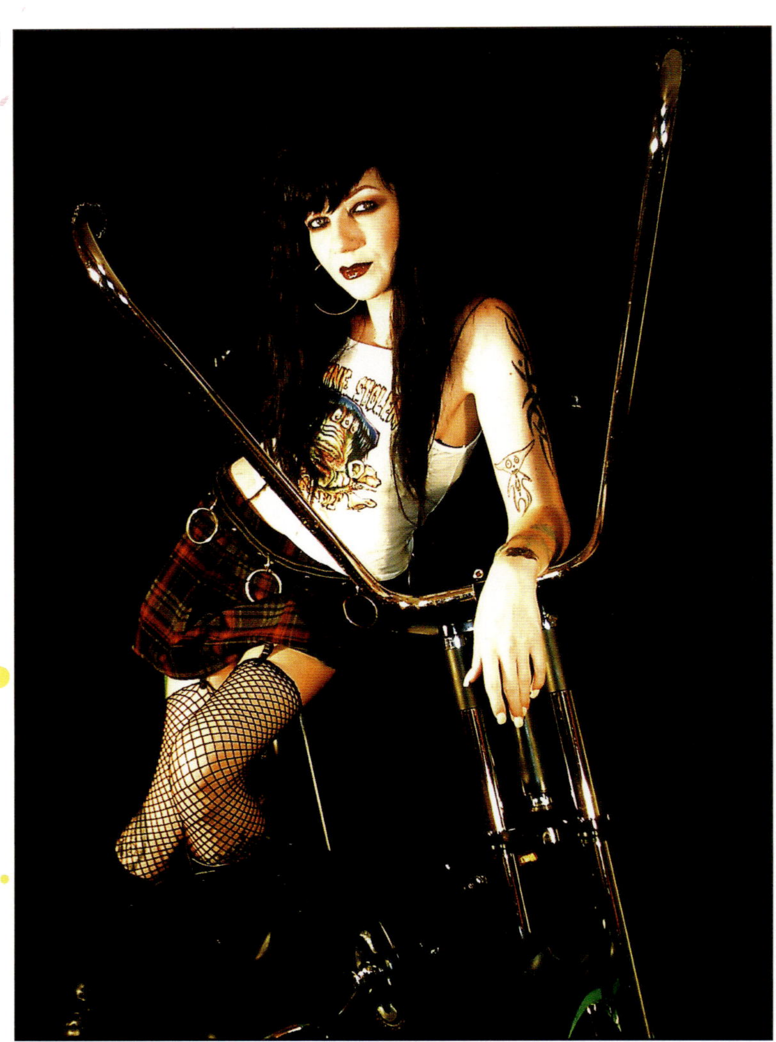

1. Kali modeling *Genuine Stolen Parts* airbrushed t-shirt with kustom Electra Rat Fink cruiser. 2006.

2. *Social Outcast.* Airbrushed child's t-shirt. 2007.

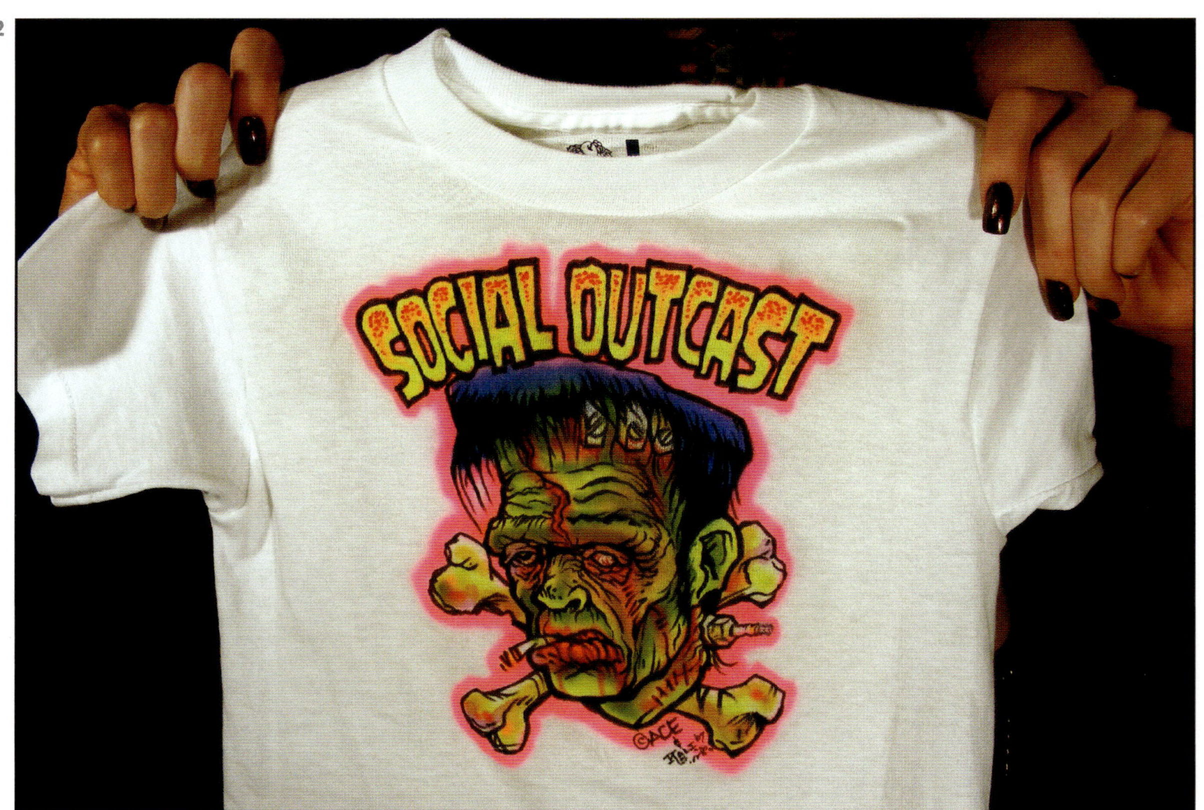

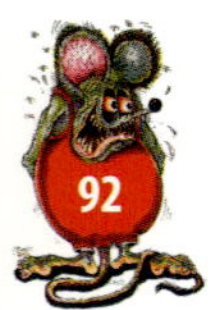

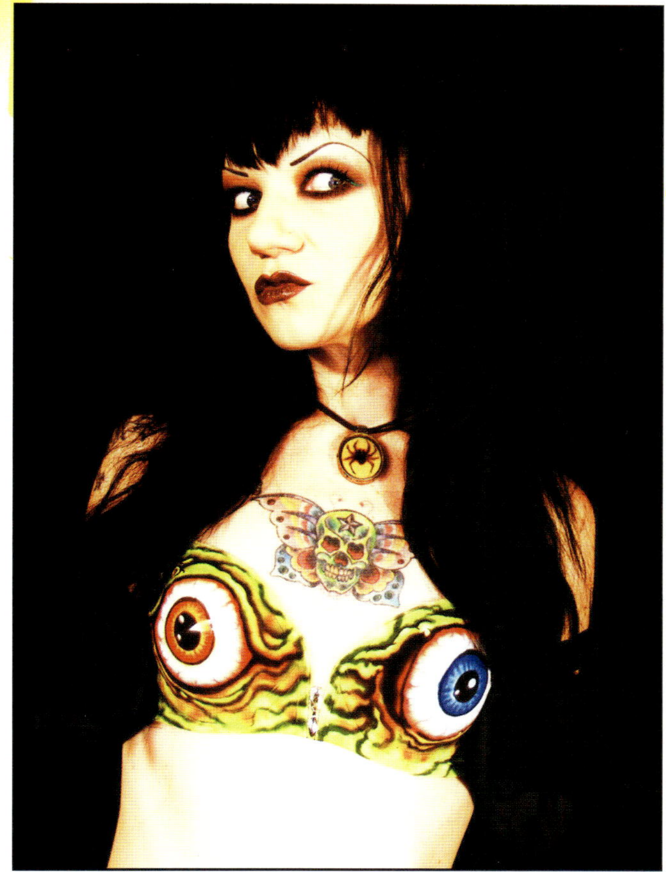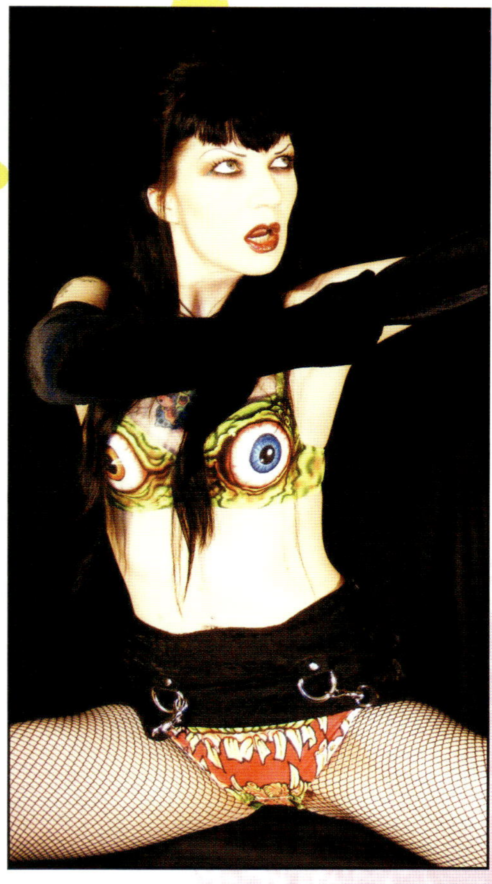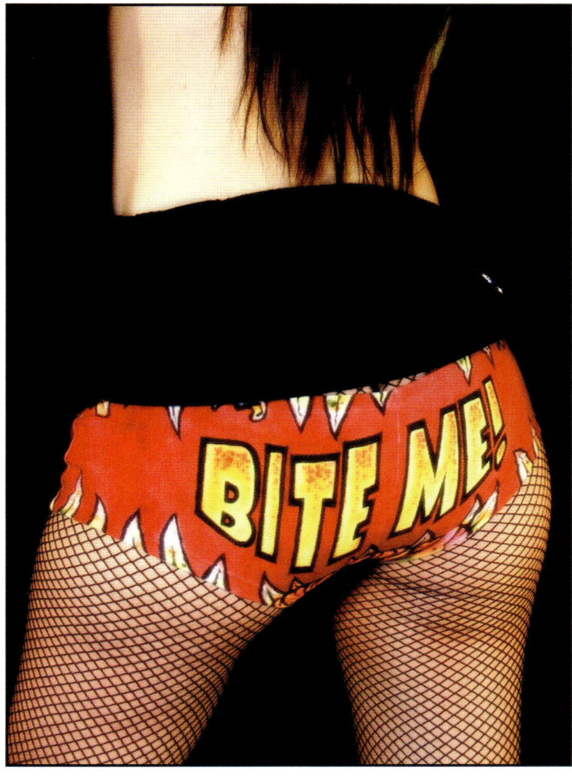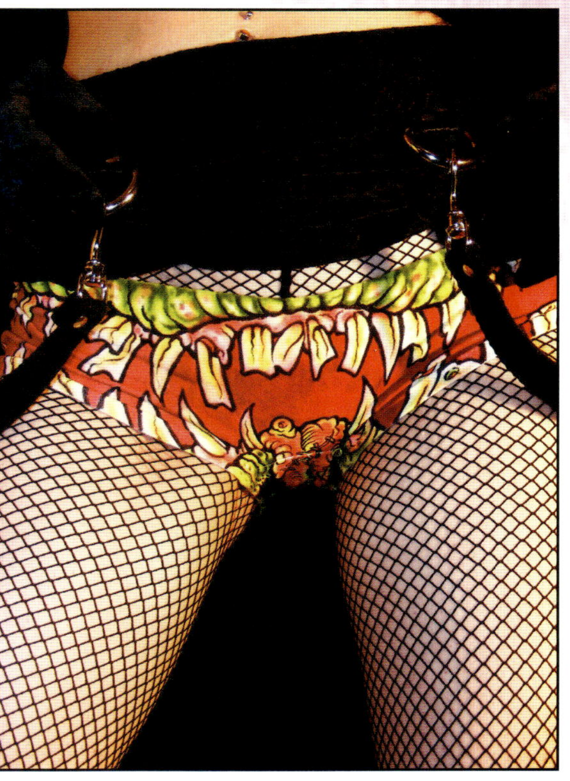

BITE ME! Monster Bra & Panties. Airbrushed acrylics on fabric, 2007.
Model: Kali. Part of the Bite me! Eat Me! Lick Me! collection.

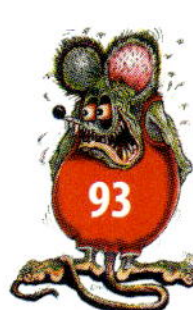

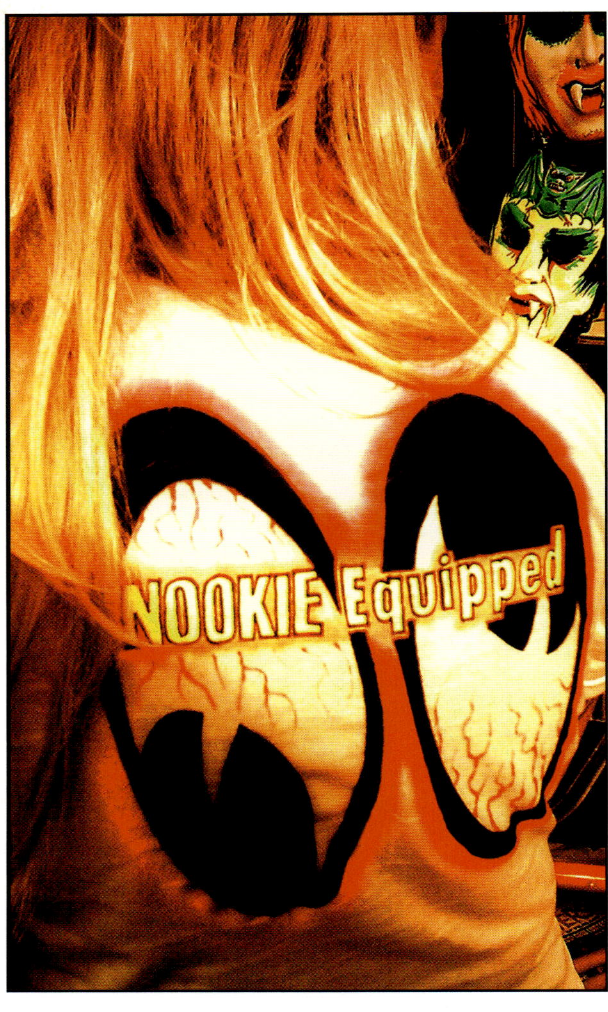

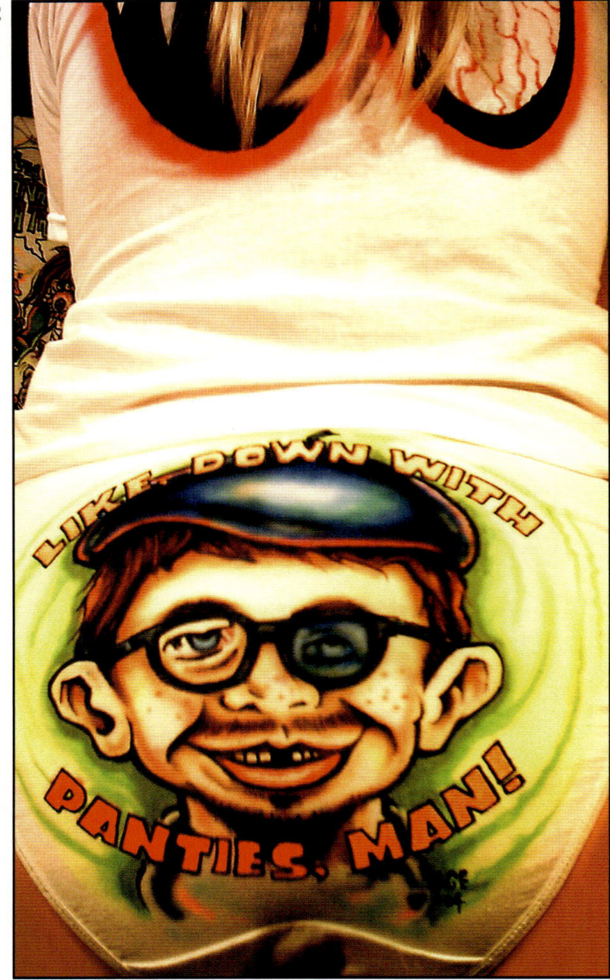

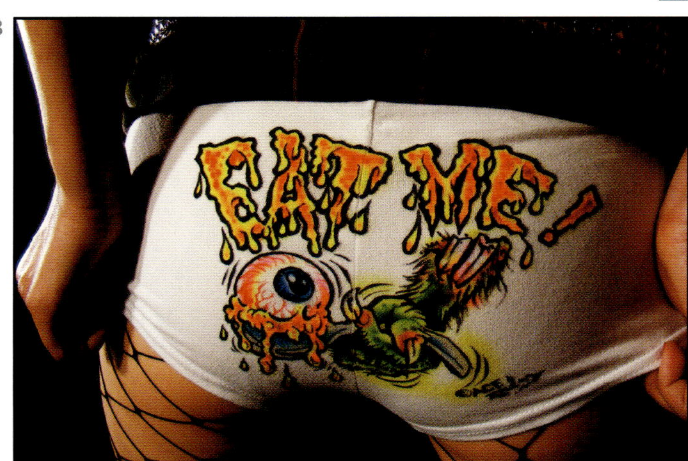

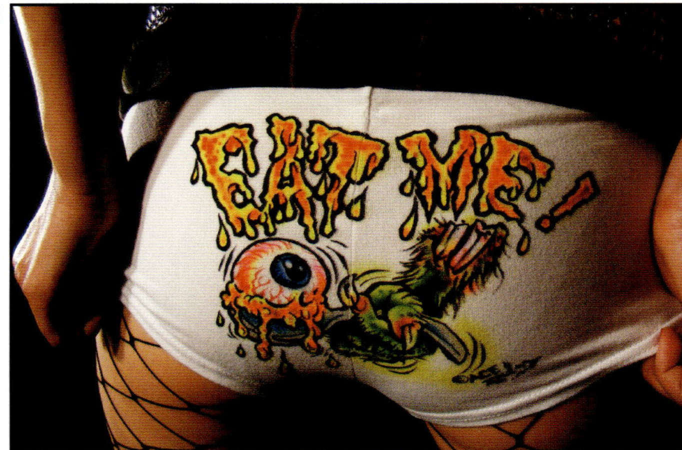

1. *Nookie Equipped.* Airbrushed girly t-shirt. 2003.
A good-natured parody and tip of the hat to an old Roth Studios in-joke.

2. *Like, Down with Panties, Man!* Airbrushed panties. 2003.
A blonde Kali gets cheeky here with a selection from the Melvin
Koznowski line of lingerie [in a larger size and with more coverage
than I usually take . . . HUMPH! —Kali] . . .

3. *Eat Me!* Airbrushed panties. 2007.
Model: Patti Waggin.

4. *Property of Johnny Ace Studios.* Airbrushed panties. 2007.
Model: Lucy La Loca.

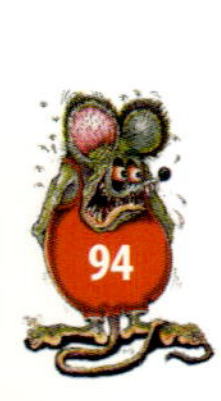

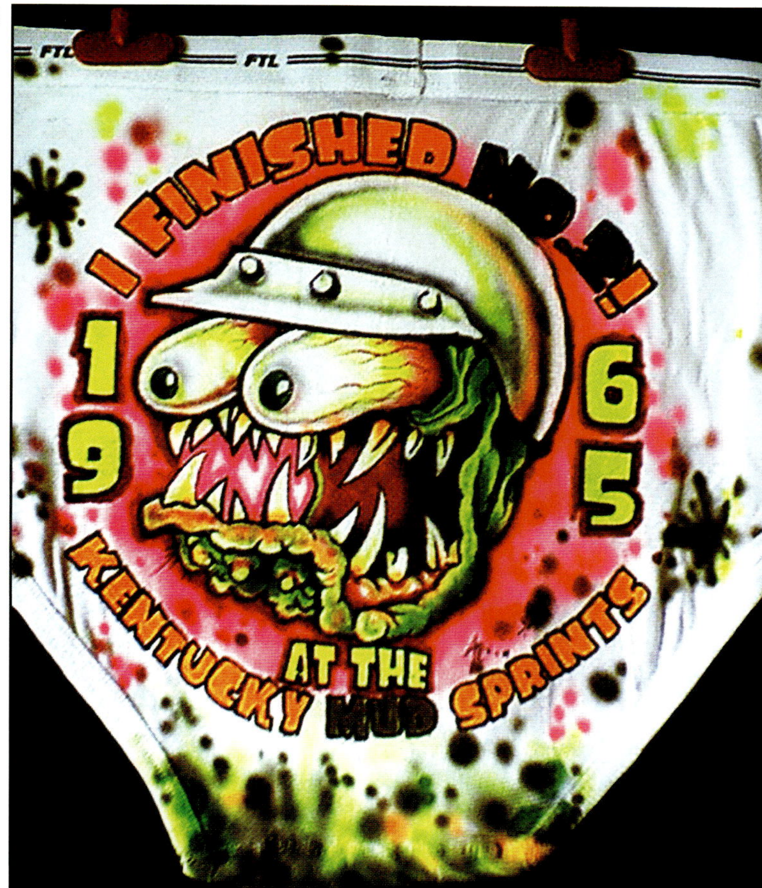

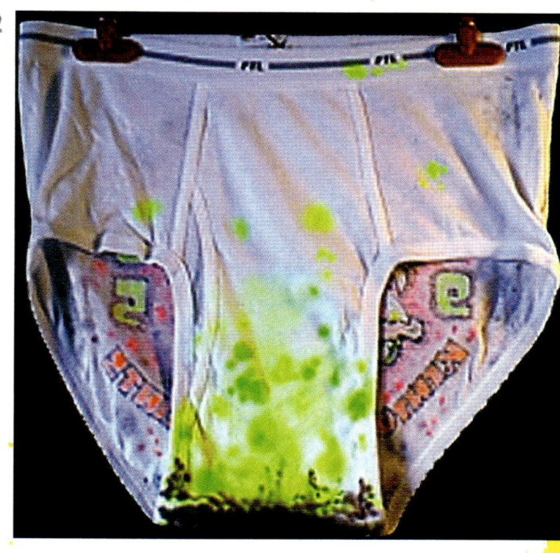

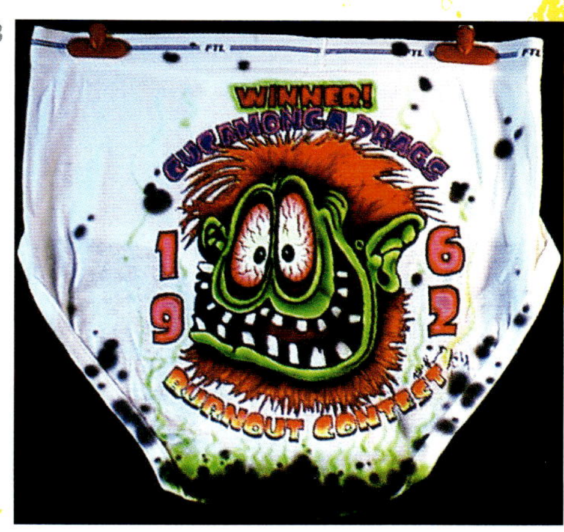

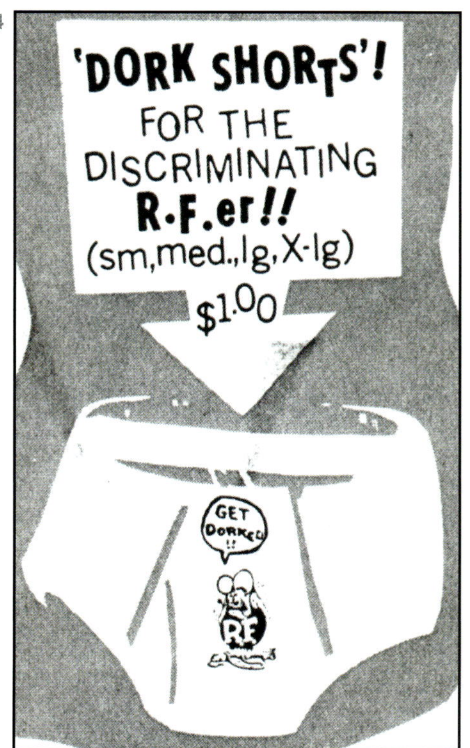

1. *I Finished No. 2! at the 1965 Kentucky Mud Sprints.* (Exhaust Side) Airbrushed giant UNTIDY tighty-not-so-WHITEYS. 2003.

2. *I Finished No. 2! at the 1965 Kentucky Mud Sprints.* (Overflow Side) Airbrushed giant UNTIDY tighty-not-so-WHITEYS. 2003.

3. *Winner! 1962 Cucamonga Drags Burnout Contest!* (Exhaust Side) Airbrushed giant UNTIDY tighty-not-so-WHITEYS. 2003.

4. Detail from Roth's *WILD! STOKE! CRAZY!* Monster Catalog. Circa 1964.

Big men's underwear is just funny. No matter which way you slice it. The inspiration for these came from Roth Studios' 1964 catalog, which featured "Dork Shorts" for the "Discriminating R.F.er," a quote from the legendary Kenneth "Von Dutch" Howard (which not only relates to THIS, but the art world in general); too many late-night, caffeine-fueled, monster-shirt painting sessions; and some *Ren & Stimpy* thrown in for good measure. There were also some abstract theories and observations on art collectors, surrealism, and the true stories of art lovers wanting to buy Ed's used paint-splattered shirts and pants—not to mention our own curiosity as to just WHO would exactly buy these damn things (these dastardly drawers) once we offered them for sale. For these tasteful examples, we got the largest whiteys we could find at the time—and no, no one here at Johnny Ace Studios actually wears these wide-awake nightmares. We feel sorry for anyone who might have actually pondered this question (seek help if you did) . . . Please enjoy this quote from a personal hero of ours:

"It all ends up BROWN! You take every color of paint in this building and stir it up in one can, and you WILL get BROWN . . . That explains a lot of things."
—Kenneth "Von Dutch" Howard

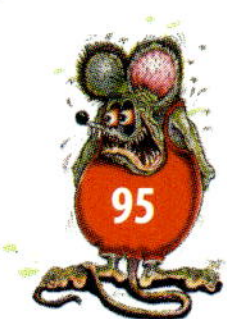

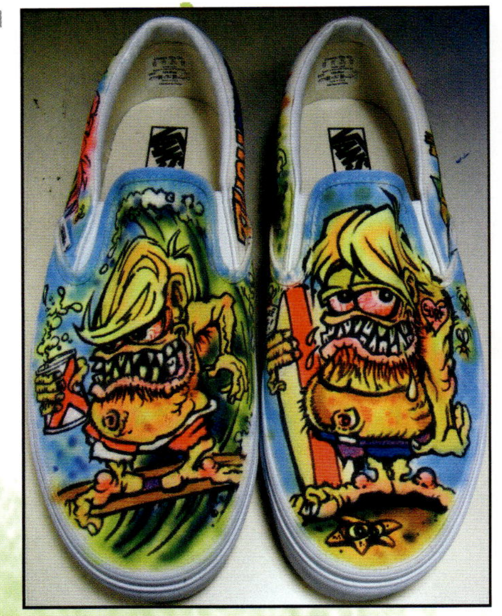

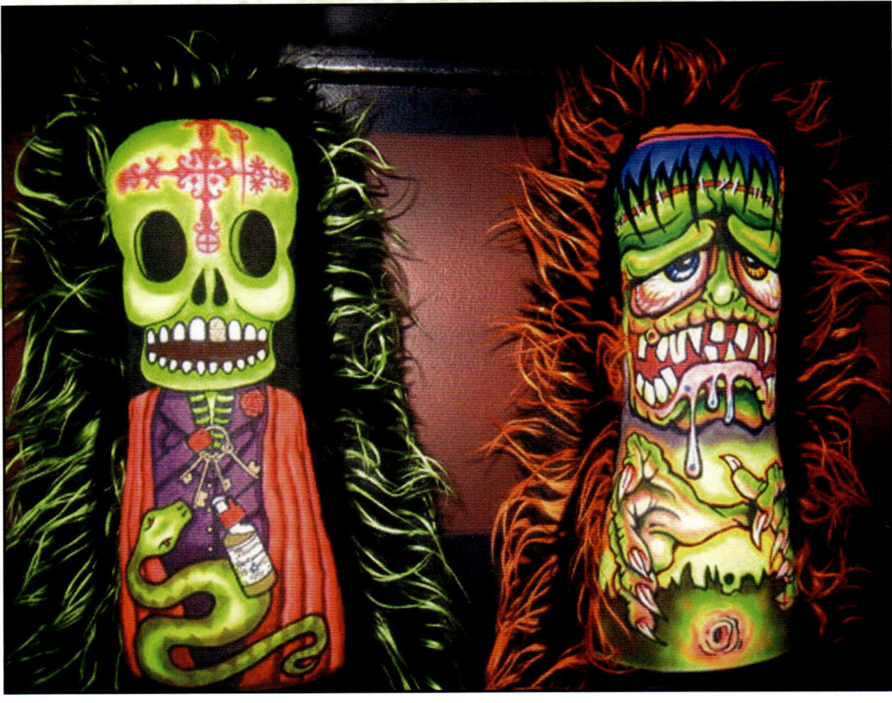

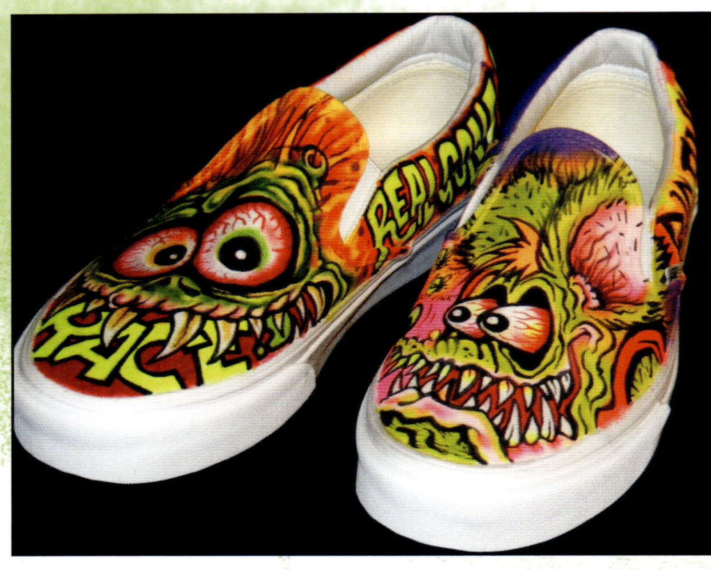

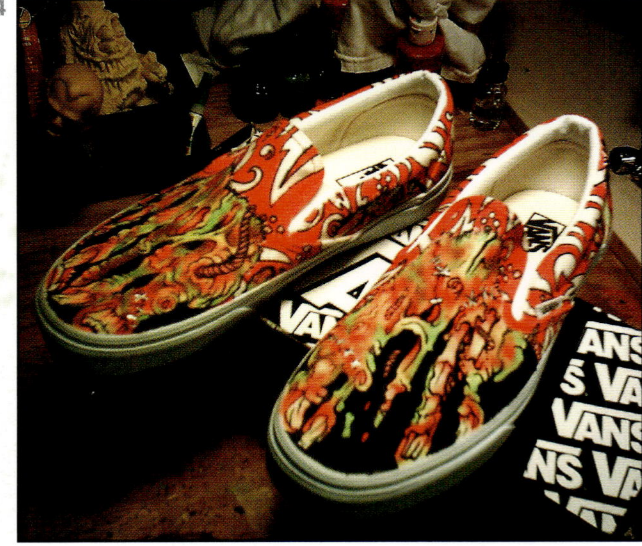

1. *Surf Slobs.* Custom airbrushed Vans. 2007.
   Collection of Murphy Graham.

2. *Legba Ghede*—Kali, 2005. **FrankenPunk**—Ace, 2005.
   Showroom NYC, Circus Punks Exhibit, 2005.

3. *Real Gone Gasser!* Custom airbrushed Vans. 2007.
   Collection of Preston Root.

4. *Zombie Skate.* Custom airbrushed Vans. 2006.
   Collection of Cliff Graham.

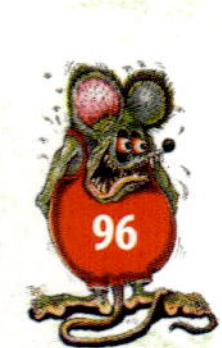

WICKED 1-SHOT
A GRIM GALLERY OF PERVERSE PINSTRIPING

"...for this I had deprived myself of rest and health. I had desired it with an ardor that far exceeded moderation; but now that I had finished the beauty of the dream vanished, and breathless horror and disgust filled my heart!"

WICKED 1-SHOT
A GRIM GALLERY OF
PERVERSE PINSTRIPING

. . . for this I had deprived myself of rest and health. I had desired it with an ardor that far exceeded moderation, but now that I had finished the beauty of the dream vanished, and breathless horror and disgust filled my heart."

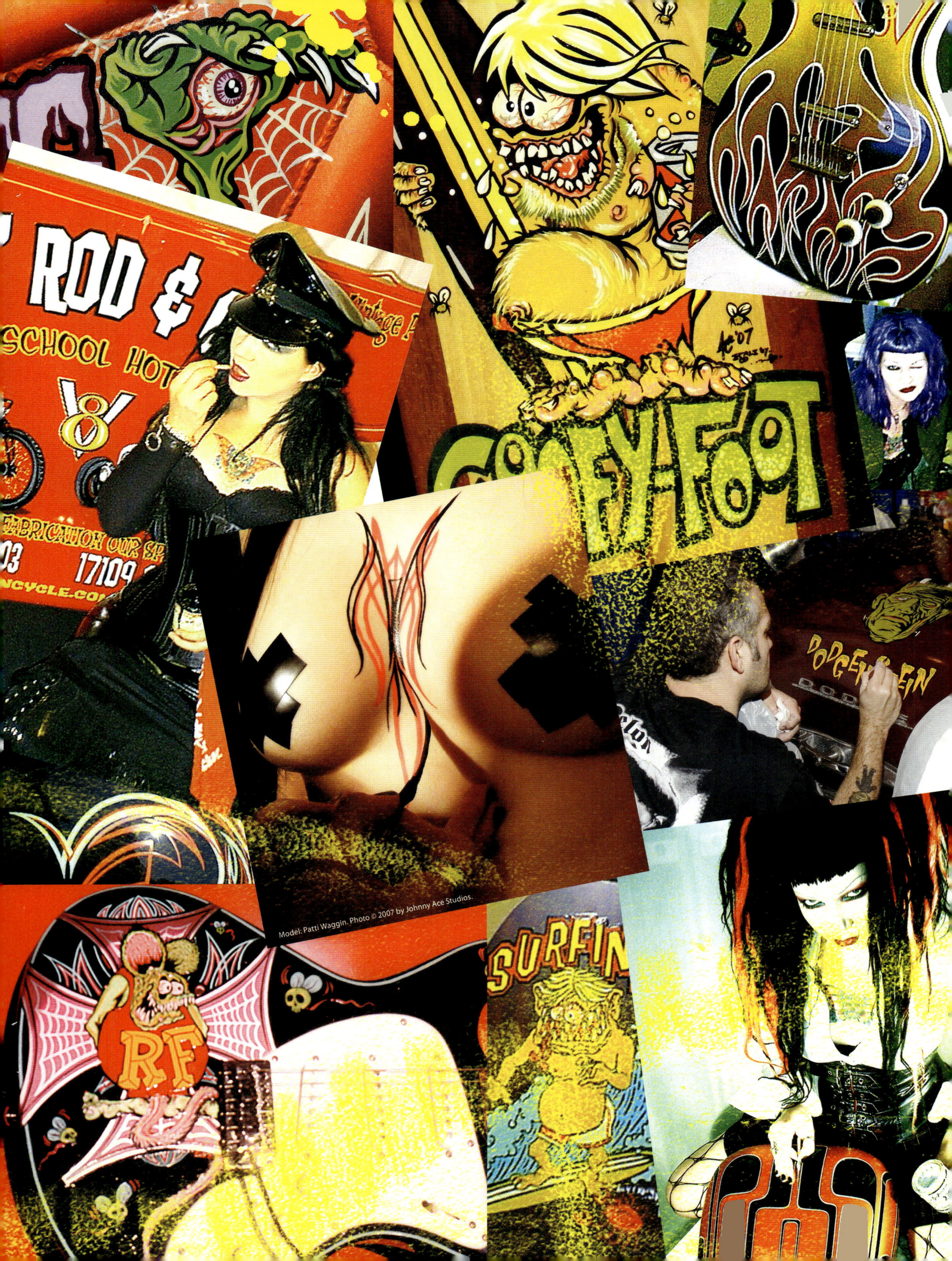

Model: Patti Waggin. Photo © 2007 by Johnny Ace Studios.

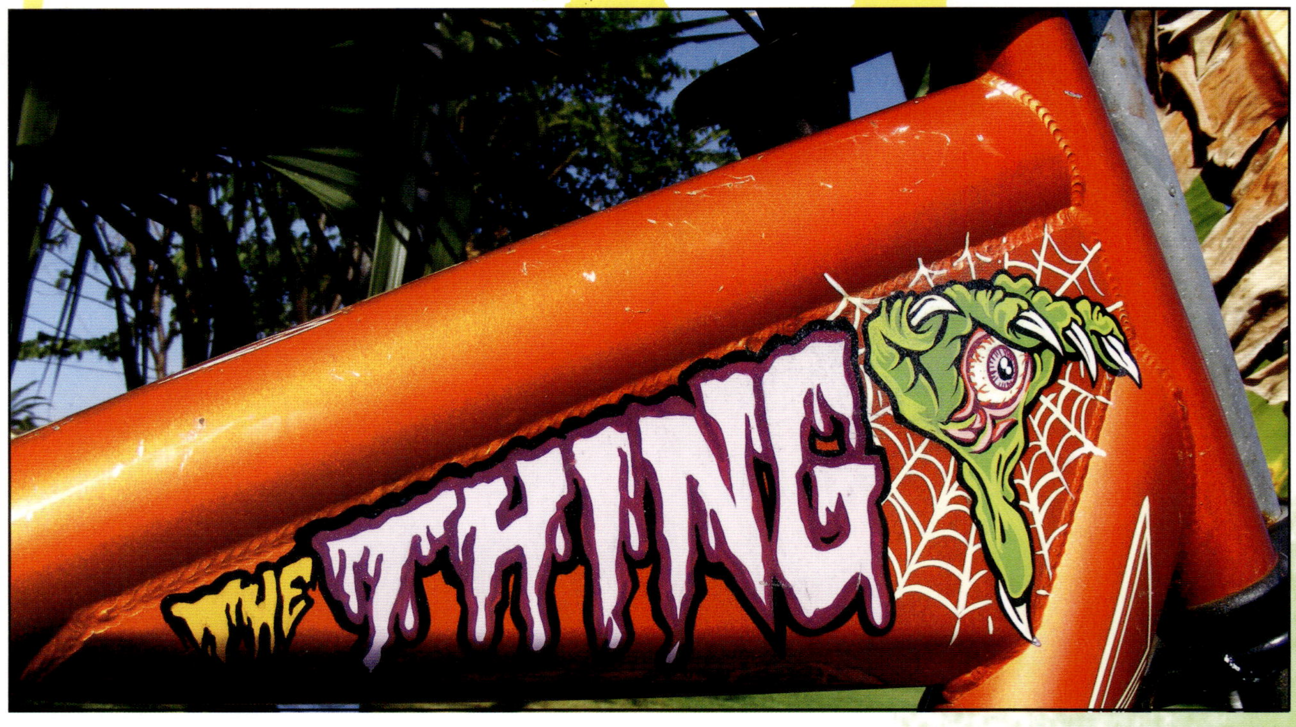

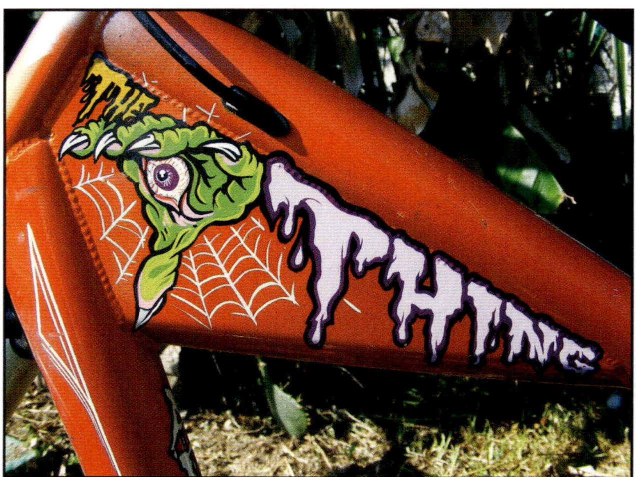

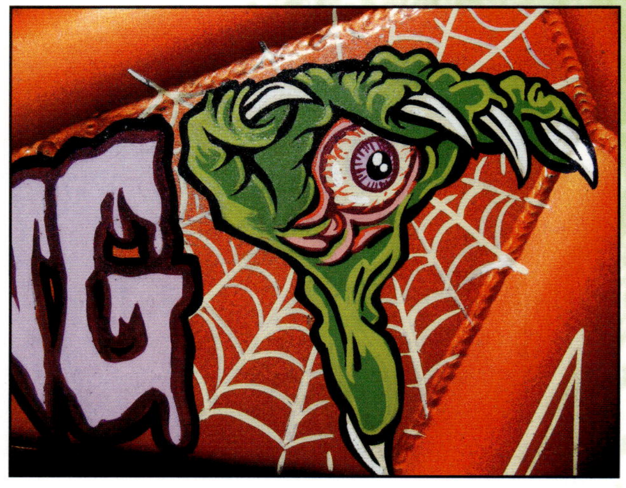

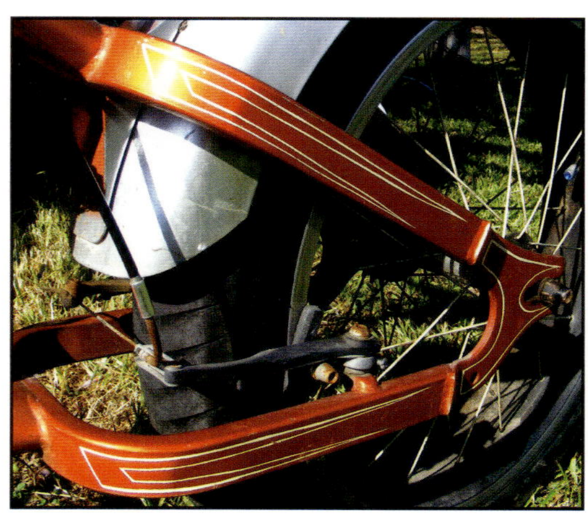

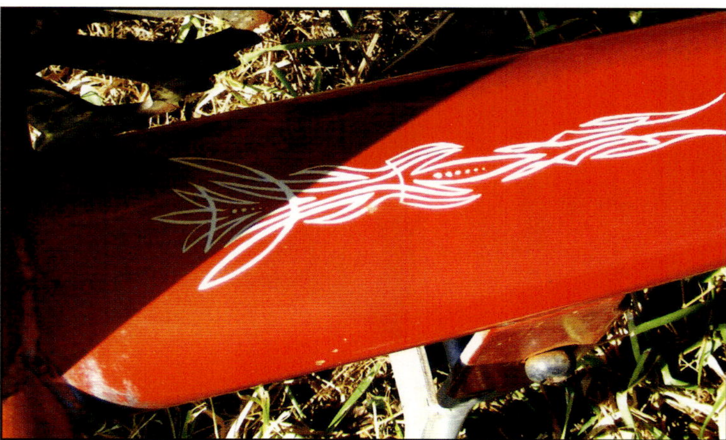

The Thing. 2006.
1-Shot enamel. We covered this Schwinn Chopper kid's bike with tank graphics and frame pinstriping. The logo itself was inspired by a favorite story from a 1952 pre-code Marvel horror comic.

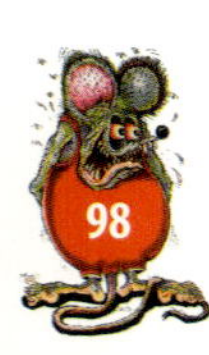

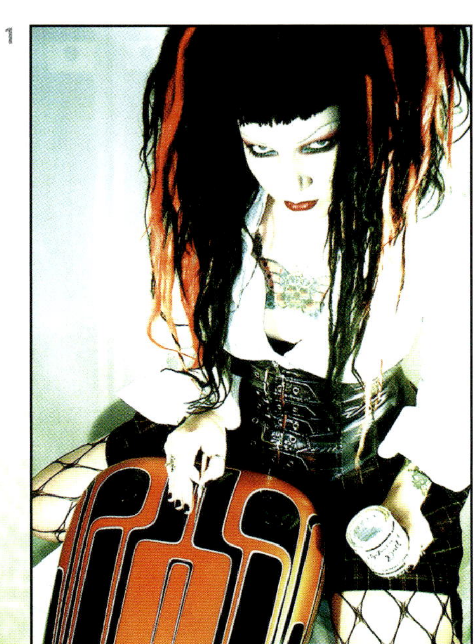

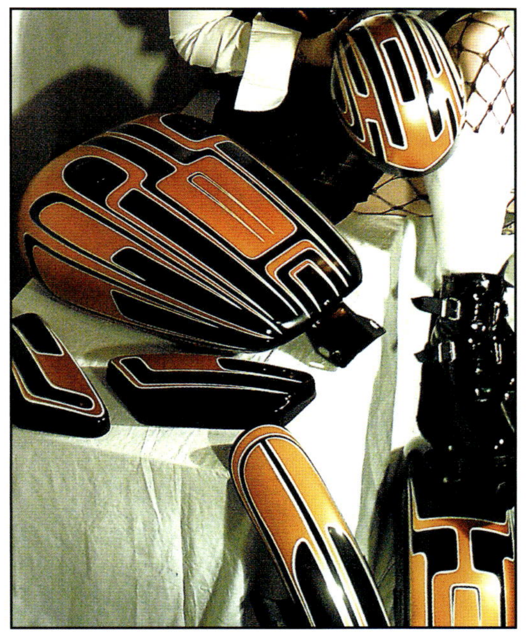

1. Kali laying ivory pinstriping over the scalloping on this group of tangerine metalflake Harley FXR parts.

2. Custom Triumph chopper fender and tank with "Dead Man's Hand" graphic by Ace and fender striping by Kali, entitled "The Incredible Edible".

3. The cobweb pattern and side pinstriping on "Dead Man's Hand" were laid in with red and white 1-Shot over black semi-gloss by Kali.

4. Kali striping another Triumph tank at Hans' Rod & Cycle, Houston, Texas. January, 2005. She held the title of official house pinstriper here, which was a highly respected garage dedicated to traditional hot rods, customs, and bikes.

5. Yet another photo of Kali working on a Harley, in the dead of winter, even! Johnny Ace Studios' Monster Rally '03 Party.

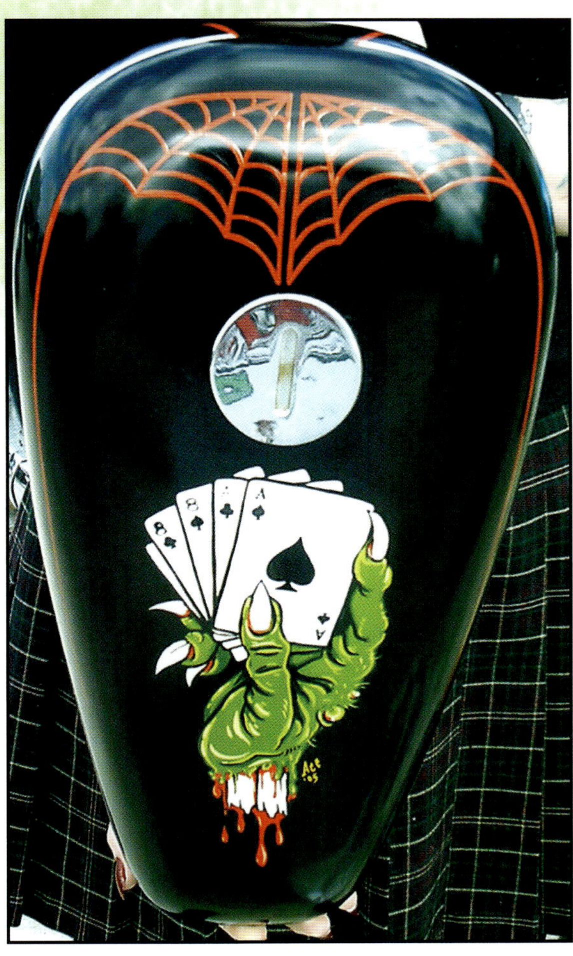

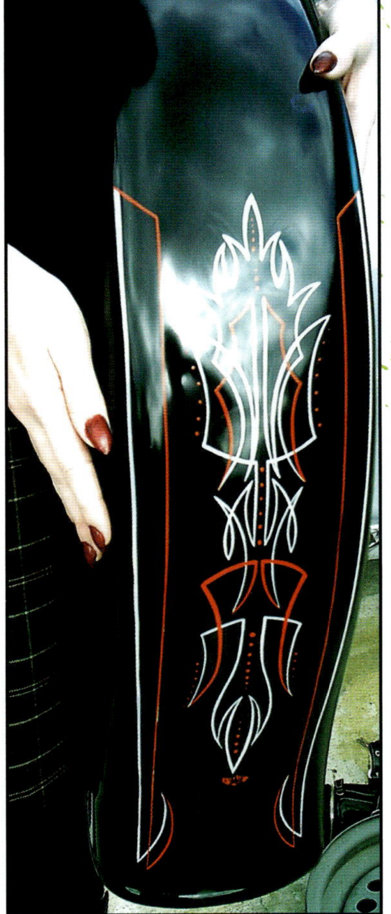

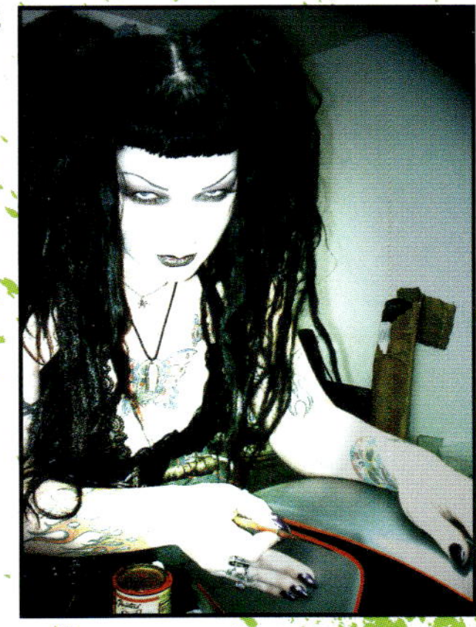

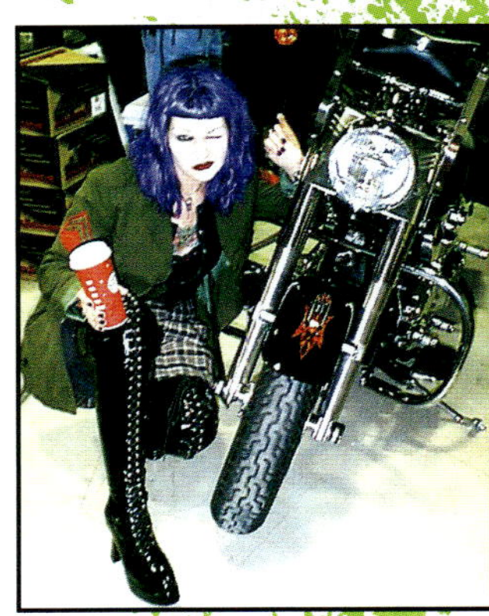

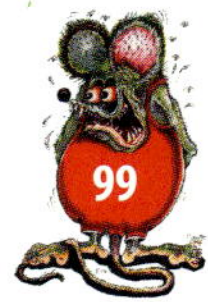

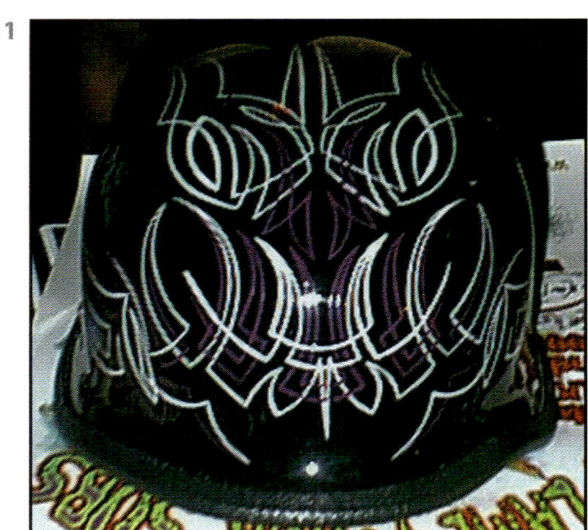

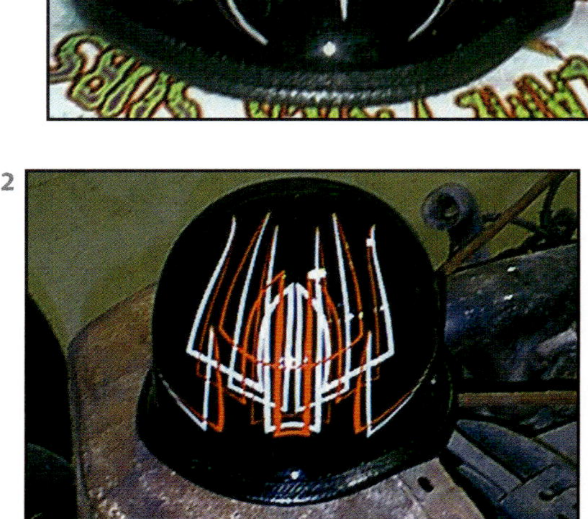

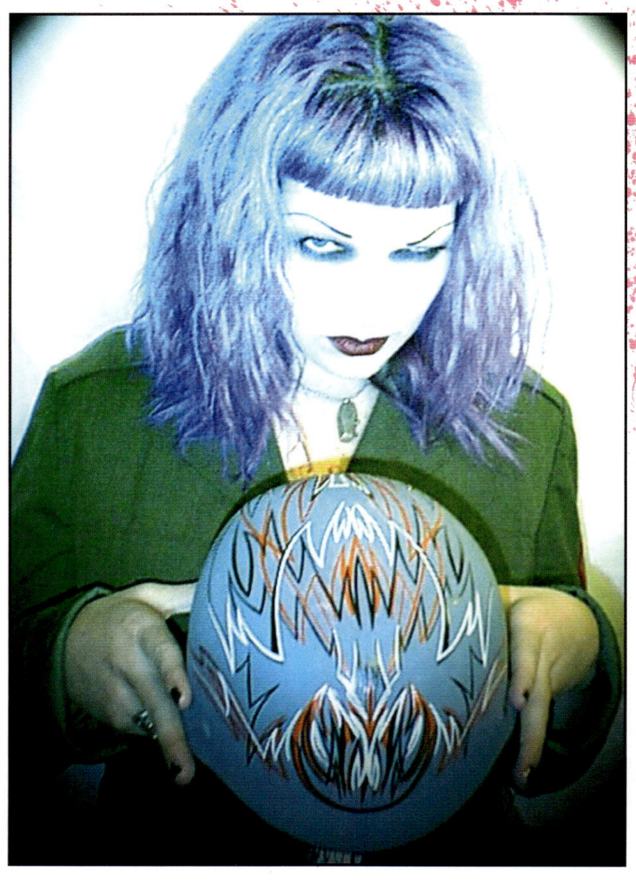

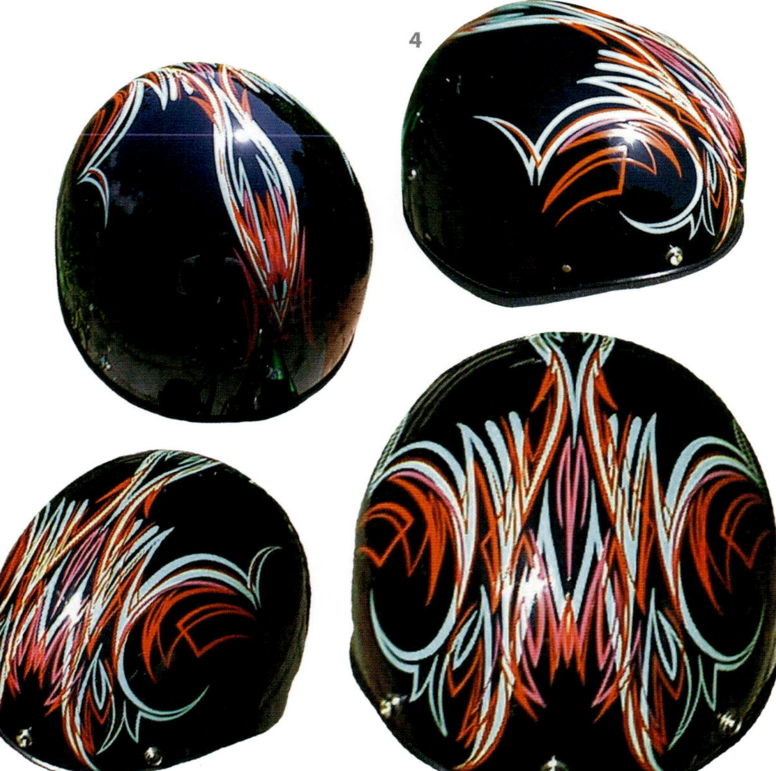

German-style helmets have long been a popular novelty item. Roth advertised them as "Surfer Helmets" and "World War III Air-Raid Helmets"! *Drag Cartoons* sold a fibreglass version "Surfing/Pit Helmet" called "Der Sauerkraut. " In more recent times, both DOT-approved (as well as non-DOT-approved) styles have become very popular . . . These are among our top-requested items.

1. *Wonder Wart-Hog (Ode to Shelton).* 1-Shot over gloss black. 2003. By Kali.

2. *The Mad Viking.* 1-Shot over gloss black. 2003. By Kali.

3. Kali with *Surf Bat No.1.* Grey primered German-style helmet with red, black, and white 1-Shot. 2002. By Kali.

4. *The Martian Mantis.* 2003. 1-Shot on black vector helmet. By Kali. "I don't like to stencil or grid my designs . . . I like to just go into zen mode and let the design happen. When I'm through with the piece and I'm letting my eyes adjust to what I've just made, Johnny will take a look with a fresh eye and name the art based on what he sees. The designs are really organic when you let them happen . . . So insects and biomorphs tend to appear, and the segmented features fit right in with traditional disc-grinder, arc-line forms." —Kali

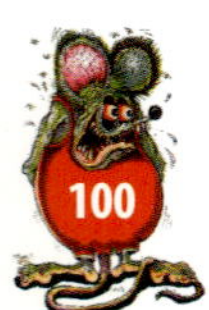

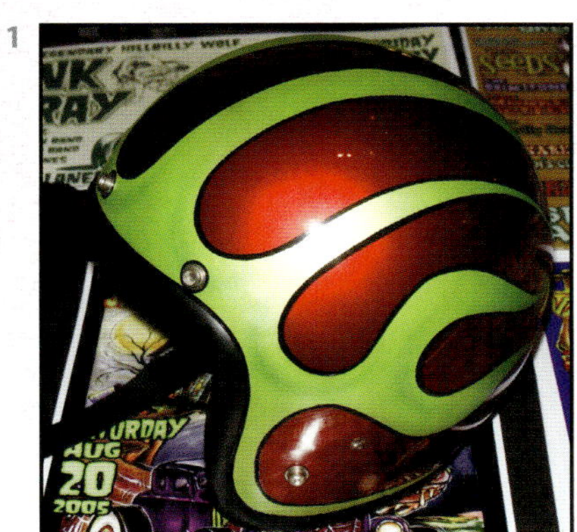

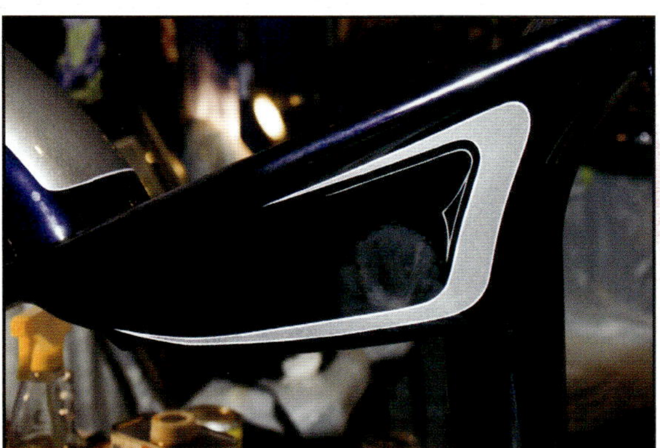

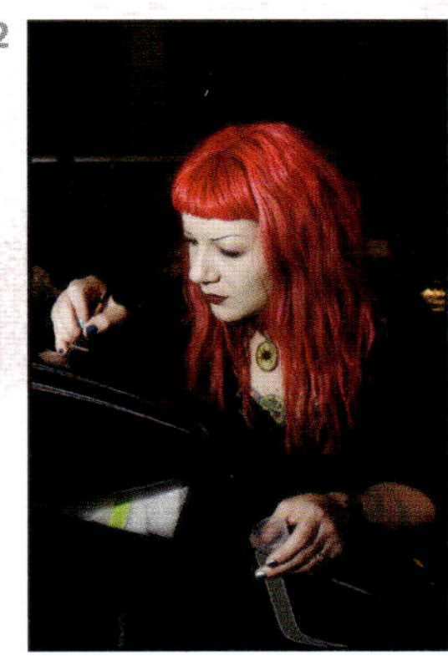

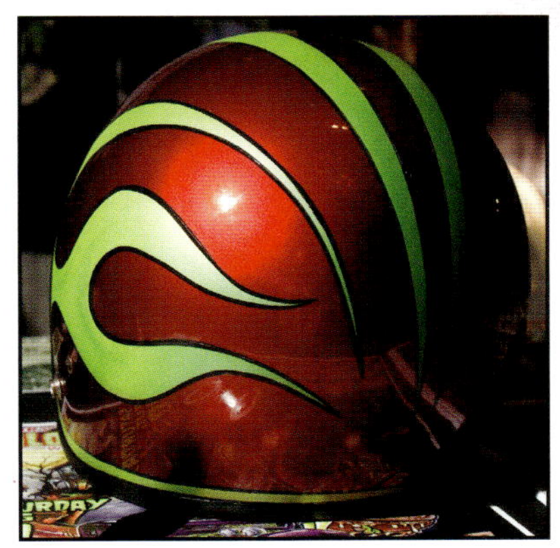

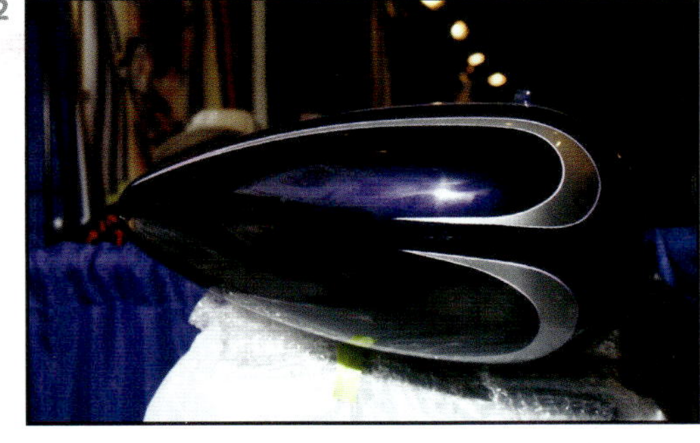

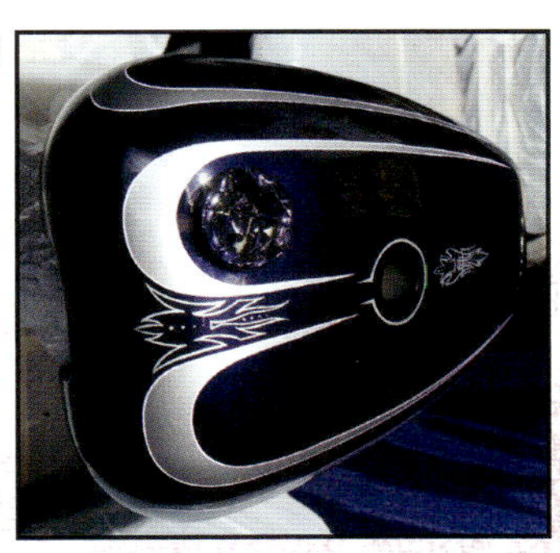

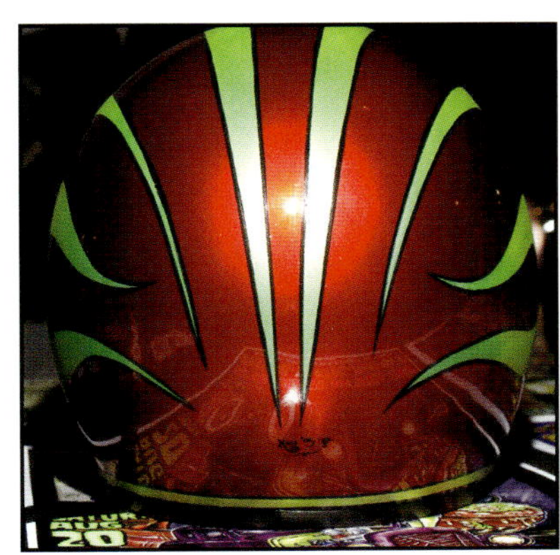

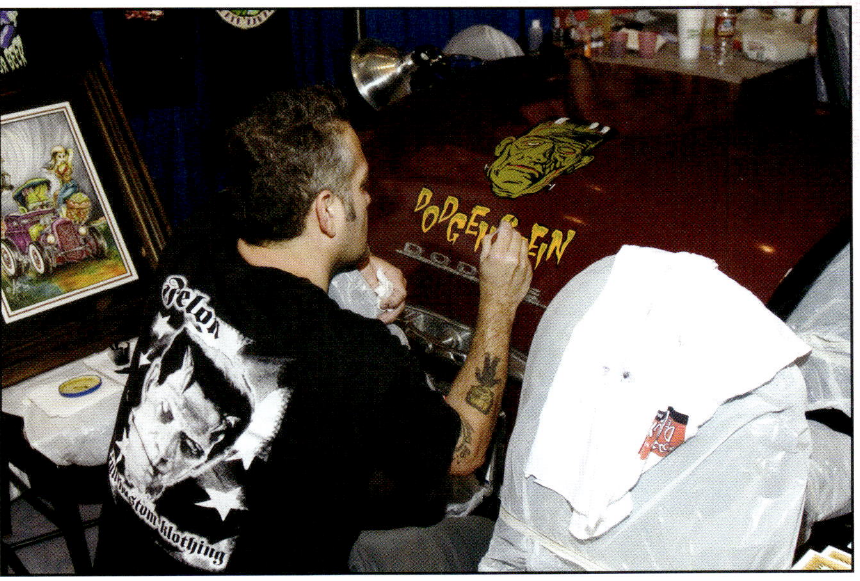

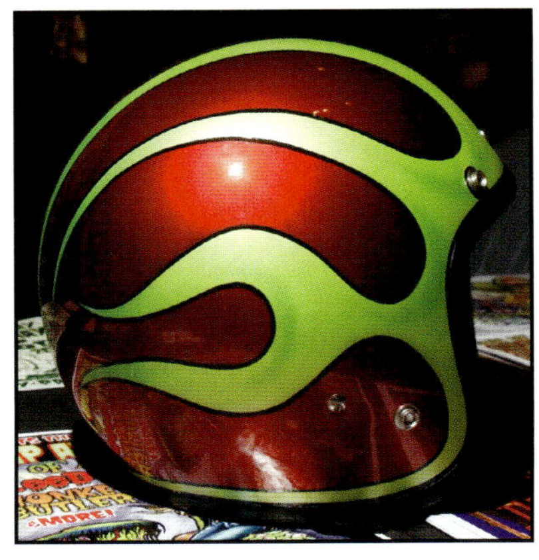

1. Red metalflake DOT-approved helmet with pearlescent monster-green scallop/flames and black pinstriping by Ace & Kali. This helmet was inspired by a photo of Don Garlits wearing a helmet with this design in the November '66 issue of *Car Craft*. We liked the scalloping and flame combination so much, we had to do one as well! Photos © 2005 by Brandon Gouthier Photography.

2. Purple with ruby pearl and silver metalflake scallop Triumph custom chopper tank, fender, and frame from Hans' Rod & Cycle, featuring metallic silver and light violet striping by Kali. Pinstriped at Live Fast 2005—Houston, TX. Photos © 2005 by Brandon Gouthier Photography.

3. Ace providing valuable product placement space for Felon Clothing while working on *DodgenStein* (Frankenstein on Dodge deck lid) at the 2005 Live Fast Hot Rod & Tattoo Convention—Houston, TX. Photo © 2005 by Brandon Gouthier Photography.

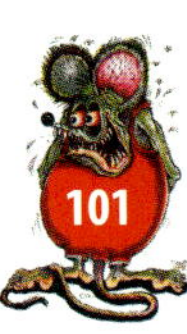

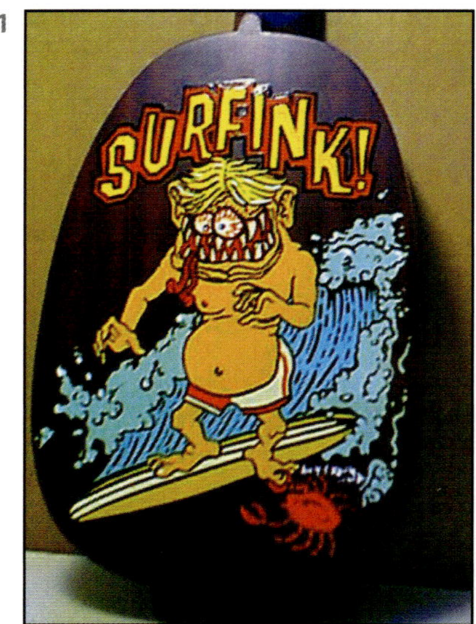

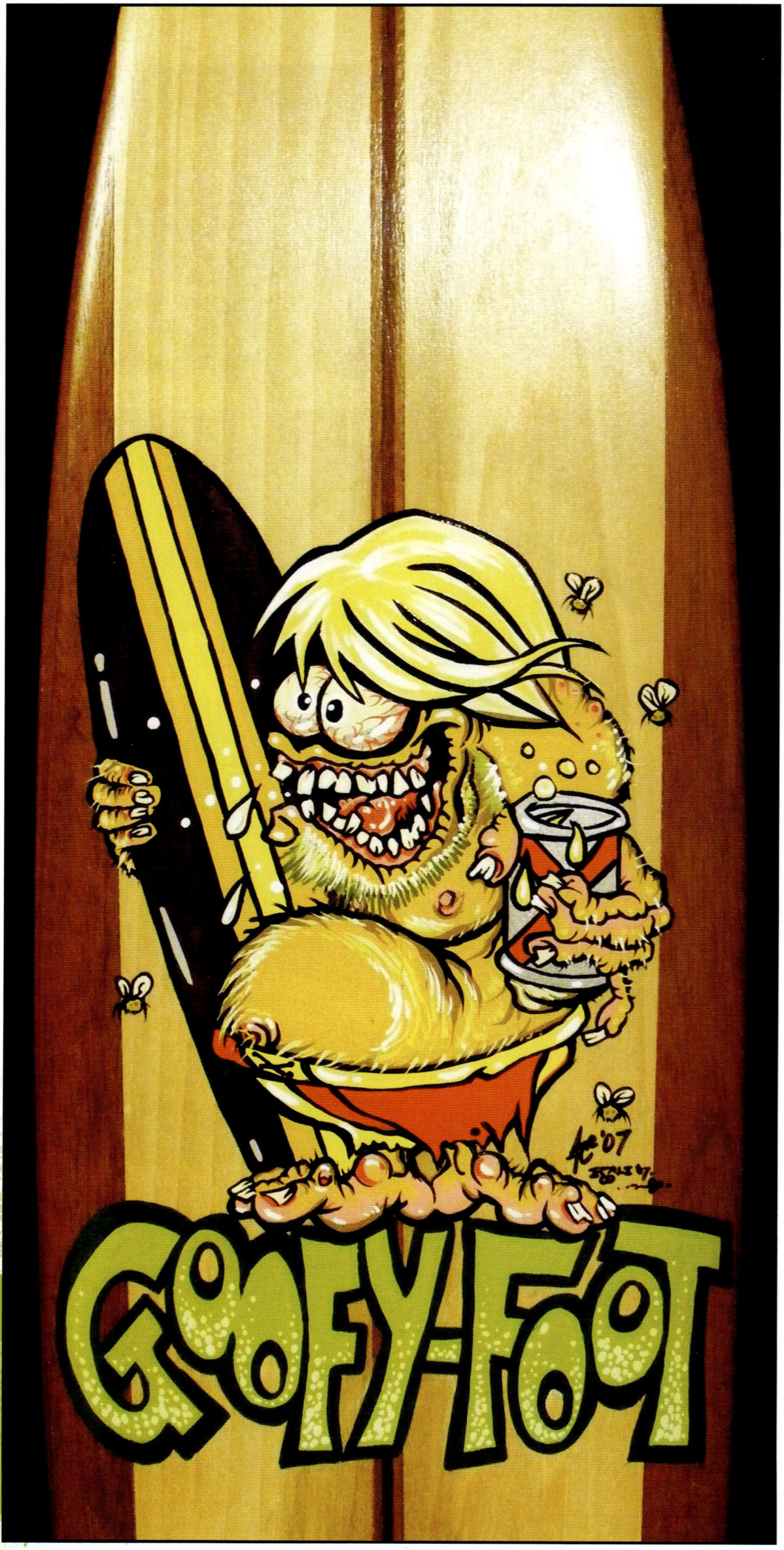

1. *Surfink Uke.* 2004.
Here's one that you surfabilia collectors will have a helluva time finding out there, due to the fact of an EXTREMELY low run of these particular ukes . . . We know for a fact that they are extremely rare, because this is actually a one-of-a-kind painted by Kali with 1-Shot! The graphics were intentionally rendered to represent the appearance of a waterslide decal. Collection of Murphy Graham.

2. *Goofy Foot.* 1-Shot over wood. 2007.
This leering, beer-soaked character is one of our crew of "Surf Slob" characters, who are directly influenced by all the fat, rotten-toothed, girl-chasing hairy monsters that Big Daddy Roth and Mouse gave us. This graphic was done on a pristine longboard. Collection of Murphy Graham.

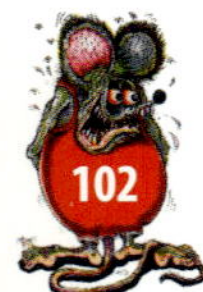

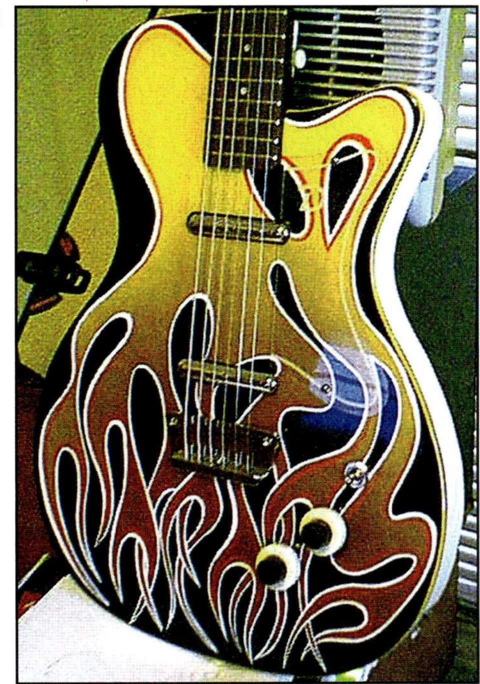

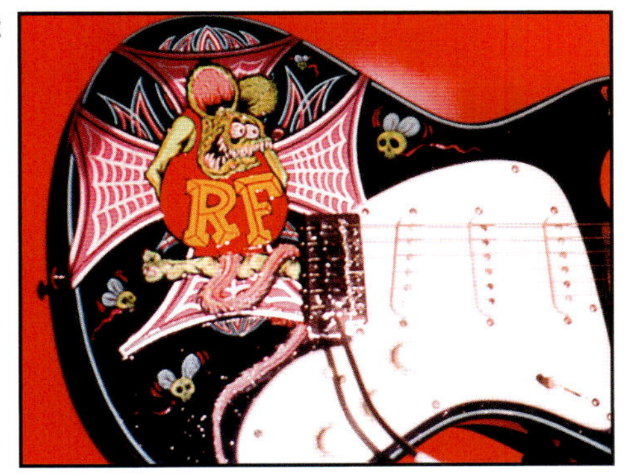

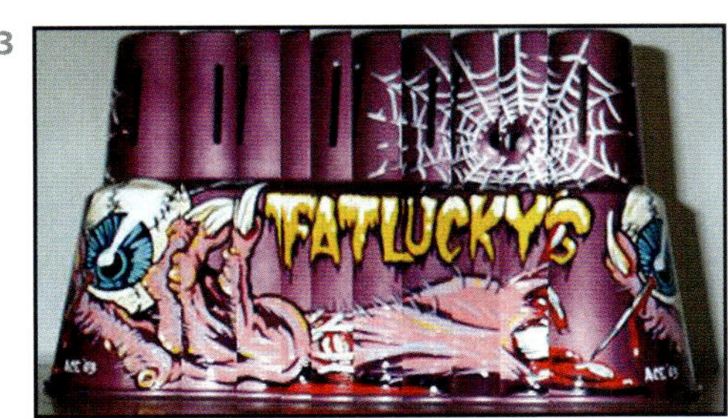

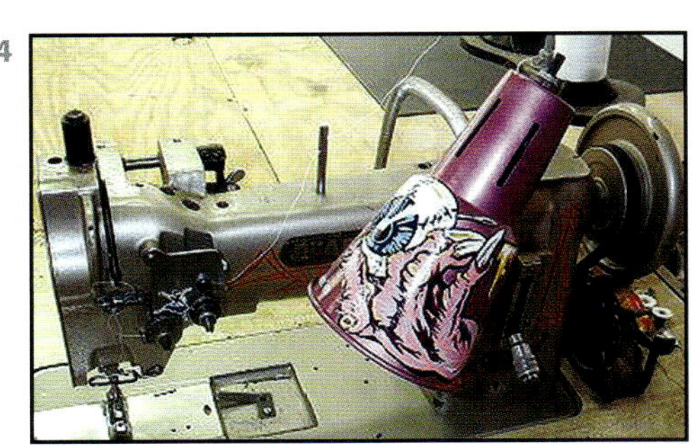

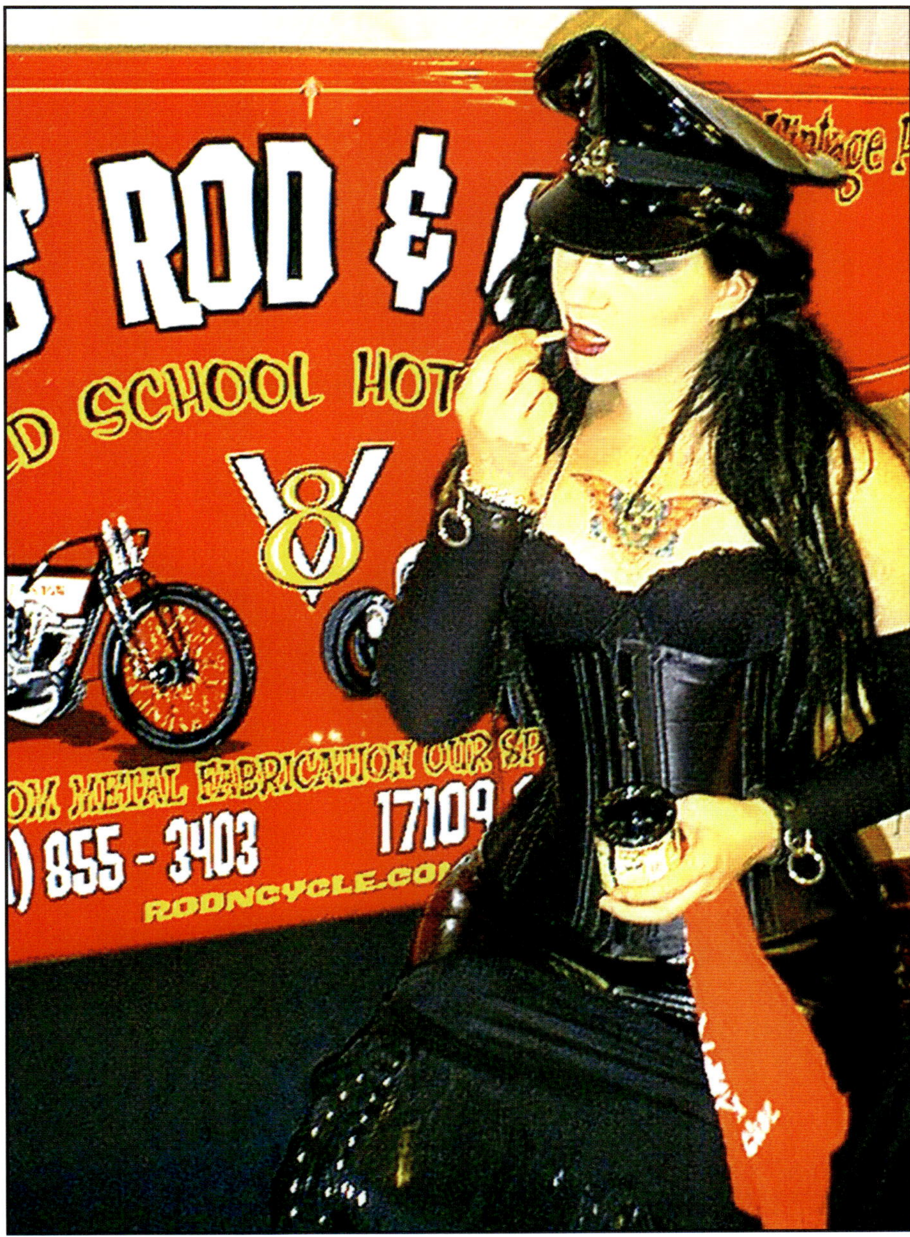

1. Rattle-can and 1-Shot flamejob on Danelectro guitar. 2001.

2. Custom Rat Fink graphic on Danelectro. 2002. Collection of Kevin Michaels of Curse.

3. Photo turnaround of Fat Lucky's lampshade. 2003. Photo courtesy of Shaun Johnstun.

4. Custom lampshade with PFAFF 145 sewing machine owned by master automotive upholsterer and hot rodder, Shaun "Fat Lucky" Johnstun. Photo © 2003 by Hank Cash, www.SouthAustinSpeedShop.com.

5. Kali working on 16-gauge rolled sheet metal shop sign for Hans' Rod & Cycle. This extremely heavy hollow sign was welded together to a rod lip and meant to be displayed high above the garage entrance doorway. Our graphics featured a Harley Board Tracker and roadster. 2003. "Once I had expressed to Ed my desire to learn traditional pinstriping, he gave me one of his own personal brushes, a Mack 00, which I used until it was down to a few frayed hairs. Ed also taught me to avoid pre-planned sketches and work with spontaneous creativity. Let the thing you are painting tell you what to paint. I'm also really big on symmetrical pieces . . . I don't like asymmetrical freeform . . . It's just not my thing." —Kali

"It'll come to ya' when you get the paint on the brush . . ." —Ed "Big Daddy" Roth

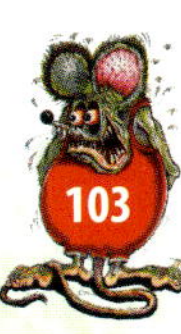

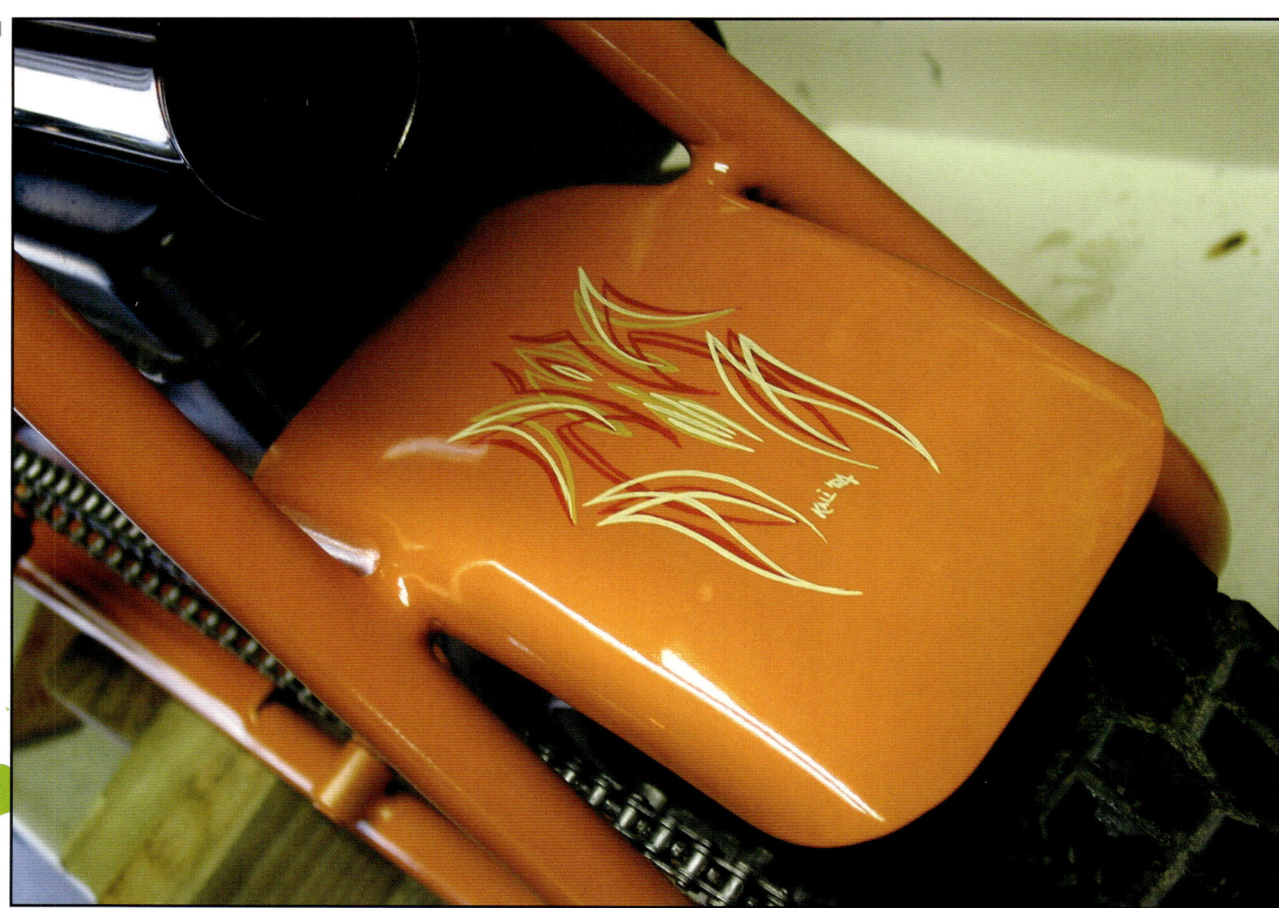

1. ***SQUANK!*** 1-Shot, Minibike fender pinstriping detail. 2004. Photo © 2004 by Blake Burwel.

2. ***KNIF from URANUS.*** 1-Shot enamel on wood panel, 3"x5". 2003.

3. ***Surfin' Skeeter.*** Burgundy-purple metalflake over silver iron cross with pinstriping on German-style helmet. 2003.

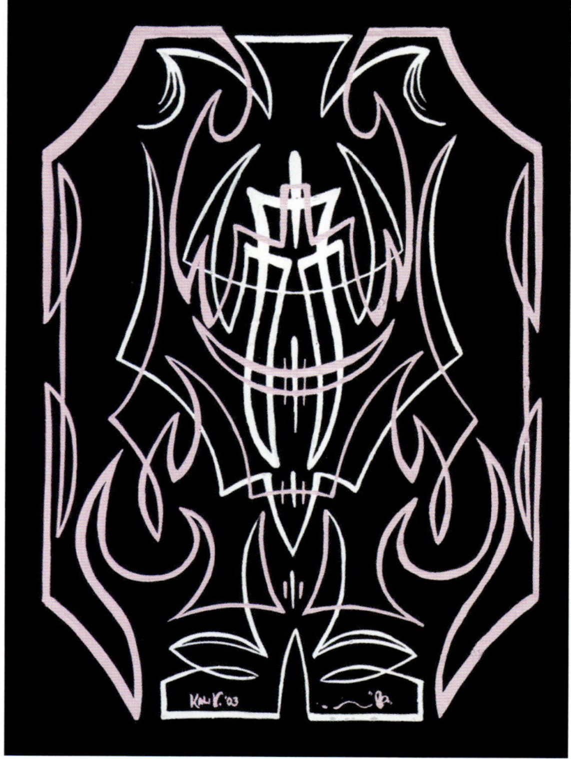

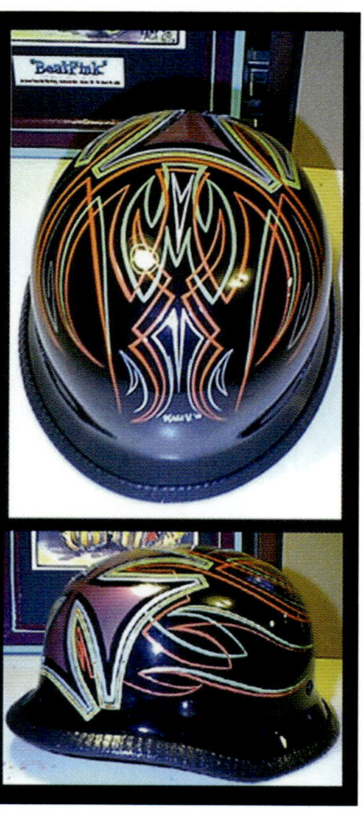

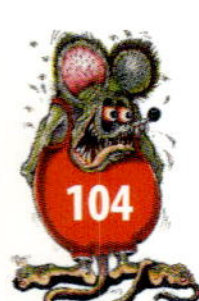

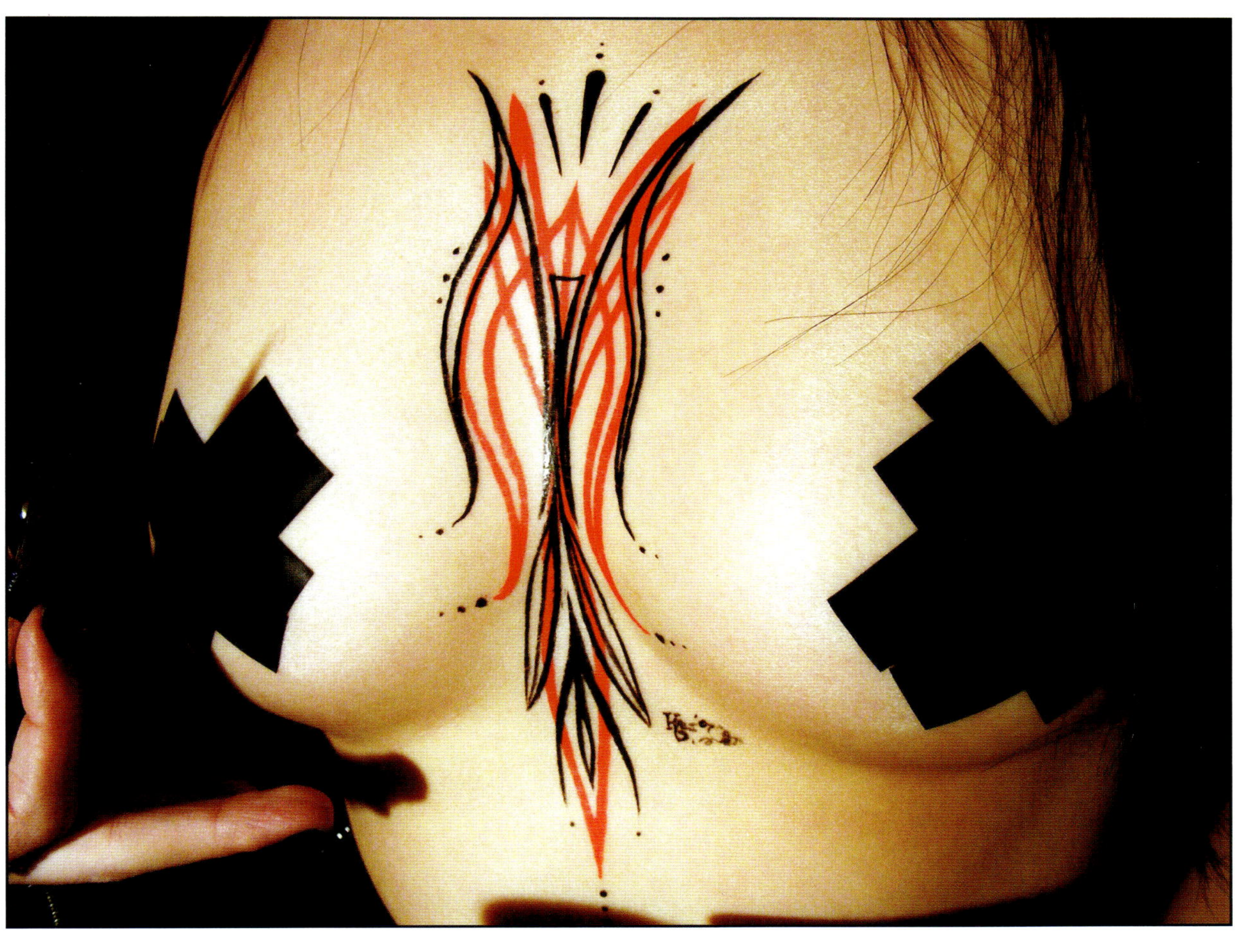

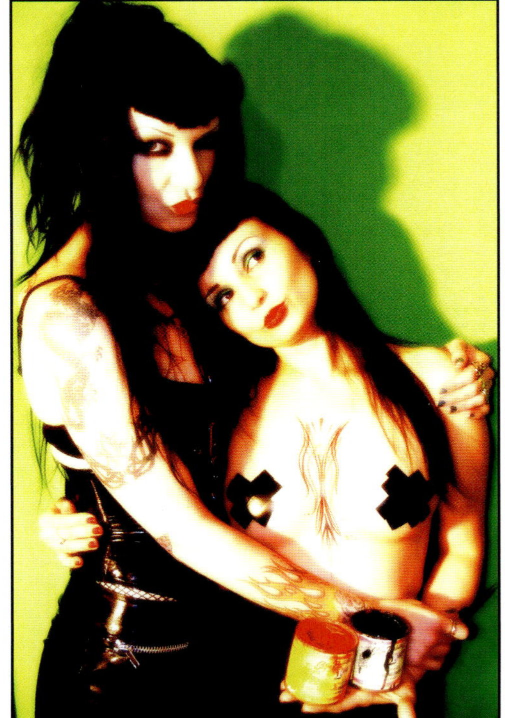

Kali painting on Patti Waggin, 2007.
(Do NOT try this at home—professional stunt model and lead paint!)

Kali shown pinstriping the feminine form, something she has done many times for promos and ad shoots. Striping a naked girl is our direct reference to the story that Von Dutch, one of our artistic idols, was captured on film in an obscure cult documentary of sorts, *You Are What You Eat*, 1968. This loose compilation of scene "happenings," circa 1966–1968, is not only purported to feature Dutch briefly but also contains such visuals/sounds as The Electric Flag, kids in German helmets, topless go-go dancers, cameos by Frank Zappa and Tiny Tim, and more . . . We wonder how Dutch wound up in this? Cheers to "The Father of Modern Pinstriping!"

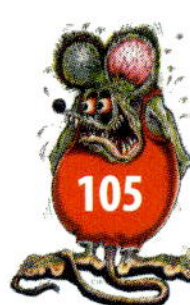

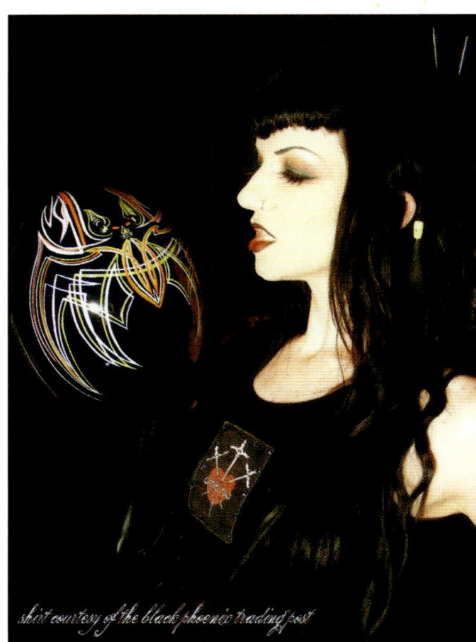

Basil Batty's Brain Bucket. 2007. Kali Verra.
1-Shot over airbrushed Frankenstein on helmet
(Frankenstein by our pal Mike . . . Thanks, buddy!)

After a two-and-a-half year absence from
pinstriping, Kali was apprehensive about picking up
her brushes again. Years of increasing battles with
nerve damage, fibromyalgia, worsening scoliosis,
and neuropathy led to loss of dexterity and chronic
hand tremors. Kali made a decision to overcome
these obstacles and created this design right out of
the gate with no warm-up or practice . . . The name
refers to the term "Brain Bucket" for helmets by
skateboarders, bikers, and drag racers alike and as a
nod to Basil Wolverton's classic "Brain-Bats of Venus."
Kali's love and natural talent for the art form taught
to her by Roth will always be there—and is damned
hard to suppress, despite physical challenges and a
field seemingly dominated by male hype.

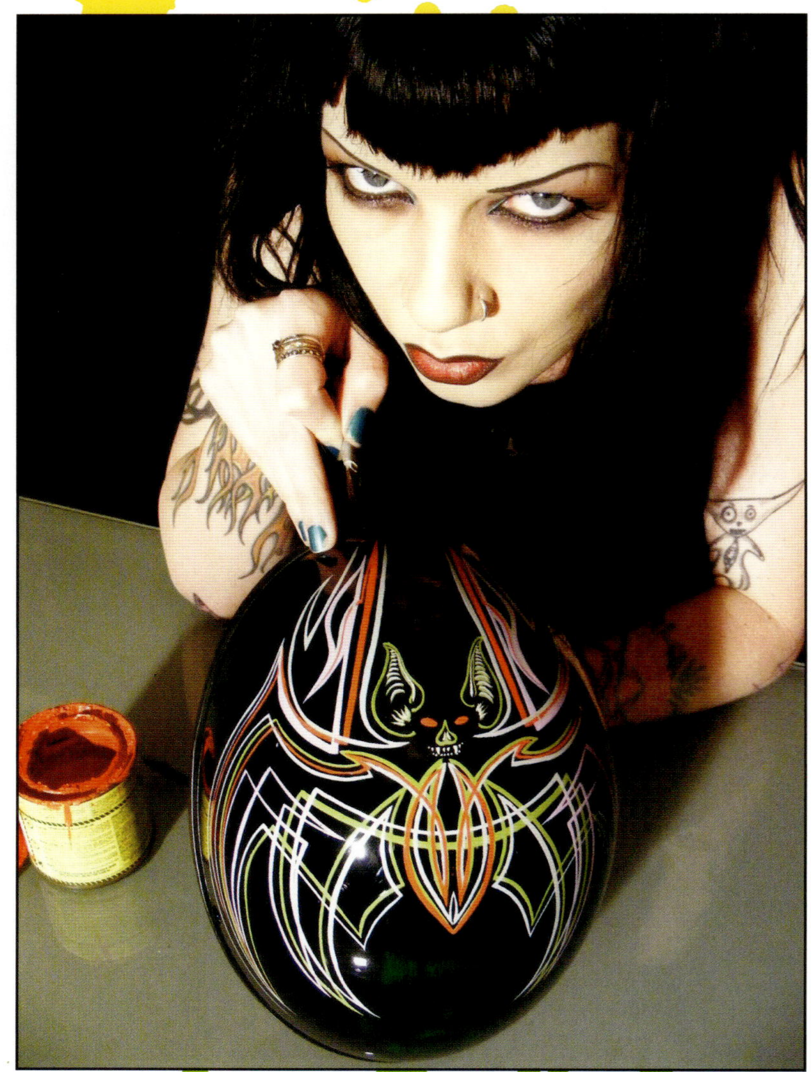

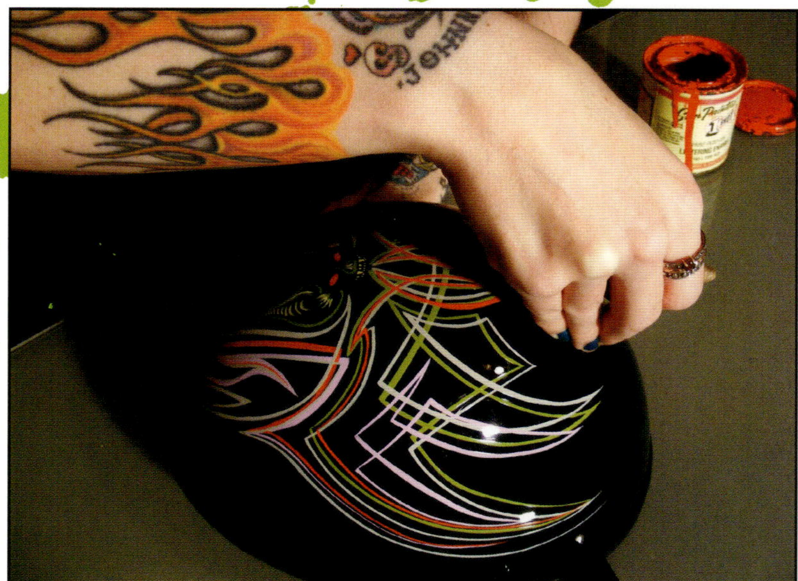

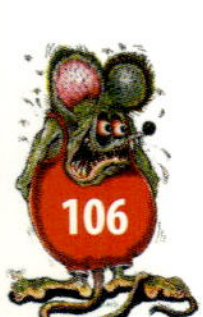

INTERVIEW

What are your personal origins?

Ace: I was born in Texas the same year as the original Aurora Frankenstein model kit.

Kali: I was put together the same year as the Aurora Monsters of the Movies kits. I grew up in Los Angeles and came to Texas years ago.

Describe some of your earliest artistic influences.

Ace: As a child, I had a habit of drawing strange, long-haired vampire women in my Dr. Seuss and P.D. Eastman books, along with bats, haunted houses with broken windows, and Ben Cooper-style skeletons. At around age seven or eight, I used automotive model-kit spray paint to create a life-sized woman in a bikini and bubble-flip hairdo on the side of an abandoned shack. I also took notice of the comics and magazines of the day—local stores had the quaint little habit of displaying all of the monster, men's adventure, hot rod, and nudie mags together . . . It's not hard to understand how all of this affected me.

Kali: My earliest influences included all of the *verboten* gore flicks of George Romero, Lucio Fulci, Mario Bava, Dario Argento, and the like . . . Infamous '70s made-for-TV horror movies such as *Trilogy of Terror, Summer of Fear*, and my personal fave, *Midnight Offerings* . . . Elvira (Oh, those Sundays with the little black-and-white tube . . . PIGS . . . EEEEK!) . . . I was fascinated by Edward Gorey, Gahan Wilson, Charles Addams . . . *Fangoria* magazine was a regular purchase (who DIDN'T want all of those neato props in the stories and ads?!?) . . . The earliest artistic endeavor I can recall was my front-porch tattoo shop: I had a brand new set of Crayola fat markers . . . I had all of my friends come over, I sat in a lawn chair and one by one, each buddy got a "W" with two dots and a "Y" underneath it on their arm . . . Naughty, naughty little shit, me! Heh heh . . .

It will be apparent to anyone holding this volume that you both have a multifaceted career that has achieved notoriety for gig posters, airbrushing, sculpture, and many other types of media. Let's begin with your poster work . . . How did this phase of Johnny Ace Studios start?

Ace: As luck would have it, I started becoming disillusioned with what I was being taught in school right about the time Alice Cooper, The

New York Dolls, and Kiss began trampling young minds with platform monster boots . . . Everyone around me resembled every bad '70s cliché you could imagine. Roth Studios had closed its doors three or four years earlier, disco was beginning to infect the unprotected, and in a couple of years, four guys from New York would kick-start a clear vision in my head of wanting to combine raw punk energy with the beloved monster comics of my childhood.

If I would have to list the major catalysts of my original progression into posters and flyers, it would be a clear realization that what I wanted to do art-wise wasn't being done or offered, and the opportunity to actually do was wide open in the world of early punk/skatepunk/surf contest gigs and events.

I had always remembered how cool Wally Wood and Jack Davis album-cover art was, with titles such as *Dracula's Greatest Hits, Monster Rally,* and *Zacherle's Monster Gallery* . . . In my mind, the combination of music and monsters was there from the beginning and seemed completely natural.

Under the pen name of Johnny Childish, I toiled continuously from the late '70s to approximately 1990 doing any and every type of assignment where I could utilize my influences. As for the pen name, I chose Johnny Childish as a smart-assed response to teachers and some long-forgotten girlfriend's parents who were fond of pointing out to me that "the life of a skateboarding, monster-drawing punk rocker" certainly was unfit for their daughter to be involved with and was completely selfish and "CHILDISH."

Kali: Um, yeah . . . the '70s . . . I was hanging out with my Big Wheel and Kiss rekkids and Kiss phono. (Uh . . . yup . . . and the dolls, too . . .) Deep dark secret: Wonder Woman Underoos. Seriously.

It seems strange how during my youthful skate-punk days, I saw and admired my future husband's work in *Thrasher* magazine. Even stranger are the events that led to our one-in-a-million chance encounter in NOWHERESVILLE, TEXAS. But here we are, folks . . . years and years later . . . haven't been apart longer than a day in all this time.

What type of work did you do in the '90s?

Ace: I took a big break from doing gig posters about 1990, only doing

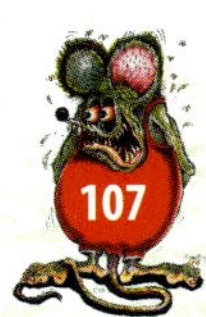

scattered and very selective pieces when the opportunity arose. I spent two or three years working in the seminal computer game industry, but let's face it, I'm not a "team player." Besides, I had begun working with Ed "Big Daddy" Roth in the early '80s and continually worked for him heavily throughout the '90s, so there wasn't much need to freelance. Kali and I contributed a lot to the early days of the garage-kit hobby before it became corrupt with greed, thievery, egotism, and self-importance . . . But we spent the majority of our creative energy with Roth.

Describe your career with "Big Daddy" Roth.

Ace: I was aware that Ed was slowly building a comeback in the early '80s. He had still been presiding over the Rat Fink Reunions on the West Coast and had started placing small ads in hot rod magazines for Rat Fink merchandise. It was a comeback that started snowballing with bands seeking out Ed's imagery (The Birthday Party, Stray Cats, The Necros) and a whole generation of artists such as The Pizz, R.K. Sloane, Steve Fiorilla, Mark Balfe, and myself, who not only never gave up the faith, but made it our mission to keep the Roth Studios legacy alive in our work . . . and to continue that tradition by actually working for Roth Studios and paying plenty of dues.

Kali: When I ensnared Johnny in my devious web of feminine wiles, he had already been working for Ed for many years. Ed knew we were an immediate team, so he put me to work in the beginning on keeping track of correspondence, business, character development, package design, ringing the bell in the tower, sculpting work, and more. Ultimately, in the years to follow, we got to help set up and tear down his booth at car shows, load and unload his rig, sell merch, listen to Roth fart, snore, belly-laugh at *The Three Stooges* at five freakin' AM . . . I personally got barked at for smoking, got to polish show-car chrome, and most importantly, got schooled in the traditional art of Von Dutch-style pinstriping by Pops.

Ace: Let's just say I consider our career with Big Daddy as the most wonderful and priceless experience Kali and I have shared in our years as a business team, studio, and couple. I set out in my youth to seek out this hero and learned a great majority of what I know about life, art, renewal, and determination . . . Everything Kali and I accomplish in the future will, in some part, have grown from the gift of having known Ed Roth.

Kali: I'm grateful to Ed for instilling in us a great respect for Kenneth "Von Dutch" Howard—an originator, oddball, paint-splattered philosopher, and seriously freggin' funny guy . . . The same description applies to Big Daddy—he was my mentor, I was his "adopted daughter." I'll always remember him letting me call him "Dad" . . . and him really BEING a Dad.

How does your airbrushing work tie into your career as Rat Fink artists?

Ace: We both do what we like to refer to as "traditional monster shirts" . . . Traditional as far as Roth Studios is concerned, that is. Guys like Von Dutch and Dean Jeffries were doing abstract characters and monsters on personal clothing with an airbrush in the mid-'50s. Von Dutch reportedly did his for personal expression and use, while Jeffries advertised his own pinstriping services and painting . . . Roth, in addition to an early pinstriping career, began utilizing monsters and almost Picasso-esque airbrushed characters for himself and his ever-growing customer base. This type of hot-rodding, monster-shirt fan was the sort of customer that Ed correctly predicted would be attracted to his exploding career as a groundbreaking show-car builder. Roth would continue to attract customers for his airbrushed shirts with the promise of a new wild show car each year. The shirts helped pay for the creation of each new fibreglas masterpiece that came out of Roth Studios. After years of doing airbrush shirts one at a time by himself and with a revolving door of young talent, Ed ultimately figured out how to screen-print monster shirts at an incredible rate, and one-of-a-kind airbrushed monsterpieces faded into the background.

I personally always held a great affection for this art form and drew and airbrushed my own monster stuff even as a teenager. I did individual shirts and flags for friends while in the Navy, countless shirts, skirts, Vans, and such during my punk years, and saw the continuation of this method of artwork as the natural thing to do while working for Roth . . . a continuation of Studio tradition, in my mind. Of course, Kali and I continue this art form partly out of habit, but more because we still hold that tradition very tightly.

In addition to your notoriety as Roth's top official artists, your gig poster work has exploded over the last ten years. What made you focus on this art form again?

Ace: Ed was aware that I had done poster work and called upon me to do not only comics, but various Rat Fink Party flyers (however, R.K. Sloane did the lion's share in the '80s). Even though Kali and I were extremely busy and employed around the clock by Ed, bands and venues would inquire about our illustration work—some venues remembered my earlier gig posters, and new clients were attracted by our Roth Studios work and occasional personal projects. Despite some of the downside of working in that business, there were enough interesting bands and names involved that it was hard not to want to take on some poster work again.

We would like to thank Mel Stultz for making a great opportunity happen for us while he was running Asbury Lanes. In addition to the last Link Wray tour, we achieved a career goal of doing a Ventures gig, The Seeds, several more Dick Dale gigs, and others. This is the type of atmosphere that we hope an aspiring poster artist can acquire—we certainly enjoyed it.

We suppose that our work is in demand because our influences have come full-circle again . . . All those horror comics, monster movies, and toys are held in very high esteem by older and younger punk, skate, goth, deathrock, rockabilly, etc., circles. It goes to prove that the "class-Sicks" never die! The pointed bangs and "Lily Munster hair" that were utilized even in the Johnny Childish days can be found from So-Cal to Japan. And, of course, the fascination with monster girls and sexy witches that began in the '60s and '70s with us still influence a new wave of artists every year.

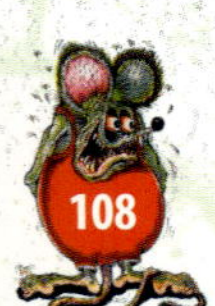

What influences you these days?

Ace: Kali, of course! I see in her everything that influenced me as a monster-crazy ten-year-old boy; an over-caffeinated, adrenaline-pumped twenty-something skatepunk; an optimistic, tradition-loving thirty-something Rat Fink; and especially now, as an inspired, still monster-crazy forty-something . . . who finally found "the monster's mate." Every time you see a cat-eyed siren with a huge Jiffy-Pop bee-hive, a monstrous bubble-flip, or Vampirella-style long black hair with bangs, you are looking at my muse.

I'm also very much still inspired by all the unheralded artists who painted the covers for the notorious Myron and Irving Fass Publica-tions: *Weird, Horror Tales, Terror Tales*, and others. The bloody monster battles and ultra-sexy stitched-up vampire women held an energy that struck a continuous chord with me from grade school, on through my punk years, all the way to the present.

Even though those titles were reviled by most Warren readers, I bought and learned from everything—Skywald, Marvel, Charlton, *Cracked*, and more. Along with my beloved ECs, I turn to these others for inspiration even today.

Kali: I'm highly influenced by music, movies, individuals, things . . . Thinking of Frances Farmer or Diane Arbus can send me off on a creative jag. As can William S. Burroughs, Frida Kahlo, Charles Bu-kowski, prosthetic limbs, Marie Laveau, pretty boots, Boris Karloff . . . I get caught up in a thought, and it will drag at me until I DO some-thing about it.

Listening to anything from old Hardcore, Punk, and D.R. (Circle Jerks, Black Flag, The Bags, The Ramones, 45 Grave, X, Bad Brains, Catholic Discipline, etc.) or to The Pixies or The Breeders (Kim Deal's voice could shame an angel), Sonic Youth (Kim Gordon's voice sounds like a gut-punched angel's), Nina Hagen, Legendary Pink Dots, Diamanda Galas, Tiny Tim, The Kingsmen, The Mummies . . . to Maria Callas . . . to '70s glam . . . to '20s Creole . . . It's all fuel and inspiration!

I love to watch a good flick to get a creative jolt, too. Being a child of the late '70s/early '80s, I have a natural proclivity for over-the-top Italian gore . . . it's in my DNA! George Romero is a longtime hero, and we both have a great love for his movies, unwavering DIY way of getting shit done, and utilization of film as mouthpiece for social com-mentary. I love silent horror (Edison's *Frankenstein, Vampyr, Caligari,* etc.) as well as old fantasy and sci-fi (Jean Cocteau's *Beauty and the Beast*, Georges Méliès films, *Metropolis*, etc.). Any classic Universal and RKO horror is a given. '70s made-for-TV horror movies REALLY tickle my pickle . . . the cornier the better! Stuff like that is PURE CREATIVITY GOLD to me.

Other things that inspire me: coffee, good pens, a freshly sharpened pencil, trimming a new brush, an inadvertent paint buzz, the thought that *someday* Lancelot Link is gonna be on satellite TV . . . (C'mon, Boomerang . . . you know Captain Planet can take five.)

—Johnny Ace & Kali Verra
Finksville, 2008

TOOLS

BRUSHES/ACCESSORIES

Mack striping brushes #00 & #000

Mack Virus #1 & #2

Mack lettering quills #1, #2 & #4

Mack Ed "Big Daddy" Roth signature series brush #00

Mack outliner #1 & #4

DC flatliner brush #00

Grumbacher striping brush #00

Paasche syphon-feed airbrushes

Roth Flake Bomber spray gun

Roth Bazooka flake gun

PAINT

1-Shot Sign Painters enamels: full range

Roth Metalflakes: Standard, Trippin', Monster, Baby, and Lil'

Roth lettering enamel: "Ace & Kali's Monster Green."

Createx Auto-air: bases, fluorescents, pearls, iridescents, and flakes

Createx airbrush colors: opaques, pearls, fluorescents, and iridescents

Testors enamels

House of Kolor: various airbrush colors and striping enamels

SCULPTING

various dental and custom-shaped tools

various epoxy putties

Pro-Mat (out of production)

top-secret polyclay mix formula created in-house *insert mad scientist laughter here*

MISC. ART SUPPLIES

Design art markers (out of production): full range

Pantone Letraset Tria markers: full range

Prismacolor art markers: full range

Prismacolor pencils: full range

Alvin Tech-Liner drawing pens: all sizes

various bristol and crescent papers & boards

various canvases

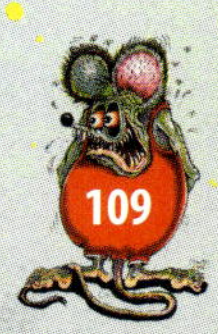

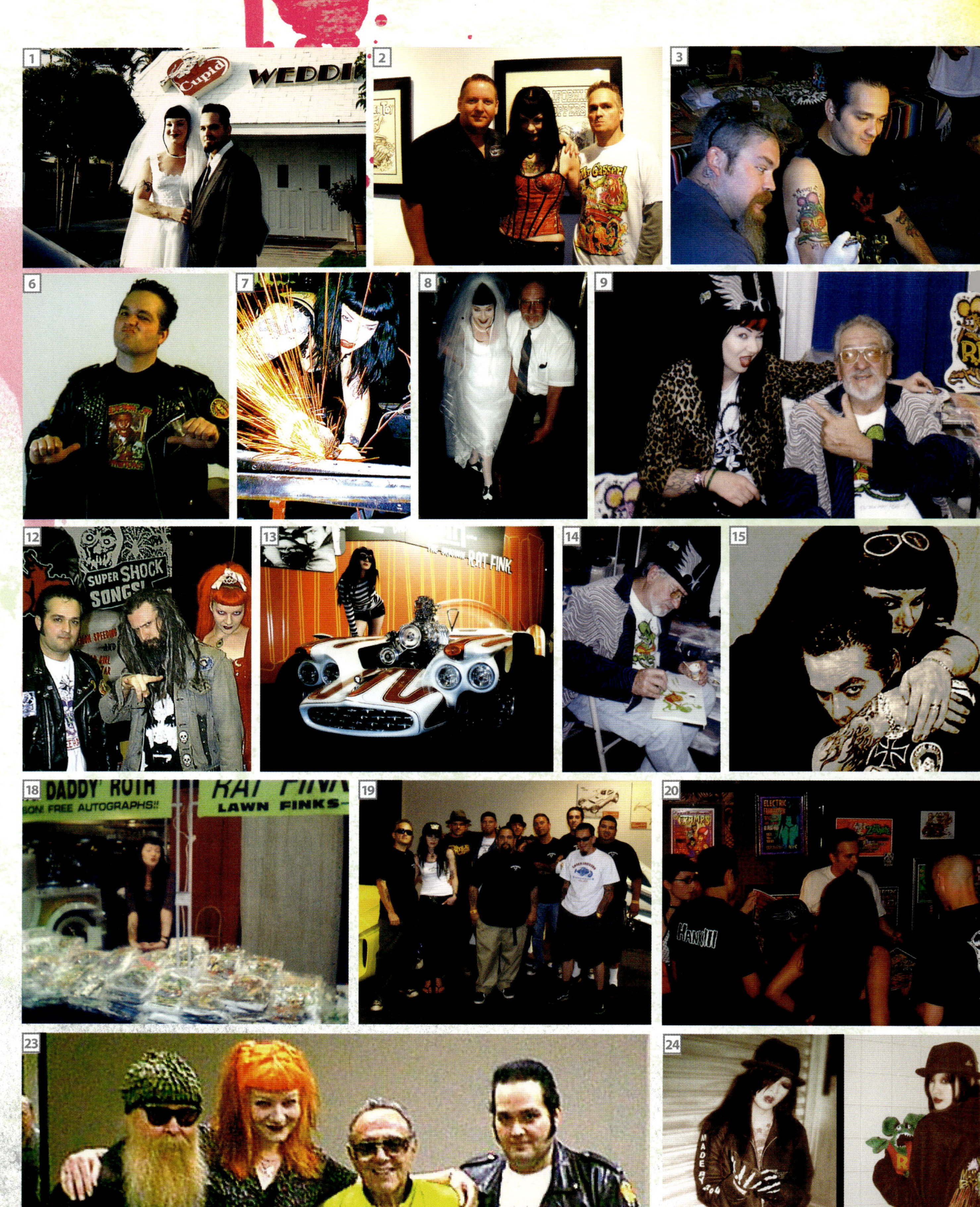

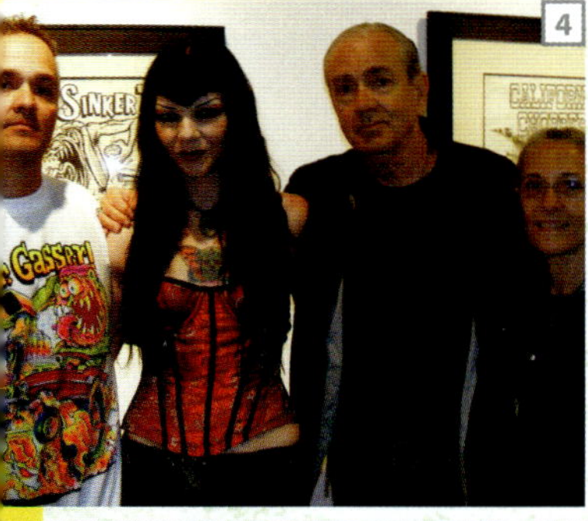

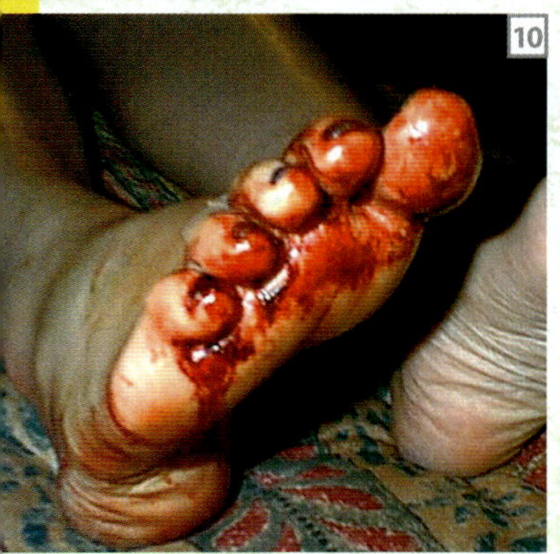

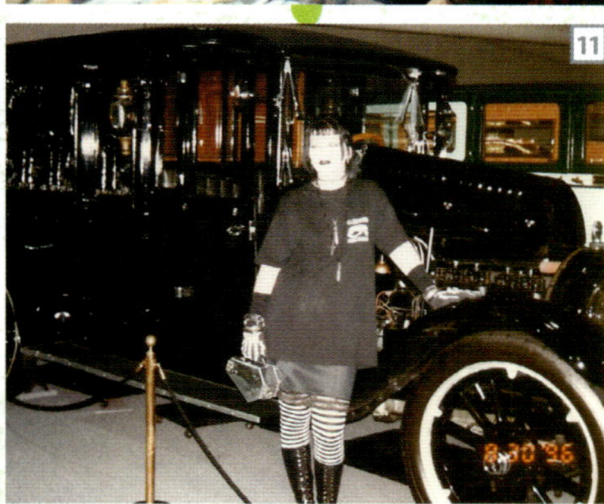

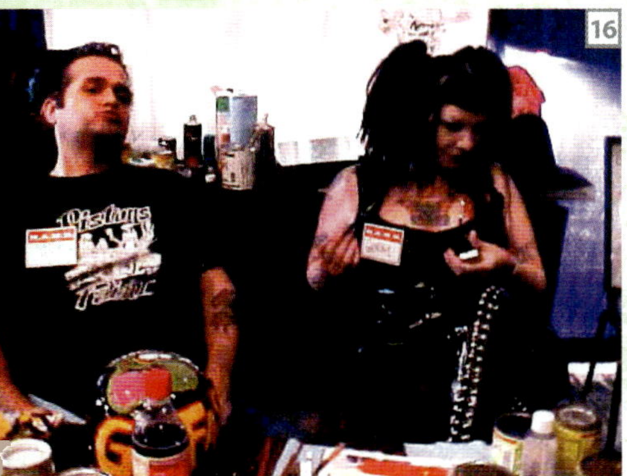

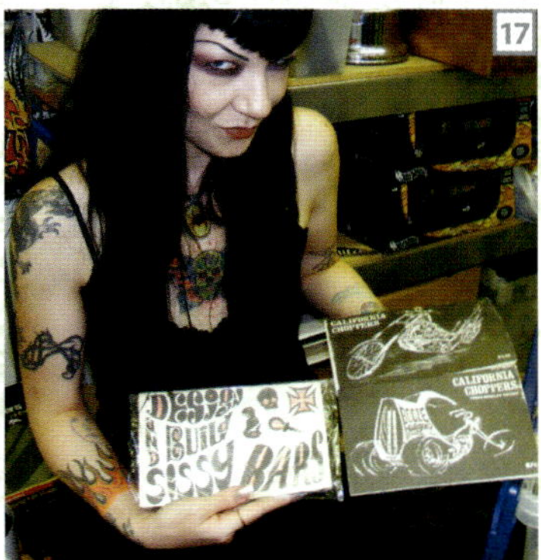

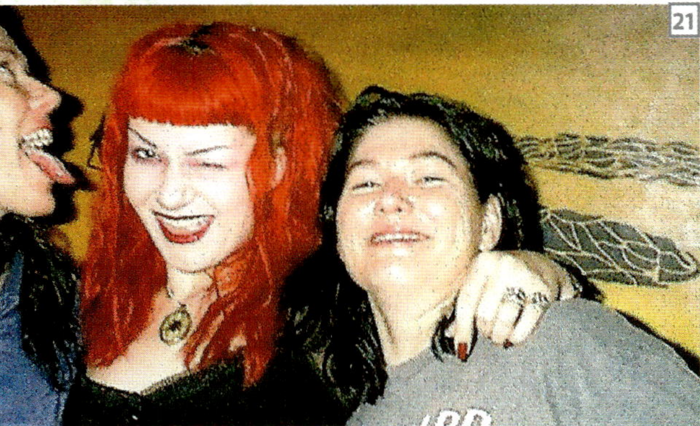

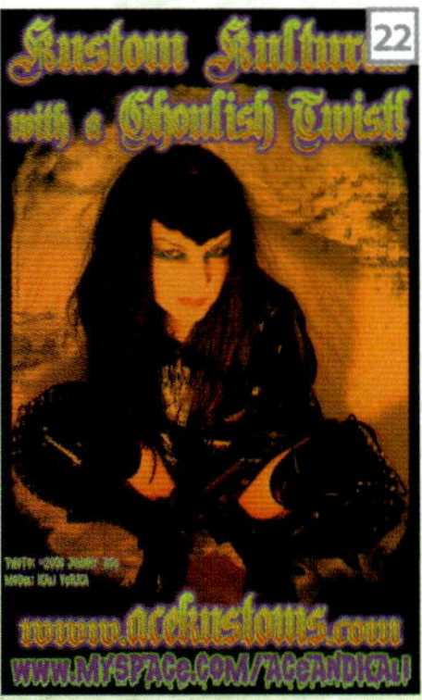

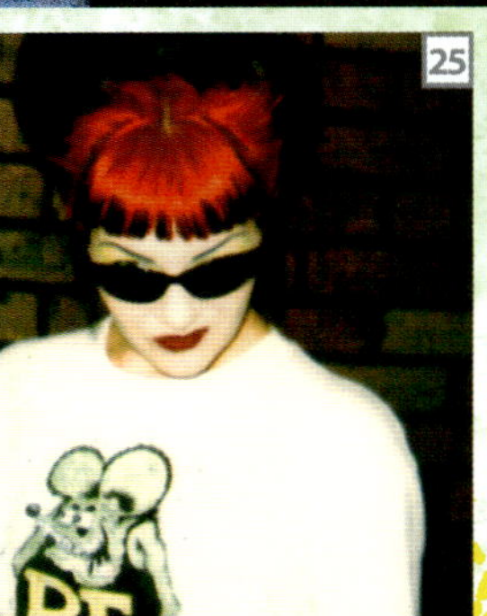

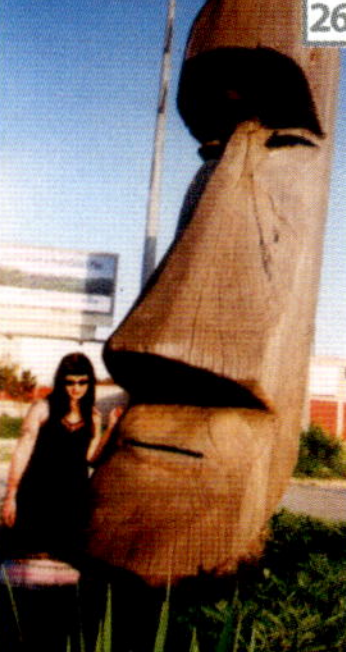

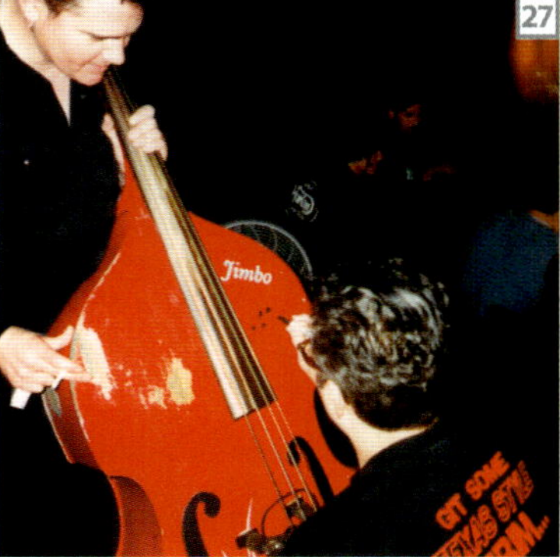

1. "I DO!" July 13, 1999.

2. Darryl Roth, Kali, Ace. Luz de Jesus Gallery, June 2007.

3. Dennis McPhail & Ace. Live Fast Tattoo Convention, 2004.

4. Ace, Kali, Robt. Williams, Suzanne Williams. Luz de Jesus Gallery, June 2007.

5. Ace, The Bonebad Crew & Nakata. Rat Fink Party. Burbank. 2000.

6. Ace loves Screamin' Jay Hawkins, muthafuggas! 2003.

7. Kali, Mistress of the Spark. 2004.

8. Kali & Roth—Battle of the Fink Feet / 11 vs. 13EEE! 7-13-99.

9. Kali & "Pops." World of Wheels. New Orleans, January 2000.

10. Kali's piggies. "It's allllll fun and games . . . till someone gets hurt." Dallas, August 2003.

11. Kali. Natural Museum of Funeral History. August 1996. (Kali says, "That's not a shirt, it's a TENT! What was I thinking?!?")

12. Ace, Rob Zombie, Kali. Houston, 2002.

13. Kali w/Beatnik Bandit. Petersen Automotive Museum. Los Angeles, June 2007.

14. Ed in New Orleans, January 2000.

15. "Love Finks!" 2003.

16. Ace and Kali (Hi hotos, my name is Germ x 2). Live Fast Tattoo Convention, 2004.

17. Kali at Darryl Roth's archives. Bell CA, 2007.

18. Kali at Roth's booth. Houston Autorama, November 2000.

19. Ace and Kali with The Road Devils C.C. So-Cal chapter (with German Road Devil visiting—for flavor). 2007.

20. Ace collecting cash (featuring future Ace Studios booty model, Patti Waggin, at far left). Texas Rat Fink Party III, San Antonio TX, 2004.

21. Kim Deal, Kali, Kelley Deal. (Kali says, "FUCK! I'm a BREEDERS SANDWICH!!! WHOOT! WHOOT!"). Houston, 2002.

22. Crouching Kali—hidden chonies! Promo photo, 2006.

23. Billy Gibbons, Kali, George Barris, Ace. Houston Autorama, November 2001.

24. Jian Ko modeling Ace & Kali "FrankenFink" jacket by Made By Monsters. Photo by Chris Kong. 2008.

25. Kali in R.F. tee workin' a wild Jiffy Pop. 1997.

26. Kali w/a tiki . . . a really big tiki. Um, BIG. Dallas, 1999.

27. Ace and Jimbo Wallace / Rev. Horton Heat. Houston, 2001. (Dude, draw me a Rat Fink on my bass!)

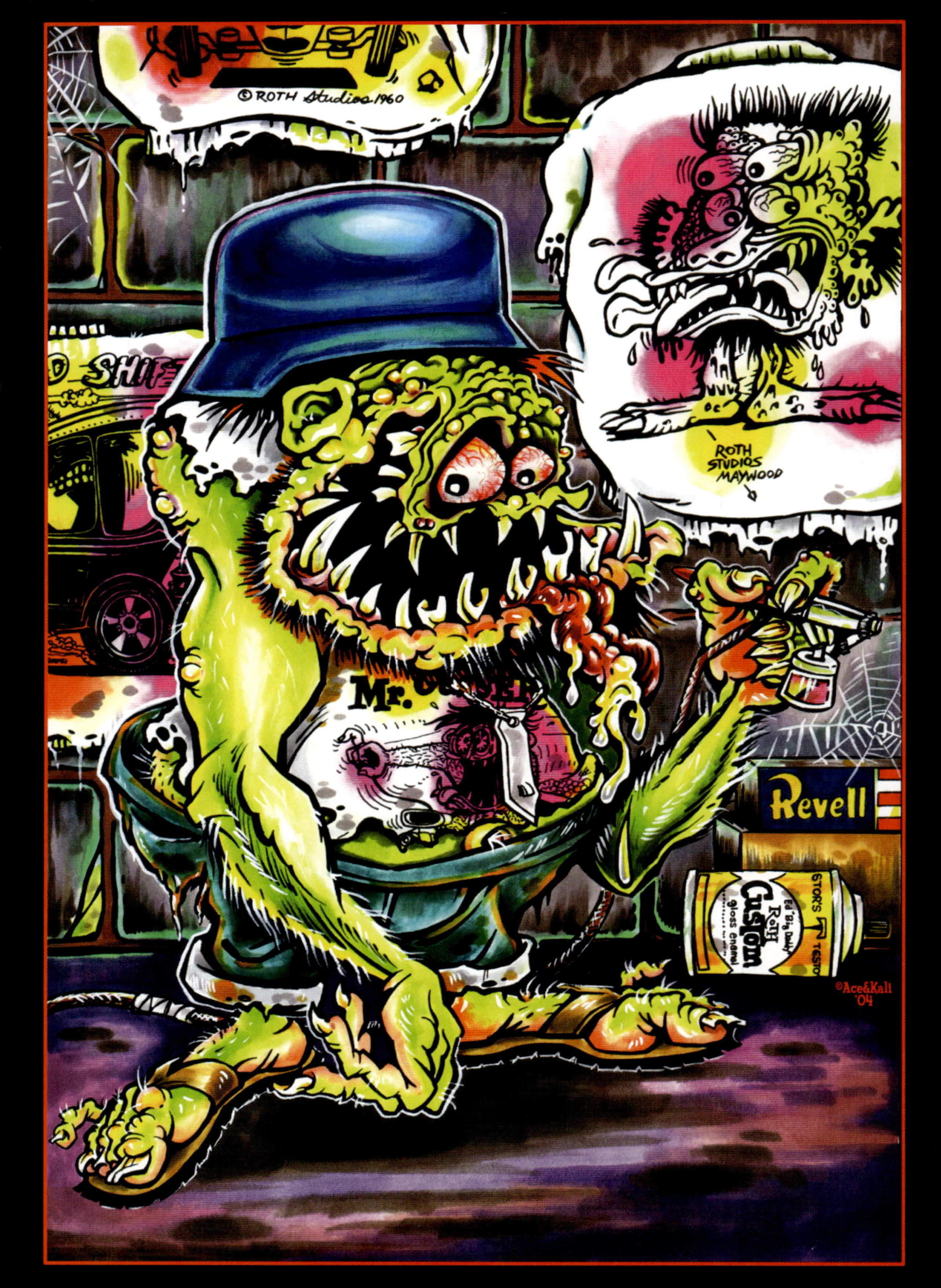

SwetFink. 2004.
One of our many tributes to the golden age of fluorescent paint, styrene plastic, grease, spray cans, fibreglas dust, and dead flies. Based on an obscure Roth Studios character design, "Chevy Lover."

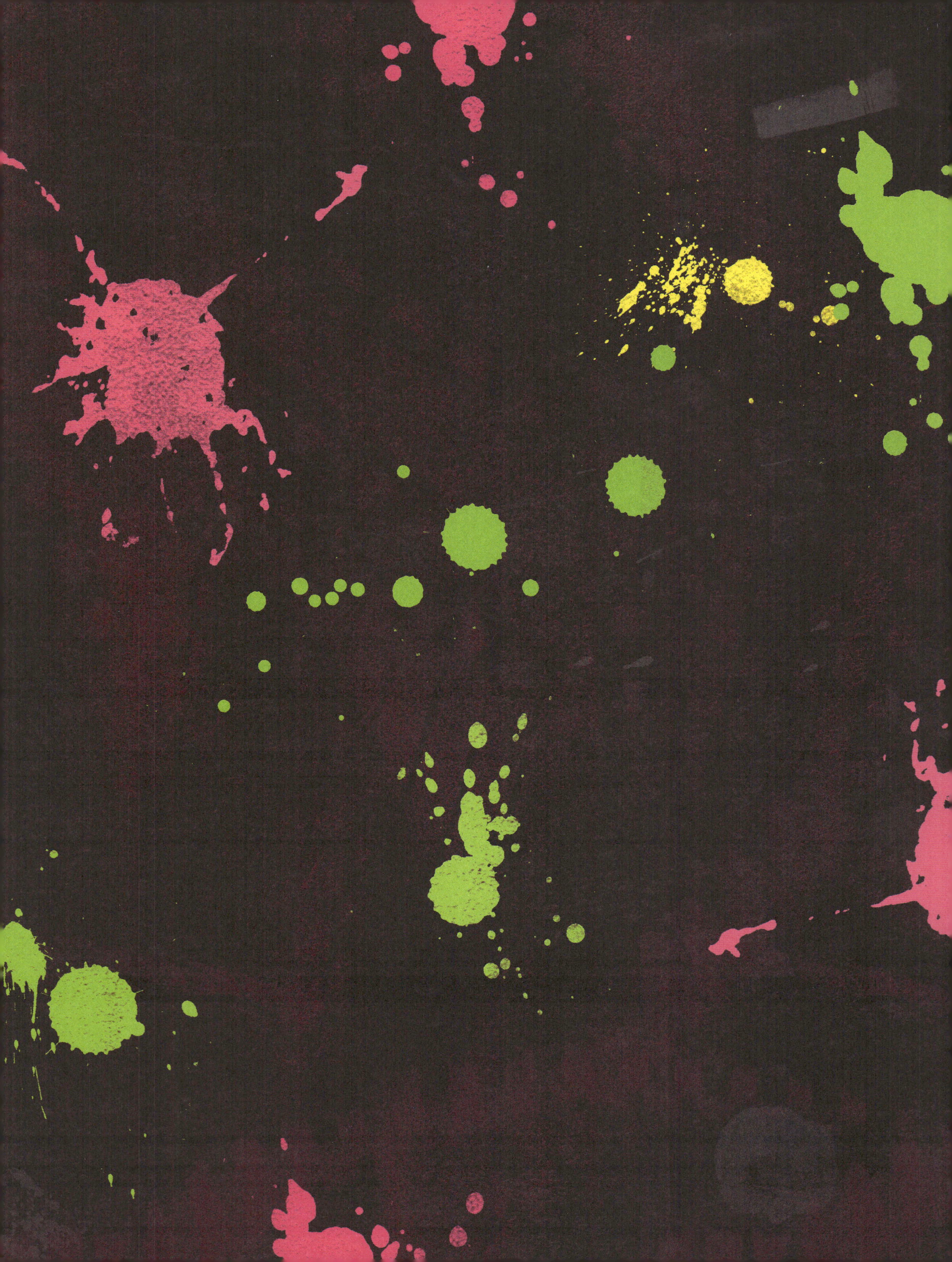